# THE CLASSICS
# OF **WESTERN**
# **SPIRITUALITY**

# THE CLASSICS OF WESTERN SPIRITUALITY
## A Library of the Great Spiritual Masters

# Late Medieval Mysticism

## OF THE LOW COUNTRIES

EDITED BY
RIK VAN NIEUWENHOVE, ROBERT FAESEN, SJ,
AND HELEN ROLFSON

PAULIST PRESS
NEW YORK • MAHWAH

Cover Art: Rogier van der Weyden (c. 1399–1464) was the leading Netherlandish painter of the mid-fifteenth century. His *Virgin and Child*, shown on the cover of this book, was painted between 1436 and 1438 and now hangs in the Museo del Prado, Madrid. Photo credit: Scala / Art Resource, NY.

*Cover and caseside design by Cindy Dunne*
*Book design by Lynn Else*

Library of Congress Cataloging-in-Publication Data

Late medieval mysticism of the Low Countries / edited by Rik Van Nieuwenhove, Robert Faesen, and Helen Rolfson.
    p. cm. — (The classics of western spirituality)
  Includes bibliographical references and index.
  ISBN 978-0-8091-0569-4 (cloth: alk. paper) —
  ISBN 978-0-8091-4297-2 (pbk.: alk. paper)
    1. Mysticism—Benelux countries. 2. Mysticism—History—Middle Ages, 600–1500. I. Van Nieuwenhove, Rik, 1967– II. Faesen, Rob. III. Rolfson, H.
  BV5082.3.L38 2008
  248.2'20949209024—dc22

                               2008010844

Published by Paulist Press
997 Macarthur Boulevard
Mahwah, New Jersey 07430

www.paulistpress.com

Printed and bound in the
United States of America

# CONTENTS

# CONTENTS

# Editors and Translators of This Volume

RIK VAN NIEUWENHOVE is lecturer in theology at Mary Immaculate College, University of Limerick, Ireland.

ROBERT FAESEN, SJ, is a theologian in the Ruusbroec Society of the Faculty of Arts and Sciences of the University of Antwerp, Belgium.

HELEN ROLFSON is associate professor of theology at Saint John's School of Theology Seminary in Collegeville, Minnesota.

For our parents

# ACKNOWLEDGMENTS

The editors gratefully acknowledge the collaboration of Marcel Cock, Thom Mertens, Kees Schepers, José van Aelst, and John Van Engen.

We would like to express our gratitude to Professor Bernard McGinn for his assistance in seeing this project through publication and for his advice, encouragement, and friendship. We would also like to thank Joan Laflamme for her professionalism and expertise in the editing of the manuscript and preparing it for publication.

# GENERAL INTRODUCTION

The spiritual tradition of the Low Countries, mostly written in Dutch (or Flemish, which is the same language as spoken in Flanders, the northern part of present-day Belgium), must rank, together with the German School, as the most important vernacular tradition in Late Medieval and Early Modern Europe. Names like Hadewijch, Beatrice of Nazareth, and Jan van Ruusbroec immediately come to mind. While the works of the aforementioned authors are increasingly known outside the world of scholars active in Flanders and Holland, if only through English translations now widely available, the same cannot be said of the authors included in the present book.[1]

None of the works included here has ever been translated into English, and some of the writings included have never been translated into any modern language (including modern Dutch); indeed, some have never been published at all but exist only in manuscript form.

We have included a number of authors who were immediately associated with Ruusbroec's monastery at Groenendaal, near the Zonien Forest outside Brussels. Willem Jordaens (d. 1372) knew Ruusbroec (1293–1381) and translated some of his works. Nevertheless, his *Kiss of Mouth*, a masterpiece of mystical theology, reveals the voice of a creative, scholarly, and independent author. Jan van Leeuwen (d. 1378), the "good cook" from Groenendaal, wrote some spiritual treatises and a fierce attack on Meister Eckhart. Jan van Schoonhoven (d. 1432) represents (and facilitated) the transition of the Ruusbroecian mystical tradition, located in Groenendaal, to the Modern Devotion, a lay movement inspired by Geert Grote, with Windesheim as one of its main centers.[2] We have included a short Latin commentary by Jan van Schoonhoven on a sermon preached by Nicolas of Strasbourg. Finally, a short *Defense of Ruusbroec* by an anonymous author (presumably not directly associated with Groenendaal) is also included.

The most popular work of the Modern Devotion is undoubtedly *The Imitation of Christ* by Thomas à Kempis, which is widely available in English translation. Works by a number of other authors, including Geert Grote and Gerard Zerbolt van Zutphen, have been translated by John Van Engen in the present series. We have therefore opted to include only the following pieces by authors from the *Devotio Moderna:* some extracts from Hendrik Mande (d. 1431), and part of an anonymous work called *Bedudinghe in Cantica Canticorum,* which is usually associated with the circle of the Modern Devotion.

An important contribution to the spirituality of the Low Countries in the fifteenth and sixteenth centuries was made by the Franciscans. *The Mirror of Perfection* by Herp (d. 1477) must rank as one of the most important channels through which the spirituality of the Low Countries was disseminated throughout Europe in the Early Modern period. It may not be a particularly original work, but the way it selects and shapes its sources (especially Ruusbroec) results in a work that is more original and forward looking than is often thought. A number of anonymous, more devotional works put the suffering of Christ at the heart of their prayerful meditations, especially *A Ladder of Eight Rungs* and *The Nine Flowers of the Passion,* taken from a treatise called *Indica mihi.* Another little treatise, *A Sweet Meditation,* has a dramatic flavor that sets it somewhat apart from these two works. Perhaps Gerard Appelmans' *Gloss on the Our Father* should be included in the Franciscan environment too. Some have argued that Appelmans (who was a hermit) might have been influenced by the Dominican tradition,[3] but we find very little evidence for this claim; some of his teachings appear more Franciscan.[4]

Finally, we included a number of significant women writers of the fifteenth and sixteenth centuries. The reader will be able to become acquainted with a beautiful extract from the beguine Claesinne van Nieuwland on the superessential life. Another major author included in this section is Alijt Bake (d. 1455). We included a number of poems by Suster Bertken (Sister Bertken) (d. 1514). A number of female writers wrote anonymously. First, there is the intriguing author (d. 1540) of two major works, *Die Evangelische*

*Perle* (The Evangelical Pearl) and *Tempel onser zielen* (The Temple of Our Soul), in which traditional allegorical readings enjoy a late renaissance. According to Kees Schepers, the anonymous sermons he uncovered (and published here for the first time) may very well originate from the same circle. The two letters by Maria van Hout (d. 1547) are very different again and more recognizably modern.

There is a rich variety in the present collection. There are a number of more "traditional" mystical-theological writings that look back to the classic age of Ruusbroec (for instance, Jordaens, but also the author of the *Pearl* and the *Temple*); some focus almost exclusively on the sufferings of Christ (for example, *A Ladder of Eight Rungs*); and there are devotional texts that shy away from the more daring trinitarian speculations of Ruusbroec's time. Is it then possible to identify a number of themes that are shared by some, if not all, of these authors?

Predictably, those authors who still draw explicitly on Ruusbroec display a number of shared themes. We enumerate five. First, the role the Persons of the Trinity play in the transformation of the human person is a recurring theme in the work of different authors such as Jordaens, Herp, the author of the *Temple*, and in the anonymous sermons Kees Schepers uncovered: the Spirit transforms the will, the Son transforms the intellect, and the Father transforms the mind or memory (in the Augustinian sense). Second, their anthropology is also trinitarian, and often directly indebted to Ruusbroec (for instance, the distinction between the so-called *essential* union of the soul—the ground of the soul where God exercises his continuous creative activity that bestows being upon us—and the *active* union of the soul as the seat of the three faculties). We find this, for instance, in Chapter 13 of *The Temple* and in the writings of William Jordaens. A third element shared by at least some of these authors (and closely associated with the first two points) is their rejection of quietist states (especially in Jordaens and Herp). A fourth element is the emphasis upon the humanity of Christ. This too was a theme that was of significance to Ruusbroec, but later authors of Franciscan provenance exploited it in a manner that must strike modern readers as perhaps somewhat extreme (*A Ladder of Eight Rungs; Indica mihi*). Finally, there is the continuing importance of allegorical readings in a number of authors included here.

Ruusbroec's most voluminous work, *Die Geestelike Tabernakel (The Spiritual Tabernacle)*, is a major allegorical meditation on the way the Tabernacle (mentioned in Exodus) was constructed. This allegorical inclination flourishes again in the author of the *Temple* and in the sermons that Kees Schepers translated for the present volume. An original point is that the liturgical year itself (rather than the life of Christ, which it reflects) is seen as the main object of allegorical readings.

Perhaps all these themes are shared by other traditions too. However, the emphasis with which they are developed (especially the trinitarian dimension) and the often explicit textual dependency on Ruusbroec's writings on these issues sets the School of the Low Countries apart from later Schools, such as the School of the Spanish Carmelites.

We wish to extend our gratitude to all those who kindly agreed to contribute to this volume. John Van Engen translated and introduced Alijt Bake; Marcel Cock translated Jan van Leeuwen; José van Aelst translated Suster Bertken; Kees Schepers translated *Bedudinghe* and four anonymous sermons; and Thom Mertens translated Hendrik Mande. All the other contributions were translated and introduced by the editors (Rob Faesen: *Defense of Ruusbroec* by an anonymous author, Claesinne van Nieuwland, the *Temple*, and Maria van Hout; Helen Rolfson: *The Evangelical Pearl* and Gerard Appelmans; and Rik Van Nieuwenhove: Willem Jordaens, Jan van Schoonhoven, *A Ladder of Eight Rungs, Indica mihi (The Nine Flowers of the Passion), A Sweet Meditation,* and Hendrik Herp).

We also wish to express our gratitude to the Mary Immaculate College Research Directorate for its financial support to Rik Van Nieuwenhove, and to Mary Cunningham for her detailed proofreading of parts of the manuscript.

Finally the editors would like to express their gratitude to Professor Bernard McGinn, editor-in-chief of the Classics of Western Spirituality, for his editorial assistance and advice, his generous support, and his ever-perceptive comments, which greatly contributed to this book.

# Willem Jordaens
## *The Kiss of Mouth*[1]

### (De Oris Osculo)

*The text translated here from the Middle Dutch is usually known under its Latin title* De oris osculo *(The Kiss of Mouth). L. Reypens attributed it to Willem Jordaens. Jordaens was born in Brussels around 1321, was ordained, and studied at the university (probably Paris). He must have joined the Augustinian canons at Groenendaal around 1352, and he died in November 1372. Jordaens therefore came into immediate contact with Jan van Ruusbroec, who was prior in Groenendaal until his death in 1381. Like so many others who came into contact with Ruusbroec's person and writings, Jordaens was influenced by Ruusbroec's mystical theology. He also translated a number of Ruusbroec's key works into Latin, including* Die Geestelike Brulocht (The Spiritual Espousals).[2]

*Apart from the influence of Ruusbroec, with whom Jordaens shares a trinitarian orientation and a rejection of quietism,* The Kiss of Mouth *also reveals the scholastic background of Jordaens.[3] Combining intellectual rigor with a theological emotion and profundity reminiscent of Augustine's* Confessions, *this work must rank as one of the most beautiful spiritual works of the Late Medieval period. It is our hope that the present translation will prove an incentive for others to translate the work in its entirety. (About one-third of the text, namely chapters 1–3 and the final chapter 11, is translated here.)[4]*

*The ascent to the kiss of mouth between the soul and God is preceded by a courtship: first, there is loving mutual gazing* (ondersien) *[chapter 1]; second, a loving conversing [chapter 3]; third, mutual befriending; and only then the kiss of mouth ensues. This scheme is, in turn, crisscrossed by another one, obviously inspired by St. Bernard's* Commentary on the Song of Songs. *Before the soul can please her Bridegroom, she must be adorned with humility and virtues. Chapter 2 therefore discusses the kiss of the two feet of our Lord: the foot of truth and the foot of mercy.*

1

*The soul is now sufficiently prepared for the loving conversing with Christ [chapter 3] and she requests to kiss the hands of Christ [chapter 4]. The right hand symbolizes the thirst for justice and the strength to perform acts of justice, while the left hand stands for the sword of inner peace, which protects the soul from adversity [chapter 5]. Chapter 6 contains an excursus on the common life—Ruusbroec's ideal of charitable activity and contemplation, and a critique of quietism (a recurring theme throughout the book). Chapters 7–10 pave the way for the kiss of mouth by developing a number of important theological themes, such as the significance of the sacraments, the role of the humanity of Jesus and his redemptive activity as the way toward the divinity, and a discussion of the Trinity. Through the operation of the Holy Spirit and the Son the soul is drawn into the knowledge of the hidden Father—a theme we will encounter again in the work of Herp. While the Son draws the intellect, and the Spirit draws or pulls the will, the Father draws the soul into union in two manners: through faith, and through purity of heart (quoting John 14:29 and Matt 5:8). The soul is now prepared for the kiss of mouth, described in chapter 11 (translated below).*

*This kiss takes place in a perfect unknowing of God. In this life the soul is stuck between a knowledge in similitudes, which no longer appeals to her, and the knowledge of glory, which she has not been granted yet. Dwelling in this darkness, the soul hears the whispers of the Word spoken by the Father, keeping her from abandoning herself to sleep in the darkness (another opportunity for Jordaens to criticize quietism). Relying on all too inadequate words, Jordaens attempts to describe this whispering, during which the Bridegroom gives his mouth to kiss to the soul: "Lord," the soul beseeches, "give me a kiss, for in the darkness we can kiss even when we cannot see each other" [para. 216]. This kiss symbolizes the transformation or deification of the soul.*

*This union between God and soul occurs on "the active level." Here Jordaens is again indebted to Ruusbroec, who first made a distinction between the essential being of the soul (that is, God's continuous creative presence in the soul) and the active unity or existence (that is, the soul as a living core of the faculties, namely mind/memory, intellect, and will). Given the fact that we have been made in the image of God, Jordaens, like Ruusbroec before him, draws on trinitarian theology [para. 221] to make this anthropological point. This allows him to return to one of the recurring themes of the book: his rejection of passive, quietist mystical states.*

2

*Whereas the quietists pursue an inactive, passive emptiness, Jordaens attempts to make clear how we can find enjoyment and rest in the midst of our active knowing and loving of God.[5]*

# THE KISS OF MOUTH
## Introduction

1.   The heart that is filled with love can hardly contain itself; it has to express itself in the only manner it knows, it reveals itself using the only signs it is familiar with to the one it loves. When it loves with sincerity, and when it is filled with faithfulness and favor toward its beloved, it desires to receive the same response from him, and demands a sign of love in return. This is why, in the Song of Songs, the bride, that is the loving soul, feeling replete with affection and willing to do many works and bestow many signs of love, demands a major sign of love and speaks out from her inner riches: "Let him kiss me with the kiss of his mouth" (Sg 1:1). If this mistress had not possessed the fullness of love, it would have been rather bold to have spoken before she had been kissed and before she had been spoken to and exerted herself in love. We can, however, safely assume that she had attained the stage of love that leads to the kiss of mouth.

2.   In natural, worldly love, which mirrors the divine love, we usually distinguish three stages before we arrive at the kiss of mouth. The first stage is a loving gaze, and here love takes root. After this, there is a loving conversing, while the third stage is acting toward one another in friendly manner. Finally, we attain to the kiss of mouth. Since we, being coarse, can only attain truth through likenesses, we can see that we only attain to the kiss of mouth, which symbolizes supernatural grace and superessential union with God, via these three stages.

Thus, first there is a loving gaze, namely, an awareness of the majesty, the opulence, the goodness, and the lovability of God in the light of faith and the holy scripture.

The second stage is a loving conversing, the showing to God of our desire and craving to love him on the one hand, and God's response to us that he wants to receive us in his love, on the other.

In the stage of gazing, having become aware of God's majesty and power, on the one hand, and our own insignificance and unworthiness to love such a great Lord, on the other, we fall down with Mary Magdalene at the feet of our Lord, and we deplore and grieve over our imperfection and faultiness. Then the Lord requests us to kiss his feet; he gives us a sweet sense of his grace and his mercy, and a clear insight into the truth of a spiritual life.

The third stage is a loving activity, namely, to perform in a pious manner works and practices of love in God's honor. Now God raises us from his feet in order that we would not remain at that stage forever, and he offers us his hands for kissing. His hands represent justice and peace, and he addresses us in the same way as he spoke to Magdalene: "Go in peace" (John 8:11), which means: practice justice under the protection of my peace. In the kissing of this hand of God the wise soul hungers and thirsts so much for justice that she becomes filled with love and desire to taste God. Blessed are those who hunger and thirst after justice for they shall have their fill (Matt 5:6). Now God raises the hungry soul toward his countenance in the purity of her spirit and gives her a burning desire to kiss him, which means to be united with him in love; and he gives her the courage to request, from the fullness of her desire, to kiss his mouth, and to say with the bride of God: "Let him kiss me with the kiss of his mouth" (Sg 1:1).

In short, the wise soul, who loves in a prudent and honest manner and who wants to engage in courtship without much resources of her own, first practices a loving gaze between herself and God. After this, she lovingly converses with him when kissing his two feet, which represent the grace of his mercy and the perception of truth. Hereupon a loving activity ensues, with loving deeds, when kissing both hands, representing his justice and peace; this will make the soul worthy of, and in a position to request and to receive, the kiss of his mouth.

The above-mentioned feet and the hands of our Lord are linked by the prophet in the Psalms as follows: "Mercy and truth have met each other; justice and peace have kissed" (Ps 85:11).

# Chapter 1

*The loving mutual gazing of God and soul*

3. Now then, my soul, if you desire to be kissed with the kiss of his mouth you should first practice the loving gazing. Make use of the reasonable eyes that God has given you to perceive him. Purify them from the whims of alien pleasures, from coveting the things of this world, from the darkness of irascibility and envy, from the haze of pride, from the winds of vainglory, and purify them from every alien image, in order that they may become a clear mirror in which the beauty of your beloved can cast his image, for you cannot see your beloved in this life in any other way than in a dim reflection in a mirror and through likenesses, as St. Paul says (cf. 1 Cor 13:12).

Now observe that God is in his essence an eternal, single goodness, which contains within itself all the good, non-bodily, properties that you will find in an accidental manner in creatures, such as goodness, wisdom, power, and so forth. Properties that are separate in creatures are unified in him; and properties that are finite in creatures subsist in him in an infinite manner. For he is immeasurably powerful, wise, and good. Properties that creatures received from him in a multiple and accidental manner, are one in God and are his single essence itself, and he has not received them from anybody but his own eternal nature. These properties are truly present in God and identical to his own essence, but they utterly transcend the comprehension of mortal creatures. That is the reason why the loving soul who has gazed longingly at the divine beauty has to negate from God all these properties insofar as they exist in creatures, and attribute them to him in an unnameable and incomprehensible manner. For the power, the wisdom, and the goodness that they are able to name and comprehend are totally unlike God's being. They name and understand them as they encounter them in creatures, that is, in a finite, divided, multiple and accidental manner, while God's being is infinite, undivided, single, and essential in himself and all creatures. This explains why the wise souls in their intellectual gaze view God as an utterly incomprehensible nameless nothing. Still, in reality God is a superessential unfathomable something. However, because the reasonable eye of the soul cannot comprehend or name him, it believes that, according to its manner of understanding, God's being is nothing rather than something. You can compare it to our bodily eyes that look into darkness and assume that they see nothing rather than something, while as a matter of fact they do see something, namely, the unilluminated air. This is why God is darkness according to our manner of perceiving him but not in himself, for "in him there is no darkness" as St. John says (1 John 1:5), but he is pure, single intellectual light, which blinds our reasonable eye so much with its brightness that it assumes that it sees darkness rather than brightness. Similarly, when a bat looks into the sun, it becomes so blinded by the unbearable and incomprehensible brightness that it assumes it sees darkness rather than light, while in truth it is of course a light.

This is the darkness in which God dwells, as scripture puts it, and where he withdraws from our reasonable eye, and this is why her highest object is, in her view, nothing rather than something, and her highest knowledge is an unknowing, as St. Dionysius states,[6] until that time when grace will be transformed in glory; illuminated she will then see in the light of glory the pure glorious light of God's essence.

4. Although all this is true, God nevertheless reveals himself to the soul that sets out. He reveals himself in the mirror of her reason, in spiritual images, and in likenesses, as an immeasurable eternal goodness, wisdom, power, riches, mercy, beauty, and so forth, so as to lead her to the highest knowledge of his unknowability, and to show her that he is lovable beyond all creatures, and to allow her to find in him in an infinite, incomprehensible, and unified manner all she can grasp in creatures in a finite, comprehensible, and manifold, and scattered manner.

5. It is you, then, my soul, whom I address, you who are most intimate to me and to whom I am most closely tied: when I behold you, I behold God and all things in God; if I were to lose you, it would be of no avail to me if I were to gain the whole world; open up your reasonable eyes, as I said earlier, and observe: you will find in God in an immeasurable manner all the lovability you could ever find or hope to find in creatures. You will find that, in the generosity of his goodness, God has bestowed upon all creatures every good

property you are likely to find in them, in accordance with the receptivity of each to God's being, which is the subsistence of all accidental properties. Everything that does not exist of its own has a subsistence from elsewhere; this is the reason why the being of creatures is not their own but God's. Because the being of creatures does not exist of its own, God must be its subsistence and support.[7] We can therefore state that God is omnipresent, not in the sense that he needs anything, but all creatures need him as their own subsistence and support.

6. Every support that is coarser than that which it supports, supports it from outside inward: thus the cask supports water or air. However, the support that is more refined than that which it supports, supports it from inside outwards: thus the soul supports the body. Now, given the fact that he is more refined and onefold than any thing that is being supported, God is therefore more intimate and nearer to any creature than the creature is to itself,[8] for he is an inner support of all beings, just as the soul is more intimate and closer to her body than the body is to itself, for the soul is the inner support of its being and its life.

If this is true, and it is true, then you, my soul, should never seek pleasure or delight outside yourself, when you have such an immeasurable treasure, such an incomprehensible depth of riches, beauty, and nobility within yourself. Empty yourself of all creaturely images, and observe with onefold eyes the support of your being, which is God; take note of his infinite treasure of all that is good, and remain there, without seeking to obtain or get any external pleasures. Then you may be stirred amid your loving gaze toward loving him.

7. Even though God is a generous, common[9] lover, he still wants to see how his beloved pleases him; if she is to his liking, properly adorned with virtues, and if she is so desirous to taste him that she begins to please him, then he will look at her lovingly and receive her in his love. If her desire is rather lukewarm, and not adorned with virtues, then he will look at her with merciful eyes, and by his grace and her willingness she will be made pleasing. Examine yourself, my soul, and see whether you are adorned with loving, humble fear to please such a great loving Lord who is entitled to throw you in the pit of hell because of your unlikeness and,

what is more, could let you return into nothingness, if he were to withdraw his support, given the fact that he continually keeps you in existence. Examine whether you trust his generous goodness with the certain hope that he will help you with his grace and his mercy to adorn you in his love as much as you need.

8. He especially notices the two virtues of fear and love in his beloved. As the prophet says in the Psalm: "God takes pleasure in them that fear him and in them that hope in his mercy" (Ps 147:11). Examine whether you are willing to suffer or endure for his sake, for that pleases him and elicits his mercy. For he spoke to Moses, "I have seen the suffering and the endurance of my people, and I have come down to release them" (cf. Exod 3:7–9). Examine whether you have obeyed his commandments, and whether you are willing to abandon for his sake the manifoldness and delights of the world: this particularly pleases him, as the prophet points out: "Hearken, O daughter," he says, "and see and incline your ear, and forget thy people and thy father's home, and the king shall greatly desire thy beauty" (Ps 45:11). Examine whether your thoughts are righteous, for the prophet says in the Psalm: "The eyes of God are upon the just and his ears unto their prayers" (Ps 34:16). Examine whether you have an inner desire and an incisive longing to please, to love, and to serve God, and a right judgment in his service and his love. For the prophet says in the Psalms that the young calf with horns and hoofs pleases God (Ps 69:32). I take the young calf to mean the soul that first sets out and who offers herself up for the service of our Lord. The horns symbolize her longing and desire, and the split hoofs her reasonable judgment, which splits all her works in two, examining whether they are good or evil, honorable or dishonorable, pleasing or displeasing to God. But above all, examine whether you are deeply humble. For humility is such a great adornment of the soul that Mary, the Mother of God, who keeps silent about all her virtues, speaks out that God regarded the humility of her (cf. Luke 1:48). Through the prophet Isaiah he says, "Upon whom but the humble man will my spirit rest?" (Isa 66:2). Observe, my soul, whether you are adorned in such a manner, that God will look at you with such loving eyes as if there was no other creature in the world to bestow his love upon but you. This will entice and

8

stir you to love him as if there was no creature left to love, or that God could love, but only God and yourself alone.

10. But it seems to me, my poor soul, insofar as I can see, that you are not adorned with any virtue, but rather covered from head to toe with all kinds of sin. Look at yourself and see whether your head, that is your will, is not tainted with pride, self-centeredness, and lacking in self-abandonment toward God and your superiors. Look whether your reason is not infected with an inflated opinion of yourself; your irascible power with anger, impatience, and cruelty, vindictiveness and mercilessness; with envy and inordinate fear and sadness. Examine whether your concupiscent appetite is not infected with lustful inclinations, inordinate love for creatures, people, and earthly things, with disorderly longings, hopes, and contentment. Examine whether your inner mind does not seek in all its activities vainglory, honor, and praise, gain or pleasures; examine your external senses, whether you have not used them for your pleasure instead of honoring God in a proper manner, especially your eyes, which often inspire you with disorderly inclinations as they often show you the manifold beauty and splendor of creatures. Still, you have often heard and read how deep the prophet, King David, fell because of inordinate sights, leading him to commit adultery and murder. Given the fact that even a man as holy as David fell so deep because of inordinate sights, you should be particularly mindful of this danger, as you are exposed to so many inordinate sights. Indeed, I am fearful that, even if you do not succumb in external deeds, you succumb often within with inordinate desires, and remember that our Lord has said that a man who covets another man's wife has already committed the sin in his heart. If you use the other senses in an inordinate manner, they too will lead to similar inclinations and desires. This is why the prophet calls them windows through which death enters into our soul (cf. Jer 9:21). The holy Job makes a similar point, "I made a covenant with my eyes that I would not so much as think upon a virgin" (Job 31:1), which means, I want to use my senses in an orderly fashion, so as not to allow them to induce images upon which my thoughts would dwell in an inordinate manner.

# Chapter 2

*The soul's humble kiss of feet*

11. Now then, my poor soul, given the fact that you are ugly and unadorned, you cannot please God nor can he look at you with the loving, friendly eyes with which he gazes at his well-pleasing beloved, wounding her with love (cf. Sg 4:9). What you need is for him to look at you with merciful eyes, so as to adorn you with virtues and grace: without him you cannot have or do anything good.

Therefore, prostrate yourself at his feet, which I have mentioned earlier. Moisten the left foot of truth with your tears and lament the fact that you are unadorned and that you live in breach of the divine commandments and counsels, the teachings of the holy scriptures and the holy life, the wisdom of your conscience, and your reason, which are rules of the eternal truth. Dry this foot with your hair, that is, with sorrow and dissatisfaction over your life. Kiss it with your mouth, that is, yearn with inner desire to lead your life in accordance with the rules of truth. Anoint it with sweet-smelling fragrances, that is, have a loving trust that God will assist you with the grace of his mercy. Without this anointment the foot would be too barren to kiss. For if anybody looks at the rules of truth he utterly fails to live up to, given his weakness, and if he does not detect in himself the confidence to trust in God, then he might stumble from fear and doubt into utter despair.

You must then moisten the right foot of God's mercy with inner, loving tears, so as to receive his grace and a sweet desire to live according to the truth. Dry the foot with humble dedication to his generous goodness and kiss it with inner desire so as to receive in all your deeds and practices a delicate, inner longing and a loving, sweet intent focused on God. You should not anoint this foot, for mercy is itself an anointment.

12. Look, my poor soul: you should kiss these two feet of our Lord with humble, loving desire, and you should never kiss one without the other. For he who, with a desire for the true state of a saintly life, wants to kiss and contemplate the foot of truth only, no matter how humble and truly saintly he attempts to be; no matter how obedient toward God and his superiors; no matter how hum-

ble and detached amongst people for God's sake; no matter how benevolent and generous toward all people in need and toward the community; no matter how patient and equanimous in the midst of adversity and suffering; no matter how moderate in his needs; no matter how prudent and cautious, when using his senses and in all his doings and comings, against the ploys of the enemy, the vanity of the world, and the indulgences of the flesh; no matter how upright in his thoughts; no matter how focused upon God with loving praise, prayers for his grace and assistance in attaining a life of sainthood, with devotion, gratitude, and flowing love. He who thus contemplates and desires to live while kissing the foot of truth but not the foot of mercy through which he would desire, request, and obtain with humble prayer the assistance of grace and the divine mercy, and the delicate desire to fulfill all the rules of God's truth— he will often fail in many points.

13. Because, "Without me," the Lord says, "you cannot do anything" (John 15:5). As St. Paul states: we are not able to think something of our own accord but all our ability is from God. When we realize that we cannot live up to the rules of truth by merely relying on our own abilities according to our own desire, and we do not look for God's assistance and grace, we begin to despair of becoming a perfect, holy human being. For he who, solely relying on his own strengths, wants to climb up the tree of life, which has been planted in the paradise of the holy church from the beginning of the world, is bound to fall, and the higher he hopes to climb and the more noble the fruit he wants to taste, the deeper he will fall. God has requested the angels, that is, his graces, to guard the tree of life, lest anybody arrive at the tree of a holy life and taste its fruit without his permission and the assistance of the grace and mercy of God. For the angel, with the fiery sword of his fury, keeps away those who want to approach the tree of life by their own strength, without a humble request for the assistance and grace of God.

14. He who kisses the foot of truth should therefore also kiss the foot of mercy. On the other hand, he who wants to kiss only the foot of mercy, and who wants to rely solely upon the grace and the mercifulness of God, and who, by merely relishing the inner sweetness and the pleasure of his devotion, thus becoming unmindful of himself and the rules of truth—such a person is in danger of becom-

ing overconfident and reckless in his life, failing to live his life in accordance with the grace he has received. He does not turn toward God and fails to dwell in God's presence with humble fear, and a loving reverence, but in a brazen and audacious manner he presumes that he is a child favored by God, who bestows the sweetness of his love upon him. Because of his overconfidence and self-righteousness he often fails on many issues, having become reckless and imprudent in all his comings and goings, and he uses his outward senses for his own delight rather than in accordance with truth. Given his self-confidence and self-assuredness, he will, as he has grown used to delights, turn toward external delights if his inner mind cannot find delights within. Indeed, given the fact that the soul is onefold and cannot simultaneously enjoy two contrary delights, it will, if it does not turn within, all too often be tempted to seek delights in external objects and squander its inner delights. At that moment, God will withdraw the foot of mercy and allow the soul to wander in its alien delights, in order to correct the soul and to reveal its sickness, as long as his mercifulness deems appropriate. He then offers her the foot of truth, and he reveals her wanderings and her unlikeness, and how great her need is to blend her inner delights with humility, and her delight with holy fear. He will make clear to her that she is not to become too self-assured in this life, in which temptations and snares abound, but always to be watchful, and not to rely on her inner feelings of delight but rather to use them devoutly in fulfilling the rules of truth with delicate gladness for God's sake.

In short, we should not kiss one foot without the other, but we should kiss the foot of truth with a delicate desire to live according to the rules of truth, and the foot of mercy with humble, holy fear to be forever watchful and mindful of impedimental consolations and delights.

15. Observe, my soul, how often you have kissed one foot of God only, and especially only the foot of mercy. Remember how often you have enjoyed an inner delight so great, and so sweet a devotion to live in accordance with the truth, that you assumed that nothing could hinder you and that, as a consequence, you became reckless in relation to external sensual attractions. Indeed, often you have been captured by delights and sensual consolations, and the

inner delights and the foot of mercy were therefore withdrawn from you. Be mindful lest the foot of mercy is taken away forevermore, and the foot of truth kicks you into the pit of hell.

# Chapter 3

*The loving conversing of God and soul*

16. When the soul who first sets out, wets the feet of our Lord with tears, and dries and kisses them, and when she has a clear idea of truth and a delicate desire to live according to the rules of truth, our Lord lifts her up somewhat, and allows her to sit with Magdalene at his feet to listen to his loving words. He now shows her his loving countenance, that is, his sweet presence, richly endowed with all kinds of goodness. When revealing himself like this, he demands love in return, and says: "Love me, for I am lovable above all creatures. Everything good and lovable that you may find in a scattered, manifold, and finite manner in creatures, you will find in my onefoldness as simple and infinite. They have their lovability from me and it is only accidental in them, while I have this love from myself, and it is my own essence and nature. Relinquish all creatures, and love only me, for I am a loving mirror and reward of love, and myself an infinite love." In this manner God speaks to the soul when he lovingly reveals both himself and his riches that surpass all creatures to her inner eyes, which at this stage are brightly illuminated.

17. This stirs the soul and, enkindled in God's love, she gains confidence to respond to her beloved who first bestowed love upon her: "I have, Lord, found in myself that my whole life, yes, the eternal, blissful life of all reasonable creatures, consists in the love and the clear knowledge of him whom one loves. No creature can have a fulfilling life without love; and an unfulfilling life is more resembling of death than of life. I notice that eternal death consists in failing to love. This occurs as follows. If we love creatures, the lovability of which is accidental, finite, and scattered, and these creatures lose their lovability, our love will perish too. Or if the state of the soul changes because of the death of the body, her prefer-

ences and sources of pleasure will accordingly change, and that which pleased and delighted her earlier, will now become displeasing and unpleasant to her, and she will lose her love. If she remains like this forever she is, in accordance with our faith, in eternal death: to be without love amounts to an eternal death. This is why St. John says, 'He that loveth not abideth in death' (1 John 3:15).

18. "Thus, Lord, love is the source and cause of life, and perishable love is the source of a perishable life which is followed by eternal death. Eternal love, however, is the source of eternal life, consisting of eternal delights and imperishable glory. Now, love can only be imperishable if both lover and beloved are imperishable and unchangeable. But you alone, Lord, are imperishable; for your lovability is eternal, infinite, and you alone are your own love; and therefore your love is not accidental and unchangeable, for love is your own essence and nature. Seeing that love transforms the lover in accordance with the nature of that which he loves, so too, Lord, the soul that loves you will be transformed according to your nature as essential love. This is why St. Peter says, 'Our Lord has done great and unfathomable things, making us partakers in the divine nature' (cf. 2 Pet 1:4). I therefore observe that only he who loves you and perseveres with this love unto death will not perish and become unchangeable. For you are unchangeable, and he becomes transformed with your eternal unchangeability, and thus he comes to possess an eternal love, which is eternal life.

"Therefore, my dearest Lord, my beloved bridegroom, I therefore want to follow your advice and fulfill your request to love you only, for you please me above all creatures in my inner spiritual delight. But you know that the one who loves becomes sweet beyond compare when he experiences a loving response from his beloved. Therefore, Lord, if you want me to love you, respond to me and give me your love to taste, so as to allow me to love you with the profound hope of enjoying you in the fullness of an all-pervasive love."

19. The Lord answers: "Do you doubt my love? Is there any person on earth who longs to be loved by somebody he does not want to love in return? Not loving somebody may not be unusual but refusing to return love is unnatural, unless there is a major cause not to. How then could I, eternal love by nature, be such an unnat-

ural lover that I would refuse to love that person whom I long to be loved by? 'I love them that love me' (Prov 8:17), my wisdom says in the scriptures. My love makes me demand your love, and my love is the cause of anybody loving me. For 'My delight is to be with the children of men' (Prov 8:31), scripture says, and for that reason my love is not really responsive but rather an eternal prevenient love, for I have loved my elect with a love from all eternity. Love me, therefore, without doubting my love, and let this be a certain feeling and a true sign of my love: that you love me with desire, that you renounce the world, that you annihilate all sinful inclinations of your sensuality, that you abnegate your own will, and that you gladly perform your virtues in my honor. For without my prevenient love and without the sweet taste of my grace you cannot do any of these.

20. "If you desire a different idle feeling, be it spiritual or bodily, outside the practice of love and virtues, then you misperceive what you long for in reality, for idle[10] feeling is not a true taste or sign of my love, nor of yours, for it probably has an alien cause, and it comes and goes, according to the disposition of your nature. Nevertheless, many people are of the opinion that they do not love, and that they are lukewarm, slothful, and imperfect in all virtues when they do not have such a feeling, and that they have been forgotten and abandoned by me, and that I do not love them. They then become reluctant to perform virtues, and unmindful of themselves. When they have this feeling, they are brave, and they are of the view that they love deeply and are willing to perform all kind of virtuous behavior, thinking themselves to be saintly. When, however, they lose this feeling, they fall into despair again, and become dissatisfied with their life, becoming slothful and careless. All this is the result of kissing the foot of my mercy only, enjoying the sweet taste of my grace in idleness, failing to put my love to good use for the sake of my honor, with proper judgment and prudence.

21. "Therefore, if you want to have a genuine feeling and sweet taste of my grace, make sure you perform essential deeds of love and attain perfection of virtues; a sweet taste and a genuine feeling will then ensue and always accompany these. Be utterly humble; my grace is all-living water, springing forth from the living well of my mercy, always wanting to run downward—this means, in

humble hearts—and it cannot remain on mountains—this means, on proud hearts. Empty yourself from all alien images and inordinate love. For my Holy Spirit is like the sweet air that will fill every void that has been made for me, but that will be driven out rapidly by earthly love and alien thoughts, like earth and water drive out air from a cask. Wipe yourself dry through the exercise of love and the performance of virtues, of all alien pleasures and temporal consolations, for my holy love is a burning fire, igniting and setting alight in praise and love hearts seasoned with innerness and tasteful devotion. This is a genuine taste and a true sign of my love."

22. The soul answers: "Oh, Lord, if I understand you correctly, I am not familiar with, and unable for, the true taste and the sweet feeling of your love, for I am slothful and lukewarm in loving you, and imperfect in every virtue. Every virtue meets so much opposition and dissimilarity in me, that it often recedes, or performs its work with much difficulty, and I taste very little, or none, of any virtue. My imagination is full of alien images, and is being flooded with dissimilar, manifold impressions of earthly things that drown my heart in the joys and sorrows, the pleasures and displeasures of creatures; and your grace, your sweet spirit and your burning love find me unreceptive and indolent. Indeed, your grace does not find in me a valley of humility in which it can reside, but a mountain of pride, on which it cannot dwell; and your holy, sweet spirit does not find in me a receptive void it can fill; rather, my heart is so full of the water of earthly impressions that the sweet air of your spirit cannot enter it, as scripture says: the Holy Spirit will withdraw himself from thoughts that are without understanding (cf. Wis 1:5).

23. "Your burning love does not find in my heart any seasoned dryness it might ignite for it is flooded with the waters of alien loves and sensual pleasures. Therefore I can only cry out with the prophet in the Psalter: 'Save me, O Lord, for the waters are come in even unto my soul' (Ps 69:2). St. Peter, my Lord, walked on water, drawing on your power, showing that your grace can raise people above the manifoldness of impressions and above all sensual love and earthly delights. Yet St. Peter was not very steadfast and was succumbing under the force of the wind that blew against him, and he had to cry out: 'Lord, save me!' (Matt 14:30), for he began to sink. This reveals that nobody in this mortal life stands or pro-

gresses in such a steadfast manner without your assistance and your helping hand, as St. Peter did, lest he sink. For he often encounters manifold winds, that is, many temptations, which overwhelm him so much that he often begins to sink in the water of pleasures and displeasures, the joys and sorrows, which make him cry out: 'Lord, help me, put out your hand lest I drown!'

24. "Now I am utterly washed over with the water of unsteadiness and manifold impressions, and I am in danger of drowning. The waves of pleasures and displeasures, joys and sorrows, happiness and distress, throw me inordinately up and down, and I therefore call out: 'Lord, help me, stretch out your hand, and pull me out of these waters of unsteadiness, and make me walk above all manifoldness of sensual impressions, and allow me to kiss your hands, that is: to do works of righteousness in the still satiety of your peace; for in kissing your feet I do not find anything else but the living desire to live in accordance with the rules of truth, with the help of your grace and mercy.'"

See, my poor soul, this is the loving conversing between God and the soul that has first set out. Now the soul speaks, having observed the splendor of a spiritual life in a reasoned manner. Then God addresses her from within as truth, and this mutual conversing is as diverse in the mind as there are diverse ways of perceiving the truth within.

Entertain, therefore, my soul, a loving conversing with God. Freely reveal your neediness to him, and pray that he may raise you from his feet to his hands, that means, from the desire to live in accordance with truth to performing deeds of righteousness. The sweet feeling of his mercy will make you perform loving deeds, namely, in the exercise of love, and in the satiety of inner peace.

# Chapter 11

*The kiss of mouth*

199. Now I would like to show you, my poor soul, how you can attain the kiss of mouth from God, which is the most supreme fruit in this life. For everything that I have said so far is nothing but

a mutual befriending[11] between God and soul, in images and like-nesses, in accordance with the knowledge of the quiddity of God that we can attain in this life, that is, with which we understand what God is. But the kiss of mouth between God and soul occurs in the perfection of the knowledge of what God is not, and this is a perfect unknowing of God. We can reach this as follows.

200. I have said earlier [no. 135] that we can know the quid-dity of God in three ways. Two of those are possible in this life, and the third one in the eternal life. Of the first two I have spoken ear-lier to the best of my meager abilities; the third one we will receive after this life.

The God-loving soul desires above all to see God in his naked, glorious essence, and she constantly cries out, full of inner desire, with St. Philip: "Show us the Father, and it is enough for us" (John 14.8). With the prophet it calls out in the Psalter: "Lord, show us thy face, and we shall be saved" (cf. Ps 79:4; 8:20). Even if the soul were to encounter the onefold image of the fatherly essence in which the soul could quietly dwell in the inner vision of the mind, as I have described earlier, nevertheless, when she realizes that all her knowledge and vision merely consists of images and likenesses, and that she merely knows God's attire but not his countenance— for she tastes that God is not at all what the intellect or mind can imagine—she then strips her intellectual eyes from all images. She strips them from lowly corporeal images, and from supreme divine images, and she does not want to retain the image of goodness, wis-dom, threeness or oneness, divinity, or the image of onefold being. For she tastes that all these images, no matter how elevated they may seem, do not reveal God as he is in his inner self but only in accordance with our intellect and comprehension.

201. For this reason the soul climbs with her mind in a darkness devoid of images. Here she stands in a perfect unknowing of God, between two tables: between the knowledge of the quiddity of God, and starvation. The lower table, through which she knows and loves God only through created images, does not appeal to her. The higher table, through which she knows and loves God in his naked, glorious essence, is not open to her as long as she remains in this mortal life. For she has understood the word that God spoke to Moses in the

scriptures: "Man shall not see me and live" (Exod 33:20). Similarly, St. Paul says, "Eye has not seen, nor ear heard, neither has it entered into the heart of man, what things God has prepared for them that love him" (1 Cor 2:8) and "We see now through a glass in a dark manner; but then face to face" (1 Cor 13:12). Likewise, St. John says, "We are now the sons of God; and it has not yet appeared what we shall be, for we shall see him as he is" (1 John 3:2).

202. With this she tastes that she cannot attain the glorious knowledge of God in this life, unless God works miracles. She knows that her intellective eyes must become glorious first through the light of glory, as the prophet speaks in the Psalter: "Lord, in thy light we shall see light" (Ps 35:10). This means, it is only in the light of glory, in which and through which our intellect will be glorified, raised, and made receptive of a deiform knowledge, that we will see the glorious light of your divine essence. This is why the soul makes her abode in the imageless darkness of her mind, before the unmediated unknown presence of the glorious Godhead. For here, without the intermediary of images, the glorious light shines into the darkness, but the darkness cannot comprehend it, as St. John says (John 1:5). This is because the darkness has not yet been glorified. When that happens, she will comprehend the light in the light, and the soul will be raised to the higher table, where we eat and drink God; that is, she will know and love God in his naked and glorious essence as long as she patiently desires to dwell constantly in the darkness underneath the higher table.

203. The soul had previously made her abode with the Father in the onefold mind in the presence of the Fatherly being, and she regularly visited this dwelling, consisting of peace and quiet beyond all activity, throughout all her works and manifoldness, and frequented it with a onefold vision. Similarly, she now makes her abode in the dark nothingness of her mind, underneath the higher table, before the unknown presence of her beloved.

But even though she may have made her abode there, she is still anxious to please her beloved and to befriend him in all the ways that I mentioned earlier, and even more so. But throughout all activity (onlede) she frequently visits her dwelling with a onefold transition of her mind beyond all images and likenesses, beyond all the possible ways of naming God, and after all activity she returns here, enjoying rest in peace and in empty dark nothingness, as if in her own dwelling. Not that she is inactive *(ledich)* there, but she has there an inactive activity *(een ledeghe onledicheyt)*. That means, a loving desire to see the glorious countenance of her beloved, and to sit at the higher table, where her beloved shall wait on her, as he promised in the holy gospel (cf. Luke 18:37). Here he himself will be food and drink, and everything that the glorious hunger and thirst may desire.

204. This desire consists of three things. The first is a sorrow over everything that lies beneath this darkness, for there she cannot find God but in images and likenesses whereas she desires to see God's selfhood. This is the reason why she is also lovingly saddened over the darkness in which she dwells, at least until God shows himself. The soul knows that her failure to see God is due to herself, for God is in himself a glorious light, and "in him there is no darkness," as St. John states (1 John 1:5). This is why God in himself is more comprehensible for intelligent beings than any creature. Nevertheless, our knowledge of God is deficient, either because our intellective eye is not capable of knowing God when only relying on its natural light, or it has not been made ready yet to see God through the light of glory. To draw a comparison: as the sun is in itself more visible than any creature, given the fact that it is the fountain of all sensible light, nevertheless our bodily eyes cannot look into the sun, because of their weakness and inability. This is why the soul sorrows over its darkness, for she perceives that she is characterized by weakness and inability.

205. Here you may learn that those who glory in this darkness are in error, believing that they have become deified, and no longer desire or consider themselves in need of knowledge. The Son of God, who does not speak untruth, speaks to his Father: "This is eternal life: that they may know you, the only true God, and Jesus Christ, whom you have sent" (John 17:3). If eternal life consists in a glorious knowledge of God, how then can those who are inclined toward eternal bliss and possession of eternal life by grace, charity, or even by nature, glory in this darkness, which is a pure unknowing of God, and a nothingness of thoughts? For all darkness is nothingness. "What manner of joy" Tobias asks, "shall be to me, who sit in darkness, and see not the light?" (cf. Tob 5:12). How could it pos-

sibly go together: to love the light, and to glory in the darkness? How can somebody love God or any creature, and simultaneously glory in the unknowing of him whom he loves? Does not love always want to know the one she loves, and does she not err as a blind person without knowledge? As Christ says: "He that walks in darkness does not know whither he goes" (John 12:35). For this reason it is to be feared that they glory more in themselves than in God. For they are of the opinion that they have climbed above all creatures and have attained such a great perfection—which in reality is only a pure emptiness of the mind devoid of all images.[12]

206. The wise, loving soul makes her dwelling in the dark nothingness of her mind because she considers her knowledge of God in images and likenesses too deficient and merely metaphorical, and this is why she prefers to be beyond all images. She does not glory in the fact that she attained the darkness, which, as she very well knows, is due to her weakness and the inability of her intellective eyes, as I explained earlier. Rather, she glories in this, that she has transcended and renounced all creatures, and that she stands in the immediate glorious presence of her beloved, who casts his rays on her darkness even though her darkness cannot comprehend his glorious light. She dwells in the darkness more out of sorrow and need than out of pleasure and abundance. For she is seated between two tables, hungry and thirsty. This sorrow is one of the three things that the loving desire of the soul perceives in itself.

207. The second one is an ardent desire to see the glorious countenance of God and to enjoy it in complete love, never satiated until she has full knowledge of God. When the soul stands in this fiery, permeating desire before the unknown but immediate presence of God, she is being spoken to with a hidden word, as we find in the Book of Job, and her ears receive the veins of its whisper (Job 4:12),[13] that is, the secret inspiration of the spoken word.

208. This hidden word is the Son, the eternal Word of the Father, which he speaks to the soul in the dark nothingness of her mind, in which he dwells with the Son and the Holy Spirit, as the Son made clear: "We will come to our beloved and we will make our abode with him" (cf. John 14:23). Here the Father speaks his eternal Word, not in images or in likenesses, which have been expelled from here, but in his glorious light, which the Father always speaks.

But this remains hidden to the soul. For even though the light shines in the darkness, the darkness does not comprehend it (John 1:5). The Wise Man says about these words spoken in the darkness of the soul: "For while all things were in quiet silence and the night was in the midst of her course, thy almighty word leapt down from heaven from thy royal throne" (Wis 18:14–15). In the darkness of the mind all creatures remain silent, and the dark night runs her course (that means, its state of life), which is in the midst or the middle between God and creatures, between the highest and the lowliest table, as I said earlier [cf. no. 202]. There the almighty Word of God leaps from its royal throne of the Fatherly heart, from which the Word is spoken without intermediary.

209. In speaking this Word the Father whispers into the soul's ears (this means, in the secret perception of her desire) many secret inspirations, with which he keeps her alert and awake. This keeps her from surrendering herself to sleeping in the darkness, as those people do who reduce all things to silence in their darkness, including their desire and their love, passively surrendering themselves to pure emptiness and inactivity (ledicheyt). As their mind has become a dark nothingness through utter, idle inactivity, so too they become an utter nothing in all their faculties through an utter and total inactivity and emptiness (ledicheyt) of their selves. Because they have become an utter nothing, they consider God also a nothing. For God responds to each creature in accordance with its receptivity. Therefore, when they have become a nothing, God responds to them as a nothing, for when the darkened mind has become a nothing, it receives God as a nothing.

For the light shines in the darkness, and the darkness does not comprehend it (cf. John 1:5). This is why these people call God a nothing, whereas in truth he is a divine entity and the everything. I am fearful that God will consider for all eternity those who pass away in this nothingness as nothing, because they will be unknown to him for all eternity.

210. But the wise soul makes and possesses her darkness out of noble love for her beloved and not for herself, as these people do. She is not inactive or empty, but she practices a loving desire that contains three aspects: a loving sorrow, an ardent desire, and a certain hope that she will attain what she desires.

She receives this hope from the secret whispers of the Word that is being spoken to her.

211. A man blind from birth may have great desire to see the external beauty of creation. But whatever people tell him about it, he can only receive it with great desire but without images and likenesses, for he cannot imagine what he never saw. Similarly, the soul receives the veins of whispers with the ears of her desire, without images or likenesses. For the whispers inspire the soul with the incomprehensible glory of God's essence, which she never could imagine, unless God were willing to reveal it to her. Even though creatures may remain silent in her, she cannot. She rather whispers with great desire, and all the more freely after she has been addressed first.

212. Even though this mutual whispering occurs without words or images, when we want to discuss it, we have to rely on words that evoke images. For we cannot find words that describe this whispering without evoking images. Nevertheless, the soul receives these whispers with a desire free from images. Therefore, my soul, in order to give a brief description of this whispering, I must have recourse to coarse words, so as to incline you to this high desire lest you allow yourself to sleep in the darkness in which you find yourself.

213. The divine Word spoken into the soul whispers to the soul in an inexpressible manner free from images as follows: "I am the beginning and end of all creatures. I am the essential goodness and the perfect bliss that all creatures desire, each according to its nature and mode. I am full of immeasurable glory and riches that eye has not seen, nor ear heard, neither has it entered into the heart of man, what things I have prepared for them that love me (cf. 1 Cor 2:9). I will generously share these with them, and I will satiate them beyond their fill."

214. Then the soul whispers in reply with even more intense desire, saying: "Blessed are they, Lord, who dine and drink at your table for they know you clearly, they praise you with gladness, they are immensely grateful, they love you ardently, and they enjoy you with full pleasure. I am seated underneath your table, in dust and darkness, and I have no light. I thirst for a clearer knowledge of you and I hunger to perfectly love you, and I unreservedly desire you. If

I have found favor in your sight, Lord, then allow me to say with Moses: 'Show me thy face, show me thy glory'" (cf. Exod 33:13).

215. Her God whispers back: "I will show you all good (Exod 33:13). I will show you myself but not while you are in this present state of life, for no man shall see me and live (Exod 33:20). It is not good to take the bread of the children and to cast it to the dogs (Matt 15:26). You are still beneath my table, like the dogs, and it is not yet appropriate for you to eat of my food or drink my drinks. But when the time comes I will raise you up and seat you at my table (cf. Luke 22:29–30), and I will give myself as food and drink in abundance, and I will put you as my beloved bride in the embrace of my divine arm in eternal rest."

216. Then the soul whispers in reply: "Behold the handmaid of the Lord; be it done to me according to thy word (Luke 1:38). I want to live in high hope, O Lord, trusting in your word. Be mindful of thy word in which thou hast given me hope (cf. Ps 118:49). I will gladly lie underneath your table as a little dog, in patience and desire full of hope, and I will gladly eat the crumbs that fall from the table (cf. Matt 15:27), saying with the bride in the Song of Songs: 'I sat down under his shadow, whom I desired: and his fruit was sweet to my palate' (Sg 2:3). Likewise, Lord, your bride speaks: 'Thy breasts are better than wine, smelling sweeter than the best ointments' (cf. Sg 1:1–2). This means, your friendly whispers and the sure hope with which you nourish and console me are better and more satisfying than the wine of knowledge through images, and they smell and taste better to me than the most noble taste I could get from knowledge through images. I am therefore more than ready to renounce that kind of knowledge and taste, and suckle your breasts. But if you do not want to clearly reveal your glorious countenance to me, then I beseech you in the way your bride beseeched you when she said: 'Let him kiss me with the kiss of his mouth,' for the breasts are better than wine, more sweetly smelling than the best ointment' (cf. Sg 1:1–2). Lord, give me a kiss, for in the darkness we can kiss even when we cannot see one another."

217. Then our Lord offers her his mouth to be kissed, which means, his immediate, unknown and lovable presence. She lets go of all desires and whispering, and she inclines her mouth, which means her naked, imageless presence, with a loving immersion of

herself into God. Here God and the loving soul kiss, for the soul becomes one with God without intermediary in a union of love, and she becomes God with the whole Godhead, or to put it more accurately, she becomes deified with the whole Godhead. It is easy to say this but it is subtle and difficult to comprehend fully, and even more difficult to feel it beyond comprehension.

218. But even if we feel this beyond comprehension, reason is at pains to understand what love feels. Sometimes reason will find truth, and sometimes it won't. For reason is prone to error, especially in those things that are beyond it. But those who are enlightened by God should find the truth without erring. I am not one of those, I am sorry to say, but pray for me and my soul. I will explain in what follows as much as I can.

219. You should know that the soul has a twofold existence.[14] The first one is according to her essential being, and here the soul is a spiritual substance. The soul will retain this aspect without change for all eternity. Even though the almighty God could annihilate the soul, or turn it into another creature, as happens in the sacrament of the Eucharist, in which the substance of the bread is being changed into the Body of our Lord, nevertheless the almightiness of God cannot change the substance of the soul into his own substance. For that would amount to making another God, which he cannot do. Therefore, nobody should be of the opinion that the soul could become God in a substantial manner.

220. The soul has another existence as active being, and this consists in the perfect activity of her perfect powers. This existence is the adornment and perfection of the first existence. For the soul has not been created as an empty substance without activity, like a piece of timber, but to work in a live manner. In this existence is the proper nobility of each soul to be found. In accordance with this existence she has been made in the image of the Holy Trinity, as I explained earlier, and it is according to this existence that the soul becomes blessed or lost. This is why St. Paul says, "And if I do not have charity, I am nothing" (1 Cor 13:2). St. John says, "He that loveth not abideth in death" (1 John 3:14). This means, he who does not exist according to the true existence of his soul is, so to say, nonexistent or dead. According to her essential being alone, the soul is nothing but a dead piece of wood that bestows on the body nothing

25

but mere existence without any lived experiences. All the holy angels are named in accordance with their perfection, each according to his own active existence.

221. The divine essence consists of these two modes of being in his onefold divine being. For it pertains to his essence or being, to be active. If the essence or being of God were merely an essence as essence, without anything else, then the divine essence would not be blessed. Essence as essence does not know or love, and yet it is in those activities that all bliss is to be found. But essence as intellective, active nature knows itself perfectly, and that is the Father. Essence as spoken object of the intellective nature is the Word or the Son. Essence as spirated love from the Father and the Son is the Holy Spirit. Because these three pertain to God, God enjoys bliss. God does not know or love himself outside of himself, and this may somewhat make clear that, if God is to be blissful, he must be threeness and oneness.

222. For this reason we can say that those who claim that the most noble life on earth or the most blissful life in the heavenly realm is to be found in an empty [or unhindered] rest *(eenre ledegher rusten)* without activity or beyond activity, are in grave error.

I am happy enough with their claim that unhindered rest *(eenre ledegher rusten)*, if properly understood, is the most holy and the source of highest bliss. But I definitely reject the fact that they situate holiness and bliss beyond activity or without activity. For inactive emptiness *(werckeloese ledicheyt)*, in a pure being of the powers, is compared by St. Paul to nothingness, and by St. John to death, as I just mentioned [no. 220]. But I do teach that the perfection of the active existence of the soul consists in some kind of free resting *(in eender ledegher rusten)*. For the most profound rest and the noblest inactivity *(ledicheyt)* that the soul can enjoy in this life and in eternal life, she attains in the perfect activity *(volmaecten wercken)* of her perfect powers when oriented toward pleasurable objects.

223. In the sensible powers you will notice something similar. When the five senses are properly disposed and have pleasurable objects in front of them, then the senses find their rest *(ruste)* in the very fact that they are active. Indeed, the soul would suffer major unrest *(onruste)* if she were to be prevented from engaging in this activity. So the soul enjoys more rest when engaging in these activ-

ities than when she abstains from them. For it comes natural to the soul to engage in activity, whereas abstaining from it is due to fragility and weakness of nature. For in this life our instruments (such as the senses) cannot engage continually in activity due to fatigue. This is why nature demands us occasionally to abandon our activity, and this is why we need inactivity and rest *(ledicheyt ende ruste)*. Thus the instruments or senses do not rest for the sake of rest and inactivity in their own right but because nature and the soul in our nature need them, having engaged in tiresome activity. Nevertheless, this kind of rest *(ruste)* and inactivity *(ledicheyt)*, and the pleasure we draw from it, is less perfect and less pleasurable than the rest we enjoyed amid our initial activity, when our powers were still fresh and not yet worn out. For the soul never enjoys as much rest or pleasure in inactivity *(in niet werckene)* as she enjoys in activity *(in werckene)*, and in the former case she will be more unrestful *(met meere onleden)* than when she engages in pleasurable, restful activity *(rustelijc werck)*. Nevertheless, all the rest *(rusten)* that the soul enjoys, and the pleasure she derives from non-activity *(in niet wercken)*, can only be obtained through being active *(overmits een werck)*. For to delight in something or to take pleasure in it is an activity of the desirous power.

224. The same applies to the inner faculties of the soul. For the higher faculties, in which all bliss and sanctity mainly reside if they are well-disposed and have God as their object of enjoyment in this life and in the eternal life, are most restful in the midst of the activity they engage in. The soul will never find as much rest or enjoyment in the complete non-activity of her faculties as in their complete activity. If the soul is properly disposed she will enjoy in this activity more stillness *(ledichlijcker)* and less unrest *(min onleden)* than if she were to refrain from this activity. The fact that she at times in this life refrains from this activity is due to the weakness of her mortal nature or to her imperfection.

225. You will thus understand that true, unhindered rest *(ghe-wareghe ledeghe reste)* does not consist in non-activity *(niet-werckene)* but in the perfect active existence of the soul. And true activity *(onledicheyt)* consists in the perfection of an active existence. For as long as the powers are not perfectly disposed toward their activity or as long they do not have an enjoyable object in front of them,

they operate with difficulty and in a laborious manner, and this is true activity [in this life]. Indeed, although the soul cannot in this life attain perfect rest or stillness *(ledicheyt)* of its active existence, this perfect stillness and rest will be attained in eternal life, when the soul will blissfully rest in all her activity, and she will never rest or enjoy stillness without being active. For fruition, the most supreme and final rest *(ruste)* and stillness *(ledicheyt)* that the soul can enjoy, is an activity of the faculty of love. No matter how you want to call this rest, if the soul does not feel or perceive this rest, it is as if she does not exist. If she perceives this rest, this very perception is an activity of the knowing or loving faculty.

226. This is why I hold the view that they who seek their highest bliss in an utterly empty rest *(een puer ledeghe ruste)*, in sheer non-activity *(een puer niet wercken)*, are in grave error and in danger of losing eternal life. For they annihilate their active existence, in which consists the perfection of the soul, both in sainthood and in beatitude, and they seek their sainthood and beatitude in an utter nothingness, which could better be called damnation.

227. Moreover, you should know that the active existence of the soul, in which the powers reside as in the essence of the soul, is in itself imperfect. The powers that reside in the substance of the soul are also imperfect. For the powers are not active in themselves but they are materially and formally united with their objects, either with or without intermediary. All the powers that use images, such as the imagination, memory, reason, and intellect, are united with their objects in a mediated manner. Others, such as hearing, smelling, tasting, touch, and the inner desirous power (both the highest and the lowest), are united in an immediate manner with the objects that in-form[15] them. For the ear receives the sound that it hears, and the nose the smell, without intermediary. The same applies to the other senses. But the faculty of love, residing within us while its object is outside, cannot be in-formed by its object in an immediate manner: the creature that resides outside of it cannot come within it, and the faculty of love cannot go outside toward the creature. Therefore, if its object is not present to it, the faculty of love is carried toward its object by receiving its image through the imagination or the memory, and through those it becomes in-formed with its object through the intermediary of that image.

228. But if the external object is present to it, the faculty of love will ignore the inner image, and it will carry itself toward the object that is present to it, and unite itself with its form without intermediary, as best as it can. The unity between the faculty and the object that in-forms it is as close as the unity of soul and body. Soul and body are themselves united as form and matter, making each one of us a single human being. Similarly, faculty and object become one as matter and form become one insofar as the receptivity and the nature of matter, or faculty, allow for.

229. For each faculty is being in-formed in accordance with its receptivity and its created nature. And this nature[16] makes it active in accordance with its form, just as the soul forms the body in accordance with its receptivity and the activity for which it has been created. If a faculty were in-formed with an object, it could call itself in accordance with its form, and state: "I have become this thing that in-forms me"; and the faculty would be active in accordance with its specific form, and it could not be active in any other way. If the bodily eyes are in-formed with a creaturely image that imprints its image on the mirror of the eyes, the eyes could say: "I am this creaturely thing insofar as it imparts its form on me and bestows its image on me, and as long as this thing imparts its image or form on me, I cannot see any other creaturely thing." If every faculty speaks like this the whole soul speaks according to her active existence.

I have said these things to help you understand the union between soul and God through love, which is the kiss of mouth.

230. Now pay heed. I mentioned earlier [see no. 6] that God's essence is more intimate and nearer to the soul than the soul is to herself because God keeps all creatures in existence. Nevertheless, God is only present in the essential being of the soul, and this divine presence does not make the active existence of the soul blessed or saintly.[17] The reason is that this divine presence is not present as an object, which alone can in-form the active existence.

231. If then the rational faculty of the soul knows God through forms and similitudes, the faculty of love carries itself into God as reason conceives of him, and this image in-forms the faculty of love, and it loves God through this image and in accordance with this image, be it goodness, wisdom, or being. Nevertheless, the faculty

of love often carries its single just intention through all images and intermediaries into God.

But when the soul, with the aid of its faculty of love, has climbed beyond all images and likenesses into the dark nothingness of her mind, God is present to her in the fullness of his divinity without intermediary.

232. Each faculty is embedded in the single substance of the soul as its support and essence. The soul possesses its active existence in the faculties with which she is active, and it is with these faculties alone that the soul becomes one with God through love, and becomes in-formed with God, in the fullness of his divinity, in accordance with the receptivity and nature of the faculty of love, as matter becomes in-formed with its own specific form. Thus God and soul become one spirit, as body and soul become one person. This always occurs according to the active existence of the faculty of love.

233. This union between God and soul is properly called becoming one spirit, for God is a spirit and so is the soul, and the union takes place through the activity of love, which is spiritual in nature. This one spirit is God according to its form, and soul according to its matter. Because the form is intrinsically more noble than matter, and because matter only attains its perfection through its form, and all the activities and operations occur through the specific form, the union of form and matter is often just called after the form. This is why this one spirit can be called God, and it is indeed God according to its form. The soul can therefore say: "I am God in the fullness of his divinity, not according to the essential being of my substance, which remains unaltered, but according to the transformation of my active existence, which I possess in my faculty of love." This is why St. Paul speaks in a subtle and careful manner, "He who is joined to God is one spirit" (1 Cor 6:17). This joining of God and soul retains the distinction between the two substances of God and soul. For nothing is joined to itself, and the union of the spirit occurs through a transformation of the soul, as I have explained earlier.

234. Even though the soul is now transformed without intermediary into God in the faculty of love only, in the eternal life she will also be transformed without intermediary in her rational faculty into the glorious form of the divine being, as I explained earlier [no.

204]. Then she will be God in the active existence of her rational nature. Through the glorious supreme faculties the interior and exterior sensible powers and the body as a whole will be transformed and glorified with God with intermediaries, and thus God will be all in all, as St. Paul says (1 Cor 15:28).

235. Even though we can say, with the views expressed here, that the soul is God, it would be more accurate to say, the soul has become deified *(ghegodt)*. For we do not say that the body is the soul, but rather that the body is animated by the soul.[18] Likewise, St. Paul did not say: "He who is joined to God is God," but rather "one spirit." Therefore, although this one spirit is God according to its form, and although it is active in accordance with the demands of its form, which is God, it is not in all aspects in accordance with the nature of the form, but also in accordance with the nature of the matter, which is the faculty of love. For although God is omnipotent, omniscient, and mindful of all things, the soul does not operate like this. After all, the faculty of love is not made for these kinds of activities, but this faculty has only been created to love. This is why the soul loves everything that her form, which is God, requests her to love, and ultimately this is nothing else but himself.

236. Again, even though God loves everything that he loves immeasurably with an infinite love, which is he himself, the soul does not love in an infinite manner, for she is not infinitely transformed into God but only in accordance with her receptivity, which is finite. The receptivity of the faculty of love is finite according to the magnitude and mode of charity, which predisposes and habitually transforms the soul with God as her own object. When charity grows, the receptivity of the soul grows, and she becomes ennobled and engages in more noble works.

237. In this God resembles the light of the sun, which transforms the air into its own brightness, without any increase or decrease of the light in itself, as much as the receptivity and the purity of the air allows. Similarly, in the eternal life the rational faculty will become transformed through the form of the divine essence, in accordance with the nature of this faculty, which is to know, and its receptivity. This receptivity is now determined by the deiformity that only the faculty of love, and none of the other faculties, attains in this life. As its receptivity grows, the receptivity of

the other faculties grows likewise. As its receptivity for glorification grows, the other faculties will likewise become glorified. It is for this reason that the wise soul makes her faculty of love engage in activity, for the faculty of love in turn sets in motion all the other faculties, allowing charity to grow. It is this charity that makes the soul receptive and predisposed toward deiformity. Through charity, which is the divine form that dwells within the soul and supernaturally predisposes her, and to the degree that the soul possesses charity, she becomes deiform, and thus she constantly possesses in an essential and habitual manner her divine form.

238. When the soul knows and loves God as an object and in an active manner with intellective images and likenesses, she becomes actively transformed by this deiform object in both the intellective and loving faculties. But this is through intermediaries, and not according to the fullness of God. For the fullness of the divinity cannot be grasped or captured in intellectual or conceptual images in this life. She becomes, however, transformed by the goodness, the wisdom, or the essence of God, as these are the forms in which she knows and loves God, as I said earlier [nos. 129, 131–32].

239. But when the soul sinks down through all images with a single intention[19] into God, and when she abides beyond all images and likenesses, from the most humble to the most elevated names for God, in the divine namelessness, in the unimagined dark nothingness of her mind, and when she has become utterly blind, then the soul loves God without intermediary in pure, intellective unknowing. For God is present to her in the fullness of his being, without intermediary. Here she becomes actively one, transformed, deified, and God without intermediary, in the active existence that she possesses in the fullness of her substance in the faculty of love.

240. Here the God-loving faculty engages in her own activity, which is called love, in accordance with the demands of her form, but to the degree of her transformation. In this activity she has and possesses an unhindered, enjoyable rest *(ledeghe ghenuechelijcke ruste)* as in her own supernatural deified nature, as much as is possible in this life. Here happens to the soul as happened to the bride in the Song of Songs: "I sleep, and my heart watched" (Sg 5:2). This means, in the fullness of my active existence, I enjoy an unhindered

non-activity *(eenen ledeghen niet-werckene)*, with the exception of my faculty of love, which, alone, watches in its activity, symbolized here by my heart. As the bodily heart bestows life and form on all the members of the body, so too the faculty of love bestows life on the other faculties and transforms them in accordance with her own form. The faculty of love commands or prohibits the other faculties to be active in accordance with its own will, which is synonymous with the loving faculty itself.

241. All this occurs beyond time and place. The knowing faculty is used to images, and it cannot comprehend anything in this life without images. Therefore, when it hears words of this kind, which usually and mainly refer to sensible things, the rational faculty generates images in accordance with the normal everyday meaning of these words, which is especially to be avoided in spiritual and supra-rational practices. Of course, we are obliged to use words when speaking of spiritual things, as we lack a proper vocabulary. Nevertheless, words such as *climbing*, to be *beyond*, or to be *below*, and so on, should not be understood in a narrow sense but in accordance with the nobility of the things they refer to. Similarly, when we speak of light or darkness, we should exclude all connotations of sensual light or darkness, for otherwise we would often mistakenly presume to encounter a divine light, or the true darkness of the mind, which is a pure unknowing, which we cannot imagine or capture as it is. It would be nothing else but a sensual fantasy about sensual light or darkness based on a simple image.

This is then how the divine kissing between God and soul takes place, beyond time and place, in the dark bareness of the mind devoid of all images, where God is present to the soul. God is present in an essential manner to the soul, as the natural subsistence of the soul,[20] and as her object, that is, as the one whom she loves above all creatures in herself and in himself. The soul does not love God outside of herself or outside of God, but only in a deiform union of mutual kissing beyond time and place.

242. See, my soul, now I have explained, in writing, how you will enjoy with God a mutual seeing *(ondersien)*, a friendly speaking *(vriendelijck onderspreken)*, a mutual befriending *(vriendelijcken)*, and a divine kissing *(ondercussen)*. If you fulfill this, aided by God's grace,

through works, you will preserve yourself and me; if you do not want to do this, you will throw me and yourself in damnation.

243. Now read and observe,

> Live and be active,
> See something and yet nothing
> Befriend and speak,
> Praise and yield,
> Know and love,
> Desire and be blind,
> Whisper and kiss,
> Work and rest
> God in God
> In accordance with the law of love
> May it grant you the eternal reward,
> The Father and the Son,
> And the Holy Spirit.
> Amen.

# Jan van Leeuwen
# Two Treatises:

*What Pertains to a Person Poor in Spirit[1] and*
*The Erroneous Teachings of Meister Eckhart*

*Jan van Leeuwen, from Affligem in Brabant, was a lay brother in Groenendaal until his death in 1378. He was the first cook in the monastery, and his writings are somewhat lacking in intellectual rigor and originality and are at times long-winded. He is mainly remembered as a critic of Meister Eckhart. His critique of Eckhart has more historical than doctrinal relevance. Anyone who reads his little book* Een boexken van meester Eckaerts leere daer hi in doelde, *translated here as* The Erroneous Teachings of Meister Eckhart, *soon discovers that he merely adduces ad hominem arguments, and totally fails to engage with Eckhart's teachings in their own right. Nevertheless, his critique is significant from a historical point of view, for it reveals that at least some of Eckhart's works were known in Groenendaal. Indeed, in this little treatise Jan van Leeuwen incorporates a major extract from Meister Eckhart's Sermon 105 (in DW 4). The main objections he raises against Eckhart are (1) Eckhart admitted to his guilt at the end of his life—which is a rather uncharitable interpretation of Eckhart's* Rechtfertigungsschrift *or* Defense;[2] *(2) Eckhart explicitly states that his views are new and not shared by other theologians—hence, Jan van Leeuwen concludes, they must be wrong; (3) Eckhart's views are unscriptural and untraditional; and (4) Eckhart is a proud man who does not care what kind of damage his teachings may inflict on his audience.[3]*

*Jan van Leeuwen's treatise* Wat dat een armen mensche van gheeste toebehoert (What Pertains to a Person Poor in Spirit) *is less belligerent and more balanced. It is one of his more focused, concise, and attractive writings. He compares the spiritual life to a blacksmith's workshop. The Mastersmith is God, the anvil is Christ. The iron symbolizes the simple being of the soul, while the different hammers represent the inte-*

*rior powers of the soul. Jan van Leeuwen identifies a number of phases in the transformation of our soul: first, there is the active life; second, the interior life; third, the contemplative or God-seeing life (these traditional divisions had already been adopted by Ruusbroec); and also a fourth phase, called* ghedochsamheit *(surrender or renunciation).*[4]

# WHAT PERTAINS TO A PERSON POOR IN SPIRIT

## Chapter 1

*The person poor in spirit*

Some scholars have raised questions and have spoken about poverty of spirit, wondering in what exactly poverty of spirit consists. And some scholars, theologians, and others, well versed in science and theology, have expressed different opinions on this issue, in their own ways, according to their own insights, to the best of their abilities. Among the views expressed we encounter the following: somebody who is poor in spirit is somebody who does not want anything, who understands nothing, and who desires nothing.[5] This is what some scholars have stated, but there is little value in this claim, hardly anything, or even less than anything, for no saint has ever stated this; nor do we find anything of this kind in the holy scriptures.

I therefore tell you above all else: a statement that contradicts the holy scriptures or that contradicts in certain aspects the teaching of our holy mother the church, should be rejected. Yes, even if the view expressed were to appear to be pleasing to God, I would still hold on to the holy church, and if the opinion contained something that went against the holy church, I would rather disagree with God, if that were possible, than disagree with the holy church or the Christian faith, in which I live and die. For our holy church is not like a tiny mustard seed.[6] She is, in the unity of the Christian bond with Christ, rooted and founded in God, and as firm as God himself is. The holy church is so strong that no person could ever subject or destroy her, not even to the degree of a mustard seed. For the invincible power of God and of the church are one. Because God cannot be conquered or subjected by any power, the church, too, in truth, cannot yield to anybody. For the church is founded upon Jesus Christ, the almighty, indestructible cornerstone between God and humanity. It is on this, you should remember, that the church is founded, and she does not grow or wither away in response to, and she remains ever unaffected by, exterior circumstances.

The body of our dear Lady Mary was the womb or the forge in which the stone was shaped; Christ was, and still is in the spiritual sense, the anvil upon which all saints and virtuous people smash their hammers. The hammers symbolize our inner active powers, with which good people humble and raise themselves toward God, with ever-renewed powers of eternal praises. As you are aware, a smith does not rest his hammer. Rather, he raises it and hammers the glowing iron. For the iron lies on the anvil between the anvil and the hammer blow. The hammer inflicts the smash, and the iron receives the blow, thereby becoming more pliable between the hammer and the anvil.

From this similitude we can develop in a spiritual manner four points relevant to our examination of the person who is poor in spirit. The one who wants to become poor in spirit can actively ponder these points with a mind enlightened by God and examine for himself the specific nature of each point. We will first examine the specific nature of the hammers, and we will consider what our inner, spiritual hammers are, with which we hit in a hidden manner. Second, we will also pay spiritual attention to the nature of our inner iron, for hammer and iron each has its own specific nature. Third, we will examine the spiritual anvil, on which our heavenly Master, together with his servants, forges. Fourth, we will consider how we should willingly surrender the iron into the transforming hand of our heavenly Master, allowing God, Master of all, to exercise as much power over our spiritual iron as he sees fit, thereby transforming and reshaping us with his Intellect. Thus God can imprint his Intellect and his eternal Wisdom into the ground of our soul and essentially reshape us by leaving the imprint of his image in us. Indeed, the Mastersmith holds tight to the iron and freely handles it in order to ply it and reshape it in accordance with his art and insight.

The servants, who stand around, have to do the heaviest work, for they have large, heavy hammers with which they have to hit hard. Nevertheless, they receive the smallest wages, for they are usually only trainees who have to remain in apprenticeship for three or four years. To the degree that each apprentice progresses and assimilates the art and the expertise of the master—and some will make more progress than others—he will be employed and promoted. A just master will employ his apprentice and, in accordance with the ability of the apprentice, he will show him due recognition, as long as the apprentice does not become boastful. The master should be mindful of this lest the apprentice gets notions and becomes full of pride.

The masters have different kinds of apprentices. Some leave their master after a short while but others, who are talented, learn quickly and are diligent. Others again may remain with their master throughout their lives but to no avail; they remain inept and incompetent because they are so slow they fail to grasp the intentions and the lessons of their master. Others again become masters in their own right and become his equal. The same now applies, in a spiritual sense, to ourselves and God, as you will see.

By referring to the four points that I mentioned earlier, I now would like to introduce you into a general active state of life, which in principle pertains to all people.

# Chapter 2

*A spiritual explanation of these points and the specific nature of a spiritual armory*

The hammers signify the inner powers of the soul, while the iron that is placed between the anvil and the hammer represents the simple essence of the soul. The anvil represents the simple essence of God, while the master, who turns the iron as he sees fit, signifies the operation of God in us through his own hand.

First we will discuss the spiritual inner hammers, which are numerous and typical of a good and honest person. For a smith has many hammers at his disposal; some he uses for one purpose, others

38

for another when exercising his craft. Some hammers are small, others big, and others again are claw hammers for plying and securing nails. Thus we have different hammers, and other useful tools pertaining to our spiritual armory.

In order for our heart to cleave to God in a durable and firm manner, we have, through the grace of God, twenty-five hammers at our disposal, sometimes less, sometimes more, depending on the ways God interiorly illuminates us.

The first hammer dispels and chases away all sins from us. The second hammer instills us with respect for the worthy name of God and makes us trust in eternal life. The third one is pure and genuine confession, whereby we open up our heart before a priest. If God finds us guilty, we must purge ourselves from sin. The fourth hammer that beats in our hearts is a bitter remorse until death over all our sins as we contravened God's will. The fifth hammer that beats in our hearts will be a right intention and a proper confession of God and our holy church in Christian faith until our dying day. The sixth hammer that we will feel beating in our heart will be mutual faithfulness and love for God and our fellow men.

The seventh hammer that beats in our hearts will be a firm determination to perform all our exterior and interior good deeds mainly for the sake of God's honor. This is a genuine kind of penitence or renunciation, which well pleases God. The eighth hammer that beats in our hearts assists us in carrying Christ's suffering and sorrows in our heart. The ninth hammer makes wealthy people donate alms and sustain the poor in the community. The tenth hammer that beats in our hearts has a solid head and signifies that we must obey the Ten Commandments and the new law, which we are requested to keep by the church. The eleventh hammer will strike us hard and assist us in resisting all evil temptations, day and night. The twelfth hammer is very dear to me: it bestows a simple life of holiness, and this induces an ever-increasing feeling of bliss and glory.

The thirteenth hammer results in performing our works with reasonable insight, guided by God. The fourteenth hammer, with which we will strike, assists us in refraining from indulging or turning toward idleness, the mother of every evil. The fifteenth hammer that operates in us signifies that we will always attempt to do good things for God's sake—thus we will keep his commandments. The sixteenth hammer that beats in our hearts effects that we engage in good works, both interiorly and exteriorly, for God's sake. Thus we receive grace. The seventeenth hammer effects this: anyone who chastises his body in severe acts of penance every day of his life will be rewarded for this on the youngest day [that is, the day of judgment], and he will be kept from harm in soul and body.

The eighteenth hammer blow is a source of great joy: anyone who worships God with spiritual exercises that are pure and honest will constantly be adorned with new grace. I also would like to single out the nineteenth hammer: anyone who wants to worship God totally and utterly should not be attached to earthly things. The twentieth hammer blow is our surrender to God, which should be genuine and not contrived, with a strong handle, which chases away from the heart all earthly love. The twenty-first hammer blow is invaluable: the person who has renounced earthly love can become a pointer to God for all of us. The twenty-second blow I praise even more: if I can turn all people to God I can honor God in all things. The twenty-third blow means that anyone who can honor God in all things will be like a soaring eagle. Thus he can effortlessly transcend all earthly things.

The twenty-fourth hammer blow will be twofold in us. In the highest part of our spirit we will be so caught up in fervor and so greatly elevated, and in the lowest part we will be so detached from earthly things and they will leave us so cold and indifferent, that nothing, neither death nor life, shall be able to separate us from the love of God or the love of our Lord Jesus Christ (cf. Rom 8:38–39).

The twenty-fifth hammer blow will strike us in a fourfold manner and is to be praised as the highest of all virtues. In these four rungs or modes we will connect all our hammer blows and worship God with all our powers. At the end of this we will hand the glowing iron of our spirit immediately to our Master. When we have struck all our heavy blows and when we have utterly surrendered our spirit to God, the iron becomes entirely reshaped and made straight. All our fervent powers, oriented toward the heavenly realm, will yield to receive God's news and, conquered, we will trustingly surrender ourselves, allowing God to dispose of our spirit and reshape or reform it. Here all steadfast striving for spiritual perfection becomes truly fulfilled.

# Chapter 3

*The characteristics of a spiritually elevated person who has renounced himself and all things*

Now we will further examine the distinctions in the fourfold rung, and show how these four modes cohere in a spiritually elevated person, who was made to renounce himself in all things, good and bad.

Nobody should pass any remarks—this I desire and state beforehand—unless he is a devout person, raised in loving desire and in modeless knowledge beyond reason, able to receive the holy and single operation of God's highest brightness. May all those people who, in accordance with the dearest will of God, have come to know good and bad times, sweetness and sourness, understand me.

Now then, the first rung by which we become utterly detached resides under the interior powers of the soul. The second rung, however, by which we practice all virtues within us and outside of us, will be within us. The third rung will lead us to God without return. The fourth rung will be a unique resting in God beyond us and outside of our active intellect. There we will become an essential or superessential rest in God, and be God with God.[7]

In the first rung and above us in the highest rung beyond the other rungs, in these two rungs we will be utterly poor in spirit. In the two intermediate rungs, however, we will be both rich and hungry and thirsty, desirous for God and all virtues, now and for all eternity. For we have to experience both spiritual wealth and spiritual poverty; one without the other is not good. For our Lord said, as the gospel teaches us, that those who hunger and thirst after justice will be blessed for they shall have their fill (Matt 5:6). Similarly, he said in the same gospel that the poor in spirit are blessed, for theirs is the kingdom of heaven (Matt 5:3).

# Chapter 4

*The characteristics of perfect poverty*[8]

Now, we will deal with the topic of perfect inner poverty of spirit. We only have an eternal dying with an eternal death, and another death. Between these two deaths we will hunger for God, with a living hunger that is immense and vigorous. For between dying to ourselves and dying to the world, our self-centered will is killed off and vanquished, and all virtues are gained.[9] Again, the more we die to the world and abandon it in its brokenness, the more we will hunger for God.

If we want to enjoy perfect poverty in the highest part of our spirit, and possess it with God in an essential way, we should pay heed to the nature of the lowest rung, which resides beneath our interior powers. Its nature consists in this—that we will have turned our back on all earthly hindrances and all obstacles; we will have died to them and overcome them through the grace of God. Thus we will not be attached with selfish love to anything that God ever created, and we will be able to turn freely inward, while nothing will hinder the free converse between God and our enlightened intellect in the pinnacle of our mind.

Therefore we will be careful and make sure that our inner peace of mind is not being disturbed or troubled by anything. We should not be focused, in an inordinate manner, on exterior, earthly things, in any degree—not even to the degree of a mustard seed, or for any reason whatsoever. This involves a daily dying to oneself, a source of much pain.

# Chapter 5

*The second rung*

This leads to the second rung, which is wholly within us. We will never abandon this rung, neither here nor in eternity. All our interior spiritual powers will be utterly focused on God. By praising, worshiping, and honoring God with our interior powers that incline toward him, we will stand in his holy presence. Our different powers, in their activity, will not yield to the impetuosity of our desires. But there and also here we will have recourse to images and various modes, each with knowledge of a different virtue.[10] With all good people on earth, united in love, and with all the saints and angels, we will adhere to the incomprehensible majesty and divinity of God. Thus we will reach out toward God, without ever reaching satisfaction, with an eternal and hungry longing in our soul for the unattainable satiation of God.

In this manner we will dwell before the eyes of God, serving as ordinary servants, in the inner life and in the unrest of ardent love, which lives in our heart and which does not allow us to linger or to rest. Our ardent and hungry desire, intent upon God, cannot be fulfilled or satiated, as long as it feeds on alienating images. For the soul who surrenders herself in her essence to the love of God, all things are too oppressive, too limited, and too narrow, because, no matter how strongly our surging desire strives and drives us toward God with our works, we nevertheless cannot fully satisfy God or ourselves in the most interior part of our spirit.

# Chapter 6

*The third rung*

Therefore, we will now pay heed to the third rung. If we want to satisfy God and become recollected in the most interior part of our spirit, and if we want to feel and taste his divine, simple freedom, without intermediary, we must transcend ourselves and all otherness in a nude contemplation until we enjoy a blissful rest in God, where God is truly seen and contemplated in the spirit, spirit with Spirit, in a onefold manner. There our love for God will become a constant, still love.[11]

As often as our love transports us into knowledge beyond reason or without reason, it will raise and elevate us beyond grace in an ever-increasing brightness, in which God dwells in an inaccessible light. Nobody can reach God here, unless he abandons all his knowledge and insights. All fortuitous knowledge that we ever acquired remains behind, beneath the purified and simple entrance of our mind.

Thus our rational faculties must yield here and abandon their activity because they undergo the operation and the essential, holy, and divine "in-spiration" of the divine Trinity.[12] Nobody else can receive, understand, or feel this but he who is gradually made to transcend himself, without himself, into an imageless mode beyond modes, beyond all possible interior consecutive practices.

You now understand the difference between the inner, spiritual person and somebody who is raised to a God-seeing life.

# Chapter 7

*The fourth rung*

Now we finally need to know about the fourth rung, which I want to praise above all else. In what does perfect and pure poverty of spirit consist or reside? What should we, in abnegation of ourselves in response to God, be like? How will we feel when we have willingly renounced ourselves and all self-centeredness in order to allow spiritual inner riches in virtue to accord equally with voluntarily espoused poverty of spirit?

All perfect holiness consists in this, namely, that we can be both poor and rich. Suppose that we are bereft of God and every consolation, interiorly and exteriorly abandoned, that we can only rely on ourselves, and that God wants us to serve him by relying only on our own resources, then we should, without complaining, feel as fine in desolation as in consolation, and we should relate to either of these without personal preference, in accordance with the dearest will of God. Thus we feel interiorly in such a manner that God can do with us whatever and how he pleases. We will then freely and happily allow whatever God in his eternal and unwavering providence sends us, whether sweet or sour, joy or affliction, life or death. Even if we were to be sent to hell and were barred from the heavenly realm and all that pertains to it, it would be for us all the same, as we would be without preference and in total accord with the dearest will of God. We should never want or prefer our own comfort, but we should only want to love God with an ever-increasing love, and to abnegate ourselves, to subject ourselves to God's will, to surrender ourselves, and to humble ourselves beneath God and all creatures in a true and patient renunciation. This is the way of our highest bliss, which can be found in our spirit, and which is rooted in love, and with which we bring all righteousness unto perfection and unto the inexhaustible Good, which is God himself.

Therefore, you must notice, this voluntary, patient renunciation can be understood in two ways. One cannot attain one form of renunciation without the other, nor can one originate without the other. One kind of renunciation is made possible by drawing on our own resources; the other kind draws on God's resources and our trust in him.

Now consider the first kind and see how we must subject ourselves to God's decision and dispensation. Nothing will then be too heavy a burden for us or too hard to bear in Christ's name, or to suffer, for the sake of God's love and honor, whatever tribulations and afflictions that may befall us. All of this we will receive out of God's hand: sweet and burdensome, wherever it comes from, and whomever bestows it upon us, unto death, even if it came from the devil and his henchmen. When faced with adversity or misfortune we will not be obstinate or unwilling, shielding ourselves from the free dispensations of God, but we must utterly renounce ourselves in humility, unto the deepest abyss of hell. Thus we must subject ourselves to God's will and refuse him nothing, not retaining anything for ourselves. Whatever he pleases to do, or not to do, with us, we should allow to happen, for the very reason that this is what he has ordained. Thus our reason must succumb; if we want to renounce ourselves, our reason must yield.

Now may God and the honorable name of our Lord Jesus Christ, the only-begotten Son of God, through whom I believe in all holy things in the unity of the Christian bond of the holy church, be blessed and believed. Fully trusting in the grace of God I hope to attain eternal life through him, his death, and his merits. Anyone who teaches you otherwise remains in damnation without further ado. May God keep us from the pains of hell.

All perfect poverty of spirit is fulfilled and consists in this: without muttering we will surrender ourselves freely and utterly to

God's transformative activity, and nothing will be too heavy a burden to us, no matter what he pleases to do with us. In this manner all things will be beneficial to us. Amen.

# THE ERRONEOUS TEACHINGS OF MEISTER ECKHART

## Chapter 1

Meister Eckhart of the Dominican Order was a devilish man. He spoke and taught in a mad and unreasonable manner, as I will show soon. Indeed, I hope to make clear to you how and why we should refute and reject his erroneous opinions.

Nobody seemingly wise and learned has ever spoken such foolish things; from a certain false perspective he too appeared wise and learned, but in reality he lingered in the dark, devoid of true Christian faith.

Eckhart taught the following in a sermon he preached:[13]

The good works, which a person has performed while he lived in mortal sin, come to life again with the time in which they were done.[14] I will now show this as it truly is [he said], because I have been asked to make my meaning clear, and I will now do this. But it goes against the teachings of all the theologians now living.

All theologians say that as long as a person is in a state of grace, all his works are worthy of eternal life. This is correct, and I agree with them, because God performs these works in grace. The theologians also hold that if a man falls into mortal sin, all the works he performed while in mortal sin, are dead, just as he himself is dead, and they are not worthy of eternal life, because he is not living in a state of grace. In this sense the view expressed is true, and I agree. The theologians also claim the following: if God restores to grace a man who repents his sins, all the works he ever performed in a state of grace before

46

he fell into mortal sins will arise again in the new state of grace and live, as they did before. I share this view too.

But they also teach that those works that the person performed while in mortal sin are eternally lost—the time and the works together. And with this, I, [Master Eckhart], am in total disagreement. I assert the following: of all the good works that a person performs while in mortal sin, not a single one is lost, nor the time [in which they occurred],[15] if he is restored to grace.

Observe: this goes against the teachings of all theologians alive today.

Now pay heed to what my words imply, then you will grasp my meaning.

I declare roundly that all good works that a person ever performed or ever will perform, as well as the time in which they occurred or ever will occur, are both lost: work as work and time as time, [and that anytime a good work is performed or will be performed, both the work and the time will be lost.][16] I say further that no work was ever good or holy or blessed; and no time [or work] was ever holy or blessed, nor ever will be, neither the one nor the other.[17] How then could a work be preserved if it is not holy? If therefore the good works [and also the time in which they occurred] are altogether completely lost, how could those works be preserved that took place in mortal sin and the time in which they occurred?[18] I declare, however, that both are lost, good works and time,[the evil and the good], the one with the other, work as work, and time as time.[19][...]

Now I have said that of all good works a person performs while he is in mortal sin, none of them is lost, neither time nor works. And that is true, in the sense in which I shall explain, although it is contrary to what all theologians now living teach. Now observe the true meaning of this.

If a person performs good works while he is in mortal sin, he does not perform the works from out of that mortal sin, for those works are good and mortal sins are evil.

He performs them rather from the ground of his spirit, which is good in itself by nature; because he is not in a state of grace, however, the works do not, in themselves, merit heaven at the time of their occurrence. Nevertheless, this does not harm the spirit, for the fruit of that work, free from work and time, remains present in the spirit, is spirit with the spirit, and perishes as little as the spirit perishes. But the spirit empties its being by working out images, which are good, just as truly as it would were it in a state of grace.[20] Although the spirit does not receive the heavenly reward by these works, as would be the case if the person were in a state of grace, nevertheless it creates the same readiness [for union and likeness].

# Chapter 2

*The proof that Meister Eckhart erred and was mistaken in many views*

Notice now that I include nothing further from Eckhart's sermon, and leave many wrong things aside. The more one comes into contact with his teachings, the more they are a source of shame and blasphemy for those who hear them.

Eckhart was undoubtedly a real unbeliever. I bet my soul on it. Eckhart revealed his true nature in his erroneous teachings and the many devilish and faithless opinions to which he stubbornly and willfully held onto until his death. Thus he resisted with an obstinate and haughty pride all the theologians who lived at that time.

In this perspective it is easy to show, yes, even by referring to his own teachings, that in his heart he was a proud and conceited individual, possessed by the devil or even a horde of devils. This is beyond doubt and utterly evident. For he was a conceited person, proud in his heart. Whatever external impressions he may have conveyed or whatever anybody may have told you about him or his teachings, all this does not matter a farthing. Meister Eckhart had as many true teachings as a toad, and there was as much truth in him as there is love and charity in the devil. Many persons who harbor a proud heart within hold their head low without, and so it was with the false and deceitful Eckhart.

I hope to show in different ways that Eckhart was a proud, vain, and conceited person. This is not an easy thing to do for me, for I am only a simple, unlearned person who never benefited from a proper education. I hardly dare to go against a teacher who is generally considered to have possessed the art of divine wisdom. I am also convinced that Eckhart was one of the most intelligent men alive, from the point of view of natural reason, without supernatural grace, and one of the most cunning. But on the other hand, he was also an unbelieving fool in every respect, and according to the Christian law of the holy church he was nothing but a madman.

Yes, as I hope to show further by referring to the teachings that Eckhart himself openly taught, so too I hope to show in four or five ways that he was in his heart a conceited person. I also want to show that, when Eckhart's end drew near, many of his heretical views were censured by the Roman Curia. Having encountered opposition to his teaching, Eckhart for the first time deferred after his views had been examined and refuted, and he admitted at the end of his life that he was guilty of teaching falsehood and heresy against the holy church. And this was and still is obvious proof that Eckhart had until then held false teachings.

Now observe the second way in which I want to prove the mad pride of Eckhart. Eckhart foolishly had the audacity to oppose single-handedly all living theologians. This was undoubtedly the greatest pride I ever heard of. For I do not entertain the notion that all theologians on earth would be mistaken, just as I cannot or should not entertain the idea that the holy church could ever be mistaken on a single issue. Indeed, one learned master could be mistaken, no matter how great his expertise in theology, as was the case with Eckhart, but it is impossible that all masters alive collectively err or teach falsehoods. I do not believe that God would allow all masters to err. Therefore, it follows that it was Eckhart who was in error, when, in his sermons, he went against the opinions of all the learned masters then alive. For we should not believe the teachings of a master, or even of two or three masters, if all other masters disagree with him or them. Similarly, we should not believe the conceited Eckhart when he held views that were contrary to those of all theologians.

Even more important is the third manner with which I prove that Eckhart was a haughty individual. Only Eckhart had the audacity to preach and declare things that no saint ever dared to think or say and that he could not prove at all in any degree by referring to the holy scriptures, not even a jot. From this it follows that his teaching was false and lifeless. The holy scriptures are not so bland or poor that we cannot find proof [for true teachings.] Therefore, Eckhart's teachings were nothing but conceited and cursed pride, which he could not substantiate by adducing scriptural proof. For we should only give credence to those theologians and their teachings whose teachings can be confirmed by the holy scriptures. If something is taught that is contrary to our mother the holy church or does not accord with the holy scriptures, you should not give credence to these theologians and their teachings, and you should not follow them, even if they were to speak with the tongues of angels (1 Cor 13:1) or had insight into heavenly mysteries. Even if they had full knowledge and expertise in herbs and earthly things, and even if they worked great signs and wonders, raising the dead or making perish everything that lives, and more than this, if even the Holy Spirit were to speak through them, do not trust them, for the voice of Christ is not with them.

Christ himself said to his apostles that they would receive the Holy Spirit from him (John 15:26; 16:7; 20:22); Christ did not say anything more or anything less about this. The fact that the Spirit came from Christ may suggest that the Holy Spirit needed Christ, but this should be understood as follows: The Holy Spirit receives, and had to receive, his divinity from Christ because Christ is united with the eternal Word, which also taught the apostles. All good people who receive their life and foundation from the in-dwelling of the Spirit through our only Lord Jesus Christ, do likewise. But the false and deceitful teacher Eckhart did not do this, for he was too proud.

I would like to show this in a fourth manner. Eckhart taught many falsehoods and wicked heresies to the people in many places. It is more correct to say that he misled the people and taught them errors than to say that he taught them the straight road of God to the truth. Because of his teachings many people err to this day.

Also, he could not care less if anybody felt offended or annoyed by his false teachings. This is a clear indication that he was an arrogant person who never received supernatural charity. It was typical of Eckhart that he could not be concerned about other people's salvation. No matter how much simple souls were damaged by his teachings, he could not care less. I hold it as certain that Eckhart never gave a genuine sermon; whatever he preached was, in reality, always false and erroneous. For how we should love God, ourselves, and our neighbor in loving unity was lost on Eckhart. Moreover, he directed people on how to find a simple bareness beyond reason and without reason only, without performing good works or religious practices; he even considered these unnecessary, and that too was false.[21] But we will proceed beyond reason and with reasons and without directing anybody, for reason and discursive knowledge should always be subject to bare truth and remain so through our only Lord Jesus Christ who, with all the saints, stands before our incomprehensible God.[22] There everybody who lives a life of virtue learns, while acknowledging his difference and distinction from God, the holiness of other virtuous people and their works, and the rewards that adhere to this holiness. In this way anybody who lives a holy life models his own life on that of another holy person and examines that life thoroughly. But you should know that Eckhart did not want to speak to people about the small and humble things necessary for salvation or how they should carry the blessed virtues of our Lord Jesus Christ in their heart and remember them for all eternity. Surely, it should not be above anybody, no matter how saintly he is in this life or in the hereafter, to ponder the virtues of Christ, his holy death, and his merits. Nobody can be too elevated or saintly for this, even if he were to be transported every day a thousand times beyond himself and caught up into heaven, as Paul was caught up into the third heaven (2 Cor 12:2). Paul himself did not consider himself too great or too good to ponder the suffering and holy virtues of Christ. Yet I take it that Paul is one of the greatest saints in eternal life besides Christ and our dear Lady, who never committed a sin. Granted, Christ himself openly said that John the Baptist was the greatest who ever had risen among the children of men (cf. Matt 11:11). Perhaps this was said because John became sanctified in the womb of his mother, or perhaps because John in his infancy was the most holy at that moment. But whether he remained the most holy person after the apostles and Paul had arrived, I leave for God to decide, who alone knows. They will sort it out among themselves.

Let us be united and be one in love. And let us carry the precious and loving suffering of our Lord Jesus Christ in our heart; thus we will be shielded by God from Eckhart's scourges and his false, reckless teachings. Thus God will instill the Holy Spirit in us. Above all, let us without failing be obedient to God and God's grace, and listen to the holy church during Lent and during celebrations, in good demeanor and with good deeds. Thus God will strengthen us with his grace, both interiorly and exteriorly, with good works. For God has requested the following from priests, clergy of lower rank, and from all people in general: that they keep the law in a pure and proper manner. All, great or small, are held by this—if they act against it they will suffer the pains of hell.

# Chapter 3

*What one should teach the common people and how priests, lower clergy and spiritually minded persons should live*

All people should live in accordance with the commandments of God. They should be taught these commandments in a manner that they themselves can understand, aided by prevenient grace. Priests and lower clergy, you should note, must fulfill two demands. The first is that they live a just life, setting a good example for laypeople. The second is that they teach them the path to God and to the life of our Lord Jesus Christ and the saints. For these two points, namely, living a holy life and teaching holiness, together and truly exercised, are generally the two most useful things on earth; indeed, these two things, a virtuous life and spiritual instruction, are the most precious things to speak about.

Four points pertain to these two things, as God's saints testify. The first is that one should warn people about the chilling Last

Judgment and the pains of hell. The second is that one should remind them of God's justice and the manifold torments that will be inflicted upon them in hell on account of their sins; some will suffer more than others, depending on whether they, in a sinful manner, gave in to their fleshly lust here on earth. Third, people should be taught how to turn away from sin and vice, and how they should turn to God and virtue. One should praise to all people of good will the kind mercy of God, and thus one will arouse their zeal by reminding them of the great reward of eternal life. Also, one should capture the attention of people and instruct them about the manner in which we should go to God through the suffering and merits of our Lord Jesus Christ. For we must spiritually unite all the Christian faithful with the Father in true devotion to God's Son. Christ himself told and taught us in the gospel that nobody can come to the Father but through him (John 14:6). For when we recall Christ the Son of God to our mind unto the pure and onefold countenance of the Father, the Son of God, the Second Person, co-equal with the Father, is constantly and immediately begotten from the Father as his only Son in the pinnacle of our spirit.[23]

Notice, this brings the fourth manner in which spiritually minded persons should be enticed to go, as I mentioned earlier, into the single interiority of our Lord Jesus Christ, who leads ourselves and all things into eternal life. We cannot enter eternal life in any other way than in the manner that Christ himself spoke of and taught about in many places. He himself states, as it says in the gospels, "I am the Way, the Truth, and the Life" (John 14:6).

This is undoubtedly why we always must be raised into grace and glory through the holy interiority of our Lord Jesus Christ. If we want to see eternal life, we also must worthily glorify him in our heart, remembering all of his merits. For when we glorify him and his precious death in our heart, he likewise will glorify us and assist us in our need. If it is the case that we spiritually long to dwell in Christ, he will dwell in us. This will be necessary for us if we want to hear Christ's voice and to follow him all the way out of this sorry world.

# Chapter 4

*How we will hear Christ's voice in seven interior touches*

Observe now further. In a few short words we want to explain how we will hear Christ's voice in true obedience to God and the holy church. For this purpose we can avail through God's grace of seven operative signs of inner touches, or perhaps even more.

The first and least touch is bitter sorrow in our heart, whenever we have done something sinful or something that went against God's will, and the resolve to never sin again. This resolve always accompanies genuine sorrow over sins. The second touch in our heart then ensues: we must sincerely trust that God has remitted and forgiven all our sins through his inexhaustible mercy and through our Lord Jesus Christ. The third touch is this: we will obey and conform to the holy church until our death. The fourth touch is that we will preserve within, like ourselves, all people through charity in union with God. The fifth touch consists in this, namely, that we will always carry the suffering and the manifold merits of our Lord Jesus Christ in our heart and thus raise our heart to heaven whenever we pray to the Father for something our soul needs. The sixth touch is that we seek above all to honor God before and after our works. The seventh touch is that we patiently endure whatever affliction befalls us. Thus we will patiently and meekly submit ourselves freely and obediently to God's will, no matter what he decides to inflict upon us. Amen.

# Nicolas of Strasbourg
## *The Sermon on the Golden Mountain* and Johannes van Schoonhoven, *Declaratio*[1]

*Jan van Schoonhoven was born in 1336 or 1337. He studied in Paris and entered Groenendaal in 1377, that is, four years before the death of Ruusbroec. He is mainly remembered as the author of a treatise called* De Contemptu mundi *and as a staunch defender of Ruusbroec's thought against the critique of the Parisian Chancellor Jean Gerson.[2] Jan van Schoonhoven was also instrumental in facilitating the affiliation of Groenendaal with Windesheim, one of the main centers of the Modern Devotion, founded by Geert Grote. Jan van Schoonhoven also wrote a* Declaratio, *or brief exposition, on a sermon preached in Leuven by Nicolas of Strasbourg, a Dominican. This sermon has been preserved in Latin and Middle Dutch in a number of different versions and is included here, followed by the* Declaratio *by Jan van Schoonhoven. The main focus is on the cross of Christ as the source of our salvation—a theme that was, of course, also of central importance to the Modern Devotion.[3]*

## *NICOLAS OF STRASBOURG,* THE SERMON ON THE GOLDEN MOUNTAIN

The lector of Strasbourg preached the following sermon in the chapter house of the Dominicans in Leuven. I want to share a truth with you, and I want you to pay careful attention. I would not want to fail to understand this truth even if I could possess the whole world. Anyone who keeps this truth in mind until the time of his death will be spared hell and purgatory. Three points are essential for this.

First, you should feel remorse for all your sins, and they should instill you with a grave sense of sorrow. Second, you should confess your sins whenever you have the opportunity or the occasion. Third, you should do penance even if it is only saying the Hail Mary; if you cannot do this, the priest should admonish you to keep your thoughts focused on God and to pray along the following lines: "O Lord, how huge is my sin and how small is the penance you have set me," and you should not fail to do this.

I would like to encourage you by making a comparison. Once upon a time there was a lord, a king, who possessed a mountain of powdered gold as large as the town of Leuven, and he spoke as follows: "I make this mountain available to all who are in debt, and they can come and shovel as much as they like and pay their debt." If there was somebody who owed five shillings and was unable to pay it but who did not draw on this mountain available to all would such a person not be considered stupid or lazy? Now, listen people, to what this mountain, available to all, symbolizes. Our Lord Jesus Christ wandered on the face of the earth for thirty-three years, and every single day he was alive, every step he took, sufficed to redeem a thousand worlds; every single wound he suffered was worth a thousandfold worlds. To what purpose his sufferings and pain, every single drop of blood of his body? To what purpose all the virtuous works he performed on our behalf—for Christ, laboring in pain merited our remuneration, for he himself did not need it? This is the golden mountain that I spoke of earlier. It is from this mountain that the thief who hung on Christ's right side at the cross drew and discharged his debt.

Now, why is it that of two people who die in similar sins, one goes to heaven and the other goes to purgatory for forty or a hundred years? It is because the former drew on this golden mountain, that is, the merit of Jesus Christ. The other one, who went to purgatory, drew on his own resources, for he lacked the knowledge of this golden mountain and of the merits of Jesus Christ. For this reason you should ponder in your heart: "O Lord, how huge my sins, and how little the penance that has been set for me. O heavenly Father, I know and admit that I have lived and acted against you, and that my guilt is so large that neither I nor anybody else can redeem it. O heavenly Father, I only want to redeem it through the works that your only Son did for my sake, through every sorrowful step he took for me, through all the deep wounds he suffered because of me, and through his red-colored blood he shed for me, and the precious death he endured for me. These I offer up to you, heavenly Father, to make satisfaction for all my sins and as a recompense for all my wasted time, and to repay all the good things that you, Jesus Christ, have done for me. Amen." This is the treasure and the golden mountain of the holy church. You, human person, should ponder this with genuine confidence, and see: you will never enter hell or purgatory.

Seven points are important in this regard. The first one is that it pleases our Lord more and is more advantageous to us, that one person laments over his sins, than one hundred Davids psalmodizing without inner devotion. The second is that it is more pleasing to our Lord and more advantageous to the human person that he would like to be a better person than he is; on account of this our Lord is willing to release him from thirty years in purgatory. The third point is that it is more pleasing to our Lord and more useful to the human person that he praises our Lord in whatever he does; this person wants to acknowledge that our Lord is above all the saints, as the pope is elevated above all others. The fourth point that is more pleasing to our Lord and more useful for the human person is that he, for the love of our Lord, should refrain from speaking idly; for this our Lord wants to give him a greater reward than if he were to fast for seven years on bread and water while failing to abandon idle talk. The fifth point is that we should for our Lord's sake abandon looking at things with idle curiosity. Our Lord is willing to give us a greater reward for this than for giving away one hundred marks and earning our own bread without abandoning idle looking. The sixth point is that we should be willing to endure a hard word for the sake of our Lord. For this reason our Lord desired to make us wise as Paul, who was elevated into the third heaven. The seventh point is that we should be patient in all our sufferings without complaining, and that we offer our sufferings to God alone; thus we will receive a greater reward from God than from living a hundred years of a perfect life.

# *JOHANNES VAN SCHOONHOVEN,* DECLARATIO

An elucidation of the previous sermon by brother Johannes van Schoonhoven.

Well-beloved father, I have enumerated a number of key points as a clarification of the truth of this German sermon, which you have passed on to me to be examined, despite my inexperience and lack of expertise.

The first key point is that we must put our complete hope and faith in the merit of the life and passion of our Lord Jesus Christ, without which we cannot be saved, and we should not put any faith or have any confidence in our own merits or works; for all our merit is rooted in the merit of Christ—whether we perform acts of penance or acts worthy of eternal life. For we are not worthy to be absolved from our offenses against the Creator, or to receive the immeasurable reward that is God himself, if not for the merits of the God-man. As St. Bernard puts it, writing on the Song of Songs: "Lord, your passion is my ultimate refuge, my only remedy; for while we are lacking in wisdom, falling short in righteousness, found wanting in sanctity, and failing in merit, your cross comes to our rescue."

The second point is the following. Even though we may be contrite and repentant, nevertheless we still carry the disease and the remnants of sin within us, unless we have a most perfect contrition and are inebriated with the love of God, like the thief on the cross; if we want to be healed we should be cleansed in the blood of Christ and be submerged in the merit and pains of Christ. For the passion of Christ is like a vast ocean in which we quench our thirst and from which we can draw everything that we lack in sanctity and merit. As St. Bernard says: "But as for me, whatever is lacking in my own resources I can draw from the wounds of my Lord Jesus Christ, which overflow with mercy. And there is no lack of clefts by which they are poured out. Through the clefts of his body the mystery of his heart is revealed to me. They pierced his hands and feet, they opened up his side with a lance, and through these fissures I can suck honey from the rock and oil from the flinty stone—I can taste and see that God is good."[4]

The third key point is that nothing is more salutary and beneficial to a person to whom death draws near than to remember the suffering of Christ, to commend one's spirit to the Father, and to surrender freely into God's hands one's dying will, allowing God to do with it as he pleases and sees fit, relying on nothing else but on Christ and the merits of his life and passion. As Augustine said in his book *On the Meditation of Jesus Christ:* "All my hope resides in the death of my Lord. His death is my merit, my refuge, my salvation, my well-being, and my resurrection by which I am saved and liberated." And further: "The multitude of my sins does no longer frighten me when I recall the death of my Lord because my sins cannot conquer his death."[5]

In my view this lecture and sermon were preached in order to make people aware of the truth that the most accomplished spiritual achievements consist in this, namely, that in their time of death they turn toward the memory of the passion of Christ and trust solely in Christ and the merits of his passion and his saints.

The fourth point is this—and I hold it to be utterly true: anyone who, at the time of his death, with a fully contrite heart and humble devotion seeks refuge in the merits of Christ and his passion; and who, moreover, through renunciation of all sinful love of self and immolation of self-will has brought himself into the passion and suffering of Christ; such a person will immediately, without spending any time in purgatory, ascend into heaven, cleansed from all sins.

In my view the speaker wanted to convey this insight above all else in his sermon, which can be briefly summarized in the following words: "If anyone with a certain hope and faith turns toward the merits of Christ, and fully relies on them, he will reach heaven without spending time in purgatory."

# An Anonymous Treatise on Ruusbroec's Teaching[1]

*The following text is a translation of an anonymous, untitled commentary on some difficulties met in Ruusbroec's teaching. The commentary is known in only one version, namely, that of a fifteenth-century manuscript that contains four treatises of Ruusbroec (Averbode, Archive IV 101, olim Library 101 F 3, in Ruusbroec studies known as ms e).[2] The text must have been written before the period from 1440 to 1450, as this is the dating of the manuscript, and the textual quality suggests that the version in ms e is not the original text. Nothing is known about its author, but evidently he was very familiar with the teaching and the works of Ruusbroec. Moreover, he was familiar with the criticism that Chancellor Jean Gerson had formulated in his famous letter to the Carthusian Bartholomew Clantier, and that which Gerson had mentioned in his* Theologia Mystica I, 14. *But the anonymous author mentions other objections that were not formulated by Gerson—which supports the claim by Jan van Schoonhoven that several readers made critical remarks on Ruusbroec's works. Not surprisingly, the present text mainly concerns the "union without difference" and the unity of the Persons in the divine nature. The author refers to the third book of* The Spiritual Espousals. *Very correctly he points out that Ruusbroec does not speak of an ontological fusion of God and man but of a life communion with Christ, which implies a radical openness in the core of the human person to the divine Other.*

## AN ANONYMOUS TREATISE ON RUUSBROEC'S TEACHING
### [Introduction]

In the name of the Lord, amen. So that no one who reads this teaching or hears it when read shall take offense at it (so that this nourishment of life becomes for him a poison; for it is a noble divine truth provided that it is understood out of the origin from which it is spoken),[3] I explain here some distinctions to help you understand some sentences that at first might seem quite obscure for some people. I explain it, though my understanding is dark and my language is unrefined. For my explanation, I do not rely on myself but mainly on the mercy of our Lord, on the authority of faith and the holy scripture, and on the teaching of saints and masters of divine science. And I am ready to give priority to the truth and to the insight of anyone else who may understand it better.

# [No Fusion between God and the Human Person]

First, in this text it is often stated that good persons are one with God, and, especially in the third part,[4] he [Ruusbroec] says that contemplative persons are the same as what they contemplate,[5] without difference or partition.[6] Therefore, it should be known that the soul of a human person (or any creature) can never be one with God to such a degree that it is transformed into God or vice versa, as, for example, food and drink are transformed into human flesh and blood, or like the union of body with soul. That would be contrary to truth and to faith, and it would be contrary to the simplicity of the divine nature. And there can never be a union of man with God in one person, because this is only given to the human nature in our Savior Jesus Christ. This is never given to any creature, either angel or human being. The creature is eternally other than God, in person, nature, and being.

# [Three Unities between God and the Human Person]

## [The First Unity]

Next, it should be known that there are three kinds of union that human persons can have in God, mainly through the grace of our Lord. The first and the most humble one, without which no one can please God, is that the human person is totally conformed to the will of God. This implies that one loves the unchangeable good (namely, God) more than any changeable good (namely, ourselves and all creatures) and all that God can give, apart from himself. The order of justice demands also that one should love honorable good (namely, the virtues) more than useful good (namely, physical life and all that is useful for this life), so that one never despises virtue or lives contrary to virtue, neither for death nor for life. The order of justice demands also that one follows more the order of reason than that of sensitive appetite or pleasure. The judgment of reason is that one mainly loves things as far as they are good, and consequently one should love most that which is in itself good and is the cause of all good, and one should love it for itself. One should love other good things because of this [supreme] good. Those things that are most similar to this supreme good should be loved immediately next, and so on, from the highest to the lowest. The order of justice demands also that we should never freely choose to do or to omit something against the commandments or prohibitions of our Lord. This is the first unity, and without this unity no one can be saved.

## *[The Second Unity]*

The second unity can be had in this mortal life through the influx of God[7] and by renouncing ourselves and all things. This happens when the human person responds to the influx of God's grace in such a way that he does not possess himself or anything as his property in any way, but he offers himself continuously to God for everything that God wants to do with him as a free, unhindered instrument, without demur. However, God wants to strengthen him in his sufferings over himself and all creatures. However painful and hard it may be for his nature, it is joy and gladness for his spirit. He is free and detached from every consolation and every feeling that God could give, apart from God himself. He yields himself strongly, with flaming love-desire, to the loving influx of God, so that he knows nothing but love. If a human person experiences this and has arrived at this point, then he has truly died to himself and is united with God, without separation. But because of our sinful bodies, in which we are clothed, people who are in such a condition cannot protect themselves; sometimes they cannot avoid falling into venial faults. But these venial faults are in these people, as far as their turning inward to God is concerned, like a drop of water in an oven of fire.

## *[The Third Unity]*

From this second unity comes a third one, namely, a contemplative life in which the spirit is one with God without distinction. When the noble, loving spirit has responded so closely with love (by dying to himself and to all divine gifts) to the inward drawing of God into the mere being of his mind, when he does not experience anything else but the loving drawing inward of God and his own active love, then he enkindles himself through these two[8] in the mere being of his existence, and he wanders in an unknowing, a modelessness, and a darkness (because all existence—as existence— is bare and without image). God possesses all existence as his own dwelling place, and therefore, when the spirit, in the simplicity of its faculties, in its bare existence, has lost itself, by sinking away from itself, then an incomprehensible brightness is revealed to him in this darkness. And that is the Son of God himself. And this brightness shines through and transforms all spirits who are actively turned inward in the bareness of their existence. And the eyes of the spirit are so widely opened in this brightness that the spirit does not know anything other than this brightness that it contemplates, and by which it contemplates. And thus, the spirit becomes this brightness itself, without difference. It receives this brightness, purely and without similarities, and it is per-illuminated and transformed by this brightness; therefore, one can say that it is this brightness itself, namely, without intermediary. This is indeed a characteristic of the simplicity of God: it cannot be known as it is, except by itself, namely, when it informs the understanding and illuminates it, so that it [the divine simplicity] is known and understood by its own being. No creature, however simple and noble it may be, can be united in its being [existence] with another spiritual creature without intermediary, because in all spiritual creatures there is a difference between existence and essence. But that is not the case in God.

Since the spirit, in this contemplation, does not know anything but this brightness, which it contemplates and by which it contemplates, and since it contemplates itself and all things in this brightness as one life and one truth with this light—because "all that was made, is life in Him,"[9] says St. John; all things, that is, live in this light, being the eternal image of everything, and living in God, and being precisely what God himself is—therefore one can truly say that the contemplative person is the same as what he contemplates and as that with which he contemplates, without separation. I cannot give a more precise explanation of this unity.

## [The Three Divine Persons and the Unity of the One Divine Nature]

Next, in this teaching it is said that the divine Persons yield and become the groundless simple bareness of the divine being. Also in other places in his teaching, he [Ruusbroec] says that the Persons, each according to the proper characteristic as Person, flow away and whirl away in modelessness, in the modeless being of God. Now, it should be known that one should not understand these words as if the Persons sink away from themselves in essential unity in such a way that they cease to be in their existence as Persons. That is impossible, as he [Ruusbroec] testifies in other places in his teaching. Neither should one understand it as if the Persons, in their existence as Persons, do not at all know and love the divine being, because they are this being itself, and their knowing and loving is precisely their being. The Father, the divine origin, knows himself and gives birth to the Son. In this birthing by the Father, the Son receives all that he is. If the Father did not know himself (all that he is), then the Father could not give all that he is to the Son, and then the Son would be less than the Father, and the Father and the Son would not be both eternal in their being—and that would be against our faith and the holy scripture, in many places. The same thing goes for the love by which the Holy Spirit comes from the Father and the Son. So that one understands this teaching correctly, one must know that God behaves differently relative to his essential being and his personal being. Indeed, in his

64

personal being, he has modes, according to the specific way of behaving of the divine Persons, as he [Ruusbroec] has proved in this teaching and in many other places. But in his essential being, God behaves as a onefold simplicity, without modes and without distinction. This means that the divine Persons yield, and flow away and whirl away in the bareness of being, because, according to essential being, they are one, without modes and without distinction. I cannot give further distinctions or explanation about this point.

# Gerard Appelmans
## *Gloss on the Our Father*[1]

*We know next to nothing from external evidence about the author of this remarkably dense mystical commentary, known as a gloss, on the Our Father. The author, a hermit of Brabant, was apparently well versed in scholastic philosophy, which he employed to speak eloquently of the relations of God to man in trinitarian and christological terms. It is estimated that he lived between 1250 and 1325. This gloss is the only work attributed to him; any other information on his life or his writing has been lost to history. A copy of the manuscript was found in the Rooklooster monastery of Augustinian Canons Regular, situated near Groenendaal, site of the Augustinian monastery of his contemporary Jan van Ruusbroec.*

*That the Our Father was a frequent and beloved subject for commentary by spiritual writers is attested to since early patristic times. It is at once an exercise in meditation and a vehicle for teaching sublime truths of the inner life, using "the perfect prayer."*

*For this translation we used the edition by Leonce Reypens, SJ, in* Ons Geestelijk Erf 1 *(1927), 83–107.*

## GLOSS ON THE OUR FATHER

This the gloss on the *Our Father* by brother Gerard
    Appelmans,
who lives near a city called R***,[2]
and there, in a forest, does rigorous penance.

Jeremiah says, "Thou shalt call me Father, sayeth the Lord."[3] For this reason our Lord Jesus Christ teaches us to adore and to pray to the Father in the Our Father.

# GERARD APPELMANS

## I. *The first word [we will discuss] is* Father.

How do we understand that word? The Father, in the fecundity of his nature, and out of the fecundity of his nature, is speaking that word to himself, engendering the Son, another Person of his own nature, in all-perfect likeness to himself, and, in a fatherly way, recognizing the other Person as Son. This nature neither engenders nor is engendered, but, by engendering, the Father extends the fecundity of his nature in the power of his essence.

In this same birth, the Father, in the omnipotence of his Godhead, is creating for himself, giving life and essence to all creatures; [giving] a substance to all creatures; by his divine and fatherly might maintaining everything that has life and essence in a creaturely way. Thus, the Father is a Father to all creatures. Nevertheless, there is absolutely nothing in common either of his substance or of his nature with angels or with humans or with any other creature whatsoever. One who understands this word thus adores the Father in these words. Next, you shall hear what adoration is.

Now note what it is to adore the Father: a rational, interior, pure, loving acknowledgment to the Father of his divine paternal quality. Note yet a little more precisely what adoration is. When the Father has possessed the whole breadth of the rational soul and has taken over and absorbed the essence and eternity of the soul and all its powers into the fathomless divinity of his glory's lordship, the soul sinks from one abyss into the other, and from something into nothing. Here, God becomes the Father of his own self, in himself, in the soul. This is true adoration on the part of the soul.

## II. *The second word is* our.

How do we, as rational creatures, understand that the Father is ours? The Father, in the fecundity of his nature, and out of the fecundity of his nature is speaking that word for himself and engendering in an all-perfect likeness to himself the Son, another Person of his very nature, acknowledging the other Person as Son by nature, in a fatherly way.

From the beginning, the Son of the Father, who is born of the divine nature, is acknowledging to himself that he is born from the

Father, acknowledging the Father in a sonly way. In this continuous birth of the eternal Word, that eternal Word is receiving his person-hood from the Father. That eternal Word is not co-engendering it from the Father but is receiving—in relation to him, in his continu-ous birth—his personhood; in the birth from the Father, all that the Father knows in his fathomless eternal wisdom is flowing out with the Son and is continuously born in the Son, with the Son knowing it in a sonly way. The Father acknowledges the paternal sons of his grace in a fatherly way. Here we are his sons and he our Father.

### III. Who art

In this word all created spirits are silenced and must acknowl-edge that we know nothing. And this is the very highest that human reason can understand: to know rationally and love lovingly [the fact] that we absolutely cannot understand God as he is in himself. Thus, in this word, he teaches us to adore and to acknowledge that fathomless excess that God himself is, exceeding all created spirits.

Still, we may get some vague idea of what God the Father is. He is a fathomless flame of the fruitful nature of the entire Godhead, flowing in, flowing over, bearing fruit of the fruitful nature of the entire Godhead, and he is a fathomless source of the Holy Trinity and a root and a stem of the entire Godhead's omnipotence, extend-ing the wonders of his omnipotence by the Holy Trinity's working wonders in the powers of heaven. And this is a glimpse of the essence of the entire Godhead.

### IV. Who art in heaven

In the natural visible heaven with its ordering of your omnipo-tent eternal wisdom.

And in the heaven of the rational soul with its fathomless out-flowing of your mercy and of your goodness and with the ordering of your eternal wisdom and with the image of your Holy Trinity and with the fruitful discourse of your fatherly heart and with the loving brilliant in-burning of your Holy Spirit and with the omnipotence of your entire Godhead, for where there is anything of God, there he is totally.

And in the empyrean heaven, a pure substance and a calm rest. Are you the self-same? We [humans] know only creaturely things.

## V. Hallowed be thy name

The Father's name is the Son; and if the Son were not the Son, then the Father would not have his fatherly name. For everything that the Father, [being] Son in a fatherly way, is bestowing, he bestows in the Son.

And also, if the Father were not the Father, then the Son would not have his sonly name. For everything that the Son, [being] Father in a sonly way, is bestowing, he bestows in the Father.[4] Thus the Father is in the Son and the Son in the Father and the Holy Spirit is in them both, and the Name is hallowed in himself.

Now, by God's grace, we are all sons of God and the name of the Father. Now if the name of the Father—which we are by grace—should be hallowed, then, the naturally hallowed name of the Father in us [should] be hallowed, acknowledged as holy and beloved, and then we, the name of the Father by grace, are united and hallowed in the name. And that this shall be accomplished in us, the Son teaches us in this word.

## VI. Thy kingdom come

Nothing is added to or subtracted from the Father, for he is all-sufficient in himself and lacking nothing, for the Father's kingdom is the Son, and all whom the Father, from the source of his Godhead, knows and loves [are] blessed in a sonly way in the Son, with the Son, in the continual birth of the Son, bestowing what is the Father's, in a sonly way in the Son.

And that this may come within us and be accomplished as the Father has known and loved to accomplish it from all eternity within us by his divine grace—that is what the Son teaches us, namely, interiorly to adore and pray to the Father in these words.

## VII. *Thy will be done on earth as in heaven*

God the Father is a totality and a Heaven of all heavens, and the will of the Father is his knowing and his loving and his understanding and his working. Now, just as the will of the Father in heaven is known and done in itself, and is to be done in us, so it is done. If this is to happen, we must leave it to God in simplicity and die, together with all that we are, to what our reason may know both by grace and by nature in God and in creatures. We must stand simply, poor of will, simply immersed in and given over into the hidden, unknown, knowing will of the Father as he is in heaven. And then our free will is taken from us and in the will of the Father it becomes the will of the Father as it is in heaven, for we neither desire nor love any other will. And then we are one body with Christ, and a son in the Son, and one spirit with God. And this happens here on earth, where the soul is in the earth of the body, in part and briefly. But hereafter, when our body rises up and possesses beatitude with the soul, we possess purely the Father's own [property] as a son in the Son, and the unique, unchangeable, eternal will of the Father in us has become "ours" on the earth of the body: one, eternal, and unchangeable as he is in the heaven of the majesty of his grace. And that this may happen in us, the Son teaches us in these words.

## VIII. *Give us today our daily bread*

How do we understand that this bread is "ours"? As it is the property of God the Father, from the nobility of his perfection, to give and to forgive, so it is our own by his divine grace to receive his gifts. Why does he now teach us to pray for what is his own? For we have nothing whatsoever of ourselves, but all that we have from God, we have by God's grace. And since the gifts of the Father are so noble, he teaches us to pray interiorly and to adore the Father in great humility of spirit, and to prepare and to be prepared to receive the noble gifts of the Father.

Now note whose day and whose daily bread. There are three kinds of days. The first day is temporal and flows away with time. On this day, "our daily bread" means all that we need. For this reason he teaches us to pray to the Father for his eternal glory and for our eternal rest. Now, he says "today." In this word he teaches us to wait wisely in great humility for the judgment of God the Father and to contemplate our unstable temporal life in such detachment from temporal things that we have not possessed with God's will and in God's will, unto God, as if this day, "today," were our last day, and God, in the last hour of this day, would pronounce judgment over body and soul, and we were aware of this.

The second day is spiritual; that is, a true right reason that is enlightened by divine grace. For just as the temporal day has absolutely no light were it not illuminated by the sun, so also the created reason would have no light were it not illuminated by divine grace. And just as our bodily eyes cannot perceive the distinction of physical things unless they have the aid of an accidental light, so also the eyes of reason cannot know how to distinguish divine truth without the assistance of divine grace. What is our "daily bread" on this day? In the innermost part of the soul, the Father speaks his Word eternally, and the discourse of his Word has a pure reason and a capacity for being received by our reason, and that is "our daily bread." And we receive this same holiness in all God has ordained, in the holy sacraments, in faith, and in modes, and in this temporal day. And we will enjoy him blessedly above faith and above time and above modes in this "day" of eternity. We now have a rational inner foretaste of this enjoyment in the faculty of reason, and that is the second daily bread. Before I go on in this way, I will speak of the reception of the holy sacrament. Whoever receives it worthily is purified of all sin and assured of eternal life.

The third "daily bread" is a pure contemplation of divine truth with clear distinction and that which God ordains in this holy Christendom. In addition, it is all that which, from the beginning of this world to the end, is a help and a support for us, so that what the Father knows and loves to accomplish in us may be accomplished in us for his divine honor.

Now we say "today." In this word he teaches us that we should receive the noble gifts of God the Father so purely that we possess absolutely nothing of our own in God's own "us" than that which we, in God's will, have possessed unto God, as if this day, "today," were our last, and in the last hour of this day, God would pronounce judgment over flesh and spirit, and we were aware of this.

The third day is God, who is a perfect day of all days and our daily bread. In this day is our eternal blessedness and God is our blessedness. How will we enjoy this bread? As he knows and loves and enjoys himself in the all-perfect holiness of his essence and of his nature and of his entire Godhead, so also he wills to give himself to us, according to our capacity, to know and love and enjoy in the all-perfect holiness of his essence and of his nature and of his entire Godhead by the nobility of his good pleasure.

"Today": one God, one being, one spirit today in this new now. And thus we are receiving that Light from the Light, that Light with the Light, that Light in the Light, the Light of lights, in this eternal new now of the eternal day, "today."

Now you have heard about the day, and about the daily bread, and how it is ours. Now note: "give us." In these words, he teaches us everything that human reason or angelic reason ever understood or ever shall possess, namely, that we, adoring, know the Father rationally, and love him lovingly, and simply acknowledge the divine quality of the Father—which is to give. For just as the Father, in speaking, engenders, in a fatherly way, by the fecundity of his nature, so in engendering he gives and bestows everything that is his, in the fecundity of his nature, to the Son, in a fatherly way; in this same birth he creates and gives life and essence, of a divine sort, to all creatures. Thus, it is the property of the Father to give and to sustain all creatures.

"Us." In this word he teaches us to accord to our fellowman all the good that we accord to ourselves just as we accord it to ourselves.

## IX. The next word: Forgive us our debts as we forgive our debtors

Who else but the almighty God in his justice has debtors? All sinners are indebted to him. For no one should say of himself in truth that he is without sin, and so also he should not say that he has debtors; thus nobody is without guilt but God alone and those he has made innocent by his pure blood. Since this is true, it is also true that we have debtors. Note how we have them. Through grace, man is an individual rational animal. When man, then, chooses injustice through his own will, and by that self-chosen injustice saddens his brother contrary to justice, he is in debt to God and to his brother. For since every debt that creature may owe to creature is so infinitely small compared with the debt that the creature owes to God, God, out of his free justice, does not will to forgive us our great debt before we, of our free will, have forgiven our brother his small debt through love of God. And as we forgive, so are we forgiven; if we do not forgive, then we will never be forgiven. This is proper to beginners.

Next, note where we have debtors. Whoever dishonors God dishonors all creatures. Thus, the sinner is a debtor to God and to all creatures. Since it is proper to God to forgive, how can we forgive? If, by God's grace, our will is united with God's will, whatever God wills is what we will. Since God, by his mercy, wills to forgive the sinner, we thus forgive with God in union with his will. How can we know when God forgives the sinner? We cannot know all God's works, but we will simply conform our will to his will and lovingly love in all his works. Thus we forgive with God. And this is proper to good people.

The third [category] is proper to the perfect, who, in it, are followers of Christ in poverty of spirit. Poverty of spirit is to have nothing, and to have nothing of oneself. In reality, these people have everything, and they forgive most totally, for theirs is the kingdom of God, says Christ. And they are totally forgiven, for the Father forgives no one but the Son and in the Son. Just as the Son has exerted all his strength in obedience to his Father and under our burdens, and has suffered bitter death, out of love, on account of our debt, so also the true disciples in the same obedience exert all their strength for the Father's glory under our burdens in such sonly love that were it possible for them to bear our burdens as the Son has borne them, they would gladly bear them. And they bear them without and within in their sonly love. It is not the case that through their own merits they deliver us from eternal death; rather, through their merits they merit for us that we become worthy to receive the merits that the Son has earned through his holy suffering. And in the same way as Mary was a support to the faithful when Christ suffered the passion on the cross, so she was such a support to all flesh with her holy merits, restraining the Father from avenging the world's sin and the death that the Jews visited on his only-begotten Son. On the last day the Father wants to have those who, in need of him, became true followers of Christ. And if this one hour of the day were lacking to us, all our flesh must perish because of our fleshly sins.

## X. Lead us not into temptation

The Father cannot do this by reason of the nobility of his goodness. What then does the Son teach us in these words? Great humility of spirit. Humility of spirit is that the spirit should have a trembling sinking away of all that it is in its nothingness, and a confession that the unique, most holy, eternal being, God, is one. And to recognize rationally and to love lovingly lest, were God to withdraw what is his from us for one instant, we should quickly be led into the temptation of eternal death.

## XI. But deliver us from evil

Evil is something displeasing to God on our part, on the soul's part; it belongs to us and to the fallen angels alone, and is not at all proper to God; the fact that this displeasing thing is not proper to God is inherent to God from the nobility of his Godhead. Now note how it is not proper to God. From the qualities belonging to our nature neither we nor the angels have any evil; for if we had it, then God would have created both evil and good, and that is not the case. For when God fashioned all the creatures, he looked at them and they were altogether good and they were well pleasing to him. Now, evil does not adhere to us as an accident that we have received from God, but it belongs to us when we have taken it upon ourselves by our own will against God's will; and therefore it displeases God in us and is evil. Now, since we have taken this evil upon ourselves by our own will against God's will, we cannot remove it from ourselves by our own will against God's will without the grace of God. Therefore, the Son teaches us interiorly to pray and to adore the Father, that he might purify us and deliver us from all that displeases him in us. May God help us in this. Amen.

74

## *XII.*

Now I ask whether anyone can dispense with the Our Father in this age in any way? And I say: no. And I attest to this in Mary, who, within her mother's womb, was delivered from the evil of original sin and was confirmed by the Holy Spirit so that she could never take sin upon herself. Even she did not dispense with it, in any way, nor did the apostles. What do we learn in Mary's prayer? True humility of heart and soul; she, as the poorest sinner on earth, attributed to herself so little of all the wonders that God had wrought in her, for she had a purer knowledge with the eternal Word than any mere creature ever had in time. She also followed his teaching in love more purely than any creature in time.

That we may adore and pray to God the Father as his only-begotten Son knows and loves the Father in glory and us blessedly— may he help us in this by his mercy. Amen.

Pure knowledge and holding certain views are not alike. Knowledge takes place in heaven; holding certain views takes place in time. I understand this essay merely as expressing certain views and I entrust and commit both my thought and this essay to the unchangeable knowledge of God and to the community of his holy Christendom.

# Hendrik Mande
## *Apocalypse* (excerpts), *A Love Complaint*, and extract from *A Devout Little Book*[1]

*Hendrik Mande was born in Dordrecht, at that time one of the main cities in Holland. His birth year is not known, but it must have been some-time between 1350 and 1360. Mande served for some time as a copyist at the court of the counts of Holland.*

*In the late seventies of the fourteenth century the* Devotio Moderna *originated, a religious reform movement that tried to revive the "old devotion" of the first Christians. The great leader of this movement was Geert Grote (d. 1384), born in Deventer, in the east of present-day Netherlands. Grote also preached in Holland, and Mande was among his audience. Mande converted and went to Deventer and Zwolle, towns at the river IJssel. There he joined the earliest followers of Geert Grote.*

*The Modern Devotion aimed at a deepened inner life and sought to offer good pastoral care to the citizens, particularly to religiously inspired women and schoolboys. Gradually the movement was organized in several institutional "branches": Brothers of the Common Life, Sisters of the Common Life, Canons and Canonesses of St. Augustine, and Tertiaries of St. Francis. After about fifty years this phase of development was com-pleted, and the convents had united in the Chapter of Windesheim to sup-port one another materially and spiritually.*

*Hendrik Mande was initially a member of the relatively unorgan-ized Brothers of the Common Life (thus designated because they shared their earnings). Later he entered the main abbey at Windesheim, where he became a regular canon. For reasons unknown to us he was not ordained a priest. In 1431 he died at an advanced age.*

*Hendrik Mande must have written fourteen relatively small works, of which eleven or twelve survived. Unfortunately, Mande's* Book of Revelations *is lost. Apart from a number of compilations he made some original works have been preserved, such as the* Minnentlike claege (A Love Complaint), *which is translated here. The medieval manuscripts contain the works of Mande anonymously. However, we know the titles because they are listed in the biography written by his much younger fellow brother Johannes Busch (1399–c. 1480).*

*Mande is known to have had many revelations, particularly concerning deceased people. His* Apocalypse *was his most famous work dealing with these revelations, and the most widely disseminated. Mande was very interested in mysticism, as becomes clear from his work, but he probably was not a real mystic. For him, the attitude, intention of prayer, and the ardent desire expressed are more important than words of prayer. This approach finds expression in* A Love Complaint, *which is a very lyrical text, completely different from his other treatises. It is indeed a love complaint, a complaint concerning the absence, the inaccessibility of the Beloved.*

*Mande also claims that perfection can be no more than the striving for perfection: "You have to see always what God most prefers and what the utmost perfection is. And after this everybody has to strive, as much as he can. For to strive always after perfection is considered as perfection. For we may not stand still on our way; we have to go forth or backward. And not willing to go forth is going backward."*[2]

# APOCALYPSE (EXCERPTS)

It happened on Assumption [August 15] that a poor brother sat down in his cell after Prime about the sixth hour and started to meditate on the feast of that day. When he sat like this and lifted up his heart, as our dear Lord gave him from grace, he was lifted up in the spirit in some stillness and peacefulness that surpassed all senses of man, so that he had forgotten all things and himself also. In this stillness and peacefulness he heard a kind of very sweet sound that surpassed all the delights of this world. He saw there with the eyes of the intellect, not in any form, likeness, or image, but in an unspeakable way, how God is enjoying himself in himself and in all creatures, and how he is his own joy and glory beyond all that is created.

When this brother was in these delights—he wanted nothing else but to stay there for ever, because he found full satisfaction of all his senses—he heard a kind of sweet voice, just like sweet string music, and it spoke: "Go out and see the queen of heaven in her glory, in which she is received and crowned by the highest." Immediately the eyes of his heart were opened, and he saw a multitude of angels, innumerable and beyond the comprehension of every creature other than the Creator of the creatures. All of them were clothed with special clarity, each according to his ranking by God. All of them produced a sweet sound of manifold melodies that no human heart could understand unless it was given to him from above. They praised and thanked our dear Lord for the glory and clarity that he had given to his dear blessed Mother and continued to give for all eternity.

Furthermore, he saw a multitude of saints of all (religious) orders, of all ways of life, of all conditions in the world. They were intangible, and each was clothed with his virtues and the benefactions he had done during his life, some with more clarity than others. But above all this they had a special clarity and a kind of clothing made from the merits of our dear Lord Jesus Christ, who in his humanity had earned [these merits] for the sake and the bliss of those who are chosen. All these were crowned as if with golden crowns that shone like the sun in its power, though some with more clarity than others, each in accordance with his merits, with the nobleness to which he was chosen by God from eternity, and with the elevation of his life in which he exercised himself here. They went in processions and sang so that all heaven seemed to resound with this responsory: "Blessed are you, holy virgin Mary, worthy of all praising." [...]

After this he saw how the holy father St. Augustine came in great glory with the apostles, martyrs, and confessors, each according to the rank in which he was set by God from eternity. Furthermore, he saw how St. Augustine linked hand with Master Geert Grote and the prior of Windesheim to his other hand with great joy. Master Geert was very beautifully clothed with golden clothes, that is, with divine love. On top of these he had a cloak that was green on top and red underneath, that is, divine wisdom with ardent love to his neighbor. And all who through his teaching and example would come to a just life, up to the last person, were depicted on the cloak. And in his hand he had a golden cross set with precious stones, because he had begun his preachings about the mortification of nature and pleasures of the flesh, which were very common at that time. And he preached one should gather genuine virtues, about which very few people, both clerical and secular, thought at that time.

After Master Geert, Father Florens (Radewijns) and Father Johan van den Gronde came, clothed with the same garments in great clarity and joy of their heart. And depicted on their cloaks was also the order of regular (canons) that has begun now with all the brothers of Windesheim.

Father Johannes Brinckerinck was clothed in ineffable great glory, that is, with the three convents in which he had worked especially, being Master Geert's house, Arnhem, and Diepenveen. And because of the special common will that he had toward all good people, and because of his generosity in receiving guests, he wore a very beautiful stone on his chest. On it was written: "Lord, thy commandment is exceeding broad" (Ps 118[119]:96), and "I was a stranger, and you took me in" (Matt 25:35). [...]

At his other hand (St. Augustine had) the prior of Windesheim with all brothers, friars, and lay brothers who died as members of the order, everyone according to his merits in his peculiar clarity and glory. And in a miraculous manner depicted on the cloak of the prior of Windesheim were all those whom he had helped by his words and his example in living justly. And because he also loved in general all who wanted to serve God, and because he was also generous in receiving the guests, he also had on his chest a precious stone like Father Johannes Brinckerinck.

The sisters of Diepenveen he saw in so great glory that he could not express it. Ah, how happy was now the lady of Ruynen and the lady of Vreden with all the sisters who had died in all the convents. A virgin from Staveren was there, named Stijn Tolleners, who was very joyful because she had served in the kitchen at Diepenveen. After this, he saw the sisters of all the convents processing, each one clothed according to her dignity, ardor, and love.

He saw how all the virgins followed the little lamb that was led by St. Agnes. And every virgin had a little lamb, and all the virgins sang with very sweet voices: "O Jesus, crown of the virgins." This and the like was so much and so manifold that the brother could not express it. [...]

# A LOVE COMPLAINT OF THE LOVING SOUL TO HER BELOVED TO BE RELEASED FROM HER DARKNESS AND FAILINGS[3]

1.   O beloved, sweet Lord, when will it befall me that I will contemplate and enjoy you, freed from all hindrance and shortcomings? O chosen one, how long will I be kept here and will I have to stay in this darkness that mediates between us so that I can not see or enjoy you, who are the eternal light, according to my desire? O, who will give it to me that I will embrace and hold you, my Beloved? O dear and benevolent Lord, have mercy on your beloved and look with your merciful eyes upon the suffering of her heart and her desires for you. Oh, let the desiring tears of my heart that I shed before your feet, draw you—and I lie here fallen down and I cry to you with a loud voice from within saying: Oh, when will I return to where I have been? Oh, when will your beloved presence reveal itself to me? Oh, the blessed hour and time when this will happen. O beloved Lord, let the sighing of my heart move you. Forget your lofty elevation somewhat and be so humble as to come to me, for I long for you with all the desire of my heart, and you are to me the chosen One from thousands. For, dear Lord, all I see that is not you is to me a pain and a burden, though I behold the beauty and multitude of your creatures and the wonderful deeds you have done in order that we would see and know you, dear Lord, in all of this. This draws me ever more and more to you, merciful Lord, because all these cannot give any comfort or rest to my heart, but they excite and stir my inner self and all my desires more and more to you, because in the multitude and beauty of your creatures I perceive your ineffable beauty, power, and mercy. And therefore, my sweet Lord, nothing can satisfy me that is not you yourself. And therefore I beseech you, my only Comfort, do not wait any longer, but come to my soul in peace, for she thirsts very much for you, who are a fountain of life.

2.   The voice of the turtledove has been heard in our land (Sg 2:12). Your sighing and your groaning has come to me. Look, my chosen one, I am here. Your burning desire and your humble prayer

has drawn me to you. From eternity I have loved and chosen you as a dwelling in order that you should enjoy me in eternity. And therefore, my chosen one, tell me what you want and what worries you, and I will fulfill it through myself, because this is my joy: to be with you and to dwell in you in eternity. And therefore, open your heart to me and I will give what you should want or something better for you, because man often wishes things from me that, if I would give them to him, would harm him for ever. But because I take heed of the pure desire of the heart, I will change this in something better for his eternal bliss. And therefore, my beloved, put all your hope and trust in me and what you desire faithfully will befall you. Because this is what I desire: that you desire great things from me and that you trust without doubt that I will fulfill your desire or something better for you. Therefore, pray and open your heart to me and demand what you want.

3.   O my chosen One, your sweet, amiable voice has strengthened my heart so that I now have the courage to speak to you, my beloved and sweet Lord. O beloved Lord, you tell me to open my heart and to say what I want. O eternal Wisdom, are you not the one who knows every heart and to whom every secret is open? O my sweet Lord and comfort of my heart, you know what I suffer inwardly and externally, and you also know my imperfection and my deficiency in virtues. And I also notice, my benevolent Lord, that I cannot praise and thank you in accordance with my desire and my indebtedness, because I recognize myself to be so deficient and failing in fulfilling what you want most, and in acquiring virtues. This and alike, O eternal Mercy, is what I lament, because it is difficult to me to bear the darkness and the blindness of my heart, which hinders me so that I cannot behold nor enjoy you, who are my eternal light, according to my desire. And therefore, my Beloved and chosen one, my eyes are weeping and my heart is crying to you because you are the eternal light and the sole comfort and happiness of my heart: O eternal Truth, come and enlighten my heart with yourself and conduct me in your right way and give me power and strength to adhere to you and to fulfill what you desire the most, because I cannot live without you, nor do I want to. For this will be my pleasure and delight: that your most eager will always be done in me, here and in eternity.

81

4. O my chosen one, why is your soul sad and what depresses you? Raise your eyes to me, who am your salvation. I am the one who wipes out your evil as if it never existed, and who alters your darkness into light, for this is within my power. Don't you know that he is blessed who endures temptations and misfortune for my sake? You have to know truly that your good works that you do in times of darkness and hardship suit me much more and are also more meritorious for you than those you do when you think you are well and that you are in the light. Don't you know that I am with those who are in trouble and in misfortune? Then you search for me and call me, and I am most near to you (Isa 58:9). And I am the one who fights for you and protects you so that you will not become trapped (cf. Ps 27:7). Therefore, remain firm and be not afraid because I am with you and I will fight for you and take your whole burden on me. So, stand firm and let me do the fighting, because it would impossible for me to abandon him who puts all his hope and consolation in me. Don't you know, my chosen one, that this is the game of love and that I try those whom I love and that I test their perseverance? Consider my decrees from the beginning of the world and you will be consoled. If you were always to enjoy light and prosperity, you would not understand what darkness and adversity are; you would easily become proud, and you would grow conceited as if you were something and as if you were capable of something on your own, and you would forget me. And so, in order that you always remain humble and your good deeds be hidden from your self and be saved, I allow darkness and trouble and temptation to happen to you and to others, my chosen ones. Thus, they will always see what they are lacking and what they have will be hidden from them, and they will not slacken, but they will always fear and seek my assistance, and they will trust more in my assistance, merit, and mercy than in their own good works. In this way their virtues are saved and covered by humility and they will always increase and become more firmly established in me, in whom all good begins and ends.

I did not promise my chosen ones wealth and prosperity in this world, but that they will cry and be oppressed and that the world will rejoice (John 16:20). Therefore, try to work and fight bravely, and your heart will strengthen. You may have heard one of my fighters saying that this momentary and light affliction that you suffer here in time is nothing compared to the magnitude of the glory that is prepared for you if you persevere (2 Cor 4:17). For nobody will be crowned but he who fights with perseverance and bravery. So, lift up your eyes and look where those who suffered here are sitting in the glory and measureless bliss. What does it matter to them now that they were once despised, rejected, oppressed, and scorned, and that they suffered much pain inwardly and externally? All this has finished and they have received eternal peace and blessedness for this, and they are assured that they will suffer nevermore but will rejoice in eternity with me. And so, my chosen one, if you entrust yourself totally to me and abandon yourself, I will be yours completely and you will rest on me without worrying, because I do not sleep, nor will sleep, I who am your keeper (Ps 120:4).

5.   O sweet beloved Lord, look, I am completely overcome by your amiable words and I can speak or complain no more because your ardent consolation has touched and strengthened my heart so much that I am now prepared to suffer with your help everything that you, my chosen one, will allow me to suffer here and in eternity, so that you will stay with me, as you said before, and will be my keeper, because I cannot do without you, as you know. And so, my dear Lord, I offer and give myself up completely in your hands so that you can do with me everything you want in accordance with your greatest glory and honor. And because I find nothing in myself to worthily thank and praise you, my chosen one, I call upon heaven and earth, water and air with all the creatures they contain to fervently thank and praise you, my merciful Lord, on behalf of me, and exalt you for all your gifts and benevolence that you, dear Lord, showed me, poor creature, and continue to show me, and for your benevolent consoling words through which you strengthened my heart. O eternal, amiable Wisdom, who are and will be in eternity one God with the Father and the Holy Spirit, yours are praise, honor, and dignity, O supra-holy Trinity. Amen.

# EXTRACT FROM
# A DEVOUT LITTLE BOOK ON
# THE HIGHEST PERFECTION OF LOVE

## Love does not lie in the feeling of sweetness[4]

Anyone who loves God loves his deeds. God's deeds are the noble virtues. Therefore, he who loves God loves all virtue. And this love is true and full of comfort, because virtues, not sweetness, are the proof of love. Because it often happens that he who loves less tastes most sweetness. But love does not correspond to that [feeling], but to the measure in which everyone is based on, and rooted in, virtues and love. Some may have sweet longings for God, which are nevertheless not all godlike, and this happens in particular to beginners and imperfect persons who are still young. Because often what one supposes to be love is sensuality, and what one supposes to be grace is nature. For this sweetness often moves man rather to the lesser good, and less often to more good. And it [this sweetness] pays more heed to that which tastes good to him than to what is best for him, because it takes after that from which it sprang. The imperfect man experiences such sweetness as well as the perfect man, and he thinks sometimes to live in greater love because he feels or tastes sweetness, and thus it is all impure and tainted. And even if the sweetness would be all pure and godlike, which is very intricate and hard to know, still love is not measurable according to the sweetness but according to the possession of virtues and divine love. For we often find that some people are content as long as the sweetness lasts, and so their love lasts too, but when the sweetness disappears, their love ends too. And this is because they are not provided with virtues. But if the virtues are planted early in the soul and are rooted firmly with long exercises and with close care, then even when the sweetness lessens, the virtues keep their nature and always fulfill the work of love from which they have sprung. For they do not await sweetness but are concerned with how they can always serve love truthfully. They do not seek flavor but usefulness. They look at their hands, not at their wages. And they commend it totally to love and they are not any worse off,[5] as true love lies in taking all things with equanimity: sweet and sour, consolation and adversity.

*An example:* A pure revelation, which happened to a brother in a monastery, illustrates this. This brother sat once in his cell, and he was oppressed and dark inside, so he did not find any taste in what he read or meditated upon. Then it occurred to him he wanted to go in the library where the common books were to see whether he could find something pure that could hearten his mind, for instance St. Augustine's *Soliloquies* or something like that. But when he came there, he did not, given his disposition, find anything that he liked, and he returned to his cell and sat in front of the place were he used to sleep. When he was seated and meditated upon his desolation and the darkness of his heart and what he could do or read best to lose his oppression, he was swiftly lifted up in the spirit. When he was seated like this, a virtuous person came to him, whom he did not know, and brought him a book and a pen with ink. Then he handed the pen to this brother and spoke to him and said, "Write." The brother said, "What should I write?" The other person responded, "You will write *Benedicam dominum in omni tempore; semper laus eius in ore meo*, which means 'I will bless the Lord at all times, his praise shall be always in my mouth'" (Ps 33:2). Then the angel said, "Read what you wrote." Then he read, *"Benedicam"* etc., as is written here before. Then the angel said further, "Open the book and see what is written in it." When the brother opened the book, he found nothing else but what he had been told to write, that is, *Benedicam*, etc. Then the angel said: "Because you sought a book in the library that you would like to read so as to find consolation, and because you did not find something that might serve you at this moment in compliance with your desire, therefore I brought you this book, which you will read and study. And it will be satisfactory to you even if you were never to read another book. And you will find true peace in this and you will be pleasing to God if you are patient under the will of God, accept with equanimity from him prosperity and adversity, light and darkness, and try to praise him in all circumstances. Because all things he sends or allows to fall upon you and all his chosen spring of his love and serve to their beatitude, because thus it is best to them and most meritorious. If you will read this book well and you will remember my lesson, then you will find

85

peace of heart and advance in veritable virtues, because all things will turn into your profit."

With these words the brother came back to himself, and he received an extraordinary consolation in his heart from the things he had heard and seen. And he made a perfect resolution to remember this lesson all his life with the help of God, and he found much profit in this to advance to a spiritual life, after which he strove.

Therefore, it is very necessary for us that everyone pays attention to the grace and gifts that he has received from God and notes his inner admonitions so that he tries to work with the grace and tries to control and further the good of God in a wise manner. Thus he may become worthy of receiving more grace.

# Exposition on the
# Song of Songs (extracts)[1]

## (Bedudinghe op Cantica Canticorum)

Bedudinghe op Cantica Canticorum *is an anonymous Middle Dutch commentary on the first five chapters of the Song of Songs.[2] The traditional view of the innumerable commentaries on this enigmatic book—one of the shortest in the Bible—has been that it contains the expression of the mutual longing of bride and bridegroom.* Bedudinghe *was written in the early fifteenth century and became widely disseminated during the fifteenth and sixteenth centuries.* Bedudinghe op Cantica Canticorum—*literally* Exposition on the Song of Songs—*occupies a place of prominence among the many Middle Dutch expositions on the same mysterious book of the Bible. The text stands out because of its excessive length and the extraordinarily high number of extant textual witnesses. More important, however, is the attractive style of its language and the coherence of the exposition. But most important, the text attains a rare level of mystical interpretation of the Song of Songs.*

Bedudinghe *owes the quality of its content largely to its Latin source* (Glossa Tripartita super Cantica). *This text was identified only in 1993.[3] The generally held view assumed that the anonymous author of* Bedudinghe *had used a large number of sources, and as a consequence,* Bedudinghe *was considered a compilation. The one source, however, turned out to be* Glossa Tripartita super Cantica, *an immense late-thirteenth, early-fourteenth Franciscan commentary on all the eight chapters of the Song of Songs. The fact that a copy of this text still exists in manuscript Utrecht, Universiteitsbibliotheek, 334 (3 D 13) has made it possible to arrive at this identification. Had the text only survived in the other extant copies—kept in Assisi, Oxford, and Munich—the source might never have been found.*

## Glossa Tripartita super Cantica

*The oldest of the textual witnesses of* Glossa Tripartita super Cantica *is manuscript Assisi, Sacro Convento di San Francesco, 354. Writing of this manuscript started in the late thirteenth century and was finished in the early decades of the fourteenth century. The codex contains the key to understanding the genesis of the text. This is found through analysis of the complex codicological structure of the manuscript, which can only be explained by assuming that the codex is witness to "work in progress." The Assisi manuscript provides a text in which the level of completion increases as the exposition progresses. The core of* Glossa Tripartita *is probably based on a course of exegesis at the University of Paris. In its early parts, written in Paris, the text of the Assisi codex boasts a succinctness that is characteristic of such a text. The course must have been taught by some Franciscan master, since analysis of the source material of* Glossa Tripartita *leaves no doubt as to the Franciscan origin of the text. Through the years the anonymous master kept adding material to his text. At some point, however, the focus of his interest shifted. This might well have coincided with the author moving from Paris to Assisi, where he probably finished the text. The older master became less intent on Scholastic divisions and distinctions and aimed ever more at a pious reading of the Song of Songs. Thus, in his later additions, his intention came close to that of the Middle Dutch translator, who focused solely on a meditative reading of the text. The exposition on each verse of the Song of Songs became increasingly extensive as the author progressed in his exposition. In the later chapters the Assisi manuscript attains its full breadth. The complete version of the work is found in manuscripts at Utrecht and Munich, while the manuscript in Oxford represents an intermediary phase.[4]*

*The* Glossa Tripartita super Cantica *presents a triple interpretation of the Song of Songs. The author provides an ecclesiological, moral-mystical, and mariological interpretation of bride and bridegroom. They stand for God and the church, God and the loving soul, and Jesus and Mary, respectively. These three modes of interpretation are dealt with sequentially, which means that each part of a Song of Songs verse is treated in three separate chapters.*

*The Song of Songs hardly allows for historical or anagogical interpretation; therefore, the focus is entirely on the allegorical and tropological meanings—as has been the case throughout the history of Latin commen-*

*taries on the Song of Songs, from Origen to St. Bernard, from Gregory the Great to Bonaventure.*

## Bedudinghe op Cantica Canticorum

*Around the year 1420 an anonymous translator deemed the* Glossa Tripartita super Cantica *suitable to be translated and transformed into a text that would be one enormous meditation on the Song of Songs:* Bedudinghe op Cantica Canticorum. *The work was intended to provide fuel for the furnace of fiery longings that burn in the heart of the God-loving soul. The translator was facing a task of great magnitude. Not only would he have to translate the large work, but he would also have to make countless small translation decisions, since the Middle Dutch text he envisaged was of an entirely different nature than the source text at hand. Even though the* Glossa Tripartita *contained all the material needed for a text aimed at comtemplative readers, it had been framed in a Scholastic structure and was permeated with Scholastic reasoning. The translator had to sift out only those parts of his material that could be put together into a new mosaic fit for meditation and contemplation. Everything Scholastic would have to be left out. The translator executed his task effectively; once completed, the work was an immediate and lasting success in the Northern Netherlands.*

*The text of* Bedudinghe *is extant partly or entirely in over forty manuscripts, which makes it a "best seller" of Middle Dutch spiritual literature. This corpus of manuscripts can be divided into two groups, since the work exists in two versions, albeit with relatively minor differences. These groups differ conspicuously, however, in their regional origin. The original version is found almost exclusively in manuscripts from the western part of the Netherlands, while the second, contemporaneous version is attested solely in manuscripts from the eastern part of the Netherlands.*

*This regional divide between the two versions is probably not accidental. In the fourteenth century the spiritual life in the eastern part of the Northern Netherlands was dominated by the institutions of the* Devotio Moderna. *The Brothers and Sisters of the Common Life constituted the initial, lay branch of this movement, while the canons and canonesses regular of St. Augustine, united in the Windesheim chapter, formed the monastic branch. The second version of* Bedudinghe *is attested mostly—*

89

*judging from the known provenances—in monasteries, both for men and for women, connected with the* Devotio Moderna. *The text seems markedly absent in the houses of the Brothers and Sisters of the Common Life. Spiritual life in the western part of the Northern Netherlands, on the other hand, was dominated by the houses and convents of tertiaries of the Utrecht Chapter and the monasteries of the canonesses regular of St. Augustine, united in the Generaal Kapittel (Chapter General), also known as the Chapter of Sion. It is in these houses, convents, and monasteries that the first version of* Bedudinghe *is attested.*

## Content of *Bedudinghe op Cantica Canticorum*

*Known provenances of the extant manuscripts indicate that* Bedudinghe *was mostly read by female contemplative monastics in the western part of the Netherlands. Therefore, it does not come as a surprise when analysis of the content shows that female monastics must have been the audience the translator had in mind. This intended audience can be deduced from the transformation process that the* Glossa Tripartita *went through in order to become* Bedudinghe. *The translator systematically applies different transformation strategies on the source. First, there are the elements he leaves out. Everything that has to do with Scholastic structuring of the text is deleted, and so are the clearly Franciscan passages. The translator skips the mariological interpretation in its entirety. Second, there are strategies that are designed to serve the spiritual needs of the readers. These involve changes and additions. The most important changes are the following. Wherever possible the translator changes the character of the text from intellectual to devotional. Most important, however, the translator adds nuptial and relational imagery that makes it possible for the reader to identify more closely with the bride from the Song of Songs. The God-loving soul is also more clearly defined as the bride. The reader— being a God-loving soul—can read almost the entire text from the perspective of the bride.*

*The ecclesiological interpretation is usually shorter than the moral-mystical reading. The most important authorities in the ecclesiological parts are St. Bernard, Gregory the Great, and Augustine. Gilbert of Hoyland continued Bernard's commentary from Song of Songs 3:2 onward. St. Bernard again, Vercellencis (that is, Thomas Gallus), and*

*Pseudo-Dionysius the Areopagite are the dominant authorities in the moral-mystical parts. This is a truly remarkable aspect of* Bedudinghe, *since Thomas Gallus and Pseudo-Dionysius rarely occur in Middle Dutch spiritual literature. The quotations from Dionysius, however, mostly stem from the works of Thomas Gallus, whose commentaries might without exaggeration be called a commentary on the works of Pseudo-Dionysius in the form of a commentary on the Song of Songs.*

*The radical new element in the sermons of Bernard is that the bride of the Song of Songs is identified throughout with the soul, therefore Bernard's own soul, but also the soul of everybody desiring to ascend toward God, the bridegroom, and to merge with him in mystical delight. Bernard states simply: "Who is the bride and who is the bridegroom? The latter is God and the former, if I dare say so, are we."⁵ Thomas Gallus's exposition differs from this affective mysticism in that it also includes a speculative, philosophical aspect dealing with the deepest ontological level of the soul, where each created person is connected with God. The loving soul should free its innermost self from obfuscation through sin, in order to repair the connection with the divine and to experience unification with the super-essential being in a superintellectual and affecting way.*

*The longing of the bride, the ardent soul, to be united with the divine bridegroom is the one pervasive theme of the moral-mystical parts of* Bedudinghe. *It seems that through the borrowings from the sermons of Bernard and from the commentaries of Thomas Gallus, Bedudinghe attains most purely its objective of encouraging the loving soul to contemplate God and to achieve spiritual uplifting in this process. Bedudinghe is a text that allows and stimulates the reader's identification with the mystical bride; the fact it does this so effectively explains it attractiveness and success.*

# EXPOSITION ON THE SONG OF SONGS

# [Prologue]

St. John saw in the Apocalypse a book in the hands of the one seated on the throne, that was written both on the inside and the outside (Rev 5:1). This book is holy scripture, which, as *St. Gregory* says, nurses young beginners by the letter of outer history as if with milk, while by the spiritual sense, with which the book was written on the inside, it nourishes the advanced people as if with solid food (cf. 1 Cor 3:2; Heb 5:12–14).[6] *Augustine:* Holy scripture outsmarts and derides the haughty by its sublimity, intimidates the doctors by its profundity, and teaches the meek by its simplicity, for under the simplicity of the letter many ways of understanding are hidden.[7] *Dionysius:* This has thus been ordained by divine providence, so that the truth would be revealed to the believers and God's chosen, and be hidden from the proud and the rebellious, as well as those unworthy of the truth.[8] *Augustine:* The profundity of holy scripture is so deep, that if I would strive to study it from my early youth on until my old days, with receptive senses and great effort, I would at long last have to say, after I had done all I could, that I had only just begun to learn.[9] For though all people may arrive at the scriptures from the outside, there are, however, very few who succeed in properly getting into them. For if one could readily understand what is hidden inside, the truth one seeks and finds in them would be less valued. Therefore, as *St. Ambrose* says, one shall at length impress and push the words of heavenly scripture energetically into one's heart and reflect upon them, so that the juice from the spiritual food will be squeezed into all veins of the soul, and one shall bow one's head before its commands, so as to arrive at understanding through faith.[10] This book that is thus written both inside and outside one shall use as a mirror, so as to wash what is unclean, to keep clean and make even cleaner what is already clean. For this book is rich and fertile, and all pleasures and delights are hidden in it just as the manna, the heavenly bread, tasted according to the desire of each person who ate it. This taste does not lie in the words written on the outside, but in the meaning that is written on the inside; it is not found at the outside in shape and sound, but on the inside in the fruit; not in the outer leaves, but in the root of enlightened reason. Therefore, just as the night does not darken the stars, similarly the minds of the faithful who properly read the book of holy scripture on the inside cannot be darkened by the evil of the world, because one can clearly understand the will of God from it. This holy scripture *St. Gregory* compares to a river that is so shallow and dry that a lamb may go through it—meaning that a simple, uneducated man might cross it with dry feet—and so deep that an elephant—meaning a person with a very subtle mind—might swim in it, yes, even be drowned, if he does not look modestly but proudly upon himself.[11] Solomon wrote one of the books of holy scripture that is called the Song of Songs, which book is hardly if at all written on the outside, but primarily on the inside, as the doctors of the holy church write about it; and it starts: Let him kiss me, etc.

# [Song of Songs 1:1]

*This is the beginning of the first chapter with its gloss by the doctors.*

LET HIM KISS ME WITH THE KISS OF HIS MOUTH. *Bernard:*[12] Solomon made three books: in the first beginners are taught to shun sin,[13] in the second the advancing people are taught to despise the enticements of the world,[14] and in the third the perfected people are taught to love the bridegroom of their soul.[15] *Gregory:* There are three types of life: virtuous life, natural life, and a life of contemplating God. In Solomon's first book the virtuous life is taught, in which he says: "My son, hear my wisdom, lend your ear to my prudence" (Prov 5:1). In the second book the natural life is taught, how everything comes to an end, where he says, "Vanity of vanities, all is vanity" (Eccl 1:2). In the third is the Song of Songs, in which the contemplative life is taught, and the coming of the Lord and the enjoyment of him are longingly yearned for,[16] as the beginning of the book clearly proves: LET HIM KISS ME WITH THE KISS OF HIS MOUTH. "Canticum" means a song of praise and gratitude, when the heart becomes joyful from the eternal goodness of God and then bursts out with sound. Just as an external song goes up and down with notes, similarly this spiritual song of praise goes up to let the yearnings climb upward in the mind toward God, and sometimes it descends to realize one's own insignificance and to commiserate with one's fellow man.

*Bernard:* This song of praise excels through its exceptional dignity and sweetness over all other songs that we know. This song is taught only through the ointment of the Holy Spirit and through experience. For it is no outburst of sound from the mouth, but a jubilation of the mind; it is no tone from the lips, but it is inner bliss of the soul; one does not hear exterior words on the outside in public, but one senses joyful and pure movements of the mind and harmonious love on the inside.[17] *Richard:* Since this is called a song of praise, it should also go up and down like a song. For at times aptitude and much grace are given to the lovers, so they might realize what they are through the grace of God, in order that they are all the more drawn to love him; sometimes this song descends, when aptitude and grace are taken from them, so that they would know what they are by themselves and thus might better despise themselves.[18] *Bernard:* Notice carefully that Solomon starts this book with kisses. Solomon means peaceful; kissing is a sign of peace. You may gather from this that only peaceful minds are invited to understand this book, because the impure, restless minds, who cannot suppress the desires of the flesh and who do not spurn the enticements of the world, are unable to comprehend it.[19] *Origen:* I caution and advise each person who has not overcome the natural desires and has not parted from all material things to be careful to read this book and all that is written in it. Because the early fathers among the Jews had forbidden it; whoever had not attained full and perfect maturity should not take this book into his hands.[20] *Bernard:* This book was not composed by human skills, but by the Holy Spirit; and although the thoughts are difficult to understand, they are satisfying to consider.[21] *Gregory:* We should watch carefully that whenever we hear words of outer love, we do not remain on the outside, but in these exterior words we should search for what is covertly concealed in them, and when we speak of physical things, we should stay on the outside of them. For holy scripture relates to words and their meaning as an image relates to paint, and he is very unwise who sees the paint of the painting but fails to see what is depicted. And just as the chaff covers the grain, so the letter covers the sense. Therefore, a reasonable, gentle person shall throw away the chaff for the animals and try to eat the grain of the mind.

In this book there are four persons speaking to one another: namely, the bridegroom, the bride, the companions, and the young women. The bridegroom is Christ, the bride is the holy church or a soul contemplating God, the companions of the bridegroom are the angels in heaven and all the perfected men on earth. Whoever loves God perfectly is a bride, and the person who duly avows the bridegroom is one of the companions, while he who is newly commenced on the way of the saints is called a young woman.[22] LET HIM KISS ME. *Gregory:* Solomon, illuminated by the wisdom of God and the spirit of prophecy, foresaw the advent of Christ in the flesh, and he prayed and longed together with the early fathers that God the Father would let his blessed Son take on human nature as a sign of perfect love,[23] as he said: LET HIM KISS ME WITH THE KISS OF HIS MOUTH. *Bernard:* Always when I reflect on the ardent desire of the early fathers for Christ to be present in human nature, I become melancholy and ashamed and can hardly hold back my tears, so greatly saddened am I by these times and the unholy tepidity that now reigns. For the manifestation of his love through his human presence pleases us not nearly as much as the hope for the future did the early fathers,[24] when they said: LET HIM KISS ME WITH THE KISS OF HIS MOUTH. The longing for the wedding between the Word of God and human nature is expressed by this, a wedding to which we are not invited without a wedding dress, that is, without inner knowledge of the divine truth. For wise men, as it is written, store up knowledge (Prov 10:14), and it is the glory of God to conceal the word (Prov 25:2) because the more gloriously he reveals himself to the mind, the more subtle and intimately he is sought. Therefore, it is honorable and praiseworthy for those who live well to examine the secrets of the scriptures, but when they hear words of human love, they should so to speak place themselves outside of mankind. Because the holy scriptures are a burning mountain, any animal-like mind that touches it and wants to understand it as he wishes will be stoned with the rocks of a gruesome spiritual judgment.[25] Thus we shall learn the ardor of divine love from the old words, and pray, yearning with the holy church, that the Father will kiss, comfort, and enlighten us with the presence of his Son.[26]

In this kiss there are two lips on the side of the bridegroom, namely, his divine and human nature, and two lips on the side of the bride, that is, the states of the perfect and the feeble, on whose behalf our mother, the holy church, through these words longs for the union of his divine and human nature in the person of Christ, so that the desire of the perfect people will be satisfied and the feeble will be strengthened in their faith. *Bernard:* For two reasons this kiss was given to us and presented at the beginning of the text, namely, that the joyful face of the holy scriptures might more easily attract us to itself with love, and that we would with pleasurable effort look for what is hidden in it.[27] The mouth is a door to the body and means the Son of God, who is a door to the spiritual body of the holy church, and this is proven by the door to Noah's ark, by which mankind was saved in the flood (Exod 6—8). For whoever did not enter into the ark drowned in the flood. Similarly, nobody is saved who does not enter through Christ into the community of the holy church. The opening of the door reveals to us what is in the house; likewise, through Christ the fatherly might and height is made known to us, for no one knows the Father except the Son and anyone to whom the Son chooses to reveal him (Matt 11:27). St. John was raised to this knowledge, as he spoke in the Apocalypse: Look, a door is opened in heaven, and a throne is placed in heaven, and the Father sits on it (Rev 4:1–2). *Paul:* A great door has been opened to me, but the adversaries are many (1 Cor 16:9). The Son of God himself says: I am the door: whoever enters by me, will be saved; he will go in and go out, he will find pasture (John 10:9). *The wise man:*[28] Blessed is the one who waits daily at my door (Prov 8:34).

The mouth reveals what is hidden in the heart; similarly, the will of the eternal Father is made known to us by the Son. With the mouth one speaks words; similarly the Son himself is the first Word and the beginning of all things, for in the beginning was the Word (John 1:1). The mouth serves the whole body and keeps it alive; similarly, the body of the holy church lives through Christ. I long to be kissed with the kisses of this mouth, by hearing the teachings of the holy gospels from his own mouth. *Bernard:* Now I don't hear from Moses: I am slow of tongue (cf. Exod 4:10); nor from Isaiah: My lips are unclean (Isa 6:5); nor from Jeremiah: I am a child, I do not know how to speak (Jer 1:6); but he, about whom the prophets have prophesied, shall himself speak to me, and KISS ME WITH THE KISS OF HIS MOUTH.[29]

# According to another sense[30]

LET HIM KISS ME WITH THE KISS OF HIS MOUTH. *Vercellencis:*[31] After a contemplative soul has examined all things and desires to be liberated from all that exists and to be gloriously united with the superessential bridegroom, then she[32] demands a kiss, that is, a union or loving unification with the bridegroom, even if she would at some time have to separate again. Still she pleads together with *Job* and says: My soul has chosen a hanging and my bones desire death (Job 7:15). This hanging of the soul is a stretching out of the mind into the super-excellent divine rays. The bones are the strongest faculties of the mind, namely, the contemplative reason and the highest desires, beyond which the soul has nothing to direct toward the divine. Death is a severing or a failing of one's self. For when the contemplative mind is taken up by the purest desires to a kiss of the bridegroom, then all activity collapses and fails, as well as all strength of reason and desire, as the prophet *Daniel* says: Lord, in the vision of you all my joints in my body failed me and there was no strength left in me (Dan 10:8). *Dionysius:* This is called a death in us, when the mind parts from all things, and then, after having abandoned itself, is blissfully united with the superessential bridegroom. This death does not destroy our being, but the spark of the highest affectivity comes to participate in the divine goodness, unspeakably separated from all lowness, and it becomes deiform, transformed beyond reason—as far as possible—by divine similarity in the manner of angels. *Origen:* St. John had come to partake of God when he said: In the beginning was the Word (John 1:1). After this unification the interior soul is yearning with desire,[33] and says, LET HIM KISS ME WITH THE KISS OF HIS MOUTH.

*Bernard:* Look, how intimate and friendly this conversation is between the word and the soul that still lives in the flesh. She pleads for what she longs for, but still she does not name the one she loves. She does not say this man or that, but only: LET HIM KISS ME.[34] Similarly, Mary Magdalene did not name the one she loved, for she thought it would be clear to everybody what she carried in her heart. *Gregory:* The mind in which the soul is united to the celestial bridegroom by desire and love cannot be pleased by any comfort from creatures, but she is interiorly attached to the one she loves. She sighs, she hopes, she is afraid, no one can comfort her, because she is wounded by the arrow of love,[35] and says, LET HIM KISS ME. Without you nothing pleases me, without you nothing has any taste for me, without you nothing is sweet to me, without you nothing seems beautiful to me, without you nothing has any value to me, without you all things become worthless to me. What is turned away from you is difficult and burdensome, and your well-being is my sole and continuous desire. I do not wish to receive visions and dreams anymore, figures and similes cannot satisfy me, the revelations of the angels do not please me; I long for the one who has created the angels and me: I long for my Jesus, who is utterly desirable, above all else.[36] I do not desire rewards, I desire no letter of assurance, I desire no lessons, I desire no inheritance, but I desire that he KISS ME WITH THE KISS OF HIS MOUTH, which is a sign of love.

*Bernard:* She could not hide the fervent love that she felt and asked for great things from the magnificent. She made no long introductions, did not use imploring words, but from the fullness of her heart, as if she had been drunk, she burst out and said, LET HIM KISS ME WITH THE KISS OF HIS MOUTH. Oh, how great was the force of love, how great was the confidence in the freedom of the spirit.[37] She is not guided by reason but by fervent desire; it did not come from boldness, as love does not follow a plan, she is not held back by shame, nor is she subjected to reason, but she goes beyond all that, and says, LET HIM KISS ME WITH THE KISS OF HIS MOUTH.[38] That is, let him touch me inside, let him shine on with the light of his truth, so I do not need the external words but may naturally understand him and comprehend what my mind longs for. There are many who are afraid of God and receive the Lord in fear with good works, but who do not kiss the bridegroom, for they are not moved by love. This was made clear at the feast of the Pharisees, where the woman who kissed Jesus's feet was exalted over others, because the ardor of love goes beyond all gifts of temporal goods.[39]

# [Song of Songs 1:5]

## According to another sense[40]

I AM BLACK BUT BEAUTIFUL, O DAUGHTERS OF JERUSALEM (Sg 1:5). *Vercellencis:* These are words of the ardent soul, as it was placed at the apex of its loving affectivity in the darkness of the incomprehensible contemplation of God, and as it spoke with the uninhibited boldness of love—as someone who was praising and full of praise and drunk with the bridegroom's wine—to the inferior powers: I AM BLACK BUT BEAUTIFUL, O DAUGHTERS OF JERUSALEM.[41] I AM BLACK, enclosed in the super-excellent light of the divine incomprehensibility. Black is a dark color indicating the obscuring of the incomprehensible light. BUT I AM BEAUTIFUL, adorned with the clear super-excellent divine rays. I AM BLACK LIKE THE TENTS OF KEDAR. Kedar was the son of Ismael (Gen 25:13). The tents that he lived in had been blackened by the rain and the heat of the sun; the same goes for the holy church or the loving soul, which because of the tribulations or anxiousness they have to expect, or because of the incomprehensible contemplation of God, are called black. They could be compared to firm tents because of the vigor of their endurance. *Isaiah:* Your eyes will see a tabernacle that one will not be able to move from its place (Isa 33:20). This tent is greatly expanded love, from the sweetness of all people of good will. *Isaiah:* Enlarge the place of your tent, stretch out the skins of your tabernacle (Isa 54:2). This tent is also beautiful and adorned with holy virtuousness, as is written: O Jacob, how beautiful are your tabernacles (Num 24:5). BUT I AM BEAUTIFUL LIKE THE SKINS OF SOLOMON, with which he covered the ark of God until his temple was completed. LOVELY from the adornment of virtues and especially by the love of God. KEDAR'S TENTS, which constantly stood in the rays of the sun and in the heat that came from the east, represent the minds that are continuously stretched upward, where they receive the fiery divine rays that shine on them from the sun of justice. SOLOMON'S SKINS, which were very delightful, represent the angelic, flaming ardor of the interior soul, which pleases the bridegroom beyond all other sacrifices of the mind, because his delights were with the children of mankind (Prov 8:31). Such a soul one might well compare to Solomon's skins, because from moderation she has lost weight, from abstinence she has dried out, from love she is unfolded wide, and from the sanctity of all virtues she is beautifully colored.

DO NOT CONSIDER ME THAT I AM BROWN, BECAUSE THE SUN HAS ALTERED MY COLOR.[42] *Bernard:* The intense, burning desire discolors the soul that is still on pilgrimage in the body, just like the burning sun; when the soul would want to be near to the glorious face of God and is unable to, and when she is turned away, she suffers greatly in his absence. Who among you is so much burning with this holy love that all color of the present glory and worldly joy is a source of grief to him, and who among you despises himself in the presence of that supremely shining sun and considers himself to be colorlessly black and impure, and says, My soul refused to be comforted; I remembered God and was delighted (Ps 76[77]:3–4)?[43] I AM BLACK BUT BEAUTIFUL. BLACK outside as to the body, BEAUTIFUL inside in the image of the soul. Black as to the perishable body that blackens the soul in many ways and hinders the contemplation of God, so she might well complain with *David*: I am placed into the mire of the abyss that has no ground (Ps 68:3). Because of this the soul receives so much "blackness" from human misery, that she might say with holy *Job*: My skin has blackened and my flesh has dried up (Job 30:30). *Bernard*: KEDAR'S TENT is our body, which hinders the soul as a dense intermediary so it cannot see the uncreated light other than through its reflection in a mirror.[44] And this was what *Paul* complained about, as he sighed and said, I, unblessed human, who shall deliver me from the body of this death? (Rom 7:24). *Peter*: I am sure that the laying away of my tabernacle is at hand (2 Pet 1:14). *Hugh*[45] says to his own soul: Why do you not rather love yourself, whose appearance surpasses the beauty of all things one can see? Oh, if only you saw yourself and could see your appearance, then you would understand how much punishment you deserve when you think anything outside of you is worthy of your love. Because such is the nature of love, that by necessity you get to be like the thing you love; and whomever you are attached to by love, you will be transformed into his likeness by the bond of love. And therefore, if you love earthly things, you will become earthly; if you love God, you will become godlike. This godlikeness is, as *Lincolniensis*[46] says, a "con-formity" and "con-similarity" with God as much as that is possible, one that will occur through unmediated attachment to him. As St. Paul says, Who is united with God, becomes one spirit with him (1 Cor 6:17).

The bride is also black on the outside because of human interaction, but nevertheless beautiful inside in her celestial contemplation. *Bernard*: The bride has discoloration of blackness mixed with beauty.[47] But that comes with this life of pilgrimage, and were she to

100

say that she had no blackness, she would be fooling herself and she would have no truth in her; but in the celestial fatherland, there she will be glorious and beautiful and without any stain. Therefore, do not be amazed that she is black, because under the ruler of the world she had to wander in earthly matters. And also do not be amazed that she is beautiful, because she has received the image of heavenly likeness, so that the bridegroom says to her, You are entirely beautiful, my friend. About this blackness and beauty the prophet *Baruch* says: Their faces are black (Bar 6:20); inside they shine like the sun in the presence of God. Thus the bride is black on the outside, but inside BEAUTIFUL AS THE SKINS OF SOLOMON. *Bernard:* Solomon in all his glory did not have anything comparable to the beauty of the bride. Because what do things with outer appearance mean when you compare them with the beauty of the soul? Compared to that, everything that this world can provide is sordid and worthless. Do not look up to this Solomon, even though when it comes to her beauty the bride compares herself to his skins. But look, there is one bigger than Solomon, who stretches over the firmament like a skin. It is a very beautiful skin to see, extended wide like a huge tent, so it may span the whole face of the earth, the sun, the moon, and all the stars and everything else beneath it. What can be more beautiful than such a skin? But still, it cannot be compared with the glory and beauty of the bride, who is an image of eternity.[48] This exceedingly beautiful skin has been purified by grace, cleansed with virtue, adorned with God's gifts, perfected with beatitudes, inhabited by the Holy Trinity. *Bernard:* What are the soul's virtues other than some kind of precious pearls, which in the adornment of the bride shall shine as an eternal light?[49]

The bride is also BLACK from the persecution of evil people on the outside, but nevertheless BEAUTIFUL from divine consolation on the inside; yes, the blackness of the outer persecution is even a great sign of beauty for the bride. The external abominable abuse of the cross is a blackness, but because it is a form and symbol of our Lord God, it gives the inner man immense joy and delight. Because of that the bride knows of no more honorable and glorious thing than to help carry the bridegroom's scornful disgrace, and says with joyous voice, May it be far from me to glory in anything, save in the cross of our Lord Jesus Christ (Gal 6:14), on which our life and salvation and our resurrection depends. It is a glorious blackness that makes the mind shine, that makes the conscience pure and gives divine wisdom. Do you want me to prove how the soul can be black and beautiful? Then do not look down on Paul, who was a very discolored, pitiful human being, tortured by hunger, by thirst, by sickness, by nakedness, by hard work, by beatings beyond measure. This was what made him black. And was it not the very same Paul who was caught up in paradise (2 Cor 12:4) and because of his purity was taken up into the third heaven? O pure soul, even though she lived in a frail body, the celestial beauty did not despise to live there with her, the angelic height did not spurn her, the celestial luminousness did not scorn her. To our eyes she seems black, but in God's eyes and those of his angels she is beautiful and pure. Therefore, Paul's blackness is more beautiful than any royal, outer embellishment; no beauty of the flesh compares to her, no white, shiny skin that will wither, no color of the face that will fade, no gold, no precious stone, no perishable good whatsoever. The bride considers to be in her honor and glory everything she is ordered to do to her dishonor and shame by her enemies. She wants to rejoice in her frailty; she has no shame over any blackness that she knows to have been borne by her bridegroom. She acknowledges that he is both black and beautiful—black in the death on the cross, beautiful in his transformation on Mount Tabor; beautiful by himself, but blackened because of them. And because likeness is an aspect of love, therefore she longs to be like the bridegroom in every way.

# A Ladder of Eight Rungs[1]

A Ladder of Eight Rungs *is another anonymous Franciscan work that is more devotional than mystical-theological in character. It focuses mainly on the suffering of Christ. Perhaps somewhat marred by over-schematization, the work, translated here in its entirety, should be used as a tool for prayerful meditation rather than being merely read.*[2]

*The main body of the text is structured along the days of the week, with, in each case, many subdivisions. Monday is the day of commemorating the passion of our Lord; the second day, Friday, represents the rung of compassion; the third rung is Tuesday, the rung of imitation; the fourth, Wednesday, is the rung of amazement over the magnitude of the suffering, and the dignity of the Person suffering; the fifth, Saturday, is the rung of exultation over the fact that Christ's passion has delivered us from sins; sixth, Thursday, is called the rung of liquefaction in the fire of divine love—a love that melts our heart when we remember the suffering of Our Lord; seventh and eighth are Sunday, the rungs of gratefulness and union—a union with the virtues and works of Christ through which we become strong and rich through his merits.*

## A LADDER OF EIGHT RUNGS

Here begins a devout exercise about the venerable and holy suffering of our dear Lord Jesus Christ.

Considering that in this world there is nothing but suffering, which often makes us drift away from God, and fully aware that there is no peace but in God, in that which relates to God, or in the holy humanity of Jesus, the soul, created in God's image, speaks the following words from the scriptures: *ascendam*…: I will climb up in the palm tree and pluck its fruit (cf. Sg 7:8). This means, I will climb up in the bitter suffering of Jesus Christ, so as to taste the fruit that is hidden within it. In order for all pious children of Christ to consider devoutly the suffering of Christ, they should proceed in a certain manner, namely, by making a ladder with eight rungs, each consisting of an aspect of the suffering of Christ. Thus they will pluck and obtain the fruit hidden within this suffering—for no one can obtain this fruit unless he eagerly applies himself in climbing these rungs.

Those who want to climb into the suffering of Jesus along these eight rungs should prepare themselves as follows in three ways:

1. First, they arouse their senses to devotion and attention to the sufferings of Jesus by considering the following seven issues:

The first point that will evoke our devotion is that it highly pleases God the Father almighty and all his saints. God the Father, God the Son, and the Holy Spirit, and the holy mother Mary, all the angels, holy men and women who reside in heaven.

Second, because our Lord Jesus has requested this from us, and so too have the apostles.

Third, because the teachers of the holy church advise us to do so.

Fourth, it is righteous and fitting, so as not to be found ungrateful.

Fifth, it is necessary above all for our beatitude. The more we concern ourselves with it, the more advantageous for us.

Sixth, it produces many fruits in the soul, as we will explain later.

Seventh, it brings us into greater glory in eternal life, in the contemplation of the humanity of Christ.

These seven points will encourage us to ascend the seven rungs of the suffering of Christ. But it is not necessary to consider all these seven points every day; it is sufficient to consider everyday just one point, to rouse our heart.

2. All devout hearts should prepare themselves, through recollection of themselves, to exclude from their hearts all concern for temporary things.

3. A devout heart must select a particular element from the passion and meditate upon it, avoiding every distraction insofar as possible. When you have so prepared yourself, you can then speak with the scriptures: *Ascendam,* I will climb up.

# The First Rung—on Monday

The first rung that allows us to climb up into the bitter suffering of Jesus is called *gradus commemoracionis*, the rung of simple commemoration. This means, one should simply and literally consider what the four evangelists wrote; then, we should consider the relevant sayings of the prophets and what holy authors have allegorically said using typology. Considering this, we will firmly believe all that is written in regard to the Person who suffered:

First, in relation to his humanity, for he was truly man, mortal, with a genuinely mortal body susceptible to feel pain.

Second, in relation to what he is called in the scriptures, such as light of the world, the wood of life, the way of life, a star, a teacher, a rock, an innocent lamb.

Third, in relation to the elevation of his status and office, for he is an angel, an offering, a king, a shepherd, a judge, and a priest.

Fourth, in relation to his divinity, for he is the first Being, perfect according to his divine nature; he is eternal life.

Fifth, in relation to his Personhood within the Godhead. For he is Son of God. The eternal Word, the likeness and the unblemished image of the eternal Father.

Sixth, in relation to his properties, for he is eternal Truth, eternal Wisdom, eternal Power, eternal Beauty, eternal Goodness, eternal Life.

Seventh, in relation to his works, for he is a mediator, a savior, a healer. Consider this and climb up the first rung of meditations.

# The Second Rung—on Friday

The second rung to climb up into the bitter suffering of Jesus is called *gradus compassionis*, that is, the rung of compassion. We will climb this rung for three reasons:

First, because it deeply pleases God. For he himself calls out: Oh, all of you who pass by the wayside, see whether any pain is as profound as mine (cf. Lam 1:12).

Second, because it is advantageous to us. As St. Paul said: If we suffer with him, we will be joint heirs with him (cf. Rom 8:17).

Third, because it is highly appropriate to feel compassion for him who has suffered for our sake. Therefore, climb up to this rung; that is, feel compassion for your bridegroom, O noble soul! And so that you may be moved to compassion and to tears, devoutly consider: first, whom it is that has suffered; second, the pain he suffered and its intensity; third, the injustice, for he did not deserve to die, for he was free from all sins.

First, in relation to the Person who suffered:

- Consider his ancestry and birth; and you will see from how noble birth he was, enjoying innumerable noble features.
- Consider the constitution of this Person; he was healthy, refined, peaceful in body and soul, beautiful and pure of body.
- Consider how he dealt with people throughout his life. In relation to God he was perfectly holy; in relation to people he was full of grace and perfect in virtue.
- Consider how highly people spoke of him, as a great prophet and teacher; a healer, amazing in the miracles he performed; and a great teacher.
- Consider how he behaved when he endured pain; he was gentle and patient throughout the suffering that was inflicted upon him.
- Consider how close he is to you; he is your most beloved, everything you can wish for. He is your brother, your bridegroom, and your lover.
- Finally, consider him in accordance with his divinity, for he is the Son of God. He is the one nobody can adequately describe.

Allow the devout heart to meditate as much as it can, and as much as God's grace allows it.

Second, in order to feel compassion toward our Lord Jesus, our Bridegroom, we will now consider the sufferings he endured in their fullness. The doctors of the church describe these sufferings as very profound indeed, and we will now examine the seven reasons why this was the case. The first aspect that increased his sufferings was the cruel desolation he endured. For the Father wanted him to taste death. The Son too has given himself up in death, as Paul says. His mother, also, preferred her child to die rather than seeing the human race perish. Then there was the hatred of the Jews, and finally the greed of Judas. The second reason why his sufferings were so profound is the magnitude of the pain he endured throughout his body, lasting long and being unremitting. Third, there were the circumstances of his passion. There was the place: he was crucified in the royal city of Jerusalem. There was the time: the festival of Passover. There was the company: he was crucified between murderers. And there was the nature of his sufferings as he was stretched out on the cross. Fourth, there was the inner aspect that increased his sufferings. Christ knew all the pains that he was to suffer beforehand; likewise, he saw present and future, all the sins of the past, and that he alone had to make satisfaction for all of them. But above all, he saw the ingratitude of so many people. Fifth, he was aware of the wrath of his Father and the sorrow of his mother and his disciples. The sixth cause of the profoundness of his suffering was the divine justice that increased his suffering because Christ had to make satisfaction for the crimes of all mankind. This divine justice, however, must be seen in the light of divine love and wisdom. The seventh cause of the profoundness of his suffering was the compassion he felt in his divine heart. As Bonaventure rightly claims,[3] his inner co-suffering or compassion was more profound than his suffering in the body. He felt this compassion for his sorrowful mother Mary, and all future saints, considering the affliction and pains that they were to suffer before they were allowed into his realm. O noble soul, climb up this rung of compassion and devoutly meditate upon it so that you may share in its fruit.

## The Third Rung—on Tuesday

The third rung on the ladder of our ascent into the bitter suffering of Jesus is called *gradus imitationis*, the rung of imitation. For it will not be sufficient for us merely to have feelings of compassion for Jesus unless we also attempt to follow him in his sufferings. First, this pleases God, for he has said: "Follow me." Second, it is appropriate to follow the King of glory. Third, it is necessary to follow him if we want to arrive where he dwells. Therefore, noble soul, attempt to follow the example of the Lord and the manner in which he endured his passion and suffering.

The first aspect we ought to imitate is his profound obedience toward the Father, submitting himself to the Father unto death on the cross. Second, his profound renunciation throughout his torments. For he did not even open his mouth, as the prophet witnesses. Third, his profound love for all of us in the midst of his sufferings. Fourth, the total lack of concern for himself, for he has not spared himself. Fifth, his immeasurable generosity, for he has given everything away, without attempting to shield his body from suffering, or his noble life from death. Sixth, the profound wisdom toward his enemies, by concealing his divinity, and thereby confounding the devil. The seventh aspect that the soul should imitate is Jesus' perseverance, for he persevered unto death. Therefore, when he had fulfilled his sacrifice unto the end, he cried out with a loud voice, *Consummatum est* (it is fulfilled) (John 19:30).

Consider, O noble soul, covered in the blood of Jesus, how you will imitate your Lord, your Bridegroom, saying with the scriptures out of the fullness of a loving soul and not merely with your lips: "I will climb up into the palm tree of Christ's suffering with this rung."

## The Fourth Rung—on Wednesday

The fourth rung in our ascent into the suffering of Jesus is called *gradus admirationis*, the rung of amazement. We will climb up the ladder by considering three points: First, the infinite nature of he who suffered there; second, the nature of the sufferings; and third, the wickedness of those for whom he endured these sufferings and the wickedness of those who inflicted them upon him.

[In relation to the first point], anyone who is not utterly hardened or insensitive and who meditates on this will be so amazed that words will fail him, and he will speak with the prophet: "A, A, A, Domine mei, nescio loqui" [Ah, ah, ah, my Lord, I cannot speak] (Jer 1:6), My Lord, my God, what amazing things do I see in this palm tree of suffering! I cannot utter a word out of sheer amazement. If you want to climb this rung, you should consider the following:

First, he is immeasurably rich, for heaven and earth are his, and yet he is being humiliated as a wicked servant. Second, he is all-powerful, for he is called almighty God—and yet he suffers, is scourged, crowned with thorns, and crucified as a feeble human being. Third, he is utterly transcendent, for nothing can contain his greatness—and yet he is tortured and considered a worm; for he spoke through the prophet, "I am a worm and not a man" (Ps 21:7). Fourth, consider that he is the glory of the angels, the joy of the saints, and the eternal bliss—and yet as a doomed person he is being robbed, hurt, and oppressed. Fifth, consider his eternity, without beginning or end, according to his divinity—and yet, as a mortal human being he is being robbed and murdered on the cross. Sixth, consider that he is the eternal Wisdom of the Father—and yet he is being scorned as a fool and a madman. Seventh, consider finally how he is the most splendid, indeed the splendor of heaven—and yet he is being spat upon, ill-treated, and tortured as the apostle witnesses: "We have seen him as a leper, without beauty or form. And we have seen him as one abandoned and struck by God" (Isa 53:4). O noble soul, redeemed and saved by God's blood, consider this miracle that took place in the palm tree of the suffering of Christ. Who, having heard and understood this, would not be struck with amazement? O children of Christ, O virgins of Jesus! Climb up this rung of amazement, and consider the great miracle that lies within these seven points. Speak with a loving soul: "I shall climb up…"

Second, you must consider the nature of the pains he suffered. Third, you must consider who inflicted pain on him. For he has suffered for our sake, we who were his enemies, and who deserve to be damned for all eternity.

## The Fifth Rung—on Saturday

The fifth rung of our ascent into the palm tree of the suffering of Jesus is called *gradus exultationis*, that is, the rung of exultation. For the prophet has said: The poor will rejoice in the God of Israel, and this for three reasons: First, because through the passion of Jesus

109

we have been released from evil, namely, the evil of original sin that had condemned us to eternal damnation, from the evil of mortal sins, committed in the past and in future until the last day. For no sin is forgiven but through the power of the passion of Christ. Second, because everything that is good came from the passion of Christ, namely, the goodness of virtues, of divine grace, and of the glory of heavenly bliss. Third, we must rejoice in the suffering of Jesus because of the seven seals that have been opened with the key of the holy cross, as St. John describes in chapter 9 of the Apocalypse.

The opening of the seals is to be allegorically interpreted as the uncovering of the hidden meanings of the scripture, as Bonaventure rightly points out.[4] The first that was opened with the key of the holy cross, the bitter suffering of Jesus, refers to the fact that God almighty is amazing in everything he does. He is Wisdom beyond comprehension. Through his Wisdom he has conquered the devil. He is just beyond comprehension as he wanted satisfaction to be made for the sin of Adam and the rest of humankind. He is merciful beyond comprehension as he has given up for us his only Son to a most cruel death.

Consider this, O noble soul!

The second seal is a revelation of the nature of spiritual beings. First, of angels: how good they were to tolerate that their Lord and King was murdered on the cross. Second, of human beings: how noble and great the soul is, for Christ has shed his precious blood and given up his noble life to release it from the hands of the devil. Third, of evil spirits: for in the cross their wickedness and evil are revealed. For they persuaded the Jews to murder the innocent lamb so cruelly.

The third seal that is opened refers to the wickedness of the world. Here it is revealed that the world is a place of darkness in which utter blindness reigns. For the world has not known the brightest light, which is Jesus. It is a place of infertile barrenness, for it has not acknowledged or received the fruit of eternal life. It is a place of wickedness of all sorts, for it has condemned and crucified its Lord, the innocent Jesus.

The fourth seal refers to the majesty and dignity of heavenly paradise. For in paradise there is fullness of glory, contemplation of beatitude, enjoyment of every opulence. We had lost this state, and God was for our sake nailed to the cross to restore us to this state.

For we were no longer allowed to dwell there until satisfaction for our sin had been made on the cross.

The fifth seal makes clear how horrible hell is. For it is a place of misery and terror, full of sorrow, wretchedness, lamenting, and darkness, and this is revealed in the cross. For if our Lord had to suffer so much to remit Adam's sin, how much more will the damned have to suffer to pay for their wickedness.

The sixth seal that has been opened with the cross of Jesus is the revelation of dignity, power, and praiseworthiness of virtue. Virtue is precious and cherished, and our Lord would rather have chosen to lose his temporal life than to have acted against it. Virtue is splendid and fruitful, for he was perfectly virtuous, has emptied hell, opened up the heavens, and found what had been lost.

The seventh seal that was opened by the cross of Jesus is the revelation of the wickedness and evil of mortal sin. Before sin could be forgiven, it needed the precious treasure and the extraordinary and painful medicine of the precious and most worthy blood of our Lord Jesus Christ.

O noble soul, worthy bride of Jesus, now you have heard how the seven seals have been opened by the cross of Christ. Rejoice, therefore, in the cross of Jesus Christ. For the cross of our Lord is the key to heaven, the gate to eternal life, the road to heavenly paradise. Consider this and ponder it, and rejoice with the holy apostle. We must rejoice in the cross of Jesus. Far be it from me to rejoice in anything else but the cross of Jesus Christ.

If only we could fully comprehend what it means to rejoice in the cross of our Lord. If only we could relish its taste. Beloved virgins and prisoners in Jesus, I say to you: Every consolation and merriment of this cursed world should be a cross to us, yes even a death, as it is in truth. In order to attain this bliss, you must exercise yourself in the climbing up of this rung. For anyone unwilling to climb it will not find this sweetness. This is why the loving soul said: "I will climb up..."

## The Sixth Rung—on Thursday

The sixth rung of our ascension into the palm tree of bitter suffering is called *gradus liquefactionis*, that is, the rung of liquefaction or melting in the fire of divine love. Consider with how great a love the heavenly Father has handed over his most-beloved Son to an ignominious death out of love for you, and then your heart will melt in the fire of divine love and the red wounds of Jesus.

Now consider in seven ways the fire of love that compelled the Son to do this:

First, O noble soul, in order to melt in the fire of love, in the red wounds of Jesus and in the divine love that induced him to suffer this ignominious death: remember that this love has been there for all eternity, as the prophet made clear. With an eternal love I have loved you, O noble soul!

Second, we had not deserved this act of love. With an incomprehensible goodness he has loved us, creatures without any merits of our own.

Third, this act of love has been of great benefit to us, for everything he suffered was for our sake.

Fourth, consider the particular nature of his love. For he did not die out of a general love for humankind but out of a particular love for each individual. For the good Lord would prefer to die a thousand deaths, rather than see one soul perish through his negligence. O noble soul, consider this, for this is of major significance.

Fifth, he has suffered out of true love, and out of strong, steady, and wise love, rejecting all that would be disadvantageous to us and fulfilling all that would be of benefit to us for our attainment of salvation.

Sixth, consider how he suffered out of strong love. Who could express in words the strength of the very love that resided in the heart of our Lord Jesus and that tore and broke his heart?

Seventh, and finally, consider how out of constant love he suffered unto death for your sake, and therefore love him in return with a constant love, not allowing a creature to detract you from your love for Jesus.

Now, who has grown so hardened and insensitive in his heart that he does not melt away when considering the love our Lord displayed toward us? O divine fire! O ardent fire that ignited the heart of Jesus to such a degree that he appeared drunk and mad out of love. Ignite and melt our cold, hardened heart, in the wounds of

Jesus, so as not to desire any other joy than to burn and to become drunk in his red wounds.

Consider, virgins of Christ, these are the six rungs for climbing into the palm tree. But it will not suffice us merely to climb these six rungs; it does not suffice the loving soul merely to climb the palm tree. For this reason the soul makes also clear why she wants to climb up, namely, in order to pluck the fruit, and this will happen in the next rung.

# The Seventh Rung—on Sunday

The seventh rung in our ascent into the cross of our Lord Jesus is called *gradus gratiarum actionis*, that is, the rung of gratefulness. We will be grateful: First, because he was willing to suffer heavy pains for us. Second, because he has left us a precious example that we should emulate. Third, because of the sweet fruits hidden within the cross, namely, both general and special ones. The general ones are common to all people cleansed in the blood of Christ, while the special ones are obtained by all who exert themselves to climb up in the palm tree of the holy cross. Therefore the loving soul spoke: I will climb up in the palm tree in order to pluck the common fruits of the holy cross, namely, the forgiveness of sins; the opening up of heaven; the remorse of hell; the peace that now has been established between God the Father and the human race; the negation of the fall of the angels because the choirs of the fallen angels have been supplemented with human beings, and this took place because of the death of Christ; and the sixth fruit, that is, that eternal life will be bestowed upon us because of the bitter suffering of Jesus.

The special fruits are many, and will be given to those who especially exert themselves to climb up into the palm tree:

First, there is repentance over our sins. For Bonaventure says that nothing makes as much satisfaction as a meditation on the suffering of Christ.

Second, the cleansing of the soul. It is like the River Jordan that makes the sinful soul as pure and clean as a child of one day old. Bernard has said that there is no stronger medicine to cure the ailments of the soul as a continual meditation on the person of Christ.

113

Third, the illumination of the human mind. For this is a book of life, the school of our Lord, in which all simple hearts become wise men. This school was attended by St. Francis, Augustine, St. Clare, the angelic doctor Bonaventure, and St. Bernard.

The fourth fruit is the stirring of hope. As St. Bernard said: I know that I do not deserve to enter into eternal life but what I am lacking I will draw from the wounds of Jesus. For all my hope resides in the death of Jesus.

The fifth fruit is a heart aflame with love for Jesus. Augustine and Bernard: O dear Lord, the cup you have drunk compels me to love you.

The sixth fruit is consolation in anguish and suffering. Bernard: I have not found a better remedy against all assaults and temptations than to seek refuge in the wounds of Jesus. For there I find peace and rest without fear.

The seventh fruit is humility and growth in virtues. For Albert the Great says, It is better and more profitable simply to meditate on the suffering of Jesus than to fast on water and bread for a whole year, to scourge oneself to bleeding, and to read the Psalter every-day on one's knees.

The eighth fruit is a renewal of life in the soul. For Bernard has said, The suffering of Jesus restores people who are dead in the soul, back to life.

The ninth fruit is a sweet nourishment for the soul, for in the suffering of Jesus is contained every sweetness that can nourish the soul, as you have heard when we dealt with the rung of exultation.

The tenth fruit is that the soul becomes inflamed to serve, praise, and thank God. Bernard: All my members praise you, when I remember the passion of Christ.

The eleventh fruit is release from purgatory, or a shortening of the time to be spent there.

The twelfth fruit is the greater rejoicing in eternal life, and in the glorious humanity of Christ. For the more we are now rendered sorrowful through meditating on the suffering of Christ, the more we will in the hereafter rejoice in the glorious humanity of Christ. For Paul has said, "If we suffer with Christ, we will also rejoice with him" (cf. Rom 8:17).

These are the twelve fruits of the wood of life, the holy cross.

Pluck these, O noble soul, and be nourished. Speak with the Book of living souls: The fruit is sweet to my mouth (cf. Sg 2:3). Having plucked this fruit, you will be grateful to the Lord. Linger with each fruit, and suck the sweetness. For if you are in a great hurry you might choke, and that would not agree with you. You should also meditate on all the benefactions God has conferred upon you: he created you when you were not; he saved you when you were imprisoned; he has treated you mercifully for so long and called you out of the wicked world; and so forth. Remember the precious blood of Jesus Christ, and offer this to the heavenly Father with gratitude. When you have thus exerted yourself in this rung or state, in the plucking of this fruit, you will then begin to eat fervently. This leads to the next rung, in which you can say with the scriptures, "I will climb into the palm tree and pluck the fruit, and eat it."

## The Last Rung—on Sunday

To climb into the palm tree of the suffering of Jesus, this highest and final rung is called *gradus unionis,* the rung of union. The holy apostle said about this: He who inclines to God becomes one spirit with God. It was for this reason that our Lord Jesus prayed to his Father, saying, "O heavenly Father, I pray you, that they may become one with us as we are one with one another" (John 18:21). In order to become one with God it is necessary to climb fervently up this rung and assiduously to exert ourselves in it.

First, the union is desired by God himself. Indeed, our Lord himself, in his own Person, has prayed to the Father for it.

Second, because this union is for us, human beings, the highest honor that can be bestowed upon us. Through this union with God we become one with God, we become divine, and our works do also. Bernard: Just as a drop of water, poured into a cask of wine, becomes wine, and acquires the potency of wine, so too all the works and desires of holy people become united with the work of Christ, and thus become divine.[5] Oh, great is the fruit in climbing this rung.

Third, because this union with Christ and his works is very advantageous to us, our works become ennobled with those of Christ, and they are therefore, together with those of Christ, most pleasing to our God the Father. Also, through this union we share in all the virtues and works of Christ. For we are strengthened with his strength, illuminated through his wisdom, and we become rich through his merits. Thus we can say with Tobias, "Through Jesus our Lord, we are replete with everything that is good." The wise man too says, "Everything good has come from him." Finally, through this union, performing our works becomes a lesser burden. When God is united with us, God performs the works, and what is more, he sustains us. For it is written in the Book of Deuteronomy, "The Lord, your God, has supported you, as one used to carry children"; as God says through Ezekiel: "As a wet nurse I have sustained the human being." Anyone who hears this will be caught up in desire to climb this rung, and say with David, "It is good to cling to the Lord in this union." Therefore, when we meditate upon the suffering of Christ we will fervently try to unite all our desires, our will, and our faculties with the painful death of our Lord, in seven points:

First, O noble soul, if you want to become one with Christ, it is necessary always to maintain your vigilance, so as to be able to become one with your Bridegroom, who is swift and appears unexpectedly. Being vigilant, you will be able to say, My Lord, my God, I always wake so as to be united with you.

Second, you must strengthen your trust in your Bridegroom, and not doubt his unwavering faithfulness. Then you will say with David, putting your entire trust in him, "I trust in the Lord," and with Job, "Even if he were to slay me, I will nevertheless retain my hope in him."

Third, you must fervently desire the sweetness of your Bridegroom so as to say with David: "Like the wild deer, that is being pursued, thirsts for the well, so too I desire, my Lord, that all my works may be united with you" (Ps 41:2).

Fourth, his majesty must lift you up and you will then speak with the loving soul, "O noble Bridegroom, draw me to you" (Sg 1:4). Similarly, in Job, "My soul has desired to become one with you."

Fifth, the delight of your Bridegroom will instill peacefulness in you, and you will not seek delight in any creature but only in him, because of his beauty, and you will speak with the loving soul, "My beloved is pleased with me, and I am pleased with him." Similarly, "My beloved is beautiful, ruddy, chosen out of thousands" (Sg 5:10).

Sixth, his joy alone may gladden your heart. For he is full of glory and joy; to speak with David, "After the many sorrows of my heart, your consolations, O Lord, have gladdened my heart." Similarly, Lord, how great is the sweetness that is in you, and so on.

Seventh, and finally, in order to become one with Christ your desire for union with your Bridegroom should utterly devour you through the power that is from God. You will then speak with the apostle, "Who will separate us from God" (Rom 8:39), as if he were to say: Anyone who is so united with Christ should not fear anything, for nothing can separate him from God. No tribulation or calamity can separate them from God, for they are united with Christ, and Christ carries the burden of their sorrows, and protects them in their suffering.

But if you want to attain this union the following is above all necessary:

First, that you exclude the following four[6] intermediaries that keep you from this union. First, your own will. For nobody can be united with Christ unless his will is one with the will of God. But the will of our Lord is this, as St. Paul says, that we are holy in soul and body. If we desire and want this holiness, then our will is united with the will of Christ. The second element that we must exclude is love for the flesh, the world, and our friends. For anyone whose heart is more united with flesh or with the world will become more alienated from union with Christ. The third is to be attached to temporal things that we do not need. O children of Christ, how great the sweetness we would find in our own sweet Lord if only we made our heart pure and free of sensual things. But alas, sensual things and anxiety for them is like a heavy beam, tied around our legs, preventing us from climbing up this rung of union. Therefore, if we want to become one with Christ it is necessary to renounce all attachments to temporal things. The more fervently we attempt this, the more we will be united with Christ. But many people do not understand this, and therefore union with them eludes them. The fourth hindrance is not esteeming spiritual things. This proves a major hindrance for spiritual growth and prevents people from climbing up. They resemble pigs, searching for acorns, at the bottom of the tree;

they eat the acorns, but they do not look up. It is the same with many spiritual religious people; they receive one blessing after another but they do not raise their heads up, that is, they do not pay any heed to the favors received from God. If we want to be united with Christ we should pay close attention to the works of Christ.

Second, if you want to attain this union you should always pray to God and say with Bernard: O Lord Jesus, make me feel the love you have had for me from all eternity. O dear Lord Jesus, I would like to love you but I cannot do it without your assistance! O Lord Jesus, when will I have attained a state of renunciation? O sweet Jesus, when will I be so united with you that everything I do, think, or say is to your honor? O dear Lord, beloved Bridegroom, when will I be one with you and no longer incense you through my thoughts, words, and deeds? In these ways a devout heart can rouse itself to be united with Christ.

Third, if you want to attain this union, you must exert yourself in uniting all your practices with those of Christ, such as all your thoughts with the thoughts of Christ; all your words with the blessed words of Christ; all your desires with the holy desires of Christ; and your whole mind, your whole will, your whole memory, your exterior and interior senses; all your exterior and interior powers, all your exterior practices such as eating, drinking, sleeping, waking, going, standing, lying down, sitting, praying, reading, singing, and everything that we can do,…we will always unite those with the practices of Christ. In this manner they will please God and be a source of merit to us. A devout heart that puts its trust in God will always be united to God. It should not take a meal, not even eat a mouthful, or drink, without being united with Christ and above all with the bitter suffering of Jesus and his holy wounds. We would like all of this, but we are not prepared to make an effort, and so we fail to obtain it. It must taste sour first before we can enjoy the sweetness. Therefore, if you want to attain this union, you must exert yourself to climb. Climbing here refers to the labor necessary to attain this sweetness. You should not complain, therefore, that you are lacking in devotion; labor hard to climb these rungs, and you will be granted devotion.

For there is no better way to obtain devotion than to practice yourself in the suffering of Christ. Do you want to become free of sin,

118

rich in virtues, illuminated in the holy scriptures? Do you desire victory over your enemies? Do you want to converse in a devout manner with other people? Do you want to repent over your sins, shed sweet tears in your prayers? Do you want to persist in good works? Do you want to avoid being disappointed in the honor that people extend to you? Do you want to pass away in a peaceful manner and reign with Christ in heaven for all eternity? Then learn to practice yourself in the suffering of Christ, in accordance with this description of rungs or steps. Climb in the palm tree so as to pluck the fruit. May the fruit of this tree, Jesus Christ, grant this to you and me.

Amen.

He
Who took leave from them and headed for Jerusalem.
Who ate the paschal lamb with his twelve apostles.
Who humbly washed the feet of his beloved disciples.
Who, after having changed his apostles into priests,
    gave his flesh as food, and his blood as drink.
Who preached a long sermon and who made many pre-
    dictions.
Who talking to his disciples expressed his sorrow, say-
    ing: My soul is sorrowful unto death.
Who on the Mount of Olives prayed to his Father, say-
    ing: "Father, everything is possible for you. Take this
    cup away from me; but let your will be done, not
    mine."
Who was consoled by an angel, and sweated water and
    blood.
Who was imprisoned and put in shackles as a criminal
    by the merciless Jews.
Who was abandoned by his fleeing disciples into the
    hands of the Jews.
Who was brought as a criminal by the cruel Jews to the
    house of Annas.
Who was interrogated by Annas and cunningly ques-
    tioned by Annas about his teaching.
Who responded in a kindhearted manner but was cru-
    elly slapped in the face by a heartless servant.

Who was denied three times out of fear by the apostle
   Peter.

Who was sent, bound, by Annas to Caiaphas.

Who was declared deserving of death by the high
   priests with the aid of false witnesses.

Who, deserted by his beloved apostles, gently kept
   silent.

Who was asked cunningly by Caiaphas whether he was
   the Son of God.

Who, having spoken the truth, was sentenced to death
   because of blasphemy.

Who, having been spat upon at and beaten throughout
   the night, blindfolded, was humiliated in many ways.

Who was interrogated in a cunning manner early in the
   morning.

Who, while tied, was handed over as a criminal to
   Pilate, the judge.

Who was falsely accused before Pilate, who maintained
   that he had misled the people, allegedly urging them
   not to pay tribute to the emperor, and claiming to be
   a king.

Who patiently remained silent in the presence of his
   accusers, to the amazement of Pilate.

Who was heard by Pilate who wanted to release him,
   not having found any case against him.

Who was accused once more by the chief priests, saying: "We have a law, and according to our law he
   ought to die because he has claimed to be the Son of
   God." When Pilate heard this, he grew fearsome, and
   he brought Jesus back in, and questioned him asking
   him who he was.

Who was unjustly sentenced to death by Pilate, who
   washed his hands, and released Barabbas as they
   demanded.

Whose clothes were taken off by wicked servants who
   dressed him again, inflicting profound pain.

Who was brought to the place of execution carrying a
   heavy cross.

Whose sorrowful Mother, on seeing him, prostrated herself in grief.

Who spoke to those who, in tears, followed him: O daughters of Jerusalem, do not weep for me; weep rather for yourselves and your children.

Who was stripped of his clothes by wicked people and whose wounds were reopened.

Who was given wine mixed with gall, which he tasted but refused to drink.

Who was cruelly stretched out on the harsh cross, exposing every member of his body.

Whose hands were cruelly pierced with coarse nails.

Whose holy feet were pierced and nailed to the cross.

Who was raised up on the cross, which was then hurled into the ground, tearing open all his wounds.

Who was crucified with two murderers; one on his left, one on his right side.

Whose clothes were shared out, and for which they cast lots.

Above the head of whom Pilate had an inscription hung that read: *Jesus Nazarenus Rex.*

Who was scorned so shamefully by the high priests and the Jews who shouted: "You who wanted to destroy God's Temple, save yourself!"

Who prayed for his enemies who crucified him, saying: "Father, forgive them, for they do not know what they are doing."

Who spoke to the murderer who hung on his right side: "Truly, I say to you, today you will be with me in paradise."

Who commended his beloved Mother to St. John.

Who cried out: "My God, my God, why have you forsaken me?"

Who cried out with a loud voice: "I am thirsty," and whose thirst was quenched with gall and vinegar.

Who, having done and suffered everything that was written of him, spoke, "It is fulfilled."

Who, crying aloud, commended his spirit to the eternal
  Father.
At the time of whose death the sun was darkened, the
  veil of the Temple was torn, rocks were split, and the
  earth trembled.
At the time of whose innocent death the tombs opened
  and the dead rose.
Whose heart was pierced by one of the soldiers with a
  lance, and water and blood flowed out.
When you saw this, O Mary, your maiden heart was
  pierced with the sword of mourning.
Who was taken down from the cross with the permission of Pilate by Joseph and Nicodemus with great
  sorrow.
Whose dead body was laid in your lap, Mary, and covered in tears.
Whose dead body, anointed and wrapped in a white
  shroud, was put into the tomb.
Amen.


Beloved Jesus Christ, I submerge my soul and my body,
and I blend all my thoughts, words, and deeds into the
loving merits of your holy suffering and into the depths
of your sacred wounds. I long to be cleansed of all my
sins hoping to enjoy eternal life without intermediary. O
Lord Jesus Christ, purify my soul from all stains of sin in
the blood shed from your holy wounds and receive my
soul in the hour of death into your bloodstained, outstretched arms. Amen.

# The Nine Little Flowers of the Passion from *Indica mihi*[1]

*This anonymous work, written by a Franciscan from the fifteenth century, contains at least four distinct treatises. Included here is the so-called* Nine Little Flowers of the Passion. *The text is inspired by the Song of Songs: "Come into my garden, my sister, my bride, I have prepared some myrrh" (6:1). In the garden nine flowers symbolize different aspects of the suffering of Christ. The Franciscan influence is revealed in the echoes of Bonaventure's* De Triplici Via *and* De perfectione vitae.[2] *This work is more devotional than mystical-theological.*[3]

## THE NINE LITTLE FLOWERS OF THE PASSION

O faithful soul, bride of God, imprint this in your heart wherever you go. Now that you have labored and are worn out, hear, in order to enjoy some rest, the voice of your Bridegroom, who calls to you: "Come into my garden, my sister, my bride, I have prepared some myrrh."

This garden, my chosen friend, where the myrrh has been prepared, is nothing else but devout meditation on the suffering of Jesus.

In this garden I have planted for you nine special flowers, exceeding all flowers of this world in sweetness and potency. Isaac enjoyed the scent of these flowers when he blessed his son Jacob, saying, "See, the scent of my son is like the fragrance of the meadow full of flowers blessed by God" (Gen 27:27). It was these flowers that the bride, sick with love, desired when she exclaimed: "Adorn me with flowers. This is the garden of delight, for these flowers will never perish" (Sg 2:5). These were the flowers that Joshua and Caleph showed to the children of Israel, rendering them worthy,

among the six hundred thousand, of entering into the land of promise. These flowers, O chosen bride of God, have been called "the
suffering of your Bridegroom." The first are called all-powerful, all-
innocent, and all-holy; the second are most bitter, most humiliating, and most beneficial; the third are most rigorous, most
universal, and most lasting.

These are the flowers, O faithful soul, with which you will
strew your chamber if you want to lovingly receive your beloved
and retain him with you.

# I

The first flower refers to the all powerfulness of the suffering
of Jesus. Richard gives three reasons why this would be the case:[4]

First, because it redeems us from all sin; the all-powerfulness
of his suffering balanced out our innumerable sins. For he intended
to save all men, though not everybody was willing to receive him.
The souls, however, who are united in true faith and ardent love,
have been redeemed from all guilt.

Second, we have been saved by the death of Jesus from eternal
punishment insofar as we become receptive to his power. This is the
reason why he wanted to die: to release his people who were imprisoned in limbo. As David prophesied, "He has broken the iron
chains and opened up the copper gates." We find an analogy in
*Scholastica Historia*.[5] There we read that Solomon kept an ostrich in
his garden. The ostrich had some young, and the king put them
behind glass. When the father saw that he could not release his
young, he flew into the wilderness and took a little worm, which he
killed on the glass. Through this blood and this death the glass
broke, and thus he released the young. The glass symbolizes the
limbo of the fathers, in which the fathers dwelt for more than five
thousand years. The all-powerful Father realized that they would
not be released unless he sent his only Son into the vale of tears and
allowed the blessed body of his Son, who had assumed human
nature, to be squashed like a little worm. Through his blood and his
death the holy patriarchs have been released. Hence Zacharias said,

"You, O Jesus, have saved with your blood and death those who were cast down in the dry pit."

Third, through the death of Jesus we have been released from the power of the devil. As St. John said: "I saw another angel, that is the Son of God, coming down from heaven, having the key of the bottomless pit and a great chain in his hand. He laid hold on the dragon, the old serpent, and bound him for a thousand years" (Rev 20:1–2). This is how some feel unto the time of the anti-Christ. This does not mean that all power has been taken from the devil by the death of Jesus. It does, however, mean that his death has assisted us greatly in many ways. For through his death, grace is poured into us, and grace drives away the devil. Because of grace, too, the angels guard us much more diligently. This is why the enemy cannot overpower us, or entice us to sin, or easily deceive us.

# II

The second flower of the suffering of Christ is the innocence with which he reconciled us to the heavenly Father. John heard that there was no one in heaven or earth or under the earth who was able or worthy to open the book that lay on the knees of the almighty Father (Rev 5:3), but the Lamb that was slain; and hence the elders cried, "Lord, you are worthy to take the book and to break the seven seals, for you have redeemed us in your blood" (cf. Rev 5:9).

This book, beloved bride of God, symbolizes this world. The seven seals are the seven deadly sins that cannot be loosened by either angels in heaven or human being on earth or under earth, for nobody can forgive sins but God. This is the Lamb that John beheld and that carries the sins of the world. He carries our sins, forgiving those we have committed and assisting us not to stray from the path of life again. O noble soul, thus our Lord has saved us like a mother who sees her child fall into a fire and who immediately runs after him, pulling him out, without paying any heed to how the fire consumes her clothes. So, too, the Son of the almighty God, noticing that the human race had fallen into the fire of eternal damnation, did not hesitate to burn the clothes of his blessed body. Indeed, he fell into the fire of his passion, and there he saved us. As Paul said, "He has saved us from the powers of darkness and has put us into his realm." He who did not commit any sin or on whose mouth no deception could be found, has desired to redeem us with his innocent death.

O bride of God, this raises the question why the loving Lord, innocent and free from sin, wanted to endure such heavy suffering? There are four reasons why Jesus did this. The first reason is to reveal the love he harbors toward us. Through Jeremiah he has spoken, "I have loved you from eternity; this is why I have raised you in order to save you." This love was so astonishingly great, but hidden in the heart of God; it could not be disclosed to us except when openly manifested in the things he did for us. This is why it says in the gospel, "No greater love can anybody have than giving up his life for his friends" (John 15:13). Oh, observe his love, which makes him give up his life for his enemies.

The second reason is that in this manner he will elicit a genuine and fruitful love in us toward him. This is why Bernard says: "O good Jesus, above all else the chalice of our redemption that you drank inflames my love for you. Oh, who could fail to love you?"

The third reason is that through his suffering he strengthens us in his service. As Bernard says: When we remember his heavy burden, the bitter pain and the innumerable blows he patiently and eagerly suffered, we will turn our heart and mind to Jesus to serve him faithfully. Therefore, O noble soul, let us not loiter in our service of the Lord day or night, but let us serve the Lord with gladness of our hearts. As David says, "Serve the Lord gladly."

The fourth reason is that he would open up the heavens for us. For nobody, however devout and holy, who lived before the death of our Lord Jesus Christ was allowed to enter into the heavens. Therefore he spoke to his friends, "I will prepare a place for you that you will occupy" (John 14:3).

# III

The third flower refers to the holiness of the suffering of Jesus; this also sanctifies the sacraments. As John said, "He has loved us and has washed away our sins in his blood." As we erase letters with a damp cloth, so too the blood of Christ has wiped out all our sins and has sanctified us. As Isaiah puts it, "I am the one who takes away sins and every malice through my own will," that is to say, through my blood and my death. There are three reasons for this, for in sin there are three evils: a stained conscience; the stings of remorse; and the fury of divine wrath. In contrast, the divine blood of our Lord Jesus is pure, soothing and precious.

First, it is pure, and in this purity we are cleansed; as Paul says, "The blood of Christ has purified our conscience of all the works of death." For the fruitfulness of the sacraments finds its origin in the power of Christ's blood. When we devoutly make use of these sacraments, we will be purged from the stain of sin and delivered from every torment that may oppress us.

Second, it is soothing and healing. "Their hearts will be gladdened as if they had tasted the wine," as Zacharias puts it. For it provides spiritual consolation and comfort.

Third, it is precious and sufficiently valuable to appease the omnipotent Father and satisfy the divine justice. Paul admonishes us, "You have approached the sprinkling of blood that speaks better than the blood of Abel" (Heb 12:24). For the blood of Abel cries out to the heavens for revenge, but the blood of Christ desires and obtains grace. O noble soul, observe now a threefold miracle. The first miracle is this: whereas blood usually stains, this blood purifies our stains. Also, this blood is bodily, and yet it heals the inner spiritual wounds of sin. Finally, how can the blood of a dead man save us from death? Still, this is how John describes it in his letters: the blood of our dear Lord Jesus Christ cleanses us from all our sins.

But how can this blessed blood be so immeasurably powerful? Here, Francis of Meyronnes[6] enlightens us: "This power is undoubtedly derived from the highest blessedness and holiness of Christ. And more specifically from the infinite power of the divinity with which this blood was united as it was an essential part of the human nature of Christ. This blood was abundantly shed in his painful death. This is why our conscience is cleansed, and we have been saved from eternal death. O bridegroom of God, this blood is being shed again every time we commit our sins of old. For as we are delivered from sin through the shedding of this blood, so too this blood is being shed again through our sins. As the wounds of the slain person bleed in the presence of the murderer, so too the wounds of Christ will bleed on the day of judgment in the presence of those who slew the Lord Jesus in the damnation of their sins." O faithful Christian soul, be grateful.

Through the blood of Christ, three kinds of powerful lords have been saved, namely openly declared enemies, the old just patriarchs, and wavering friends. The first have been released from the shackles of their sin; the others from limbo; the third ones from the weakness of their faith. It is for this reason that the loving Lord has shed his blood from three different sources, namely, from his hands, feet, and side. Christ shed blood from his hands in order to release the sinner through his blessed blood from the shackles of sin and to draw him close to him. It was in this that King David rejoiced when he exclaimed: "O Lord, you have broken my ties. I will offer you a sacrifice of praise." Similarly, Isaiah, assuming the role of Christ, "O noble soul, turn to me, for I have set you free." Augustine too said, "Christ has shed his blood to extinguish our sins." Christ has shed his blood from his feet also in order to lead the old just patriarchs from the pit of hell into the heavenly realm. This is why Jeremiah says in the Book of Lamentations, "I alone have trodden the press." Indeed, his blood was shed in abundance in the passion so as to gladden many people. Finally, blood was shed from his side. His disciples were wavering in their faith; many more were tempted and had become lukewarm in faith. He therefore roused them to faith, constancy, and a good Christian life. He inflamed them with love and raised them to a new life with the ardor of his precious blood, and inspired us to follow him eagerly. Hence he spoke through the prophet, "I have become like a pelican" (Ps 101:7). For as the pelican opens his heart to nourish his young and wake them from the death inflicted by the serpent, so too Christ has wanted to save his children with the blood of his heart from eternal death inflicted by the serpent of old. O bride of God, be grateful.

## IV

The fourth flower refers to the bitterness and painfulness of the sufferings that Christ endured for the sins of others and for his enemies. Many things made the sufferings of Jesus more burdensome. There is, first, the noble refinement of his bodily constitution. For his blessed body is formed from the most noble blood of the glorious virgin, the beautiful Mary. Indeed, the sole of his foot was as sensitive as the eye of any other man. Therefore, beloved, when he, who always walked on bare feet, hit his foot on a stone, he suffered the most intense pain. It is said that the wounds of Jesus numbered 5,475. Therefore, anybody who daily prays fifteen Our Fathers will by the end of the year have prayed one Our Father for every wound Christ suffered. The second reason why his sufferings were most bitter is that he was without any consolation. The third is concern for those who persecuted him unto death. The fourth is that he endured suffering in his inner and outer members. Jeremiah, assuming the role of our Lord, said, "Oh, all of you who walk down the road, notice and see my suffering and pain—Is any suffering equal to mine?" (Lam 1:12). Bernard too said: "The head before which the angels tremble is pierced with a crown of thorns. The countenance more beautiful than that of any of the children of men is soiled with the spit of the Jews. His eyes, brighter than the sun, have been darkened in death. The hands that made heaven and earth have been nailed to the cross. The feet, of which we adore the imprint, have been thrust with nails. The body is covered in wounds. His heart has been pierced. No part of his body has been spared, except for his tongue, allowing him to pray for sinners and to commend his mother to John." The fifth cause of the bitterness of his suffering is the ungratefulness of those for whom he suffered. For this was the greatest source of grief to him: "O people, see how I suffer for your sake. I call upon you for whom I die. See what a bitter death I suffer for your sake. See the wounds I have suffered for you, and the nails that were thrust through my body. See how profound my pains are, but they increase so much more at the sight of your ingratitude."

O bride of God, many teachers of the church assert that one single thorn was as painful to the loving Lord as a stroke of a sharp sword is to us. Indeed, a breeze of the wind was more painful to him than a blow with a stick is to us. Oh, how grievously the soul suffered when it had to depart his body. Francis of Meyronnes enumerates three reasons why the suffering of Christ, on account of the infinite nature of sin, was so painful. The first reason is this. Sin had deprived us of our nobility, tainted the image of God within us, and stained the whole human nature. Second, the divine majesty had been offended. Now, this divine majesty is infinite. Therefore satisfaction had to be made in accordance with the greatness and the dignity of him who had been offended. Third, the human race had fallen into the bondage of the enemy, and we were not able to resist the enemy. Therefore, Christ had to descend into hell and to make satisfaction in an infinite manner. A mere human could not accomplish this; it was therefore necessary that the redeemer be both divine and human in order to make proper satisfaction through his most bitter suffering.

# V

The fifth flower of the suffering of Jesus is its humility and miserable character, and this for four reasons, namely, the place, the time, the company, and the cross. The place was Calvary, where one used to condemn criminals. The wise man predicted this: "We want to condemn him to death with miserable thieves and murderers." O human soul, this is why he chose to suffer in such a horrible place: to lead you into the place of eternal glory. As he said to his beloved followers: "I will prepare a place for you." This place was abhorrent, full of torture, agony, and corpses of condemned men. Similarly, due to the elevation of the mountain, his shame was even more exposed. But, beloved soul, everything that was shamefully inflicted on him will be beneficial for our salvation.

O Christian soul, the time also added to the humiliation of Christ. As Jeremiah said, assuming the role of the crucified, "O human being, my Father has invoked time against me." This happened in three ways. The first is the splendor of the festival that drew huge crowds to Jerusalem. Thus Jesus was put to shame in the presence of many and by a multitude of people. It was a time of rejoicing, and therefore his suffering was even more atrocious and humiliating. For there is a time of rejoicing and a time of grieving. The second aspect is the length of time of Jesus' suffering: from the evening until the next day at three o'clock, when he finally gave up the spirit. As David lamented, "Night and day they have laid siege on me." The third temporal aspect illustrates the ungratefulness of the Jews in the light of the gracious gifts he has bestowed upon them from all eternity. Indeed, while he was suffering at the hands of the Jews, he released their elders from exile in Egypt. The very day his soul departed his body, he bestowed a life-giving soul on them. The very same day his side was pierced, he created the mother of humankind, Eve, from Adam's side.

The company also added to the humiliation of Jesus' suffering. He was hung between murderers, and it is especially crushing to suffer in innocence among guilty people, as a king among murderers, a prince among criminals. Isaiah predicted this: "He was reckoned among the criminals." All this he suffered for you to be numbered one day among the angels in heaven. How cruel it is to suffer among beloved friends and his dearest mother. See how the sword of sorrow pierced her heart.

The cross itself added also to the humiliating character of his suffering. Jesus himself had to carry the cross on which he was to be hung. At that time this was the most ignominious death. For the Law said: Cursed is he who hangs on the cross. In order to safeguard us from an eternal curse Christ was willing to become cursed for our sake.

# VI

The sixth flower refers to the beneficial character of the suffering of Christ. Through the power of Christ's passion the divine friendship and love have once again been given to us. Through the passion the cause of divine anger, that is, our sins, has been taken away. As David said: "You (that is, the almighty God) have hated the evildoer." Now that our sins have been forgiven because of his blessed passion, his love for us has been reinstated. This is what Paul meant: "We have been reconciled with the almighty God through the death of his Son." Bernard puts it as follows: "If the Son of God had not more loved me than himself he would not have given himself in such grievous suffering for me." Oh, he loved with a perfect love, and therefore he preferred to see his soul depart from his body rather than to see us depart from God. It is this perfect love that made him cry out: "I thirst." O noble soul, remember this love of which St. Gregory and Bernard say: If the Son of Mary had had as many bodies as there are stars in the sky, and if every member had been another body in turn, he would have preferred to endure in each of these bodies the same painful passion rather than abandon one single soul to the grinding teeth of the devil. O bride of God, remember this love. Gregory said: O incomprehensible love of our Lord, which did not hesitate to give up his only Son to save the servant. As we read in the *Historia Scholastica*, this salvation is symbolized in the scriptures in the figure of Moab. His city was under siege from his enemies, and his people perished from hunger and thirst. The king loved his people so much that he offered up his only son outside the city walls into the hands of his enemies. This king represents the heavenly Father, while the city symbolizes our world full of sorrows. The king has allowed his only Son—that is, Christ—to be sacrificed outside the walls of Jerusalem. This eternal peace has been established between God the Father and the human race. Oh, let us maintain this peace.

# VII

The seventh flower, O noble soul, is the vigor of the suffering of Christ, and this for three reasons. The first is that his nature is the strongest, for it had not been corrupted by sin, as Francis of Meyronnes points out. It is also written that he did not commit any sin, and that his human nature was not subject to any ailments. He has not assumed any deficiencies apart from those that are an essential part of human nature, such as being susceptible to hunger and thirst, coldness and death. When nature is strong and vigorous, death is even more painful. Second, the death of Jesus proved the most fierce because of the harmonious relation between spirit and body. For his spirit did not covet against the body, or the body against the spirit. The more harmony and unity, the more bitter and painful the separation. Third, because of the outstretching of his limbs. O bride of God, observe what Jesus suffered for your sake from head to toes. Bernard said: "O human being, observe the grief and suffering from the soles of his feet unto the top of his head. Stretched out from the right hand to the left hand, observe how intensely he suffers in his hands, his arms, shoulders. Observe how he is being stripped, scourged, crowned with thorns. Observe how deep the scourges penetrate his skin unto the bone. See how deep the nails penetrated his hands and feet. See how the lance pierced his side, how water and blood flowed out, and how his soul departed his body." Oh, what did David say? "They have numbered all my bones" (Ps 21:18).

# VIII

The eighth flower, O bride of the Lord, refers to the fullness or universality of the suffering of Jesus. For it permeated all his members. He has made satisfaction for all humankind, from Adam unto the last human being. The suffering of our Lord matches his desire for the salvation of all people. Isaiah speaks in the person of the Lord when he says: "I have made man and I will suffer for him. I will carry the weight of his sins in my body on the wood of the cross." St. Hubert likewise claimed that Christ saw all the past sins of humankind in the present, and he saw the future sins more clearly and more distinctly than any human being can see his own sins. These sins oppressed the heart of Jesus so much that he became greatly distressed in his lower nature, dreading that he would give up the spirit immediately. This is why he bent down to pray, and his sweat turned into drops of blood that sprinkled the earth. These sins caused him so much sorrow that no intellect, human or angelic, could ever begin to grasp it in all eternity. Every single sin could cause this grief. O noble soul, every mortal sin is like an iron with five teeth that gnaw at the soul of Christ and wound it fivefold. Who can fathom how many sins have been committed from the beginning of creation unto the last man? These five wounds in the soul of Christ are the divine anger, the arousal of divine vengeance, the repulsive stain of the soul, the disorder caused in the realm of God, and the infliction of eternal punishments.

The first tooth, O noble bride of God, is the divine anger. The Son of God loves his Father and his honor. The greater his love, the more the shame of sin and dishonor caused by sin afflicted him. Because Christ has taken it upon himself to make satisfaction for the lack of righteousness of humankind, it was necessary that he endured sufferings as profound as sin was offensive to God. The second tooth is the arousal of divine vengeance and goodness. Jesus Christ is a mediator who longed for peace between God and his creature. Because of the magnitude of his love, he was saddened by the divine wrath directed at creatures because of their sinfulness. The third tooth is the repulsive stain of the soul. Christ loves above all the beauty, the nobility, and the splendor of the soul. Therefore, to the degree that he rejoiced in its beauty, to this degree he was saddened by its ugliness. Out of profound sadness and anxiety his heart became tender, and with the balsam of his blessed death he has cleansed the stain away. The fourth tooth is the disorder caused in the realm of God. As the Son of God, an almighty Lord, cherished the honor and glory of the realm of his Father, he became deeply saddened by the disorder of sin. The fifth tooth is the infliction of eternal punishments. The Son of God was the Savior of all blessed people. Given the fact that he deeply loved the peace that creatures endowed with reason enjoy in the presence of their Creator, he was equally saddened to see them separated from God and subject to the pains of hell. In this manner Christ became sorrowful over our mortal sins, and his sorrow grew with every sin committed.

# IX

The ninth flower, O friend of God, refers to the fact that the suffering of Jesus has been excruciatingly long. He suffered being confined into his mother's womb from the very moment of his conception, and he continued to suffer until he gave up his spirit on Good Friday. The very hour in which Adam was expelled from paradise, the noble soul of Jesus departed his body, and heaven was opened up.

O beloved soul, remember that heaven had been closed to us for more than five thousand years. This closure was signified by the closure of paradise, which had been closed in three manners, as scripture reveals to us. An angel guarded the gate with a burning fire and a two-edged sword, sealing paradise, restraining and terrifying us. The death and blood of Christ, however, were the key that opened the heavens; as Jerome said, The blood of Christ is the key to paradise. The water that flowed from his heart is his gracious reward that extinguished the burning fire and put away the sword that would otherwise have awaited us. This two-edged sword signifies the righteousness of God that cuts both body and soul. Paul said, "He is a mediator between God and his people, the man Jesus who has given himself up for us" (1 Tim 2:5). O soul, it often happens that the one who mediates between warring factions receives blows from both sides. This was the case with Christ, who freely embraced these wounds so as to lead us to eternal glory.

"O most beautiful among women, where is your lover, and we will seek him with you?" (cf. Sg 6:17). O faithful soul, hear what the bride says: "My beloved has gone down into the garden to gather fragrant herbs" (cf. Sg 6:1). O dearest beloved, let us not depart from this garden but let us accompany the bride into the wine press and press the little flowers we collected. Let us eagerly pluck the flowers, constantly remembering the passion of our Lord Jesus Christ, and carry them into the press of compassion. Thus we will, O beloved soul, receive the following fruits. A continual remembrance of the passion of Jesus, which weakens the temptations of the enemy, the flesh, and the world; it takes away imperfection from our soul and induces us to works of virtue. It makes us worthy of being honored by the angels, it awakes us to love, heals what is broken by sin, and allows us to share in the peace of God. It strengthens us in our struggles and heals us from every evil. It wakes us, who were dead in sin, to new life. It calls us who were lost to the straight road of joy, sweetens everything that is bitter, surrounds us with grace, and keeps us from evil. It discloses to us everything we need to understand, enlightens us in every darkness, and adorns us with every virtue. These then are the eighteen fruits that we extract from the nine flowers that grow in the garden of the bridegroom. It is unto this garden that he continually calls and invites his bride.

The taste of these fruits gladdened the bride; as she said, "In the shadow of the tree that I desired I sat down, and the fruit is sweet to my palate"(cf. Sg 2:3). When she returned into the garden and found her beloved, she cried out to him with ardent desire: "O kiss my mouth with your sweet mouth. Your breasts are sweeter and more savory than wine. O my lover, I want you to put your left hand under my head and your right hand to embrace me"(cf. Sg 4:10; 2:6). Bonaventure admonishes us to remember and meditate on the suffering of Jesus so as to imitate it. First, we should imitate his humility, patience, love, and all the other virtues of the Savior; second, to grow with compassion for him, considering the intensity, the length, and the multitude of his sufferings; third, so as to be taken with amazement at who is suffering, what he suffers, and for whom he suffers. For he is God and man, a King of kings, a Lord of lords before whom the angelic powers tremble. Do you want to know what he suffered? Go and walk in the flower garden. Consider for whom he suffered: for ungrateful people. Fourth, so as to rejoice, for he has released us from the hands of our enemies, the choirs of angels have been supplemented, and hell has been emptied. Fifth, we should contemplate the suffering of our Lord so as to grow detached from all sensual things. Finally, in order to rest in God, as David says: "In peace I will go to rest and sleep" (Ps 4:9). O bride of God, noble soul, go now with your Bridegroom to rest and sleep. Your eyes will sleep, but your heart will always wake (cf. Sg 5:2).

# A Sweet Meditation

*(on how the lost soul was found by the Son of God)*[1]

*Of all the devotional works collected in this book,* A Sweet Meditation
*(on how the lost soul was found by the Son of God) must rank among the
most attractive. It is a refreshing drama, emotionally charged, about the
quest of the Son of God for the lost soul, his human bride. After a short introduction, the Meditation opens with a heavenly council between Father and
Son. The Son is sent to earth, hides for nine months in the womb of the
Virgin, and then sets out to find the lost soul. He finally finds her, utterly
stained, and presents her in his death on the Cross to his Father. K. Ruh sur-
mises that the work is Franciscan in inspiration,[2] and this is not impossible—
although the work is genuinely unique in its kind.*[3]

## A SWEET MEDITATION

Once we know the cause of love, we are then drawn into
attaining this love.[4] In order to attain this love, one is well advised
by the words of the wise man Solomon,[5] who states, "In accordance
with the manifold riches of timber, so the fire burns." So too, the
memory of the manifold gifts of God and the benefactions conferred by our loving Lord ignite the fire of divine love. Above all,
God has revealed to the soul his incomprehensible love in three
aspects.

First, God has created us according to his divine image.
Second, he has renewed us after the Fall through his holy life, his
passion and death. Third, he has received human nature in grace
and forgiven our sins.

Therefore, the devout soul will love her bridegroom with all
her might and all her heart, not just because God has created her,
but also because he has saved her with his bitter passion, in which
he has revealed in a most supreme manner the abyss of his love for

the noble soul. For out of his bottomless, ardent love, he thirsted and desired to come down into this vale of tears in order to seek out the noble soul who had been lost.

When the eternal heavenly Father counseled that he wanted to save us from eternal death, he spoke to his only Son: "Depart, and return the lost soul to us." In response, the Word, the Son of God, yielded to his Father, and spoke: "Father, I will gladly do so. I want to be obedient unto death, in order to save the human soul from eternal death." Then the Father said: "Depart into exile, my Son, to suffer trouble, misfortune, distress, desolation and scorn. Again, depart; you are God and man and will be considered a sinner. Depart into exile, so that your noble divinity becomes united with humanity, and your divine humanity be subservient to all human beings. Depart into exile, revealing the plenitude of your gracious innocence, and discharge the debt of the whole of humanity. Depart into exile, and though you are a king, you will not enjoy much royal honor in the earth realm, and it will never be conferred upon you. Depart into exile, and foresee your suffering and martyrdom, so that it will be ever more excruciating. Depart into exile, and I will cut off your life in its youthful prime, so that your death will be even harder for you. Depart into exile, and fulfill with your deeds everything that the prophets have foretold about you. Depart into exile, and I will hand your enemies the sword so that they can do with you as they please. Depart into exile, and share your scornful death with good and bad people, or with those who want to receive it faithfully. Depart into exile, and suffer the earthly bitter death without the consolation of your Father. Finally, depart into exile, and undergo suffering for which you will never be rewarded."

The worthy Son took his leave of his heavenly Father, descended from the high heavens, left behind him his domain and his riches—that is, his glory, his royal court, and the holy angels—and he withdrew all by himself into the foreign land. He had sent angels, patriarchs, and prophets, but now he himself came down from his elevated heavenly kingdom into the deep vale of the earth.

As he descended to seek the lost soul, he first arrived in the town of Nazareth. In order to outwit the enemy, he sheltered and hid himself for nine months and remained in a confined place, the unsoiled, chaste temple of the most pure virgin Mary. He who could not be contained by the heavens, rested and took up residence in the pure body of the virgin Mary. From her all-pure blood he has, with the cooperation of the Holy Spirit, assumed human nature; he has put on the poor attire of a human *body*, covering up the glory of his power, to make sure the enemy did not recognize him.

After nine months he came out of his abode, in resemblance of the flesh of sins, hiding his divinity and revealing his humanity, born in utter poverty, a poor, naked, little child that slept its first night in a manger among the animals, wrapped up in miserable swaddling clothes. There he cried out first, calling out for the lost soul. Looking for the soul in Bethlehem, he could not find her there.

After forty days he went to Jerusalem and searched for her in the Temple, but he could not find her. Then he rushed to Egypt and went looking for her during seven years, but he could not find her. He returned and went into the barren desert, and he searched for her for forty days and forty nights amid profound sadness, groaning and shedding tears, but still he did not find the soul.

He now girded himself with a great burning love to seek the noble soul. With great desire he wandered for thirty-three years, enduring poverty and humility, making his way with great effort through forests, ravines, thistles and thorns, mountains and valleys, suffering hunger and thirst, in waking and in prayer, enduring cold and heat, in utter poverty, with great toil and labor amid derision and nameless misery; and so it happened that many a night he shed warm tears and prayed to his dear Father for his beloved bride, the noble soul, who was lost.

We can assume that many late evenings he arrived at his mother's home, exhausted by his travels, hungry and thirsty, soaking wet with sweat and tears. When his dear mother saw him worn out for love's sake, she asked him whence he came and what had happened to him. Jesus answered his dear mother: "O worthy mother, I have shed my tears throughout the night in prayer and called out for the noble soul who is lost, my chosen bride, who has been taken away from me and is now sadly lost. I fail to find her, but I will keep calling and crying out for her until I find her."

In the holy Gospels, too, we read that Jesus used to spend whole nights praying. And we may assume that he seldom or never prayed without shedding tears.

After this, Jesus addressed his disciples and revealed the ardent nature of his love for the noble soul, saying: "Now I want to go up to Jerusalem. There the Son of Man will be betrayed, scourged, mocked, and spat at, crowned with thorns and crucified, for the sake of the lost soul" (Mark 10:33–34). He therefore continued and arrived at the Mount of Olives. There he searched for her with great effort, sweating water and blood. Still he did not find the soul. He then became sorrowful in his mind. He began to shiver and said, "My soul is sorrowful unto death" (Mark 14:34). Immediately a messenger from heaven appeared, consoling him: "My Lord, be devout and strong; you will break the shackles of Adam and you will redeem the human race, and dispel the displeasure of the Father. Thus you will find the lost soul."

Now the blessed Jesus felt consoled, and he stood up, swiftly allowed himself to be captured and to be led off to Jerusalem in order to search for the soul from house to house. So he was brought to the house of Annas (John 18:13). He searched for her the whole night, in great tribulation and pain—but he did not find her. From here Jesus was brought to Caiaphas, the high priest, where he suffered much ignominy. Still he did not find the soul. He now was brought back to the house of Pilate, where he was accused by false witnesses. Still he did not find the soul. He was sent to Herod, who treated him like a fool. He was then led back to Pilate and brought into the courthouse, where he was condemned to death. Still he did not find the soul. Then he was tied to a column and mercilessly scourged. A crown of thorns was put on his head. But, tied to the column and with sharp thorns on his head, he still could not find the soul.

Then he put on his tunic, lifted the heavy cross on his bleeding shoulders, and carried it to Mount Calvary hoping to find the lost soul. But he did not find her. Then he was put on the cross and horribly stretched by the wicked Jews. And still he did not find her. Then his cross was raised, and he was lifted up, hoping to see the lost soul anywhere. But still he did not find her. Then he cried out from the cross with a hoarse voice, to be heard by all people. Thus he called the lost soul with sorrow in his heart: "Alas, noble soul. O my chosen daughter. O my dearest and only beloved bride, see how I am aflame with love for you, and what I have suffered for your sake. Do you not hear my calling and my lament? Why do you not respond? Surely you can see how I have become destitute and miserable in a poor little house, laid down between two animals, with miserable swaddling clothes, for your sake? I was driven to Egypt, seated on an ass. I have been searching for you for thirty-three years, suffering much poverty and destitution. The more I search for you, the more you elude me. But if you consider all I have done for you insufficient, I want to do even more. My only desire is that I see your face and that you lovingly respond to me."

In this manner, with great sorrow, Jesus sought out the lost soul. When everything was fulfilled that had been prophesied of him, he finally found his beloved bride. She was stained, black, and dirty beyond recognition, poor and incarcerated in a dark dungeon, oppressed, with her hands and feet tied into iron shackles, in utter misery. When he saw her in this condition, he wept and cried, saying: "O my soul, my noble creature, how has this come to pass? How did you end up like this? Your face is blacker than burnt coal. How has your splendor been darkened so much? How your beautiful complexion has changed! Raise up your eyes, look at me, and speak to me. Do not be downcast, for I will help you. I am sufficiently wealthy; just reveal your failings to me."

When the soul heard this, she lifted her eyes, feeling shame and love, for she was being chastised in a sweet manner, and she bitterly deplored and lamented her miserable state, and speech eluded her. When Jesus saw this, he addressed her as follows: "O my beloved bride, I feel deep compassion for your misery. O devout and pious soul, O soul that abandoned me and has committed adultery with many lovers, turn now to me again. For although you have often wronged and offended me, I beseech you to return, and I will lovingly receive you."

The soul answered: "Alas, woe is me, Lord. Although I am willing, I cannot bring myself to do it. I am beyond consolation or support, for I have strayed too far. I am too guilty. All is lost. Woe is me, wretched creature. Who will release me from this body of death, and remove these heavy shackles?"

Jesus responded: "Be at peace now. Through my grace and with my assistance, you will be redeemed. I am sufficiently wealthy. Just reveal your debt to me.[6] For the whole world is mine, and everything within it. For you I am willing to pledge everything in this world, as if it were nothing.

The soul spoke: "O my dearest friend, even if you were to give everything in this earthly realm, it still would not suffice to obtain my release from the cruel tyrants that keep me captive."

Jesus answered: "Heaven too is mine. Even if I may not be able to help you with all the goods of the world, I will pledge the heavens, the sun, the moon, and the stars."

The soul spoke: "All that you offer will not suffice for my release."

Jesus said: "It would greatly surprise me if I could not help you with the riches of heaven and earth. I would like you to tell me how I can help you."

The soul answered: "O noble lover, heavenly Bridegroom, return home, for I am beyond salvation. The treasure needed for redeeming me is infinite and immeasurable."

Jesus said to her: "No, favorite daughter, I have not been sent out to return without you. I have received the command of my Father that I should not return home, no matter what cost, unless I bring his daughter, my bride, along. Therefore I need to know what I can do or give for you, for I am not to leave here or to return to my Father without you."

The soul answered: "Oh, I dread to say what may be of help to me."

Jesus spoke: "Be brave, and speak freely. I prefer to give everything I own rather than abandon you."

Now the soul cried bitterly, and said: "O heavenly Bridegroom, only Beloved, you have now laid everything before me, but only one thing will secure my salvation: that you offer up your own body and soul for my sake."

Hearing this, Jesus turned aside and became sorrowful and filled with sadness. For with loud cries and tears he has been offered up. He spoke with sorrowful voice: "Be still, my beloved daughter and bride. If it must be, I will gladly die for your sake. See, here, I am willing. For my feet have already been nailed to the cross to obtain your release. I have stretched out my arms to embrace and kiss you. My head stoops down to give you the kiss of peace. The chamber of my heart is ready and open to receive you. Therefore—

come, O soul, and do not turn away from me. O pious soul, O devout soul, turn toward me."

And when death drew near Jesus cried out with a loud voice, "Father, into thy hands I commend my spirit" (Luke 23:46), as if he wanted to say: "Heavenly Father, now I have found the lost soul whom I have been seeking for so long. Heavenly Father, now I have embraced the one I love. And now I present her as a pure dove, cleansed with my blood, before your divine eyes. Ah, heavenly Father, now the moment has arrived for you to open the gates of heaven. For now I bring along the lost soul, for whom I was sent. See, the soul that was lost has now been found."

Oh, he finally found the soul he had sought for so long in the hard, cruel bed of the cross. O devout soul, pay heed. O pious soul, raise up your eyes and see what your Bridegroom, your King, your Judge, your Creator, the Crown of your glory, has suffered for your sake. For never has anybody desired so much to remain in this life, as Jesus desired to die in order to find and redeem the lost soul. If he had as many bodies as there have been, or will be, people, and if he had offered up all these bodies for us in death on the cross, this would still only have revealed a minor portion of his love. Such was the ardent nature of the divine heart of Jesus and its loving concern for the soul. Woe, woe, woe is the hardened heart that cannot be moved or grow soft before the revelation of such power and might of love in the only-born Son of God, King Jesus. O devout and pious soul, remember the great things Jesus has done for you, put them in the scales of your heart and measure them, and allow him, who, for your sake, was nailed to the cross, Jesus Christ, who is blessed in eternity, to dwell in your soul. Amen.

# Hendrik Herp
## *A Mirror of Perfection*, Part 4[1]

[Spieghel der Volcomenheit]

*Hendrik Herp (Henricus Harphius) is a major representative of the spirituality of both the Franciscans and the Modern Devotion. He studied in Leuven, and after he entered the Franciscan order he exercised a number of leading functions within his order in Antwerp and Mechelen, where he died in 1477. His main work,* Een Spieghel der Volcomenheit (A Mirror of Perfection), *was widely distributed throughout Europe through a Latin translation in 1509 and several translations in different European languages soon afterward. Through Herp's writings (especially the* Mirror*) the mystical tradition of the Low Countries exerted a considerable influence throughout Europe in the Early Modern period. In his* Mirror *Herp mainly compiles and synthesizes his sources; he does not present the reader with a work of striking originality. Nevertheless, a study that details the way he selects, interprets, uses, and transforms his sources might very well reveal a personal touch—and one that is less recognizably traditional and more modern than that of Ruusbroec or Jordaens (two of his main sources). He is more than a compiler; he integrates his sources into a coherent work that has been rightly described by Kurt Ruh as a "Summa Mystica."[2]*

*The* Mirror *is divided into four parts. The first part, which is somewhat introductory, treats the mortifications that prepare us for the spiritual life. This spiritual life itself is divided into the active life (part 2); the spiritual contemplative life (part 3); and the superessential contemplative life (part 4), translated below. Each part is structured along the same lines: preparation, adornment, and ascent.*

*The superessential union with God requires a preparation of the soul; that is, the soul must renounce everything dissimilar to God. Herp enumerates nine preparatory stages in which he describes a growing surrender of the soul to God (chapter 60).*

*The adornment consists of a number of points, such as inner peace, inner silence of the mind, loving submersion in God, and contemplation of darkness in which the spirit has died to itself and lives in God.*

*Not surprisingly, given his sources (especially Ruusbroec and Jordaens), the ascent into the superessential life has a trinitarian dimension: the Holy Spirit operates on the will or the loving faculty; the Word operates on the intellect; and the Father acts on the memory. Here our glorified spirit possesses "all the deliciousness, the riches, the knowledge, and all that it can possibly desire." Although the final pages of the* Mirror *strike any reader familiar with Ruusbroec's oeuvre almost as a collage, it is clear that Herp has, in the words of his editor L. Verschueren, "interpreted Ruusbroec in a very specific manner."*[3]

# A MIRROR OF PERFECTION, PART 4

We now turn to the third and most perfect life, which is called the superessential contemplative life. It is symbolized by Mary Magdalene, who had chosen the better part; for just as we have been created to dwell with angels in glory, as scripture teaches, so too we will be raised higher in the choirs of the angels when we grow in true perfection of virtue. For this purpose we are enlightened in divine knowledge. The superessential contemplative life has the highest grade of divine illumination. Therefore, we should ascend all the rungs of virtue, and pursue especially true renunciation, as much as we can, and thus we will make ourselves ready blissfully and profitably to receive from God the supreme influx of the superessential contemplative life. Granted, it sometimes occurs that this gift is bestowed upon those who have not even begun to prepare themselves for a life of perfection, or on those who have just embarked upon pursuing a life of perfection, or on those who have just abandoned their sinful ways, as in the case of St. Paul, who was raised up into the third heaven and saw God in an essential manner, as we will joyfully see him in eternity. Nevertheless, it often happens that after this superessential contemplation these people are put to the test with unspeakable temptations, anxieties, evil, and resentful feelings toward God, as I have discussed earlier in this book. This is hardly surprising, for they are not yet perfect in virtues and renunciations.

God has commanded us to pray, and he wants to give plentifully, but everyone must take heed and make sure that he does not pray for things that are beyond the measure of his perfection. Rather, we should only pray for the things we need for our salvation or for attaining perfection. God, who enjoys giving freely, often grants the request of him who prays so as to fulfill his promise: "Ask, and it shall be given to you" (Luke 11:9). Still, it is of no use to the one who prays to receive it, for he fails to use it properly for his salvation. Hence, these people are often handed over to unspeakable pressures of anxiety, blindness, and hardness of heart, evil, and infernal resentment toward God, as Christ said to Ananias, speaking of Paul, "For I will show him how much he must suffer for my name's sake" (Acts 9:16). In order to avoid this we must in this state prepare and adorn ourselves, and then a salvific ascent will ensue.

# Chapter 60

*The preparation for the superessential life through renunciation of will*

This preparation requires first the two previous lives described earlier. It is founded on the most perfect and noble mortification of our nature. This means that the loving soul will renounce everything unlike God and enter into a perfect likeness with God so as to see the God of Gods in Sion. We must seek this likeness in the most pure desire for self-renunciation. In order to explain this desire I will discuss nine grades and elaborate on each of them, as God has usually ordered them.

The first grade of renunciation is the one that is founded on the fear of God. Through it we desire to abandon all mortal sins. This is the first entry into the likeness of God. Just as we have become estranged from God through the unlikeness of sin, so too we return to God through the likeness of his grace and our virtues. David admonishes us to do so in the Psalms: "Come you to him and be enlightened, and your faces shall not be confounded" (Ps 33:6). But these are very few in comparison to the numbers of sinners, and their enlightenment is still very obscure, as in a haze, and they hardly discern or avoid mortal sins. Their lives are still very questionable; their conscience is fearful; their senses are surrounded with alluring temptations; their salvation is very dubious; and the enemy is very hopeful of their fall and damnation, for it seems to them that it suffices to be on one's guard against mortal sin, saying with the prophet, "Lord, enlighten my eyes that I never sleep in death lest at any time my enemy say: I have prevailed against him" (Ps 12:4–5). This is why they remain lukewarm in their illumination, and without enthusiasm. In many things they look for the comforts of nature and food for their senses. Hence their way of life veers more toward hell and mortal sins. Even when they refrain from committing mortal sin until the end, they will nevertheless have to suffer long and horribly in purgatory, for they have not made any efforts to extinguish the desire for daily sins, and their good works will be considered of little value by God because they have been performed with impure desires and intentions.

The second grade of renunciation is characteristic of those who follow divine inspirations and diligently turn away from the vanity of this world, seeking out the advice and the company of good people, who might exert a beneficial influence upon them. As David says, "With the holy, you will be holy, and with the innocent you will be innocent, with the elect you will be elect, and with the perverse you will be perverted" (Ps 17:26–27). These people are more enlightened than the first, and through this enlightenment they are drawn toward shunning every occasion for sinning. They frequent churches, listen to sermons, and visit places where they might become better persons, so as to say with David, "Your word, O Lord, is a lamp to my feet"—that is, my desires—"and a light to my paths, which I seek in order to attain perfection" (Ps 118:105). Nevertheless, these people too are often assailed by the enemy, who often attempts to seduce them, attempting to make them lukewarm and neglectful in the arduous works and practices of virtue. The reason is that they merely refrain from mortal sins and obvious daily sins, but they do not pay sufficient heed to avoiding the tricks of the enemy, to small and hidden imperfections, irresoluteness, and lack of mortifications, nor do they sufficiently commit themselves to pursuing the strengths of virtues. For the enemy has instilled in them, in a sweet and cunning manner, a confidence in, and harmful certainty of, divine goodness. Given the fact that, in their view, they have renounced much for God's sake, they become complacent and vain, assuming that they are of importance. This complacency is so subtle that they themselves do not notice it. They, therefore, become so self-opinionated—as if they no longer need anybody's assistance or advice—and thus they become very prone to spiritual imperfections.

The third grade is that of those who have even more conquered the world of the flesh, the senses, and sloth, who dedicate themselves to difficult and severe works and practices of penance in the body so as to avoid hell, shorten their time in purgatory, and arrive gloriously in eternal life. As David puts it, "I have inclined my heart to do your justifications for ever, for the reward" (Ps 118:112). These people deserve to receive the enlightenment for which David prays, saying, "Lord, make your face to shine upon your servant, and teach me your justifications" (Ps 118:12), as in the performing of exterior bodily practices and virtuous works. Nevertheless, the enemy keeps these people in blindness, and they therefore are unfamiliar with the excellence of spiritual practices. Their highest practice consists in enduring hunger, thirst, and cold; in fasting, waking, wearing a hair shirt, and in oral prayers. But they are utterly unaware of interior practices and mortification of the inner self. This is why they still suffer, and they feel drawn toward, and retain natural affections for, their friends—carnal or spiritual—and family members. They are of the opinion that this kind of love is licit, not realizing the profound spiritual damage that may ensue from it. For through it they remain anxious and restless in their hearts, for they are concerned with many things in relation to their friends or family members. They therefore never reach the inner person but are daily assailed with innumerable possessive, impure, and restless desires, concerns, and worries, which find their origin in natural love, even though they appear to be good and virtuous.

The fourth grade is characteristic of those who dedicate themselves not only to exterior bodily works and practices but also to interior spiritual practices in inner prayer, sighing, loving compassion, and yearnings, and everything of that nature that pertains to the inner person after the inner operation of the Holy Spirit. But they too are kept in blindness by the enemy, as they pursue their practices in order to enjoy a devotion and love that still pertains to

148

the senses. For in all their practices they desire, seek, and are intent upon their own enjoyment in devotion rather than the pure, naked, and dearest will of God. These people often boast about their enlightenment and the spiritual sweetness they enjoy, scorning those who succumb under the yoke of temptation. In a presumptuous manner they say or think that the word of the Psalter applies to them: "The light of your countenance, O Lord, is signed upon us; thou hast given gladness in my heart" (Ps 4:7). These people remain opinionated and full of self-will, and they fail to surrender themselves truly into the will of God. Granted, it sometimes happens that they appear to surrender themselves and everything they are and can do, and offer it up to God, full of desire for a freely embraced poverty, debasement, suffering, exile, death, and so forth; nevertheless, when they are being deprived of these sensual feelings of devotion, and these feelings turn into feelings of abandonment, and they are subject to shame, persecution, adversity, and injustice, then their lack of renunciation is revealed in their impatience, restlessness, sadness, grumblings, and so forth. For they harbor within themselves an inordinate self-love, which the enemy of hell uses to draw away their will, which, supposedly, they had offered up to God in all things. Thus they remain stuck in self-will through a hidden pull of nature. They are unaware of this but desire that God conforms to their will rather than that they utterly conform to the loving will of God in prosperity and adversity, in sensual grace and abandonment.

The fifth grade is characteristic of those who renounce their own will in the loving will of God in all their works, practices, and habits. However, because they have not practiced this state or dwelt in it for very long, they find themselves infirm and wavering, even though this is a source of grief to them. The reason is this: the desire for renunciation is not yet rooted in them through steadfast practice, and therefore they are still subject to fickleness, now renouncing all self-will, then again lacking every resolution in this regard. Assuming the role of this person, David spoke, "And I said: Perhaps darkness"—that means, adversity—"shall cover me, and night shall be my light in my pleasures" (Ps 138:11). This means, in the pleasures of flowing grace, the night—that symbolizes the remembrance of adversity to which I freely surrender myself—is my light—this symbolizes my true access to God by which I become enlightened. If these people were to abandon all attachment in their heart without any reservations, and if they were to subject themselves totally to the dearest will of God, with a complacency of heart and a humility of mind, even in adversity, then they would receive a superabundant reward, and they would become enlightened and know the most hidden paths of virtue, unknown to almost all other people.

The sixth grade belongs to those who, through constant practices and recollection of their manifold desires, abandon all self-attachment without any reservations into the dearest will of God. They become perfectly enlightened in their intellect and know that everything that happens to good people is for the good of their soul, even in adversity. This is why they speak with David: "The Lord is my light and my salvation, whom shall I fear? The Lord is the protector of my life; of whom shall I be afraid?" (Ps 26:1). Nevertheless, these people are not without failings, for they are too concerned with receiving spiritual consolation and yearn to receive it from God with possessiveness. Their intention for the enjoyment of this consolation is not pure and divine. This becomes evident in the restlessness of their heart until the consolations return, fulfilling their desire. This shows that, although praying and asking for this sensual devotion and consolation from God with a proper and honest intention is not wrong or flawed in itself, it nevertheless reveals an imperfection. For what is lacking is a pure renunciation of self. Such a person is unable to allow God to work in himself in accordance with his own dearest will, in abandonment and adversity, without any resistance in his heart. Although he acknowledges that this is a worthy ideal, he himself does not attempt to surrender himself freely, purely, and perfectly to it. This is why he does not progress in other practices and virtues, for he fails to identify adequately or to recognize the hidden inclinations of nature and the subtle inordinate desires.

The seventh grade is characteristic of those who can use their two hands in a proper manner: the right hand of prosperity and the left hand of adversity, speaking with David, "My heart is ready, O God"—that is, to put prosperity to good use in accordance with your will—"my heart is ready," to endure adversity for your dearest will's sake (Ps 107:1). For these people desire to fulfill God's dearest will in every manner, in turning inward and outward, in intentions and in love, as the shadow conforms in every manner to the movement of the body. Of this the loving soul says, "I sat down under his shadow, whom I desired: and his fruit was sweet to my palate" (Sg 2:3). You should know that God himself is the light, and the humanity of Christ is the body that casts the shadow. His profound, perfect life is the shadow under which we will aim to rest through imitating it.[4] Then the spiritual fruits will be abundant and sweet, for God enlightens these people and bestows many hidden spiritual gifts and knowledge upon them. They do not become darkened by the night of adversity and abandonment, for they stand firm on the foundation of naked love, by which they have learned to do great things and to endure grievous sufferings. David addresses these people as follows: "The darkness"—this means, adversity—"shall not be dark to you, obscuring the light of grace but the night of adversity shall be light as the day of prosperity or sensual grace. Then your darkness will be as light to you" (cf. Ps 138:12). For these people find in adversity their spiritual rest and progress. This is why they receive in a proper fashion divine enlightenment and spiritual gifts. These enrich the memory[5] with admirable hidden insights; they enlighten the intellect and ignite the faculty of loving, that is, the will, with the fire of divine love. However, because such superabundance is perilous for incautious persons, it sometimes happens that they misuse through a subtle, hidden ignorance the gifts they so often receive. For instance, unknown to themselves, they rest too much in and love too much the sensual character of the divine gifts. Thus it happens that in an inappropriate manner they do not desire to receive again the grace that was withdrawn from them; they therefore do not know that the gifts that had been bestowed upon them were used in a careless manner.[6] As long as they do not renounce this, they will not attain the highest perfection.

The eighth grade is characteristic of those who honestly surrender themselves into the dearest will of God, allowing him to do with them as he pleases, in time or eternity, stripping them of all self-attachment, ties of love, and the attractions of creatures or divine gifts. Even though they may possess temporal goods, they nevertheless remain as free and empty as if they possessed none. Similarly, they remain empty in relation to the gifts they receive

151

from God, without growing vain or exalting themselves, as if they had not received them at all. These people are usually visited often by God with great and hidden gifts through which God reveals to them many wonderful things in images, figures, and similitudes. They are close to God, although it sometimes happens that imperfect people too receive revelations in the same manner. This is dangerous for their souls, unless they gratefully resolve to grow in virtues and renunciation. However, the highest, superessential revelation that is received beyond all images and similitudes usually remains hidden from these people. The dwelling of this revelation in the soul is the supreme darkness beyond all considerations, of which I have spoken earlier, quoting David, "O Lord, thou lightest my lamp"—this refers to the intellective powers and spiritual knowledge, "O Lord, enlighten my darkness" (Ps 17:29), in which I dwell with the essential contemplation of your countenance. This contemplation is not granted to them, for they receive the revelations and gifts from God in such a manner that, so it seems to them, there is always something lacking in them. They pray to God for what they believe is lacking, even though none of these is necessary for their salvation or progress in a life of virtue. Also, they are much more desirous to receive these revelations and gifts than they would be desirous to be without them, and here lurks a hidden attachment, which God considers to be a flaw. For they should remain so empty and free from these in their heart, as if they had not received them, and gratefully rejoice in the generous mercifulness of God, praising and thanking him who honored the unworthy sinner with these hidden gifts. This person will surrender himself to God, and he will not only be prepared to do without gifts and revelations but also be prepared to face abandonment and adversity. For it is not in gifts and revelations as such that the perfect life is to be found. In these loving gifts God reveals his abundant goodness with which he draws many people who are weak-minded into a perfect life. From this we learn how we have to renounce perfectly all possessiveness if we are to attain the superessential contemplative life in a proper order.

The ninth grade pertains to those who with vigorous practices and surging desires have annihilated flesh, blood, and the core of their body for the love of God. They do not seem to have any other strength than the one their vibrant spirit exhibits. For their blood has been boiled and dried in the fire of divine love. They are not aware of this, due to the exceedingly burning fervor that totally holds sway and makes nature work and endure beyond nature. These are the dearest, hidden children of God, on whom he bestows the fullness of his gifts and graces, and whom he sometimes raises to the contemplation of his divine essence, which happens in the third state we want to discuss. Nevertheless, they have attained such a degree of renunciation that they do not rest in this for its own sake—for they are no longer concerned with their own gratification and pleasure—but they rejoice solely in a perfect imitation of the cross of our Lord Jesus Christ. They yearn more for renunciation, shame, and suffering than for consolation and exultation. For they have put their foundation and their consolation in faith alone, adorned with naked love, with which they desire to endure all adversity without any support of divine consolation, as Paul said after he had seen God in an essential manner, "God forbid that I should glory, save in the cross of our Lord Jesus Christ" (Gal 6:14). These people are drawn to this for two reasons. The first is that they desire to imitate the humanity of Christ in all things, to resemble him entirely in the withdrawal of all consolation, and to suffer both bodily and spiritual abandonment, saying with Christ, "My heart"—that is, my desires—"hath expected reproach and misery" (Ps 68:21). The second reason is that they are rooted in such humility that they consider themselves only worthy of utter abandonment, and without any trace of false modesty they consider themselves in mind and heart lower than any creature. They desire to be scorned and wronged by people in all kinds of ways and to be handed over by God into all kinds of tribulations, sorrow, anxiety, and abandonment in order to follow Christ in all things, even unto the most abject and painful death on the cross. Here you should note that, although these people have learned to glory solely in the cross of our Lord, they nevertheless do not become presumptuous in their carefreeness and unconcern, and therefore they do not obstruct any divine visitations, influences, operations, spiritual stirrings, and illuminations. Rather, they offer themselves up as willing and living instruments, as best they can, and attribute all their works to the operation of the Holy Spirit in them, so as not to be found ungrateful for God's grace. Of these people David said, "They shall

153

be inebriated with the plenty of your house: and you shall make them drink of the torrent of your pleasure" (Ps 35:9). But at other times, as they will be looking for the lowest and most miserable according to the outer man, similarly, according to the inner man they will, above all, desire pure love devoid of all felt consolations and carry whatever suffering they encounter with a heart that is both stricken and renounced. No matter how much suffering they endure, they will desire to suffer even more for the sake of God's love, continually remembering the inexpressible anxiety and renunciation of the spirit of our Lord, when he sweated blood during his prayer. For there he struggled without any support of spiritual consolations, and he triumphed devoutly in the dangerous spiritual fight that took place in his human nature. Thus he redeemed humanity and taught them to attempt to follow the same path. For in this is to be found the foundation of all perfection.

# Chapter 61

*The adornment of the superessential life explained in six points*

We now want to continue to explain the second aspect of this life, namely, how to be adorned in this state. Here you should recall that St. Thomas states in a treatise on the vision of the divine essence that the perfection of all things consists in being united with their final goal.[7] That goal of the created intellect is the uncreated, intellective light of the divine being. Therefore, the highest perfection of the intellective light of our spirit is to be united with God in essential contemplation and fruition of God. For then God is being united with the soul, as a form with its matter, or a soul with its body. Now a form cannot be united with matter unless the matter is properly predisposed to receive the form, thereby becoming receptive toward the form. For instance, a human body cannot be united with its soul unless the body first receives a proper disposition to receive the soul. Similarly, our spirit cannot be united with God in an essential manner in the fruition of glory unless it becomes first properly predisposed. This disposition in our mind or spirit is the light of glory that perfects the intellective powers to

154

contemplate and enjoy God in an essential manner. Therefore, although all blessed spirits see the divine essence in eternal life, nevertheless some blessed spirits will see God more clearly than others, depending on the predisposition they received. The spirit or mind does not have this predisposition or receptivity by nature, but through the light of glory, which makes the spirit grow in likeness with God. Therefore, he who receives most of the light of glory will contemplate God's essence in a more perfect manner, and he who has more naked, pure love will receive more light of glory and will therefore contemplate God more clearly.[8] This is why the contemplative life is considered the best in this life. For a constant contemplation of the beloved and a constant, pure, and enjoyable delight in the beloved ignites the activity of love. This love increases our desire, and it opens up the desirous spirit, making us apt to receive the light of glory, which all of us will receive in eternal life in accordance with our predisposition and aptitude. But in this life it is inaccessible to us, mortal beings.

Therefore, nobody should be of the opinion that he can attain a superessential contemplation, be it through profound knowledge, subtlety of mind, or through exercises, no matter how spiritual. Only he whom God himself, out of fathomless generosity, wants to unite with his spirit and the light of glory (which means, to illuminate him with God himself)—only he will contemplate God essentially, and no one else. But few people attain this state because of their indisposition or ineptness. For they are not inclined to prepare themselves to be adorned and to do what they can. Moreover, the light in which we contemplate the divine essence is a hidden light. This is why nobody can fully understand the things we are about to explain through learned doctrines, cleverness, or brightness of the natural intellect. For all that we can humanly teach or understand of this is far below the true feeling. Furthermore, even though this light of glory is inaccessible to all mortal people, nevertheless we must do all we can so as not to be considered ungrateful. We should always attempt to become properly predisposed and adorned in the presence of God and to do whatever is in our own power. For when God finds us properly prepared and predisposed, he will gladly and generously make us perfect. Six points pertain to this preparation and adornment, which we will receive when we do what we can to contemplate God in an enjoyable and essential manner.[9]

The first point is true, quiet peace between God and ourselves. If we want to find this peace in ourselves, we must love God so much that we, for the sake of God's love and honor, can renounce with an unconcerned mind everything that we previously loved and enjoyed in an inordinate manner. With a cordial love and vivid heart we will raise all our faculties to God in a simple nudity of mind above all multiplicity and restlessness of heart, in which the law of love is being fulfilled. Thus we will steadfastly attempt to attain an inner, elevated heart with a pure intention, which above all bestows on the heart a delicious, quiet peace.

The second point is an inner silence; that is, the intellective faculties are stripped of all images, forms, and likenesses that do not represent the beloved. For the mind must be naked and devoid of every consideration of things. Thus we will possess God in burning desire. This is easy for those who love God only in themselves and all things in God. For pure love, which is imageless, renders the mind simple and empty of all things and raises us above all things and above ourselves into God.

The third point is a loving submersion in and adherence to God, and this is fruition. For when we adhere to God with pure love, without seeking our own profit, we truly enjoy God according to grace but not according to glory. This is a pleasant and fruitful adherence, which unites us so much with the beloved God in the bond of love that we lose all attachments to created things. For we no longer desire to please or make an impression on anybody; neither can anybody make an impression on us. The touch, of which I spoke earlier, teaches us this adherence.

The fourth point is to rest in the beloved we enjoy. For where the beloved is being conquered by the lover and is being possessed in a pure, naked, essential love, there the lover and the beloved come together in love, and they utterly belong to one another in mutual, quiet possession.

The fifth point is a blissful sleep, in which the spirit melts and flows out of itself and does not know how or where, for the spirit flows into the profound abyss of divine love, not knowing itself, God, or creature, but only the love it tastes and feels. This love possesses the spirit in a simple, naked emptiness of all other things. As oil in a cloth or water in wine is being dispersed, so too the spirit flows out of itself into the beloved and loses itself in an immeasurableness so as to become receptive to the lover. The spirit then becomes with eternal love a length, breath, height, and depth of a love that nonetheless remains measureless.

The sixth is a contemplation of darkness, which we cannot grasp or understand with reason. In this darkness the spirit has died to itself and lives in God. Because the spirit has become one with God without distinction, God is its peace, rest, and enjoyment. Here the spirit is continually breathed out of itself and becomes transformed in God[10] beyond all activity and desire. If a person feels these six points in himself, he will be equally ready to engage in contemplation and enjoyment and find them as easy as living or breathing in and out. He is now adorned for the superessential contemplative life, for he has become a living and willing instrument of God, with which God can do as he pleases, whenever and however he sees fit.[11] He does not give himself credit for these works, and he remains equally prepared to willingly do what God demands or to suffer what he permits.

# Chapter 62

Let us continue a simple teaching about this person, and how he should withdraw into the secret chamber of God, and dispose himself to receive the light of glory, insofar as he can. For this purpose he should reckon himself, with profound humility, to be the worst of all people, consider himself genuinely below, and at the disposal of, all creatures, and utterly die to, and renounce, all self-will. Furthermore, he will comply with God's dearest will in all things, as the shadow follows the movement of the body, so as to allow God to work freely and without impediment in him in both prosperity and adversity. Moreover, he will raise his higher faculties, especially the loving will, with burning desire, and passionately turn inward into its fountainhead. Here he will confidently wait, knocking with his desire, as on the door of a friend, until he is allowed to enter and be made blissful—for he himself cannot do this. There is no other way to attain the essential contemplation: the Spirit of God must strip and transform us. The faculties, with which he attempts to attain bliss, are like chamberlains who lead the soul into her highest point at the threshold of the chamber of the eternal king. When the soul is raised with her faculties into her highest point, beyond all created things, and is being sweetly embraced by her lover, then the faculties must withdraw and cease all activity. The Spirit then permeates the soul and blissfully transforms the soul in many, yes, even a thousand ways. The human person then feels in his loving power a touch of the Holy Spirit as a living fountain that flows with rivers of eternal sweetness. In the intellective faculty he receives a supra-splendid, bright, intellective illumination with divine truth from the eternal sun. In his memory he feels devoid of and purified from all images, and he feels invited and drawn into the inexpressible embrace of the supreme and super-essential union with God. These are the three doors that are opened by the Holy Spirit for the loving soul, so as to allow it to contemplate and know part of the infinite treasure of God.[12] With this we end the adornment of this life.

# Chapter 63, §1

*About the ascent into the superessential life*

Finally, we want to discuss the ascent into the third life and state. We cannot describe properly and truthfully the incomprehensible, noble subtlety of the drawing of the Holy Trinity or the innumerable ways of its holy operation on us in accordance with its proper will and our preparation.

Here you should know that this ascent only occurs in response to the inner operation of God, while the soul remains beyond all activity of its own. Although the Persons of the Holy Trinity act as one and without separation, nevertheless we attribute to each Person of the Trinity its appropriate, individual operation in the powers of our soul. The Holy Spirit operates its drawing in the will or on the supreme loving faculty; the Son acts in the intellect; while the Father acts in the memory. Thus the soul becomes able to contemplate God in an essential manner.

# Chapter 63, §2

*The inner operation of the Holy Spirit*

The Holy Spirit is most intimate to us due to the outflowing of the Holy Trinity, for it is he who proceeds from the Father and the Son. This is why the loving power is being acted upon and drawn first, before the intellect and the memory. This ascension is prefigured by Moses, who was called by our Lord to ascend Mount Sinai. With all the children of Israel, Moses saw our Lord from a distance, and the appearance of the glory of God on Mount Sinai was like a burning fire in the presence of the children of Israel (Exod 19). These children symbolize those who have abandoned a worldly life and entered into the solitude of penance. But God commanded Moses to separate from the people and to climb up the foot of the mountain with Nadab and Abiu and seventy-two elders who were ordained with Moses to administer justice. Then Moses saw underneath the feet of our Lord a colorful work, as if made of sapphire stones, and as the heaven when clear (Exod 24:10).

This ascension signifies the inner operation and drawing by the Holy Spirit that the soul undergoes. Just as the thunder and lightning struck, and the earth shook before Moses was called to climb up, so too there occur in the human person a powerful operation of the Holy Spirit, fiery flames of burning love, and a considerable stirring of the body. Then the Spirit of God flows into him as a superabundant, living, supremely sweet spring, in which the loving spirit is being baptized and immersed, and raised in an inexpressible manner into a hidden embrace of divine love. Here he learns the exercise of perfect love, namely, mutual friendship and embracing, mutual feeling and tasting, pleasing and being pleased, melting in love and flowing into the beloved.[13] These people contemplate God as a burning fire; that is, they feel God's goodness as an incomprehensible, abysmal fire of eternal love, which pours into them an inexpressible, sweet, divine feeling in enjoyable love. Thus they melt into God. For God is a fire of love, infinitely great, and each blessed loving soul is as a burning coal that God has inflamed with his fire. All the blessed spirits who are united with the Father and the Son in the unity of the Holy Spirit burn as an infinite fire. Here the divine Persons too, in the unity of their essence, melt through love in the infinite abyss of simple beatitude. Here there is no Father or Son, or Spirit or creature, but only a simple essence, namely, the most simple substance of the Holy Trinity in which all creatures in their superessence become absorbed. Here all enjoyment becomes perfect and fulfilled in essential beatitude.[14]

When a person, while turning inward, has learned to immerse himself freely, purely, totally, and vigorously in the infinite love of God, so as to be absorbed by it, at that moment, as in a flash of lightning, an intellective light shines into the spirit. The spirit stands wide open with vigorous desire and admirable, loving strife between the divine spirit and the human spirit, until they lovingly embrace each other beyond all strife in a naked, enjoyable love. A rough example will illustrate this. Think of a concave mirror, which is called an incendiary mirror, and put it in the direction of the sun when it shines brightly. Then take a paper dipped in sulphur and hold it about two hand spans from the mirror in the light reflected from the mirror. If you hold it still for the duration of a Miserere, it will ignite at the point of reflection. This too happens in a spiritual manner, when we turn within and lift our soul up to God, purged of all sins, full of desire, burning love, and devout reverence.[15] Then the brightness of divine grace shines in the mirror of the soul, and it operates on it with eternal love in such a powerful manner that the mind or the most noble apex of the soul ignites with love. The mind becomes illuminated with a simple, clear knowledge above all intellective powers. The spirit becomes immersed in eternal love, dying to itself and living in God, becoming one love with love, and feeling nothing but love. It becomes free and devoid of all exercises and practices of love, merely receiving and suffering this simple, divine love that devours the spirit, and melts in love. This person does not know or feel himself, God, or any creature but only love, which he tastes and feels, and which blissfully possesses him in a simple and naked emptiness.[16]

# Chapter 64

*Of the operation of the Son in the intellect*

Second, the Son operates with his drawing in the intellect. This operation is symbolized by Moses, who was called by the Lord to climb higher up the mountain. Moses took Josue with him and told the others that they should wait for him. He climbed up into the solitude of the mountain, and a dark cloud covered the mountain, and Moses and Josue waited until Moses was called by God. He then left Josue behind in a small ravine of the mountain and climbed up into the darkness, where he remained alone for six days, until he was called again by God. This ascent denotes the spiritual act and operation in the intellect, which we attribute to the Son. It is rightly called *speculatio*, that is, to see in a mirror. For the spirit of this person has now become a living mirror, in which God forms[17] the spirit of truth, and in which he dwells with fullness of grace. God does not show himself in this living mirror, as he is in his own essence, but only in the most supreme and noblest images and likenesses. Thus the illuminated, elevated intellect acknowledges, in a clear manner without any errors, in intellective images, everything that he has heard about God, about faith, and about every hidden truth, namely, that God is highest majesty, truth, goodness, wisdom, mercy, justice, and love. Moreover, he recognizes that there is distinction among the Persons, and that each Person is God almighty. He knows that there is a unity of the divine nature in the Holy Trinity, and trinity in the unity of the divine nature, and that every Person is God in the unity of the divine being. He further recognizes that God is fruitful in the divine nature and a simple emptiness in the divine being. For the intellect, elevated and illuminated by the spirit of truth, sees God in its own mirror in so many ways, in so many forms and images, that it could possibly conjure up or desire to see. Nevertheless, the elevated intellect remains ever desirous to see what God is in his own essence. But even if the elevated, illuminated intellect were to come face to face with the essential image of God, nevertheless it could not grasp or see it because of the immense brightness, which would darken and blind the eyes. This is indeed the darkness or the shadow under which the soul sits with delight in the Book of Love (Sg 2:3). Thus, Josue walks with Moses; this means, the intellect wanders with the loving power, but here the intellect must remain behind and the loving power continue on its own. For the loving power seeks embrace rather than vision. When the loving power has entered in the incomprehensible brightness, which blinds the intellect, as the eyes are blinded by the brightness of the sun, then the soul receives above the intellective power a simple eye, opened in the operation of the loving power. This eye sees with a simple contemplation in the divine clarity everything that God is in his simplicity. What happens to the person at that moment, or what he then knows, cannot be expressed in words, nor does he himself fully know it when he comes to himself. At times the intellective eye follows the simple eye and wants in that same light to know and examine whom and what God is. But here all understanding and considerations must give way.[18] Having sensed the divine drawing, the simple eye leads the loving power forth into simplicity, so that the mind of the person is no longer in control. This occurs as frequently as the sun of justice draws our simple eye toward itself into its immeasurable brightness, in which we see God and all things without distinction and consideration, with a simple contemplation in the divine brightness.

# Chapter 65

*The operation of the Father in the memory*

Finally, the heavenly Father operates his drawing in the memory. This operation is symbolized by Moses, who was not content to merely sit in the darkness. When God called him on the seventh day and when he approached God, conversing with God as with a friend, Moses prayed to God, "Lord, if I have found favor in your sight, show me your face" (Exod 33:13). And the Lord answered: "I will show you all good, that is, myself but not in my inner essence, for man shall not see me and live. But you shall see my back parts," that is, I will show you an incomplete knowledge about me (Exod 33:19, 20, 23). Nevertheless, Moses was later allowed to see God in an essential manner. By this is signified the inner spiritual operation and the spiritual drawing, which our spirit receives from the heavenly Father. When we adhere to the loving, generous, heavenly Father with a constant and determined spirit, he allows an incomprehensible, bright intellective light to descend into the most interior part of the naked elevated mind. This light cannot be grasped by intellect, nature, or reasoning. This light is not God himself but an illumined means between God and the living spirit. This is the noblest that God creates in nature. It ennobles and perfects nature. Our simple, naked mind is a living mirror, in which this light shines, demanding from us to become like God and to become one with God. This light is called the splendor of eternal light, and it demands a mirror not tainted by any other images. It is also called the spirit of the Father, in which the Father shows himself in a simple manner without distinction of the Persons but only in the nakedness of his nature and substance. Nevertheless, God does not show himself as he is in his unutterable glory, but he shows himself to each one of us in accordance with the light that each person receives, illuminating the eye of the spirit and making us ready to receive it. Still, this light bestows on the contemplative spirit a true knowledge, with which he sees God insofar as we are allowed to see God in this life.[19] This is called true contemplation, namely, to see God in a simple and onefold manner.[20]

In this contemplation the simple eye of the naked mind does not receive any other images but solely and utterly the divine image, which the simple eye knows in itself because it receives it in itself.[21] Through the presence of the image the mirror becomes illuminated and made ready to contemplate the divine image. This image of God, which is like an immeasurable brightness, is so tasteful to our spirit, that our spirit, submersing itself into profundity, drowns into the essential brightness and becomes one with this immeasurable light, having died to itself but remaining alive in this light. Our spirit then receives this light without any intermediary, and thus the spirit becomes the very light that it receives and becomes seeing with this deiform light.[22] In other words, the soul becomes illuminated with the light of glory with which we contemplate God in an essential manner. Because this light is always being renewed without ceasing into the hiddenness of our spirit, so too our soul is always being blissfully and gloriously born in an eternal now with the Son of God.[23] Here the glorified spirit possesses all the deliciousness, the riches, the knowledge, and all that it can possibly desire. The incomprehensible, amazing things that reside in the infinite treasure of this hidden glory are utterly beyond the intellect of all creatures that are not drawn with the light of glory into the enjoyable knowledge of God. This is why it would be presumptuous to attempt to describe this. Because even if somebody had, with Paul, seen in an essential manner, he would not be allowed or be able to say or capture in images that which cannot be expressed in words.

Thus I have shown, as best as I can, the entrance to the super-essential contemplative life. But what the soul receives, when she is drawn into this, is something that needs to be considered by those who are familiar with it by having felt it within, and who have been drawn with Paul into the third heaven. To this state pertains the ninth grade of love, which is called *amor inaccessibilis*, that is, an inaccessible love. For this love leads us into the contemplation of an inaccessible light, if it predisposes us and makes us ready as much as is possible for us. The impetuousness of this love is so great that when we are utterly engulfed by it, we are being put outside of ourselves into God, and it makes us constantly drunk with the sweet taste of incomprehensible goodness, such that the exterior and lower powers are drawn into the higher powers, and the higher powers are in turn drawn into their origin, namely, the apex of the mind. Thus our spirit becomes drawn into the spirit of God, and there it is being melted. Thus it flows into the immeasurable abyss, in which it is constantly being renewed and blissfully born, so that the Father can say to the spirit, "You are my son; this day have I begotten you" (Ps 2:7). May the loving power, wisdom, and goodness of the Father, the Son, and the Holy Spirit grant us to hear this now and in time to come. Amen.

# Claesinne van Nieuwlant
## *Conversation*[1]

*We know very little about Claesinne. On the basis of the information given by the Benedictine abbot Jozef Geldof Ryckel (in his* Vita S. Begghae, *Leuven, 1631), we can deduce that she must have lived from c. 1550 till 1611. He mentions that she lived in the St. Elisabeth beguinage in Ghent, but that seems to be a mistake, as her name is mentioned in the obituary of the so-called small beguinage in Ghent (Ter Hooie). She appears to have been a rich and exceptionally intelligent woman. Complaints about her lifestyle reached Bishop Wilhelmus Damasi Lindanus, and he sent his confidant, the priest Pelgrim Pullen, to investigate. Part of this investigation was a long conversation with Claesinne, of which our text is a written report, though Pullen may have inserted an earlier text, written by Claesinne, that had served as a point of departure for their conversation.*

*Thus, though the text presents only the words of Claesinne, it is written by Pelgrim Pullen. His real name was Jan Pullen, but he usually called himself Pelgrim (pilgrim). He was born around 1520, near Venlo, and studied at the University of Cologne. As a priest, he was for several years (1577–84) rector of the beguinage of Roermond and confessor of his bishop, Lindanus, who became bishop of Ghent in 1588. Also in Ghent, Pullen was Lindanus's confidant. After the death of Lindanus, in the same year, Pullen returned to Roermond. He tried to live a hidden life—which was difficult because of his reputation as a spiritual leader—successively in Cologne, Liège, and 's-Hertogenbosch, where he died in 1608. We know of seventy-three titles of works attributed to him, though of twenty of them the authorship is disputed. In fact, only twenty-three works have been recovered until now, and only four of them have been published. The influence of Ruusbroec, Herp, and* The Evangelical Pearl *on his works is obvious.*

*The so-called* Conversation *(Samenspraak) was published for the first time by Leonce Reypens in* Ons Geestelijk Erf *13 (1939–40), 312–52, on the basis of one manuscript: Brussels, Koninklijke Bibliotheek, ms. 4920–21. A second edition with a modern Dutch translation was made by Paul Mommaers (Claesinne van Nieuwlant, Samenspraak, Spiritualiteit 22, Nijmegen: Gottmer, 1985), on the basis of Reypens's edition, but with corrections from a second manuscript: Tilburg, Theologische Hogeschool, ms 18. We used this second edition for our translation, and we have selected a central passage from the* Conversation *(about one-third of the whole text).*

# THIS IS THE CONVERSATION WITH A RECLUSE, AT THE BEGUINAGE NAMED DE HOOIJER, IN GHENT, IN THE YEAR 1587, NOVEMBER 27

## About the Superessential Life

The superessential life is that in which the spirit is lost, namely, where it is sunk away from itself into God in such a way that nothing remains to it than being sunk away. The contemplative life is a pure cleaving to God, without oneself, while God remains in himself. An active life is detaching oneself from oneself in such a way that the human person is continuously being separated from himself and pulled away, and that whatever he does, God is doing it, and God is all. In the superessential life the spirit is in nakedness, and his being is in God and is God.

Even so, in the superessential life, the human person has an ascent to God, beyond himself in God, where he is wrought by God. In his lower part the person has a working downward in his littleness, in his nothingness. If the lower person—that is, the body—would not be wrought by God in its littleness, than it would follow the highest and would be drawn upward from the earth in the air.[2]

The natural drive of the intelligence can sometimes be so strong toward divine things and God that the body follows the spirit, that is, that the spirit of the human person thus drives strongly upward naturally and the body follows the spirit and lifts it up in the air. And this can happen in a natural way.

When the spirit is spirited out in God and the body has become so obedient to the spirit that there is no conflict between

166

the two, then the body follows the spirit, is obedient and docile; wherever the spirit is, there is the body drawn.

When the enlightened spirit transcends superessentially, then the body transcends superessentially too. There, the spirit is God and the body spirit.

In unexercised persons, namely, those in whom everything has not died fully in spirit, soul, and body, it is very doubtful whether this elevation from the earth comes from God. Therefore, as long as everything inside and outside is not discarded, a person has to resist every inner or outer elevation. When it is not all divine, it is doubtful, and one should not be too much concerned about it, etc.[3]

Some people have a loving ascent to God. If they do not have a descent too, that love does not become essential. If they do not feel the loving ascent, they complain, and it seems to them that God has left and abandoned them. For them, love does not become essential. Ascent and descent should proceed equally, as long as these people are in time. Then the love, which has descended, becomes essential.

Some people are very much taken up with the intelligence and have more knowledge than work. They should leave it all and should be led into the nothingness, especially those who have too many feelings, too much light, that is, so much knowledge by which nature is fed.

Some people complain about, and lament, the persecutions in Christianity. That is good, but it is not best. Also in these things they should have an ascent to God (which is best), namely, when one complains about the downfall, the misery, and the blindness of people and at the same time one rejoices in the righteousness and goodness of God.

The human person should arrive beyond that misery, beyond sin, and be one with God, unchangeable and equal in all things.

The external person in distress and misery, and the inner person in joy—may both parts be equally practiced.

No sorrow can be so great as to see that someone is outside the holy church and that he lives in the sin of unbelief. That sorrow persists until the last day, because those people see that all that is outside will perish. Inside is the life of the truth and the light of clarity, and this can only be known by the one who bows down to the faith of the holy church. In that faith all truth is taught and understood, and not in reason, for all that reason can understand is neither truth nor light. Intelligence cannot come there.

Those who bow down to the faith of the holy church are led by the Holy Spirit, so that they work together with the church and receive nourishment from all that happens in the church, yes, even from the smallest thing that happens there. Indeed, they are led upward into the origin, where their spirit remains lost, and loses itself actively and essentially. But they do not always feel this drive or guidance. Sometimes they are left to themselves and find themselves in aridity so that they experience no taste in anything that is done there (in the church), even in the sacrifice of the Mass, and so on. Sometimes they are left to such desolation, in their nothingness and evil, that they cannot stand themselves or cannot remain present where these mysteries are celebrated. This descent is the most certain, because then nature is not seeking itself and it cannot lead its life there.

This sacrifice is a common sacrifice. Herein the person widens himself to the whole world, and considers all people, just as they are, and himself, and so he goes together with the Son to the Father.

The passion of Christ is exercised in this person by God, or such persons are exercised by God in the passion of Christ, and then they are led by God into the love of Christ, which made Christ to come down in this lament and passion. And just as Christ worked his passion out of love, they have an ascent out of love and an elevation in his love, and out of love they become loveless. Their external person takes up Christ's example, namely, how he has preceded us in poverty, misery, suffering, etc. And thus this person comes, through Christ, in the divinity and in the Father. Those two should keep pace—the one upward, the other downward—and thus an equal ascent is realized, namely, an essential ascent.

When a person has committed a sin, he should not weigh the gravity of it, as if he would try to make satisfaction. That would darken him and create an intermediary between him and God. He should prostrate himself in humility and littleness at the feet of God, because he has dishonored his God so much and has violated his commandment. One should never bother about the gravity of sins and be taken up by it. One should humble oneself, sink down before God. Then our sins do not create an intermediary in our free ascent to God.

In the high contemplation of God the spirit finds its life and the intelligence its knowledge. This should all be given up and should die. Because God is not what he gives. To see the heaven and the nine choirs of angels—that must be lost. He should have nothing that comes from God, because it is all too small. He shall want nothing and turn into his nothingness at all times. Where the spirit stands naked before God, and the intelligence in an unknowing, in such a way that everything there is "un-imaged," then only God is at work.

As long as all this, which lives in the spirit and in the nature, is not fought out, the person should not be admitted to any ascent to God or to contemplate high things or to speak (about them). He should be led into his nothingness. Out of a nothing one comes into a superessential life. The human person should contribute nothing with regard to the superessential life. He should leave it to God. This life is wrought by God, without our activity. In the superessential life nothing can hinder us but ourselves. And if something hinders us, then that is only because we have not left ourselves behind.

This life is wrought by God in the human person when this person is standing in his own inner nothingness, without any knowledge of his intelligence and without any life of his spirit (...).[4] God does not allow the spirit or the intelligence to come here, and they cannot come here, however small the hindrance may be.

The inner person can remain here in his own, unhindered by the outer.[5] The outer person can remain in his own, unhindered by the inner, as in eating, drinking, learning, writing, consoling, speaking about the times, etc., if only he does not seek himself or live, etc., in nature or in spirit.

As I said, the intelligence cannot come into that which is wrought in the spirit or beyond the spirit. The human person cannot perceive what is wrought there, as far as it is wrought there, but only as far as it is revealed to him in the spirit and in the intelligence by the Godhead, by the Trinity, etc. Then, he knows what is wrought in him superessentially by God. Here, in this superessential life, the human person can contribute nothing with exercises or activity, as this is purely wrought by God, without any share of us.

When the spirit rises up in love, in such a way that it leaves itself behind, naked in God, and when there is nothing but the pure Godhead, then there is a superessential knowledge and enjoyment in the Godhead, such as in the Trinity the Father is in the Son, etc. This knowledge is not in human knowledge, in a human mode. Here, the human person must remain outside; he is not allowed to touch it. But the human person is attracted to it, especially those who are very intelligent. The spirit and the intelligence flow toward it and have their pleasure there, and reason wants to know it all. When the human person climbs up in the divine light with his spirit and his intelligence, most likely some delusion comes with it. As soon as the devil knows that the human person is flowing toward there with his spirit and his intelligence, and that the spirit lives there, and that it is a pleasure for the intelligence, he shoots his own light in between. He gives the person much knowledge in that light and makes him contemplate high things, and in this light the spirit rejoices and the intelligence becomes lively.

If in this light the human person has no descent in the humanity of Christ, in such a way that he expresses Christ—his humility, his poverty of spirit—and if he has not all the virtues of Christ, yes, if he has not Christ's nothingness, wherein Christ existed, then this light is false, however high it may be. The person must be led away from it and be directed into his nothingness; otherwise it might turn out badly for him. If shrewd people climb up high with their intelligence into the Godhead or into the Trinity, etc., then they must also be led away from it, or else they might lose their mind or destroy their nature. The drive of the spirit is so passionate and all too active; it might destroy even ten bodies. The drive of the spirit is in some people so powerful that it lifts up their external body from the earth.

Some people have also a natural drive toward Christ; they are occupied with his birth, with his passion, etc. When a person is thus led naturally, and his spirit and intelligence have a pleasure in the exterior suffering of Christ, then he should shun all images that are produced in him, however beautiful they may be—even images of Christ's birth or of his passion. Indeed, the spirit would have its life therein, and the intelligence its pleasure and attachment, and as soon as the devil notices this, he can throw his own images into it

170

and show to the human person how Christ has suffered, how he died, etc. But to the resurrection, he cannot come. If these images do not draw the person into the inner experience that was in Christ, such as his nothingness, etc., they are false or given by the devil or produced by a weak sensibility, etc.

When these images occur, the human person should not let them enter into himself, however beautiful they may be, except as far as they lead to Christ, that is, to humility, nothingness, etc. The images as such should be rejected, and one should cleave to the truth, that is, what was in Christ and what is wrought in Christ. It is much nobler that the truth and what was in Christ are introduced without images. This truth and light can be recognized as coming from God, when nothing remains in the spirit or in nature that would give life or pleasure to them. Nothing can live close to that truth and light, or live in them, and nothing can take possession of them. And reason must yield to this light. While there is nothing in the human person that is capable of coming here—neither spirit nor nature nor intelligence—he experiences a sinking in his nothingness. Indeed, spirit, nature, and intelligence have nothing on which they can live or which is a pleasure. And if there is no appropriation, neither in the spirit nor in the nature, then it certainly comes from God.

The human person should lose everything that is born in him or is revealed to him, however high these gifts may be. The faculties can receive them and live on them. However, the faculties cannot receive or grasp God; God can only receive himself—the human person is too small. Therefore, the human person shall lose more and more, so that nothing remains, neither life nor being, appropriating, or knowing, so that all of this is God. Thus God is in what is proper to God, and the human person is in what is proper to him: in God is knowledge, life, and being, and in the human person is his nothingness, where he has arrived. He is not appropriating the things that are wrought in the "highest human person."[6] He appropriates only his nothingness.

When the spirit is standing upright, and when it loses everything, it is taken up by God and is wrought and shaped. Here, the human person cannot be active; he cannot take the initiative or even collaborate. He has to undergo God's work. Yes, he is devoured by

God into the Godhead, and neither the spirit nor the reason know this, as both spirit and reason are too small for that. Though the human person is wrought by God, he does not want to have any knowledge thereof, as it leads him into a knowledge of himself. The more he is wrought by God, the more he receives knowledge of himself, and the more he is alienated from himself and annihilated, the more he is amazed that God is willing to deal with such a poor creature. In such a person is no appropriation; whatever a person can appropriate, he loses it all, and is standing naked from all things, from God and from himself, etc.

These people have no words with which they can express what they receive inwardly. If God wants them to reveal what he works and has wrought, then that light must descend somewhat in the faculties. From there, the person can take what he can express in words. Or God gives him those words. Or those people are referred to the teachers, to find there (in their writings) the word, with which they can express, and the meaning. Thus with their reason and the spirit they remain down and do not fly too high, and consider that they are in time. A human person cannot ascend and grasp God, neither with the letter, nor with all the teachings of the holy teachers, nor with the holy scriptures. Neither the letter nor all understanding of the holy scriptures can enter into God. However, they lead us toward God.

The spirit has its life where it has its pleasure in the gifts of God or in the knowledge of God. Nature has its life in things such as erudition or eloquence, etc. The life of the spirit must be killed too. Now, the spirit can have its life both in ascending and descending. In descending, the spirit can have more than in ascending, for it thinks that this is safer, namely, humility, poverty, etc. Yes, that is because it thinks that it is in the humanity of Christ, and it thinks that who is standing in Christ is standing safely. If the person is not tested by his superiors in this ascent and descent, and if he is not approved, we cannot know whether this ascent or descent comes from God. In case it is from God, it will not be hindered by any creature. If he meets opposition, and he can endure it, he is from God. He will not be hindered by any creature if he is from God.

In case he is not from God—that is, in case this drive comes from the life of the spirit, when the spirit seeks itself, or lives for itself in its ascent or descent—then he succumbs at the opposition of the superiors or the inferiors; he does not endure and gives it up. That is a sign that it was nature or the life of the spirit, and not God. God will not be hindered. Superiors should be very careful on this point; they should not hinder or kill the spirit that is from God. We should act judiciously so that we do not hinder the spirit of God. Initially, when these people have a drive upward to God or in the Godhead, or downward into the humanity of Christ, they should be tested. One shall direct the spirit downward and tell them that it is not fitting for them to taste such high things, that it is not fitting for them while being in time, that they are sinful and failing, etc. And when the person has a drive downward, inclining to follow Christ in poverty, and when the spirit finds its life therein, one should direct him away from that, and direct him toward himself, namely, that he should mortify his shortcomings, and abandon himself.

For some find life in going outward exteriorly when they live in poverty or in misery in order to express Christ. And it seems to them that they are safe and are standing in Christ, though they are standing completely in themselves; yes, they are living in themselves.

It should all be dead, the spirit and nature. However, they should not be killed;[7] there should be no appropriation in the spirit or in the nature. Just as nature should not appropriate anything, neither joy nor sorrow, but should stand equally in poverty and in riches and in all that God disposes, in the same way the spirit should not appropriate anything, and should stand equally in all that is given to the spirit or is taken from it.

The best thing that one can do is to abandon oneself to God and to the superiors, and to appropriate nothing of what is received, whether in nature or in spirit, and to consent to what is good and to reject what is bad.

It is good that the spirit has its life both in being despised, in poverty, etc., and in the ascent of high knowledge and enjoyment of God, or in the gifts of God. But there is something better, namely, that there is no appropriation or life in the spirit, and that the spirit is naked, yes, that it has completely lost itself, and does not know, neither this nor that.

When the spirit is standing upright, directed in God, it has its life there, its taste, and its claims. And when it has there its taste, its life, and its claims, then that is creaturely; it is his own, and thus creaturely. When he is beyond, in what is not his, not seeking, tasting, etc. what is his, then that is God. Nothing can come into God except God. When he has the impression of coming into God, and when he lives there or tastes something with which he wants to remain, then he is not in God, nor is he standing in God. When a person is standing in God, there is no preference. Then the person is standing in all that God wants for him, namely, to follow Christ in his weakness and to know his nothingness. That is his highest joy; there he knows Christ and his life, and that is most pleasing to God.

The higher the spirit climbs in God—that is, the higher he is taken up in God or in the Godhead—the lower his exterior person descends into the humanity of Christ. Christ is God and man, and the one is not separated from the other. In the same way these two (movements) cannot be separated. Where the one is separated from the other, the person is an Antichrist, opposed to Christ, and he does not come to the Father, that is, in the origin. In case the person has a drive that drives both equally—the spirit in God and the external person in the humanity of Christ—then the drive comes from God. In case the spirit is driven in the one, but without the other, then it is from nature, or it is a false light that leads us to ourselves and not to the Father.

If we will taste God or know something (of him), then we need to know in Christ, that is, that we are in Christ. Christ testifies that this is true. No one knows the Father except the Son, and anyone to whom the Son chooses to reveal Him (Matt 11:27). Now, the Son reveals the Father there where the Father is well pleased, and the Father only finds his pleasure in the Son (cf. Matt 3:17). If we are not in the Son, that is, if we have not put on Christ (Eph 4:24), then we do not please the Father and do not come to Christ. No one comes to Christ unless he is drawn by the Father, as Christ teaches (cf. John 6:44). Thus, we do not know anything at all about God (outside of Christ), however high or mysterious the words we speak, or however high we are elevated. Christ is known in Christ's life. When we have Christ's life, we know Christ, or the Son. And if we know Christ, then we know the Father also, because the Father is known in and through Christ, as the One is never without the Other.

# CLAESINNE VAN NIEUWLANT

This we should know: where Christ's life is, or where Christ is, there is no appropriation concerning all that happens to the exterior or interior person. And this becomes agreeable, for the sake of its own dignity, and not because something else can be attained by it. Where something else is, Christ is not, nor his life. Where Christ's life is, there is Christ, and nowhere else. Whoever asserts differently is a liar, and whoever has another opinion is deceived.

# Alijt Bake
## *Four Ways of the Cross*[1]

Alijt Bake (1415–55) most likely grew up in or near Utrecht in a
family of means.[2] As a young woman she was active in society but also pursued an intense spiritual life, consulting with a recluse and collaborating
with a hospice sister. About the year 1440, aged twenty-five (past the ordinary age for either marriage or the novitiate), she resolved to try religious
life at a house newly founded (1431) in Ghent. Galilee had just formally
incorporated with the canonesses of Windesheim, the professed branch of
the movement known as the Modern Devotion, and installed Hille
Sonderlants, an aged veteran of the movement, as prioress. Alijt Bake,
upon her arrival, descended into great spiritual and personal turmoil:
whether to stay; whether to try the house of Colette, a reforming Clare
establishment (also in Ghent); whether to profess religious life at all.
Sonderlants, together with other sisters, attempted to impose a disciplined
ascetic regime quite other than this restless spiritual seeker either expected
or intended. Here is how Bake recalled it in 1451:

> They feared that I wanted to fly all too high, wanted perfection
> all too quickly, and so would be deceived. They counseled me
> strongly against this way and, as best they could, put me off
> from it, saying that I should turn toward getting to know my
> faults and overcoming them and toward useful acts of external
> service. This is what was proper to the young and inexperi-
> enced, not these high things. They spoke to me frequently and
> a great deal, and they scorned me and my words and acts, and
> disparaged them. And because I could turn to the things they
> set out only with difficulty, they accordingly became displeased
> with me and dissatisfied, since I was so drawn inward to the
> things that God was teaching me from within. They con-
> demned me as wise in my own eyes (eighenwijs) and conceited
> in myself, and as believing myself and the feelings of myself to

176

*be better than anyone else's, and thus stuck on myself and liv-
ing in myself and, in short, to be nothing other than a woman
who had taken herself into her own hands. Things of this sort
they said often.*[3]

*On Sunday, December 18, 1440, she acquired and read* The Book
of the Nine Rocks *by Rulman Merswin, the converted merchant of
Strassburg around whom the Friends of God had formed and to whom
Friar John Tauler had ministered. A week later, Christmas 1440, a vision
persuaded her to stay in Galilee and enter the novitiate. A more significant vision on the vigil of the Ascension in 1441 yielded a definitive spiritual breakthrough, at least as she retold it a decade later in her spiritual
autobiography. After making profession at the end of 1441, she lived as a
canoness for three years, and then was elected prioress, to succeed
Sonderlants, about March 1445. She served for ten years as head of her
community, a house slated for sixteen posts that grew to a hundred souls by
1465, certainly in part under her leadership. In the late spring of 1455
visitors from the order summarily removed her from office and also ban-
ished her, probably to the house in Antwerp. The formal concerns turned
on her mystical teachings, though there may also have been discontent
among some of the sisters. She protested her deposition in writing and
through channels, to no avail, and died in exile not long after, on October
18, 1455, aged forty.*
*In fifteen short years Alijt Bake copied, wrote, and taught: copied
materials as her way of appropriating them spiritually (especially Tauler
and Jordan of Quedlinburg); wrote materials, some quite independent in
tone, some riffs on her reading; and taught her sisters as their prioress.
Modern scholars have only discovered her and her writings in the last generation, and we possess, alas, no proper critical edition, and not even full
agreement on her corpus.*[4] *Beyond a set of conferences, or talks to her sisters, usually set at four (with no agreement even on that), we have the
lengthy second half of a spiritual autobiography (properly, "On My
Beginnings and Progress"), a letter from exile, a number of fragments,
possibly a very long work (a "teaching") on the passion, the only item to
reach print (anonymously in 1514), and the work translated here, called*
The Four Ways of the Cross. *(Virtually none of Bake's work, inciden-
tally, came with titles, most being the concoctions of her editor, Bernhard
Spaapen.)* Four Ways of the Cross, *scholars agree, had the largest manu-*

*script transmission (five copies), encapsulates the heart of her teaching, and was rooted in her spiritual struggles (with complex points of connection, therefore, to her spiritual autobiography, which cannot be taken up here). We have the work, moreover, in a manuscript widely held to be in her own hand, certainly from her own house, Galilee (Brussels, Royal Library, MS 643–44). A disputed colophon dates it to 1446, the year after she became prioress. But the entire manuscript tradition of* Four Ways *yields at least three versions, some variations slight, some significant. Spaapen chose not to use the manuscript from Galilee, the possible autograph, relegating its readings to the apparatus on the grounds that it displayed too many "mistakes" and "sloppiness" and another manuscript was "easier to ready."*[5]

*I would prefer to take an author at her word, even if that word was an early one later clarified or polished. But it is not possible here to redo the editorial work. In the main I have translated the text Spaapen presented in 1966 but opted on occasion for readings from the Galilee manuscript (as reported in the apparatus) that strike me as sounder. Alijt Bake, a passionate and original thinker, was not as rhetorically gifted as some medieval Dutch religious prose writers. She can be verbose, contorted, obscure, and not always easy to translate. Like other medieval writers, she used the equivalent of* thereby *and* therein *regularly (thinned here), and the connective* and *to begin sentences (also thinned). Bake generally employed the third-person masculine* (hij) *in the older generic sense of "man"* (mensch), *thus "person." Because she was addressing her sisters ("my beloved"), I have generally used "she." Otherwise, I have tried to be true to her language while generating an intelligible English translation. Spaapen introduced paragraph divisions and numbers. I retain the numbers, for ease of reference, but sometimes divide the paragraphs differently.*

*The* Four Ways *must date from before 1446 (the manuscript of Galilee) and may distill the heart of Alijt Bake's spiritual breakthrough on Ascension Day 1441—at least so scholars have often assumed. With that spiritual transformation, to put it now in terms of her teaching, she moved beyond the first two ways and then the third, all oriented toward ordinary souls, including the sisters who did not understand or approve of her. The fourth way, the heart of this work (also two-thirds of its length), resonates with her own deep spiritual trial, an anguishing experience of God, or rather of being forsaken, of dying again on the cross. At the end she takes up an "easier way" and relatively clearly refers to spiritual experiences among her sisters that she regarded as less than they seemed, also*

*less than the real encounter she had made her way through—a point she
did not hesitate to make more or less explicitly to them. Readers may judge
for themselves.*

# FOUR WAYS OF THE CROSS

[(1) These are the four ways of the cross that each should
enter upon who wishes to follow Christ Jesus in spirit in
order to be crucified with him in spirit.][6]

(2) The person who is crucified with inward and genuine co-
suffering in likeness with Christ, is well-armed against her Enemy
and can escape all his evil and extraordinary punishing. As it stands
written in the Apocalypse, the angel was commanded to spare no
one who did not have the sign upon his forehead.[7] This cross [the
sign]—has four points, and that signifies to us that we must walk in
the passion of our Lord in four ways if we wish to arrive at the perfection of our Lord Jesus Christ.

(3) The First Way: that in our hearts we should exercise sweetly
the passion of our dear Lord with good thoughts and try to spend our
time usefully in that. This works great benefits in those who steadily
make an effort to exercise, because they spend their time usefully and
drive away all alien illusions and useless worries. It makes the heart
full and steady and rouses the heart of a person to the love of God,
moved by devotion and interior compassion, and draws a person away
from all idleness and rashness and empty society and idle tale-telling.
She keeps herself quiet in the passion of Christ, which tastes better to
her than all other things. This way is most fruitful, as you have heard,
and makes for great readiness to progress to the next way, which is far
more fruitful if a person practices it wisely.

(4) The next way leads much higher and deeper still into the
ground,[8] with greater and more interior devotion, and draws the
heart so deeply into God, with such great co-suffering that she sometimes thinks that she is present there where the actions of the passion
took place, and that she feels them also in her, both spiritually and
naturally, the interior suffering and the exterior suffering of Christ,
sometimes the exterior alone, sometimes the interior alone, and

179

sometimes both together, which is the most powerful. (5) But that exterior natural suffering without the interior is not the most powerful, even if it should effect powerful things. Because the interior is in every way the very best and most noble, and produces accordingly more fruit because it leads deeper into God, in knowledge of the hidden secrets of God that she knows and tastes and becomes, not only according to his humanity but also according to his divinity. (6) And this penetrates all the powers of a person, exterior and interior, with such great inwardly penetrating, good-tasting feelings and co-suffering that some also receive in their [bodily] natures open signs of the passion of Christ, such as St. Francis and St. Catherine of Siena did. It seems clear that they exercised themselves markedly in the passion of our Lord earlier, before the signs were conferred upon them. And the person who thus inwardly exercises this holy passion, in such a person many a hidden wonder transpires. She knows those hidden things of which other people, who have not gone down this way, have little knowledge.

(7) This way works much fruit in human beings, above the other of which we first spoke, because this way puts to death in a person all sinful movements in her nature so that she is entirely changed into another person, just as it stands written in the Book of the Kings that Saul was changed into another man (cf. 1 Sam 16:14). Because all the things that earlier were pleasurable and desirous for him, so he thought that he neither might nor could leave them, those same things become for him now as a bitter sea and a heavy cross and a torment, such that he not only forgets all alluring desire and lust toward those things, but he also knows not to do these things and would rather die a bitter death than to do these things or consent to them. And not only does this die in him; he also cannot bear to have other people doing it. He becomes entirely unused to it and is disturbed by anyone who does it, and admonishes them and reproves them sweetly and chastises them, as best he can, that they no longer do it. (8) More, in him there is such a great desire and love for the salvation of his fellow human's soul that he would happily die a bitter, shameful death, no matter how bitter and shameful it was, for the preservation of that human being.

With this high penetrating inner compassion and love for God and his fellow human being, so a person comes to the third way of

Christ's passion. (9) Nonetheless it [the second] is the highest or the purest, and the most secure, not only in which to remain but in which to advance further, because the two others, that now follow, lead still higher, to more purity and likeness to Christ, as will be explained hereafter, if God gives it. (10) Still, the present way, however great and high and elect it may be, as you have heard, has two shortcomings or hindrances, which are most harsh and damaging; for which reason it is less than the two other ways that follow hereafter. And with this the Adversary gains power and strength over a person, to deceive and draw her toward harmful things.

(11) Here are the two shortcomings of these [first two] ways. The first is that a person is easily undone and throws herself thereby underfoot and becomes useless, because she possesses and employs no discretion in these matters but follows, without discretion, any way that strikes her and her passionate desires. In this way she so ruins and sickens her natural powers that her internal spiritual powers also are sickened and overcome, a good head and a strong heart vanquished together in great sickness and impatience, so that she can suffer nothing adverse or untoward. Thus she becomes so seriously upset that she falls into all sorts of failings and into great sins such as murmuring and evil suspicion, judging others and gossiping, and feels displeasure and dissatisfaction toward others. She becomes sour and hardhearted and worthless, also quite contrary with many little complaints, scolding anyone around her, never satisfied with what someone does for her. And thus she is wearisome to herself and all those around her, and she cannot and often will not put up with anyone else. She says, "My head and my senses are sick," and thus thinks that others must give in to her and bear with her. Over time she thereby becomes useless for all good and genuinely spiritual exercises, and people have to flatter her or coax her like a child. Look, my dearly beloved. The failing, even much more than a person can say, comes about here because the person has exercised no discretion and good judgment in [following] these ways. (12) The other point is this: Such persons remain without knowledge of themselves, and also without overcoming the ground of all self-possession.[9] And for that reason the Adversary has power over them, so he can bring them into greater illness, because, since self-possession still lives in them,

they expend accordingly greater effort and are never satisfied. But where self-will is truly uprooted and purged, there the Adversary will have no power over them. Because the Holy Spirit will teach well in the utterly pure ground how she should uphold herself wisely and with discernment and how she should employ it profitably. He has then no power arising from self-possession. (13) Because so many hidden snares lie here, this is not the highest or noblest or purest way. The more progress a person has in it, so also the far greater hidden self-possession she gathers to herself and fixes in her ground, because she thinks she has come to the very highest and has intended the very best. And for that reason she remains hanging on it and cleaving to it and uses it as her own peculiar good and will not allow herself to be counseled or taught by the Spirit of God from within or from other human beings without, because she thinks she has intended the very best that can be. And hereby such persons remain in their self-possession and do many great faults in their ground, which they recognize precious little, and thus remain outside the very best and noblest. (14) They imagine nonetheless that they have intended the very best and noblest and hold themselves to be closer to God and higher than anyone else who does not have this way—people who, however, are much nearer to God in perfect purity and utter virtue than they. Even if the others seem much poorer and dryer and barren in graces, and also have many temptations and adversities, they nonetheless come far nearer to God by way of their humble submissive ground[10] and the going out of their selves, when they pray to God both in their pleasing and their failing. And so let us use this way with wisdom and discernment so that we do not come into such a sinful life.

(15) The Third Way of the passion is more fruitful than the other ways of which we have spoken. It is measured and well-ordered and leads entirely inward into the living innermost (*die levende binnenste*)[11] of our Lord Jesus, where the spirit of a person is sweetly and gently drawn in and illumined with divine clarity. There, thus, she enters the *sancta sanctorum*[12] and sees there the hiddenness of God, which no one is allowed to see other than a person who attempts to make herself fit by way of a total dying in her ground and a total outgoing of herself in all that is not entirely pure God. And to this fittingness belong three points.

182

(16) The first is that a person must have purity of heart. This purity is such that in all her turning toward she does not seek or think of anything other than utterly pure God, to work for his eternal honor and to discover his dearest will and to bring it to completion with the help of God.

(17) The next is that she must be so humble in her ground that she may never exalt herself, above all in that great good that God shows her.

(18) The third is that she must have an assiduous diligence toward all these exercises, wherever that may take her, and turn herself with goodly gentleness inwardly to God, and take up the life or suffering of our Lord or something else that she has seen or heard, whatever it may be she thinks best draws her toward the salvation of her soul.

Then lift her heart in humble and interior prayer to our dear Lord, to render her heart and senses apt, praying God that he will reveal and make manifest to her the hiddenness of his secret wisdom and divine glory, also what his intentions and desires are, what he desires of us, and what we should understand therein for our teaching, so we might be pleasing to his eternal honor and praise. Then say, "O Lord, illumine my eyes, so that I may not sleep in death, so that my Adversary may not say 'I have had power over this one.'" Then set yourself down with a sweet and gentle heart, as comfortably as you can, and say, "Now speak, Lord, your poor servant or maidservant is listening to your voice."[13] And then take up several good exercises, of which we have already spoken,[13] but without any self-possession. And see then what the Lord will do, and perceive what he will speak in you. Where he leads or draws you, follow him there good-heartedly and simply, hoping and trusting that he will not lead you badly, because all those whom he leads cannot be deceived, and those who allow themselves to be lead by him cannot remain lost or deceived in eternity.

(19) And if it should be that he then leads you into his living innermost and into his open loving heart, into which he would happily draw all human hearts should they want to follow him, that happens best through the secret ways of his most holy passion, where he will show you the most secret treasure of his heart. These will he give you to know: how you should understand and enjoy all

things, how you should walk in the rightful truth to live rightly for him and for yourself without hindrance or any betrayal, with right discernment. And thus you would become so subtle and wise that all your adversaries could not draw near or deceive you with all their harsh evil. (20) There too nothing may come to dwell in you that displeases God, as you may well on occasion become aware. Because Christ, who is your guide and your master, will not allow you to keep it hidden. He shows it to you himself, so that his beloved will not be deceived. Because he would be ashamed of that, and may not let that be, since you trusted in him with a brave heart. And because you did not seek or intend or love for any reason other than to please him and to do fully his dear will, so your eyes are simple and your heart is pure. And for that reason he must also do fully that which he promised, saying, Blessed are they who are pure of heart, for they shall see God (cf. Matt 5:8). And in seeing God, so they see in him the full truth of all things. And for this reason, likewise, they cannot be betrayed.

(21) O most beloved, learn thus this way of fulfillment, and learn to lift your spirit inwardly up to the living innermost of our Lord Jesus Christ. Because there you will find all that is useful and needful for you both from without and within. Also, that there will be no need for you to seek consolation from any strangers, or any help outside of him, nor as well any books to study other than the loving heart of our Lord and his living innermost. There alone you will find more good and trustworthy teaching than you will be able to find in all the books of the world and in all human beings. Because he is the sweet fountain in which they must and may all dip their buckets and from which they draw if they want to have or obtain anything. St. Paul said that in Christ are all the treasures of wisdom and of knowledge to draw from (Col 2:3). You should also know that I have had no other library than this. So, what is lacking in myself or in other people, or what I find in books that I cannot understand, all that I draw up wholly out of the innermost of our Lord Jesus Christ.[14]

(22) He is mild and merciful and gives gladly all that we shall desire, so that we also always desire his honor and praise and nothing else. And if it happens that he does not give what we desire at once, still trust him nonetheless that he will give it or he will accom-

plish it himself in us when we do not know it. And thus I obtain from him all that I desire and all that is needful for me and for all my society. For that reason, my beloved, learn also to walk in this way with contentment so you may also be enlightened from within. (23) If you have these three points in you of which we have spoken, and you are thus prepared as is written above, and you have a certain easiness in the bodily nature, and in addition are nicely at ease there where the grace of God dwells in you together with the purity of heart of which we have spoken, then I know nothing that may be lacking in you of all that is useful and needful. Because this person may find a miracle, yes indeed, more than any person has found since the time of our dear Lady Mary. Because he can go walking in the living innermost of our Lord, just as a nobleman goes walking in his court gardens with his friend, and converses with him, and examines the state of all the trees and the herbs. Just exactly so does a person go walking in the living innermost of our Lord, or with our dear Lady, or any of the other good saints whom he loves. He seeks there the truth face to face and goes walking there, asking and answering, and is sweetly taught and set right about all that he desires, (24) because Christ has promised in the Gospels where he says: Ask and you shall receive, seek and you shall find, knock and it shall it opened to you (Matt 7:7). Truly, Christ does not lie. If you will then seek and knock and ask about the above-noted points, such as purity of heart and humility and diligence in these exercises, see, thus you may obtain this great light and hidden divine wisdom that will teach you all things and instruct you in all things. It will make you so subtle that all the wickedness of the Adversary, of the evil natures, and of hidden self-possession, which tarnishes the interior ground and whereby the Devil gains power over a person in order thereby to betray him, will not prevail. May you do all good exercises with proper discernment to the eternal honor of God without deceit or vexation.

(25) The evil Fiend thus flees before such a person, and looks for a way, as truly as he can, to draw other people away as well, those who would learn virtue from her, as she can or may. Because when other people come into the presence of this enlightened person, their wickedness will become manifest. Then the Enemy shames himself that he has thus become known, and he loses his power and

must depart in great confusion. See now, my beloved, if you now have this way, so may you become most fruitful to holy church, not alone in your selves but also in many other people, for whom you may be helpful and understanding with your prayers, with divine teaching and good discernment, and make them participatory, in meek and true charity, of all the good that you have received in that hidden *sancta sanctorum*, and gain thereby other people for that same place wherein you have dwelt, just as St. Paul and other friends of God have done. And thus may you become fruitful and make another fruitful.

(26) With this way you enjoy the use of the other two afore-said ways wisely and discerningly, without any deceptions and with-out any loss to your body or your senses. And for that reason hold to this way with the others. So may you remain standing, and you will learn much higher and subtler and more certain ways, that you otherwise should never know, wherein you may become most like Christ. And that is the way that follows hereafter to the honor of God ever blessed.

(27) This Fourth Way: it surpasses all the aforementioned ways and brings a person to the greatest perfection and likeness to Christ that may be in this life. But this way is very unlike the other three. Because all that was exercised in them must here be left behind, because this way does not lead upward in exercises of enlightening and of tasting and of enjoying, but downward in let-ting be and suffering and a purer love,[15] for the eternal honor of God and to his praise, just as Christ offered all his works to the honor of his eternal Father. (28) Here the good that a person had enjoyed and tasted earlier falls away and becomes entirely nothing and dies in the death of our Lord Jesus, just it was obtained earlier by way of that same death. Because for the very reason that she ear-lier went upward and desired to know and to taste, for that same reason she now goes downward and desires that she now suffer and let be. She is thereby brought into great darkness and desolation and dryness and into as great poverty and misery as she once was rich, indeed, so that she thinks that she has on occasion returned to the world and draws nearer to the gates of death than of life.[16] Because it seems to her that the very greatest sinner in the world has more taste and trust in God in her conscience by way of good

prayers or the works she does, which are very small, no matter how small they are, than she does.

(29) So she goes along in this way hours at a time, years and days, withering and drying up, tormented and shriveling up, utterly consumed in all her powers without and also within, because the bodily nature and also the reason have nothing of their own, and must die and sink into ruin from loving the death of our Lord Jesus Christ. From this there grows within a person such a great pressure that she does not know what to let be or to do or where to turn, because she is so amazingly anxious and so distressed in spirit that she thinks she must die, or that she will lose her senses, or she will not be able to bear it. Still, she thinks she would gladly suffer it for the love of God, if she knew that it was pleasing to God. But that she does not know, and she becomes sorely tempted to seek help and counsel in anything that might help and enlighten her. (30) And if she should have come to this way properly in the advancing light by way of the third aforementioned way, all this consolation and all the help and understanding that may come for her from other persons stands in opposition to this ground. If she takes some of it up as her aid, there grows in her still more anxiety and suffering than in those who have acted contrary to the truth. Because the noble ground testifies to her that it must be suffered if she is in any way to come to perfection. And for this reason she experiences great distress, that she has done the exact wrong and rather offended God from within by the very means by which she should have gained him. That is very damaging, and far more than she recognizes, for a great miracle should have happened there, had she suffered it through, because she should have been remade into the image of God by way of this interior suffering. (31) So they deceive themselves very much, those who, as soon as they feel and become aware of the anxiety and pressure within, return to what they have left and thus help themselves and drive away within themselves that reproach of God, that saving interior suffering. Then they think that it a good thing, well done; they are quit of it, and remain further in their good external appearance that they had assumed earlier. Oh, my beloved, you deceive yourselves deeply and do yourself all too great harm, and damage yourself in a very great good. And that is a great sorrow.

(32) For this reason it is also too bad that so few people come to this high and most noble good, because they remain entirely lost in things that are outward and appear good in themselves, and they do not pass over into this superessential good that goes beyond all the senses. This comes about because people want all too much knowing and co-working in things, which cannot be; because here a person cannot have co-knowing and co-working, large or small, but must allow herself to be led and overtaken by the spirit of God, and work in this wild wilderness in which she has arrived, in which she cannot stand by herself, or remain there with her own self knowing or co-working, or bring in any fruit. And for this reason she must on occasion resign herself entirely to God and let him command her, and direct all things out of right love for God until she grasps it and saves herself. She never saves herself before God himself saves her. And in so doing the true life may be born out of you, which you may obtain in no other way than by letting be and suffering, and that for the love of God. (33) Oh, this must indeed be a desert way, a wild and barren and dry way, which is altogether contrary to the others, because in the others there is always knowing and co-working, tasting and feeling. And that does not exist here.

(34) In truth, if for a time she hears or sees something that touches her spirit owing to its similitude, she would feel quite awful, exactly as if she were about to faint. It comes from the ravishing and luxurious indulgence of her spirit, wherein she will be consoled and strengthened even if the lowest faculty of reason does not know what it is, and imagines that it is temptation and should not follow it and is thus also quite undone. Oh, my beloved, I will tell you what it is and what this wants to be so that you alone will hold to this wretched way. Otherwise you can have in this no solace or help. For that reason do not drive it away but follow where it leads and suffer all that happens to you.

(35) You should stand fast in this and in still another point, which here follows. That is this: a simple inner speech *(inspreken)*[17] in the ground of a person, in the innermost part of her heart, where God himself speaks to the spirit of a person and gives her a sure testimony to what she should do or let be in all that concerns her, whether from without or from within. In this ground no deception can come, so long as she otherwise stands rightly and well ordered

toward God, because there God himself speaks and indicates to her his dear will. Should a person then perceive this and follow him in it, she will become more and more enlightened from within and strengthened to go forward in this wretched way. (36) Indeed, where a person is not well ordered toward God and in addition does not allow God to speak there and to indicate his dear will to the person—because it does not satisfy the two lower dimensions of a person, that is, the reason and [bodily] nature—she then receives nothing or she notices nothing, and the person is thus deprived with respect to her highest blessedness, remaining in whatever state or grade she is. Should all people diligently perceive and act accordingly, they would not thereby be deceived, especially those who walk in the fourth way of the cross. Because God is eternally and essentially united thereto, such that he does not separate himself therefrom, indeed even from the damned. Because just as he admonishes and testifies to and teaches a person what he should do and what let be according to his dearest will, so likewise God reproves and reproaches the damned in harsh follow-up to a person who was not subject in this life and often did not carry out his dear will.

(37) This simple inner speech is very straightforward and gentle, sweet and good-hearted, full of peace and rest, thus counseling a person, drawing and leading her toward letting be and suffering out of love for God, thus strengthening a person and consoling her in faith and hope and to trust in God and toward all virtue. This is a secret whispering into (inruinen)[18] the heart, to which reason must listen closely if it is to do and understand well what it means to communicates, and to follow it, because it speaks quietly and simply. It is a voice without words, born of God into the spirit of a person, but giving witness, awakening and renewing desire, speaking beyond any reason. But should it happen that the reason at once understands with desire and follows in order to understand what [the voice] is and what it is indicating, so may she be enlightened and gloriously instructed, her faith and hope and all her inner powers strengthened, also her natural [bodily] powers enlightened, consoled, so that she consents and follows after the reason and the spirit. Thus both reason and [bodily] nature will be drawn into the spirit, and the spirit then draws them both to God, and thus will they be all fulfilled as things demand. And thus will you be entirely

189

united with God both in body and soul, because the soul will be united to God according to the Godhead, because it is capable of grasping God, and the bodily nature will become perfect in virtue and united with the bodily nature of Christ. Thus will a person become entirely godly, to the extent that this happens. And this can always happen in all matters wherein her reason or her bodily nature or both together bow under and are overcome with respect to the straightforward and simple counsel and witness of the spirit, who is ruled by no one other than God her creator.

(38) For this person nothing is as necessary and useful as that whole encounter that is so contrary to her reason and bodily nature. For there come illusions in which she has mightily to suffer that are not from God or from human beings or the Devil or one's own illness, however wondrous and alien in appearance, yes even contrary to God and to virtue according to the test of her reason but not by the witness of the spirit. Because the spirit testifies to her all the time that it must be so if she is to come to perfect victory over herself, which she very much wishes and God wants her to have and which cannot be otherwise. So he counsels a person that she should simply and plainly let go in all things and suffer out of rightful love for God, and await good-heartedly and patiently the end of all things, believing and trusting wholly in God, that he will not leave her, and even if he should wish to leave her, that she would still in herself freely be consoled, to the eternal glory of God.

(39) See now, to this and things like it the spirit testifies from within in all these wondrous things, matters a person should closely perceive and truly follow if she wants to remain standing in this wondrous way and to increase in virtue without succumbing to a collapse of powers and an outburst of temptation and interior suffering. (40) If she well and truly does this, she has no desperation because she has help and consolation enough in these two. That is, to know that luxurious indulgence of spirit when it hears something compatible to it, when the bodily nature well would go faint, as was written a little earlier. This singular testimony of the spirit, which happens most richly for a person, and is also most profitable for her should a person perceive and follow it speedily and consent to it—from it she will quickly discover what fruit may thus come for her.

(41) Then she should see well that no necessity should drive her to run out to other people to ask for consolation and help or to learn something or to want to take on certain exercises that are contrary to this. However good they may appear or be, they will impede her and take away the genuine birth that should be happening. That would do very great harm, because God wants, with these wondrous and desolating ways, to reduce a person entirely to nothing in herself and thereby to remake her and draw her wholly into himself, or he wants to humble himself and descend into this person and himself take possession of the ground of the person, which can happen in no way so perfectly with any other exercises than to walk in this way. (42) And this does not happen in knowing or in feeling or in tasting but in letting be and in suffering, where love is exercised most highly and nobly in everything that a person might do. Such a person stands entirely loose and free from all consolation and keeping, within and without, and finds nothing that may help or console her, because she thinks that she has been overthrown and abandoned by God and, moreover, isolated from all other people and dwelt in by all sins and faults. Further, in all this she will hardly know what she should confess and can feel no remorse for her sins. If she had that, she might have received at least some consolation. This she cannot bear, and so she is intensely pained. And if she should lament her despair to someone or ask for counsel in order to gain help, there arises immediately in her a new anxiety greater than ever before, because the noble ground cannot suffer it. It objects and says that she should let it be and suffer and be satisfied with the witness of the spirit, that God will never withdraw as long as she does not will to put up resistance with a perverted will and she regularly scorns the advice of the Devil where that often goes contrary to the lower reason. (43) If she were to do that, she then would fall into greater impatience [with suffering] and into ruin altogether and take away from herself the glorious birth that should be happening there, had she suffered it through according to the testimony of the spirit. And for that reason a person should perceive from within the simple and the plain, and consent at once out of love that leads directly to honor of God, and flee at once this impatient not-suffering that is so disordered in a human person.

(44) She receives a sweet anointing in her soul and a becomingness in her bodily nature under the will of God. And so on each

journey a new birth contents the human being for a time, yes, even if the person for a time remains burdened with these most amazing temptations and this suffering that has to be, also all these alien and cursed thoughts, this murmuring and arguing against God, because he decreed so much hard suffering should come over her, and he had imposed this testing on her so long and so harshly and so variously and wondrously and strangely that the person in all these things does not know what to do or let be, because she does not know what the will of God is. If she had known that the will of God were such, she would have been, in suffering, consoled and at peace, however wondrous or great it was. But because she did not think this way since she finds herself deprived of God and all the virtues, in keeping with her assumption that he was customarily there in the other three ways, she comes to think that she is entirely misguided and deceived. And so this was for her a great and difficult suffering.

(45) The more she is in poverty and suffering, she does not see how anxious this makes her and works against her, so much so she thinks she will die or lose her senses. And see, then there comes to her sometimes a tiny witness from within, from the very depths of her ground, that testifies to her and says, "See, be at peace with this and suffer, because God has foreseen in eternity that this must be so and that you must have it so, because it is the will of God and may not be otherwise." Then it occurs to the person how often in the time of grace she has desired this from God, and similar things. These and similar things enlightened her already truly in the ground and testified fully to the spirit of the person in order to console her and strengthen her in the faith and also in the hope that a person must diligently perceive and keep herself, and so let all those other matters quickly go which are contrary to it, however good or reasonable they may appear in the person's eyes. But you should quickly follow this simple and plain witness, (46) and see what light is indicated to you wherein to walk, and then you will soon be fully enlightened, saved, and consoled in all your members. As soon as that witness is desired and consented to by you and you remain with it, all temptations and darkness fall away from you. And you will be lifted up with faith, hope, and love for God, and will be so deeply submerged in God that you become one with him. And this is sometimes even indicated with a marvelous light for which there is no expression. But for that per-

son who finds this in herself, she has something of a taste of the eternal life, which is God himself, just as genuinely as she will hereafter possess and enjoy that eternal life in unity.

(47) Here, in this light, the kingdom of God will be clearly revealed for this person, and that as perfectly and as fully as any person may obtain and taste in this life, so that this person [experiences] these two things as the testing of that luxurious spirit through which she could very nearly fall into a faint or on occasion become unconscious, as was said above. Some imagine this as temptation because it is a matter of mere feeling alone and not of knowing. If a person simply follows it without fear, she will become aware of what it was and what it meant, because it will bring her to great light, consolation, strength, and assurance.

(48) The other thing of which we have spoken [the inner speech] is better known and works in greater clarity and in a nobler light with more discretion in the reasoning powers than does the other, and it will also be renewed and united with the spirit. This is more common and more fruitful and has as such not so much expression as the first. With it a person may well remain hidden outwardly before people, if she wishes that, and be satisfied with this inner speech, and simply and plainly follow it in all dimensions and testimonies of the spirit.

Thus will she doubtless survive without fear and without anyone's help or counsel, because she has help and counsel enough in these two, so long as she indeed truly follows. They will give her light and taste enough, which go far beyond all light and taste in this poor sickly life. Oh, how high and noble is this light and taste, that go above all that was touched upon in the three ways. It goes as far beyond what was written about above, as God is higher and nobler than all angels and all created beings.

(49) And so, my beloved, always see to it that you discover in yourselves and perceive these two points written out above. Wherever you have been borne, follow him and be subject to him in all things, wherever it may lead and draw you, and so you will not be deceived or ruined, either in spirit or in bodily nature. Believe him in truth, and that one whom it has visited and has written about it and by the grace of God was first all surprised by such great wonders—and indeed still a hundred times more such wondrous things than I

193

have written to you, or indeed would be able to express in written word or by mouth, because it is not to write out with a pen or to express with the tongue, but nonetheless allows itself to be found in this. For this was not found out with regular exercises. They [other people] do not want to believe many such things but think them unbelievable and untruthful and ornamented. So, no one should judge it, but let God rule all things and let him become and work in all things and creatures, as he wishes; he does not sin. And so, if it may be so and I may pray you so, simply hold to the two points written above, and then you should not, by the grace of God that lives in you, collapse. For this is that pure, sheer work of a pure spirit that God wants to give you as consolation and as help and progress in this life to stay straight in this way, so that you may be kept in this life enlightened, consoled, strengthened. For without consolation you cannot live in this life or remain standing in these things.

(50) So, God wants hereby to console you and keep you whole. All other solace and support and help you must be rid of, as well as all busyness with work and all that still lives in you by having preferences in this or in that, or in something that someone does for you, and in matters where you have favorites in some person or in certain things, yes indeed, however great or holy that person was or how holy that work is. (51) Because the sweet Comforter, the Holy Ghost, wants to have you alone to himself and wants to preserve but two works in you. The one is idleness, and that you have to do. From within make yourself entirely idle from all that is not pure God or from anything that is not in itself authentic. It must all be rendered idle and gotten rid of. (52) Then comes the second point, which she has to do herself. That is to realize this way, here to increase in letting be and in suffering and in forbearance with all things that God appoints for us. In this way we are rendered idle with respect to what might have been a hindrance for us toward God. Then the sweet Holy Spirit is realized in us in himself and in all good things and with greater assurance. If for you the movement of the Spirit is enough, then God will make manifest to you such light and grace that for you there is no need to ask counsel of anyone else or to seek help from outside.

(53) In this way, my beloved, may you remain standing in the way wherein you have begun to walk, and not otherwise. You will

assuredly and gloriously progress in the way of the virtues without anyone's help or support, and remain unknown to people. Oh, see, my most dearly beloved, in this alien, wondrous, wild, deserted, barren, dry, poor, wretched way, more authentic good is promised than is contemplated in all the others, even if it is true that they envision and grasp in the spirit this high noble life and being. But there [with them] only matters of feelings and of beings are attained.

(54) In this way you will be set rightly in the footsteps of our Lord Jesus Christ, those he stood in that night when he had to begin to suffer his bitter passion for our sakes. Then he became so grieved in spirit and said to his Father, "Father, look upon the distress of your beloved son, and if it be possible, let this cup pass from my suffering so that I do not drink it. But still, Father, your will must be done and not mine" (Matt 26:39). Christ here thus envisioned all the suffering that was to come upon him, and he willingly gave himself over to it, even though it [touched] him in his noble tender nature so that out of anxiety and fear he would sweat water and blood. Then an angel stood by him, strengthening and consoling him, and said, "O Lord, this work belongs to you and is fitting for you alone to do and no one else, and it is a worthy thing that you alone should do this service to your heavenly Father to redeem your people." (55) Then our dear Lord stood up and went willingly to meet his adversary with a joyful face, and said to Judas, "Friend, to what end have you come here?" (Matt 26: 50). And to the Jews he said, "Whom do you seek?" And they said, "Jesus of Nazareth." And he said, "I am he, and because you know that I am he, take me alone" (cf. John 18:5, 8). Just as if he would say, "Do with me anything that you want." Then they received much power over him to do with him all that they wanted, and not before. (56) Because then he [first] abandoned himself in his ground, and then was he first abandoned from above to himself. The lowest faculties of his humanity and his reason had to suffer through all this wonder in his lowest powers. But the uppermost and highest faculties of his humanity, which were God, did not have to suffer, because they were united to the will of God and were themselves God. In addition, he was abandoned outwardly by all his friends and moreover surrounded and taken captive by all his enemies, as is well known to us all from his passion.

(57) This whole way of truth was made plain to this person in the other three ways, as she climbs and increases in the godly light and very willingly and desirously takes this way on. However wild, however desolate, however bitter, however difficult it stands before her, she is nonetheless already consoled in whatever may befall her, and she prays our dear Lord will want to help her and that he will want to accomplish this in her to his eternal honor and praise. With this interior handing over and giving up to God she is thus consoled that it will happen for her and is strengthened to carry it out, and then takes this way on knowingly and willingly with a joyful spirit and goes out to meet her adversary and says, "Friend, to what end have you come?" Because she knows that he will bring her to a saving way and to the most perfect. She follows the Spirit of God thus, who leads her with his will and knowledge, himself operating therein, and brings things so far that he on occasion hands her over to her enemies and allows them to do with her all that they want. Who are now these adversaries? They are every sort of testing and temptation and contradiction that may befall her. And so the person will on occasion be overwhelmed by the Spirit of God, beyond herself. (58) Then the person is no longer herself, and she has neither knowledge nor works. Up to this point the person was led by the Spirit of God and well preserved wherever she went. But from now on, as she is overwhelmed by the Spirit of God, she at times no longer knows and has no power to act. So now the person must abandon herself to the work of the Spirit of God in a wondrous, alien, desolate way, beyond all understanding of any who have not been so visited. Even if she has contemplated the end of these matters in the light of grace, when she comes to this point, she comes regularly to think all manner of things that she has never said, and is now deeply tempted by unbelief, because it occurs to her that it is all a deception and is beyond belief. And she is massively tempted and becomes shaken as to whether to return or seek help and counsel, as she could and might. (59) But this she may not do. She must hold herself to the faith as a devout knight for Christ, believing genuinely that it must be so if she is ever to come to her best, trusting in God, for whose sake she willingly undertook this way, that he will not abandon her, suffering happily out of love all that may befall her, and being entirely consoled, no matter from what side it comes

or how it comes, to the eternal honor of God, and holding herself to it and standing fast in it. Then she will thus be re-formed *(overghe-formt)* in God, coming as nearly as she ever can to it. Because these are three godly virtues that largely re-form the person in herself and unite her self largely to God, indeed so interiorly that there is very nearly no difference between the spirit of God and the spirit of the person, other than that the one spirit is uncreated and the other created. A person comes to all this in this life by way of the above-written wild, desolate way in Christ, and is made like him by this being completely handed over into the hands of all her adversaries, willingly prepared for all torments that come, as Christ was.

(60) Thus is the person abandoned entirely, from without and from within, from above and from below. From within she is abandoned by God without any knowledge or taste or feeling, just as if she had had nothing of God and just as if she would have nothing more but be eternally rejected by him. She has no consolation from without or from within, because the lower things have no taste for her. And should it be that she should think that they begin to taste for her, then her pressure and her suffering would become only greater. This pressure grows in her so much that she would think it very nearly unbearable, and not know where to turn. If she should turn to other humans in order to lament her desperation, she would receive no consolation, because the person does not understand her, because he has not been tested in this and often counsels very strange things that would harm her progress in this way if she were to do them. And it contradicts the anxious comfortless ground that bears her from within and does not allow her to do it. And so from this she only becomes more shaken and more wounded on all sides.

(61) Thus are they abandoned from all sides and find no solace or help anywhere, and in addition are attacked on all sides by the evil Adversary with many difficult temptations, bringing all too much despair on many occasions. And as to her faith, that is mightily attacked by people from without who load onto her many troubles and burdens, which make things very hard for her and make her think that it only helps increase her deep suffering. For if she could be alone with herself and with her own exhortations from within, she thinks she should not do this or that or that she would hold out better. To it comes as well much counsel that people say to

her, also surprising things they tell her, by which she is deeply shaken, as was said already.

(62) Third, she is attacked most of all by her own reasoning powers, which want ever to know and investigate this. That has no place here, and they want ever to contradict and test with reason and against writings, and that is not allowed here. This is the harshest foe,[19] the most evil to overcome. And if this is overcome, the others will have no power.

See, in this way a person is set in the footsteps of Christ and allows herself to be taken captive and her hands to be bound behind her back so that she does not have the use of them to resist. She must on occasion suffer all these things, just as Christ did under all his foes, or else she gains no protection from it. See, my most beloved, now you must assuredly prove yourself in this fourth way. It is the most high, over all the others, because this one exercises the suffering of Jesus the most truly, in true feeling and with genuine co-suffering from within, in the interior person, and also outwardly in the external person. (63) Such a person properly suffers and is crucified with Christ, and she dies with Christ and is buried with Christ, and there she suffers for a time hidden until Christ rouses her and has her stand up and arise and makes her public with perfect works of virtue that no one can contradict. Thus will wonders be done through the person, a saving harvest for holy church.

About an Easier Way: (64) There follows now another way that also belongs here. It follows after the ways written of above and is somewhat easier. It stands in the very same darkness as the others but does not feel such harsh suffering. That comes from the fact that self-possession, from which the other suffering arises, is better overcome and put to death in the ground, and for that reason she does not feel all such sufferings. This is, for her, hardest with respect to the reasoning powers, the very last among all the forms of self-possession and the worst to overcome. Because when all the others are reduced to nothing by harsh suffering, there remains still this reasoning power, and it wants still to grieve, complain, dispute, argue, and say: "See, I thought so, that it would go thus for me, that I would bear such poverty and barrenness and become idle of any good, so there is no hunger or thirst in me for any good from the graces, no desire in me to exercise any good, because all the desirous drawing and spiritual diligence for such exercises has been reduced to nothing in me. And that is irritating. I remain thus entirely lost and waste away sadly thus in all things good. More, in this state I can feel no sadness or heaviness of heart."

(65) This is the most difficult for such a person, to know it and not to feel it, knowing too what is written there, that those temptations are most anxiety producing that one feels least harshly. Then they think, "O Lord God, what are you up to now?" If a person could never again feel that suffering and harshness, that seeking, that grieving a total loss, then you would have no despair. If you could obtain this, your heart would be consoled. But now you have nothing, and you are forced to hope falsely, not in the goodness of God, but in your works and your great improvements. Because you can have no hope of gaining improvement, since your desire to turn toward all good exercises has entirely died in you and has gone to nothing. And you have become wholly without solace, and say, "O Lord, never was I so without any solace, because when I was in the world then I had still a little solace and hope that if I should be out of the world then I would improve my life. But now I have no solace or hope because I know no estate or place or thing that can help me toward a good end other than God alone." Oh, how have you set yourself up now! You are entirely cut off from God, and you are also now entirely miserable over it. Still, in all this I will have full trust in God and think, according to my own soul, never, easily, was I so near to God as I am now, or ever indeed was before—even if you do not know this.

(66) I will give you counsel, as to what you should do. Whenever you feel yourself thus and are in this spirit and can find nothing else and it has to be this way with you, and it cannot be contradicted by anything, see how thereby your faith collapses in you. Only then is your reasoning power overcome and not earlier. Then say to yourself: "If it has to be this way inside you, and cannot be otherwise with you for ever, I will nonetheless still hope in God and in the purpose of my works and in the good simple intentions with which I had undertaken all this, because God knows that I sought and intended nothing other than to do fully his dearest will, and that I thought that he asked it of me or wanted it. My conscience also forced me to act thus and to give my self to this. (67)

And so because I do not know anything other or better, I hope that he will look upon my good simple intentions. And if he will allow it, I will be entirely content with this and suffer it out of genuine love to his eternal praise. It is entirely worth it to me, all that I can suffer or let be for his dear sake. I am consoled by what may come of this in time or in eternity."

Oh, now, lose within yourself your hope together with your faith. Love, however, alone remains standing in the highest, and it goes in where knowledge remains standing outside. (68) See here, rend your veins and crush your sinews! And here all that is within you will come bursting forth, such that you preserve not a drop of yourself, but rather will be all upset to the eternal honor of God and for love. And with that you will do for the Lord fully and completely as much as you can. If you had more, you would give more and do more; but not you. And so the Lord must allow himself to be satisfied with this. (69) Now, this is the fourth way that belongs to the cross. This is the cross with four points of which we spoke before, which we must carry between our shoulders until death, with humility, with patience, with letting be, and with suffering out of love, to the eternal honor of God. We should also carry it in front of us between our breasts with loving contemplation and good exercises, the back of which cross drives away the serpent, that is, all sins.

Now, one can find some people that allow themselves to think that they have obtained this way and that they have already survived it, because they sometimes become aware of this withdrawal of the graces. The accustomed interiority and orientation toward God is somewhat withdrawn from them on occasion for a day or two, more or less, as things fall out. When this happens, they strive to suffer this good-heartedly and to help themselves in another way, and are thereby satisfied, praising and thanking God for the poverty that they have suffered, knowing that it must be this way and not otherwise, and in this way make their peace. (70) They also seek out many sweet little verses to help themselves. They think: "See, it must be this way. In this I must be tested, how I shall conduct myself in this, whether I will depart from God or not, whether I shall now hold to him faithfully. I will never, no matter what overtakes me, place my hope falsely and I will trust in his love." And thus they help themselves with all manner of subtle things whereby they also rouse their devotion and have devotion more frequently than if they had simply held to their first interiority. These people think they can thus help themselves nicely and also suffer, because they prefer to suffer, because poverty is luxury to them and suffering solace. As much as such people would like to draw nearer to God, they do not have all that is required. These people think that those others of whom we have spoken, who exist in such great suffering, are greatly in the wrong and in fact do much of it to themselves in their stubborn self-possession. If they could only let be and make peace with it, as they do themselves, it would not cause them the kind of distress that so shakes them.

(71) Oh, dear God, they speak truly. But that is another manner that they imagine or know, because hard persistence in such testing is altogether different, as much as clear day from dark night. Oh, if the others [the easier way] had no other testing [than this], how little should it weigh on them. They would think that it had become a beautiful day, as indeed in truth it would be, if it were to transpire thus for them. Oh, nay, dearly beloved, it is still all too far from testing. You imagine you know it, but you know nothing, because what you have and understand, is very little or nothing in comparison. But that which you know and grasp, those are transitory things, in order to open and prepare this way. It has to go far beyond testing of that sort, things that are much more and harsher, which you do not yet know or have not yet tasted, and moreover by chance will never taste or feel. But these must advance far beyond in a variety of ways before you will come to the other.

(72) Humble yourself, therefore, under the other, and acknowledge your infirmity and your great wickedness. Reckon yourself not to be that which you not yet are. Oh, if God sits with you in the other way, you would not know what it was you had, and you would have yourself in a far more ill way than these other people, if you should happen to think you could have yourself well off. Oh, nay, it is still all too far, and you must still discover where God has placed you. But not you! You are all too infirm and all too unfaithful in your ground, and the grace of God has not yet worked mightily enough in you, as would be necessary to come to this way. (73) And for that reason our dear Lord cannot do it. For he knows that you will descend into still more harmful things and be unfaith-

ful to him and forget about the noble ground. You can ill believe that it should fall out this way with you, because you think that you are totally faithful to him and that you will not be separated from him. I tell you truly, in various matters you will fall out quite at odds with him to the harm of your souls. You may hardly be able to suffer that I say this to you, and that I mean you by this. But I may not keep silent, because it is true, and I must indeed say the truth, so that people who are guilty may take note. For this will not lay any claim on those who are not guilty. And those few who are guilty, it will not lay claim on them such as to render them not guilty. God alone makes better. (74) But, still, each person knows herself, and no blue-hooded cloak hangs around God.[20] Look, I have not said this so that a person will lose hope of coming into this way, but only so that you may learn your infirmity and do not exalt yourself, so you thereby suffer no harm in your souls with respect to your saving progress. Because, in truth, that devotional feeling comes from a sickness in the bodily nature.

# Sister Bertken
## *Pious Colloquy* and a selection from her *Songs*[1]

Berta Jacobs, in literature generally known as Sister Bertken
(1426/27–1514), is one of the very few female authors we know from the
Late Medieval Netherlands. Historical research has made clear that she was
an illegitimate child of one of the famous families in Utrecht, the Lichtenberg
family. Her father, Jacob van Lichtenberg, was provost of the Utrecht chapter of St. Peter and played a prominent role in church political life of his time.
This background suggests Bertken must have had a good education. Bertken
chose, however, not to engage in the world of famous people of her time; at the
age of thirty she decided to spend the rest of her life in solitary seclusion and
for that purpose she had a cell built at her own expense at the Buurkerk, the
most important Medieval parish church of Utrecht.

Bertken lived fifty-seven years in her cell and died June 25, 1514,
at the age of eighty-seven years. After her death three prominent clerics
made up an official document in Latin that was put in a bottle and placed
in her grave. This document was translated into Middle Dutch and written in a copy of the Legenda aurea of the regular canons of Utrecht, who
kept the key of Bertken's cell. It is our only source of information on
Bertken's life. From this document we learn that Bertken always wore a
hair shirt on her naked skin with a simple gray dress over it and that she
went barefoot. She never burned a fire in her cell. She ate neither meat
nor dairy products. This testifies that she took the ascetic life very seriously.
Her way of living—renouncing the world in all respects—accords with the
true meaning of the anchorite life. The inclusion ceremony symbolizes a
burial; the cell was regarded as a grave, in which the recluse was solemnly
buried. The ascetic life was Bertken's way of imitating Christ. Both her
way of living and her authorship are exceptional and make her stand out
among the many devout women of her time.

The texts Bertken composed testify that Christ was at the center of
her spiritual life. Every day she meditated on several aspects of his life dur-

ing her long period of inclusion, and she provided herself with texts to do so. Very important in her spirituality is a long meditation text on the passion of Christ, structured on the canonical hours, which she used every day in meditation. But she has also left a vision of the birth of Christ that is generally considered to be a masterpiece. In these two texts she presented Christ as the living example, which she was prepared to follow. But for Bertken, Christ was not only the example to be followed, but also the bridegroom, with whom she longed to be united, at least in part here on earth, and in full after death. About her longing to be unified with him, she speaks most clearly in her Pious Colloquy between the loving soul and her beloved bridegroom Jesus, which is presented in translation below.

Besides these prose texts, Bertken also wrote nine songs, the melody of one of which has been preserved. It is by these songs that Bertken won a place in the canon of Middle Dutch literature. Four songs are presented here in translation. Whereas Bertken's prose is rather exuberant, with many superlatives, the style of the songs is sober and simple. In the songs we meet the whole range of spiritual themes that interested Bertken. They deal with the birth and death of Christ, his sweet name, and the problems she faced trying to die to the world and live only for him, as in what is probably her most well-known text "I Went into My Little Garden to Gather Herbs," but also in "The World Held Me in Its Power." The songs deal also with her relation with Christ as bridegroom, as, for instance, in "O Chosen Soul, Why Do You Abandon Me?" and her longing to be united with him as far as possible here on earth, which she expresses in "Now Hear, I Will Start Singing a New Song."

Shortly after her death, Bertken's texts were printed by three different publishers, namely, Jan Berntsz in Utrecht, Jan Seversz in Leiden, and Willem Vorsterman in Antwerp. The following translation of Bertken's Pious Colloquy and four of her songs is based on the Utrecht edition of "Suster Bertkens boeck," published by Jan Berntsz on June 23, 1516. A copy of this edition has been preserved in the Royal Library of The Hague (signature 151 F 9). A new edition of Bertken's texts is in preparation by a group of Dutch scholars. A description of Bertken's life and writings with literary references was published in 2007 under the heading "Jacobsdr, Berta" on the Digitaal Vrouwenlexicon van Nederland Web site.

SISTER BERTKEN

# PIOUS COLLOQUY

### THE LOVING SOUL

O glorious, illustrious princes, inhabitants of the highest free city, beholders of the most high God, who is there very miraculously and above our sight in the bottomless depth of the all exceeding brightness of the hidden, eternal unity of his most high Trinity. O you who nobly, highly glorify and sing the wondrous songs of praise of the most high King, standing before his face, full of joy and full of glory burning and glowing in love for him whom my soul loves, oh, bring word to him that I languish from love.

### THE INHABITANTS OF THE HIGHEST CITY

O devout bride, what do you desire from your beloved? He has left open for you the pharmacy with the very best herbs. He unlocked the wine cellar with the very best wines for you. Hidden, heavenly bread is brought unto you: eat and be strong, drink and be merry.

### THE LOVING SOUL

O high noblemen, is it your habit to torment the tormented soul further? Do you not know that I am searching for my beloved, that I desire only him? Show me him whom my soul loves.

### THE INHABITANTS OF THE HIGHEST CITY

O devout bride of the King of glory, be not displeased. I have come to comfort you and bring you good tidings of your beloved. He will linger no longer, but he will come to you and he will speak to you himself. His lingering is only for your good.

### THE LOVING SOUL

Oh, how long will it be said to me: "He will come, he will come." When will he come? Where is he for whom my soul yearns? Behold, my beloved comes leaping over the mountains. Awake my cittern, my harp, and all my joy. Let us be jubilant before his face.

205

## THE BRIDEGROOM JESUS

You have wounded my heart, my sister, my bride.

## THE LOVING SOUL

O my most beloved, I did not know this. If I had known that, I would have suffered your lingering more patiently. Oh, what shall I do? I should wish that the most inner being of my heart and all the powers of my soul and all my inner being were the most precious, the finest balm, sweet smelling above the fragrance of all good herbs that grow in your garden. O my beloved, my dearest love, I would be very glad to pour out myself completely with great desire to soften and sweeten your very sweet, loving, wounded heart. O most beloved, you were wounded but you still remain unharmed. O you, who know all hearts, who see through the abysses, to whom all things are revealed and not hidden, do not hold me in contempt for speaking to you thus openly as my heart feels. It cools down my heart. Love is the cause of it. You have always received with pleasure what emanates from love, and you have usually defended them against those who do not know love and judge it wrongly. This is my comfort.

## THE BRIDEGROOM TO THE LOVING SOUL

My friend, your voice sounds sweet in my ears. I have loved you with eternal love. Before you existed, I wanted you to be, and I chose you for myself to be my bride. I give you my eternal faithfulness, and I want to have your eternal faithfulness. I will never leave you.

## THE LOVING SOUL

O most beloved love, how sweet is your soul. My heart becomes soft, it is just like melting wax. There is no speech in my tongue. I did not exist, which means out of nothing you have created me. What I am, I am because of your grace. All I have ever had and still have, I have received from you. Now I take your divine truth to be my witness, that I renounce myself and all my possessions with all my will and with my total desire and I give myself entirely and completely to your eternal divine will and I profess to

be yours fully and I desire with everything to be eternally subservient to you. With your eternal truth as a witness I reject all
renunciation and desire that this will be steadfast and unchanged
into eternity. *Consummatum est.* Receive my spirit.

## THE BRIDEGROOM JESUS

O my chosen bride, long I have desired this to happen. It is my
will. Receive my blessing: I bless you in my name, may my divine
blessing rest upon you into eternity. Arise my friend and go out with
me a little. I will teach you how you can please me. I am your king,
but my kingdom is not of this world. I came into the world, but the
world did not know me. I shone into the darkness, but the darkness
did not understand me. The world despised me. I lived in the world
in great poverty and in labor from my youth onward. I was despised
and rejected by the people. They stripped me naked; they whipped
me so severely that there was nothing left unbroken in my whole
body. They did not want to have me for their king. They rejected
and scorned me and shouted "Away with him" and "Crucify him!"
They crowned me with thorns and, to despise me, they put a reed
in my hand and in derision they fell down before me and in contempt called me king of the Jews. After so much humiliation they
nailed me naked on a piece of wood and stretched me so unmerci-
fully that all my veins were torn, and they raised and lifted me up
into the air between two criminals and when I was thirsty, after
much more humiliation, they gave me a foul, bitter drink. Being so
miserable, naked, despised I tasted the bitter death and was buried
and rose again. My body was glorified and I ascended above all
heavens and I am sitting at the right hand of my Father.

My chosen bride, consider now very carefully what I have told
you and do your utmost to be my equal. Because I was very poor in
the world, you too will be poor. Because I am pure, you will guard
against all blemishes. Because I labored from my youth onward, you
too will labor. Because I have done everything out of love for you,
you will for my honor do everything out of love for me. Because I
suffered unto death, you will be obedient and persevere unto death.
You shall be humble of heart and meek, because I, your bridegroom,
was rejected by the people for your sake. Therefore do not desire to

be honored in the world, you who have become my bride. Because I meekly suffered all humiliation, all suffering, you will be my equal and be meek in all sadness and suffering that comes to you. You will pray for everything that is weak. You will not hate except evil. All that you suffer now and will still suffer is not without reason. It is known to me. I will deliver you and take you unto myself when the suffering you have to suffer is completed, and I will place you with me in my kingdom. There you will delight with me without end. My beloved friend whom I have chosen and received to be my bride, do as I have taught you and know that, even though you do not see me as I am, I see you everywhere, that you walk before my countenance, and I see all your spiritual progress. Remember this and remain as small, as poor, as meek, as humble as I desire you to be.

### THE LOVING SOUL

O my most beloved, may your will be done. The spirit is willing but the flesh is weak. May your left hand be under my head and may your right hand embrace me (Sg 2:6).

### THE BRIDEGROOM JESUS TO THE SOUL

My bride, because you recognize your weakness, and desire help and comfort from me and you rely on me alone, I will put my hand under you and hold up what is weak and let you rest on my hand. My right hand will embrace you and protect you from all harmful evil. Be of good courage and remain in peace. *In pace in idipsum dormiam et requiescam* (Ps 4:9).

# A SELECTION FROM HER *SONGS*

## SONG 3:
## I Went into My Little Garden to Gather Herbs
*(Ic was in mijn hoofkijn om cruyt gegaen)*

I went into my little garden to gather herbs,
I found nothing but thistles and thorns.

# SISTER BERTKEN

The thistles and thorns I pulled out,
I would like to plant other herbs.

Now I found someone who can garden,
He likes taking care of it.

A tree had grown high in short time,
I was not able to get it out of the ground.

He noticed well that the tree hindered me;
He pulled it entirely out of the ground.

Now I have to be obedient to him,
Otherwise he will not keep on gardening.

My little garden I have to weed all the time,
Still I can't keep it pure.

In this [garden] I have to sow the seeds of lilies;
I have to start it early at daybreak.

If he covers it with dew, the love of mine,
Then this seed will soon take root.

He loves to see the lilies, this lover of mine,
When they flower naturally and are pure.

When the red roses are among them,
He covers them with his sweet dew.

When he pours over them his sunshine,
Then all the powers of my soul rejoice.

Jesus is his name, this lover of mine,
I want to serve him eternally and be his own.

His love has impassioned me with such a high spirit,
That I don't value worldly goods anymore.

## SONG 4:
# O Chosen Soul, Why Do You Abandon Me?
*(O siel wtvercoren, waerom begeefdi mi?)*

**Jesus**
O chosen soul, why do you abandon me?
It is my sweet bliss to be always with you.
Please turn back now; my heart is open for you.
My love is immeasurable; I would love to receive you.

**The loving soul**
O you noble, beautiful of appearance, rich, mighty,
    moreover wise,
Lord above all lords, what shall I answer you?
My heart starts to tremble, please be merciful to me.
I launch into your grace; forgive me guilt and pain.

**Jesus**
Come closer, chosen one, your supplication is heard.
I see that your heart is disconcerted from sorrow and
    very dismayed.
Please rejoice with me now; always be at peace.
Come, I will serve you the very best wine.

**The loving soul**
Sorrow, pain and heavy longing have all passed away
    in me.
O very sweet Jesus, your love has done that,
Brilliant, beautiful, without measure, and it has many
    powers.
My heart starts to burn just like a seraph.

**Jesus**
Come my chosen one, enter cheerfully into my quiet.
There you will see and hear the joy and delight of the
    angels
Who are elevated in great honor with me.
That you will be their equal, that is my will.

### The loving soul

No joy can please me anymore in the whole wide world.
My only longing, O Jesus, is to behold, where you are,
Your sweet, glorious face with joy,
And to sing your praise eternally without end.

### Jesus

My beautiful one, my chosen, now be patient for a short
    while.
Take pleasure that you accommodate me.
I suffered a lot for you, please remember that
And let your will completely be absorbed in mine.

### The loving soul

O Jesus, sweet bridegroom, look at my inner being:
I have your sweet image imprinted on my heart:
Elevated on the cross, pale, bloody, and heavily
    deformed.
The flames of your love have penetrated my heart.

### Jesus

My bride, my chosen one, I am in your heart.
I hold your whole will completely in mine.
You have given me everything that was in your power.
I lovingly received that for which I waited for so long.

### The loving soul

Heart, mind, strength and senses opened kindly:
I embraced you with great pleasure and longing.
O Jesus, sweet bridegroom, though it is beyond my
    power,
I reached this stage by the power of your burning love.

### Jesus

My bride, my chosen one, please be at peace now.
I united your heart with mine out of love.
I will not leave you, nor let you be in need.
Out of love for you I died a bitter death on the cross.

## SONG 5:
# The World Held Me in Its Power
*(Dye werelt hielt my in haer ghewalt)*

The world held me in its power
With its manifold snares.
It deprived me of my strength,
It has done me much harm, before I escaped it.

I said goodbye to the world.
Its joy is done so quickly
In such short days.
I do not want to risk my noble soul anymore therein.

I see the narrow path lying open
That leads straight to eternal joys.
Nature, please do not be afraid.
I want to walk this path courageously to please Jesus.

I feel a little spark within me.
It moves my heart so often.
I want to guard it well.
Love is perfectly able to make a fire out of it.

Now you can hear a heavy complaint.
Nature cries: "Woe, alas!"
It has to give up its joy.
What it rejoiced over for a long time, it has to learn to hate.

Farewell, farewell nature of mine.
My heart has to be set free.
Complaining will be of no avail.
I want to let him in, whom my soul desires alone.

My enemies observe it closely
In secret and in public.
They lay false ambushes for me.
Therefore I have to watch by day and also by night.

I don't want to be defeated in that,
Joyfully I want to face it.
I will repulse them well.
Love is burning so heavily, they cannot harm me.

I am very confident of this:
He strengthens me with his exalted love.
His power makes me win the victory.
His gifts are so manifold, no heart can conceive of it.

# SONG 7:
# Now Hear, I Will Start Singing a New Song
*(Nu hoert, ic sal enen nieuwen sanc beginnen)*

Now hear, I will start singing a new song:
Love, Love, she wants to force me continually
To rejoice here,
But here I am down in a valley.

I hope that I still will completely grasp love.
Sorrow, Sorrow it is I will start with.
She will get me so far
To sing the song of the dove in the valley.

Now my little heart will be cheerful in suffering.
Nature, Nature, she leers on all sides.
She endangers this noble, perfect little dove.
Therefore I have to be cheerful in suffering.

I sing the song of the dove in secret.
How well, how well will I now learn to be concerned
Down here in the valley.
The little dove is frightened of everything.

Now hear, I will renounce the song of the dove.
Love, Love, she wants to live in joy
And sing with the nightingale.
Noble love will accomplish that certainly.

Love, she endures much suffering in joy.
Now hear, now hear, where will love rejoice?
In a beautiful orchard.
There love will understand the nightingale.

The nightingale sang sweetly.
The sound, the sound was beautiful to the ear.
Now love is overcome by sorrow.
How will she escape the first sleep now?

Love, she wants to watch always in joy.
Nature, Nature, you will sleep in peace.
Love cannot rest,
She wants to lament her sorrow in joy.

The joy of love is immeasurable suffering.
The song, the song she cannot forget
How far the nightingale moved away.
Love will get out of her senses completely.

The nightingale, she will prepare the way.
Love, Love, she wants to depart from here
Over hill and dale,
Where she will find her beloved in joy.

Love, she has two red, shining cheeks.
Love, Love, she welcomes her beloved with singing.
She is embraced very intimately.
Now the complaining of Love has ended completely.

Love, she is free, noble, of high birth.
Her beloved, her beloved she has chosen.
He is so wonderful.
No heart can understand the joy of love.

# The Evangelical Pearl, Part III[1]

*The inspiring text of* The Evangelical Pearl *can be situated in the general context of the era of the so-called Modern Devotion, initially practiced under the aegis of the Windesheim Congregation of Augustinians and shared with a much larger public eager for a spirituality that could nourish both lay and religious Christians. A product of sixteenth-century beguine spirituality, written in the Dutch vernacular by an anonymous author (possibly a beguine), this treatise was sometimes called* The Great Evangelical Pearl, *because it is an expansion of an earlier and more modest treatise. It was published in Antwerp between the years 1537 and 1538. Here we present only Part III, the third and last section of the book. Studies on the authorship and provenance can as yet tell us little with regard to the woman who wrote it. As a treatise bearing much sound, even mystical, doctrine on Christian life in union with God, and displaying the influence of scripture and such signal mystical authors as Jan van Ruusbroec, Jan van Leeuwen, and Hendrik Herp (Harphius), it became popular in circles of the devout and was soon provided with multiple editions in the vernacular, as well as translations into Latin, French, and German, thanks to Carthusians and Franciscans in Cologne and Paris. The influence of* The Evangelical Pearl *extended to such diverse figures as the mystical poet Johannes Scheffler (alias Angelus Silesius) (d. 1677) and Pierre Bérulle (d. 1629).*

*For this translation we used* De groote evangelische peerle vol devote ghebeden, goddelijke oeffeningen, ende gheestelijcke leeringhen... *(Antwerp: Cnobbaert, 1629).*

# THE EVANGELICAL PEARL, PART III

## Preface

*The third part of the book has many beautiful teachings and devout prayers and exercises, conducting the ardent faithful soul into the super-essential life of contemplation, where she learns to abandon herself totally, to go out of herself into her Source, and to seek the kingdom of God within her own ground, and to find it, and there to adore God in spirit and truth; annihilated in herself, she learns to be transformed in God and wrought upon by the Spirit of God, and to become outwardly and inwardly perfect like Christ.*

## Chapter 1

*An interior conversation of the soul with God; it is an expansion of the "exercise of the heart" discussed earlier in the book.*

I believe in God, that you, my Beloved, are three Persons and one true God. And you are a simple being that cannot be moved. You have omnipotence, wisdom, and goodness contained within yourself. By your omnipotence, you sustain all things. By your wisdom, you know all things. By your goodness, you love all the things that you have made.

I believe that you are the essence of all beings. You are the essence of my noble soul. You are the light of all light, and you are the light of my soul. You are the life of all life, and you are the life of my soul.

I believe that, when still uncreated, I was in your divine essence, in the memory of the Father, in the knowledge of the Son, and in the love of the Holy Spirit. And that you have made me after your own image and likeness and have united yourself to me, and that you are in the essence of my soul in an essential, genuine, and pure fashion. You are also in all humans. Just as there is a sun in which all the rays are united—the sun in the rays, and the rays in the sun, and yet it is one sun, and totally in each ray—you are one God and you possess me within yourself, and I am your creature, and I possess you within me. You are in all humankind in this way, and you have saved us all alike. Just as the sun shines upon all things with uniform strength, light, and heat, so also is the divine Sun within all of humankind, with the strength of the Father, and with the light and wisdom of the Son, and with the heat of the Holy Spirit's love.

According to the measure in which each one makes himself ready, you work within him. Just as the sun comes out and consumes all stench and dangerous humidity of everything that lies before it exposed and within reach, so also you consume and destroy within us all imperfection and the bad odor of our conscience when it is exposed before you. And then you make it fragrant, by your divine strength, light, and warmth.

Since you are thus within me—having made me after your image and likeness—you want me to know you. For what would it profit me if I had such a marvelous good and precious treasure within me, if I did not know you? For one cannot love what one does not know. If I have your image and likeness within me, would you then be an image?

*God:* No. I am a spirit, an uncomplicated, simple being and the Father of the spirits.

*The soul:* In that case, I too am a simple being! Whence then come the images within me by which I am ensnared?

*God:* you introduce them from outside; they come from created things, through the five senses, and you keep them in your faculties. But they cannot enter into the nakedness of your soul or into the simplicity of your essence where I dwell, working and resting, without images; these images and multiplicity hinder you from knowing me in you, and from becoming one simple being and one spirit with me.

*The soul:* Where, then, am I a spirit?

*God:* In the uppermost part of the soul, in the simple essence where the three faculties become one, there is that image of the soul and there is it that you are a spirit.

*The soul:* And where is it, now, that I possess your likeness?

*God:* Where the three faculties flow out of the simplicity of the essence. In their activity they show forth a likeness to the Holy Trinity.

*The soul:* How is it that I possess likeness unto you?

*God:* It occurs insofar as you turn inward to your ground in the simple essence of your soul, and become one spirit with me, and in the measure that your thoughts do not resist nor hinder what I, by my mighty power, am working within your memory, and your understanding does not darken the light that I, by my divine wisdom, am making, and your will does not withstand what I, by my goodness, am doing within you. And just as I work within you by my power, wisdom, and goodness, so also I work through you, through your memory and love. You can hinder this, change your likeness, and lose your resemblance with me if you do not put into action your good thoughts and if you darken the light and your will resists. For I have made you like unto myself in freedom of the will. With it you can pursue good and resist evil. Nevertheless, you can do nothing outside of me. This is why I am within you, because I want to help you, for you can do nothing without me. Without your cooperation, I cannot make you blessed, and I have so united myself with you and with each person that I neither can nor will be separated from you.

And if you enter this naked ground and unite yourself to me, you are enabled to become by grace what I am by nature, for I am the life of your soul and the food of your spirit. Set your mind, then, to become as a little child who is suckled and nourished on its mother's milk and who would grow on nothing else so nicely. In this way, by my holy merits, you shall become pure and clean as a little child; you shall turn inward and be nourished by the union with the divine essence. For nowhere shall you be so well nourished as where your spirit is filled with my Spirit and receives testimony that you are my child. It is there that I shall teach you all truth and reveal my mystery, and thus in your essence you shall be nourished by my divine essence.

It is there, too, that I kiss you with the kiss of my mouth (Sg 1:1); that is, I kiss your essence with my divine essence, and you feed on and are nourished by the marvelous food that is within me. And you grow in all your members (that is, the faculties and the sensibilities of the soul), and you grow so much that I can lay the burdens of my humanity upon you. Fed on my food, you become intelligent and wise, and understand my will, desires, and intentions. For your

218

memory becomes fruitful and one delight with me; your will becomes transformed and one spirit with me; you become peaceful in your thoughts, for they rest in me, and joyful in your intellect, for it knows that I am within you; you become free in your will, for it is within me. And this is how you become holy and conformed to God in your heart.

Then, you always have a joyful soul, through the merits of my joyful human soul, which has merited that you return to this image and likeness. It is my will that you should always be peaceful, joyful, and free, so that I may rest in your soul, unto my glory.

Because of this food and its fruitfulness, the soul bends and bows down before my divine omnipotence, even to the abyss of humility; the deeper she lowers herself, the more I turn toward her and enlighten reason with my wisdom, so that she can discern and choose the good. By this choice of virtue, she becomes holy. Hence the appetites are drawn to die to all pleasure, good, and honor. By this dying, the soul is rendered joyful. The irascible faculties are also calmed. I have so much desire and pleasure in being enthroned in your soul and in ruling her according to my pleasure and desires, thanks to the merits of my holy, sorrow-filled soul.

I transform and purify and cleanse your heart and body; you shall be happy and joyful to serve me. For in this interior peace of heart, you learn to deal peacefully and joyfully with all people and take your place beneath all, as I did in my holy humanity, through the merits of my holy, pure, and pierced body. And so I take pleasure in dwelling in your body.

In this way you are nourished and you grow by the food of my divine essence; you are transformed with your essence into my divine essence and with your nature into my divine nature. When you turn yourself to me and remain in me, I shall imprint on your spirit an essential, unique, eternal, divine, delightful, peaceful, and joyful essence after my own divine essence. And so I shall imprint upon your soul the interior suffering and the cross that I bore within my own soul. This cross is so noble that no one knows it except my chosen ones, who have entered into the secret wine cellar. They know it, and they know how little I obtain my intentions, desires, and will from any people, though I am in all of them. This is the most painful suffering and cross, and yet the sweetest wound.

The greater the suffering is, the more joyful the spirit; the more joyful the spirit is, the heavier the cross. The one does not diminish the other. And this I have also had in my holy humanity, for never for an instant was I free of this cross. Therefore, my chosen ones must also bear it, for the more love and longing they receive toward me, the more love they will receive for all of humankind.

*The soul:* my beloved, why is it your will to remain in my spirit, which is so unfit?

*God:* Because you should always remain in me and be one spirit with me, and always remain joined and united to the Godhead, according to my humanity. I shall render your spirit suitable, through the merits of my joyful spirit, provided that you are always united in your will with my will. And this is how I take pleasure in remaining in your spirit.

*The soul:* Why do you desire to be enthroned within my soul, since I am unworthy of this?

*God:* So that I may always judge and chide you here whenever you do wrong. If you accept it, amend yourself, and follow my counsel, I shall be a merciful judge to you in the hour of your death. And then, on the Day of Judgment, you shall be enthroned with me and judge the twelve tribes of Israel. If you place all your desires in me, and I possess your kingdom, and if it is obedient and submissive to me, then, in turn, you shall possess my kingdom in heaven. When I possess your soul, then the kingdom of God is within you. By the merits of my sorrowful soul, I render your soul worthy of this, and thus I find peace within your soul.

*The soul:* Why do you, Lord, desire to dwell in my body, which is so unprepared for such a favor?

*God:* I am always glad to make it pure and fit by the merits of my holy, pure, wounded body. If you set your heart's intention on me, I take pleasure in your body, since I may work in it and through it, as I worked through my holy humanity; I may speak in and through you and may proclaim the truth, and may have my way with you and through you. Then you can be sweet and peaceful in your conduct, follow after me, and become conformed to my humanity: in the pain of my body, so you might not seek after pleasure in your body, and so I can take pleasure in dwelling in your body; in poverty, so that you may seek no consolation here; in humiliation, so that you seek no honor here, but my glory alone.

This is how you become my only son, whom I bring forth a second time, and you become conformed to my holy humanity, if you always remain in me and I in you, with a joyful spirit, and a sorrowful soul, and a suffering body. For those who follow after my holy body have crucified their flesh with its desires and if you thus remain in me and I in you, you shall bear much fruit. Since I am thus in you and your spirit is my throne and your soul my seat, your body is my tabernacle; I will surround you with my whole heavenly host. Since I am within you, they shall gather around you; for where I am, there my servant shall also be. Then I can remain immovably within you and hold my supper within you; in this way I can receive myself spiritually in you, in the holy sacrament. For I am in you according to my Godhead, not according to my humanity; by receiving you, I can make you a participant in my humanity. Then you will be fed and entirely changed into me, and you will live in me, and I can fulfill my desires in you. For he who eats my flesh and drinks my blood remains in me and I in him (John 6:57). In this way I feed you on my flesh and wash you with my blood, and I give myself entirely to you. I clothe you with my Godhead, and you become one with me as I am one with my heavenly Father.

# Chapter 2

*On the honor God does the soul who is united to him, and how he surrounds her with every heavenly thing; what he counsels her to do.*

O noble creature, see what a great gift I give you: so that you give yourself back entirely to me, give poverty for wealth, give one thing and become one. When you thus remain one with me, all my servants, each and every one of them, are near you and care for you. Each and every one has an order and a service to which he counsels and admonishes you. The patriarchs counsel you to have an ardent desire for me. The prophets counsel you to have patience, following my example. The apostles counsel you to remain steadfast in me, with faith, and to follow my footsteps. The martyrs counsel you to bear up perseveringly in all oppression and suffering. The confessors counsel you interior worship in my service. The virgins counsel you to chastity and purity of heart and of body, and that, since you are my bride, you should always think about the things that concern me and please me. And I counsel you to remain united with me and not to break your fidelity with me, so that I may keep the promises I have made to you; namely, if you thus abide in me and I in you, we shall come and make our dwelling in you: the Father in your memory, the Son in your intellect, the Holy Spirit in your will. And we shall remain with you this way until the end of the world. And my beloved Mother counsels you to be poor of spirit, holy of soul, and pure in body, so that you will be ready and prepared for my spiritual birth within you, and so that you can be my Mother by grace, as she has been by nature. The Seraphim counsel you to let your thoughts rest in me, in ardent love. The Cherubim counsel you to let your intellect abide in me in order to know me. The Thrones counsel you to maintain your will steadfastly in me and to become a throne upon which I rest. The Dominations counsel you to be patient in your reason and to pray for those who offend you. The Principalities counsel your appetitive faculties to disdain all temporal things. The Virtues counsel you to control your anger. The Powers counsel you to be discreet. The Archangels counsel you to serve me out of love. The Angels counsel you to have done with evil, for fear of me. In this way I teach you within, and my servants teach you without. For that purpose, I have ordered all my servants to be ever at your side. Therefore, I counsel you to abide in me and to be faithful in me, for I dwell in you, so that I might effect spiritually in you all that I have done bodily.

# **Chapter 3**

*How God wants to fulfill all the great feasts in the soul, and wants to renew them in her always.*

I was born once in the flesh for your sake, so that I could always be born spiritually in you. All the other great feasts that were outwardly celebrated by me should also be fulfilled spiritually within you, where they should be celebrated, since you should constantly have and carry in your heart my whole life and sufferings (everything that I underwent, gave up, taught, and suffered for your sake), as I bore it in my heart for your sake, without departing for an instant.

In this way it is always Good Friday within you, and you are spiritually crucified and you die every day for my sake and are entombed in me; you entomb me within yourself in the grave of your heart, and you anoint me with the oil of dying to yourself; you enfold me in the winding sheet of your conscience that I have cleansed by my death and passion. This is how I shall rise in you and through you, and bring you to life out of death, and make you joyful out of suffering, and thus it shall always be Easter within you; I shall go down with you into Hades and bring the souls with me into my joy and glory. With them, you shall be one celestial spirit and rise mysteriously with me in the innermost essence of your soul. And your life shall be in heaven with me, for I am in you. In this way, you shall celebrate and carry out my ascension within you. Thus I shall renew your heart with my graces, enkindle it with my love, and endow it with my sevenfold gifts. Thus you shall fulfill the great feast of the sending of the Holy Spirit. You shall always keep Sabbath in your spirit and celebrate the memorial of all the feasts within you, and ceaselessly honor the Holy Trinity in the unity of the divine essence that is united within your essence. It is the essence of every essence and the light of every light, and the life of every life. It is the life and the light and the food of your spirit and transforms your essence into my divine essence; thus you shall always maintain within yourself the memory of my presence and keep Sabbath and rest in your spirit, so that I may rest in you, and you in me, and you may always have my rest in your spirit and my reality in your body, and thus you shall be simple in all multiplicity and abide in my divine union, as I did, according to my humanity, and as did my beloved Mother.

# Chapter 4

*How we should stay simple in all our religious exercises in the essential unity of God.*

No one can describe a perfect circle if the compass stays fixed on one point. The circle is the reality of my Holy Trinity; the point is my essential unity. So also, you can accomplish no perfect works unless you abide with me in my essential unity, and I with you in this reality. Then all your works shall be perfect, if you abide in me and I in you. If you desire my help in all you do or undergo, I work with you and you abide in me. In all outward activity you shall perceive my inward activity, for I sometimes find more satisfaction in working within you while you are engaged in outward works; you also would be more satisfied than after your rest. Therefore, do not neglect your outward works. But preserve the inward rest of the spirit and peace of heart and the control of your five senses, and the uprightness of your conduct in all multiplicity, whenever you are among people, and so you get to be both contemplative and active.

I am always at work and at rest in stillness. Thus you shall never lack me within you, for all that you do, you do for love of me; you eat for the sake of my love, realizing that it is I who give it to you so that you get strength from it to spend in my service. The mouth eats food and all the members of your body are thereby fortified; you cannot maintain yourself without food for the body; just so, your soul cannot for an instant do without my spiritual food, which is I myself. Your mouth takes in the food, that is, I feed your essence on my divine essence, and I give you to eat the food of my love. As often as you desire it, you are fed on my flesh and blood. I transform you spiritually into me, and you lose your own name. In this way, for the sake of my love, you rest with me in the chamber of your spirit, in the arms of my love, and I watch over you, and my servants guard you. And when you awake, you enter into simplicity, simply, in the innermost ground where I have awaited you in order to give you all good and to teach you new things. There, you shall learn my mystery, for it is there that you are the most receptive. And then you shall immediately address my Majesty, speaking with loving inspiration.

# Chapter 5

*On the first address to God in the morning.*

My Beloved, who are you? You are the one, eternal, immutable, supreme Good. I believe in God, that I have been for eternity in your immutable goodness, and that you are now in me. Now I give myself once again entirely, as a living sacrifice, as when I was as yet uncreated in you. And now praise yourself in me and through me, for I can do nothing outside of you; for that reason you have united yourself to me, for you want to help me. Therefore, I pray you, help me to accomplish all that is pleasing to you. Father, into your hands I commend my spirit, in the wisdom of your Son, and in the love of the Holy Spirit through whom you do all things, so that you might do with me whatever you please. Since I am unworthy, I pray you make me worthy; by the merits of your joyful spirit, that you might remain in my spirit; by the merits of your holy sorrowful soul, that you may be enthroned in my soul; by the merits of your holy wounded body, that you may dwell in my body; and by your holy merits, let your Godhead appear in and through me. Drive out of me all that is a hindrance to you. Since I am not worthy to receive you, and my soul hungers for you, then take yourself unto yourself in the holy sacrament, and transform me totally into you, so that I may be someone after your own heart, and give myself over to you entirely.

*God speaks:* My beloved soul, since you thus give yourself wholly over to me, I shall adorn and clothe you with my holy merits, so that I may make you worthy, and I shall praise myself through you. Since you can do nothing outside of me, you should always say: "Lord, open my lips and my mouth shall declare your praise; God, come to my aid, and make haste to help me" (Ps 69:2), and you should always read your hours giving all your attention to their meaning and for my honor, as I have ordained it by my friends and saints, and so I shall reveal to you there many a hidden ground and meaning. Afterward, you should pray for pardon for a neglectful life, and for having badly kept your Rule, and for having fruitlessly displayed the appearances of holiness. You should pay for all of this by my holy life and bitter sufferings. You can thereby become once

225

again as clean and pure as when you were baptized and when you made profession. Through the merits of my pure wounded body, you should pray for mercy, for you have often besmirched the purity of your body; through the merits of my holy sorrowful soul, you should pray for mercy for the disobedience of your soul; and through the merits of my joyful spirit, you should pray for mercy for not having kept poverty of spirit very well, so that from now on, you may become and remain pure in body, obedient in soul and poor in spirit. Since I am then in you and you in me, the vine, nothing is more useful or blessed for you than to remain in my presence and in the knowledge of my holy triune unity, triple in personal reality and one in my divine essence. It is there that your face, the image of the soul, is made luminous, for I have fashioned you after my image. Therefore once again receive my likeness; when you remain united to my divine essence, I may work according to my Holy Trinity in your three higher faculties, and by my majesty, make your memory fruitful and glad; by my wisdom illumine your intellect, and make it wise and understanding in order to know both yourself and me; by my goodness, enkindle your will in my love and make you one spirit with me, transforming you into myself as iron in the fire and making you entirely virtuous so that I may be enthroned in your soul and work with her in the lower faculties; work in your soul, making her entirely pure: thus you possess my likeness. And when you place your will, desires and intentions in me, and not in yourself, and only delight in and do my will, desires and intentions, I live in you and you in me. This is how you should frequently entreat and address me.

*The soul:* My Beloved, what is your will, your desire, and your intention now?

*God:* It is that you should abide in me and I in you; that with my help you should keep my counsels gladly and zealously and keep your vows according to your Rule, statutes, and customs; that with my help you gladly fulfill what you must do by obedience; that you do it happily and be submissive and helpful to everyone. You should always watch and pray to become conformed to my holy humanity. At all times keep in mind what I have suffered for you, so that you might follow me in this with all patience and obedience. Always remain with loving inspiration in my divine essence. In order to enkindle the fire of the Spirit, you should at times pray very ardently. Always gather my bitter passion into your heart. Bear it in all your bodily senses; bear all my virtues and obedience in your soul; be poor of spirit, recollected and exalted in mind; in this way you always remain essentially peaceful. Thus you possess a paradise in your soul. You remain essentially pure in your body. In this way you have an apothecary of every fragrant herb within you, for I am the medicine for all wounds: against pride, you have my humility; against avarice, my poverty; against luxury, my suffering, and so on for each wound as my holy life and passion shall teach you.

# Chapter 6

*How we should transport ourselves into God, so that God may work in us.*

A person should thus divest himself of everything, direct himself into the noble ground of his soul to the eternal truth, and transport himself entirely into God, in spirit always resting in the divine Unity and so becoming one spirit with God that he never lacks God.

He should always keep his heart busy with the passion of Christ, so that he always mirrors himself in the image of Christ; thus he is transformed and established as a living replica of him in his five senses and in all his conduct, so that God may find a reflection of all his works in him and may work unhindered through him. In this way a person abides in the Ineffable, insofar as he lets himself, his will, desires, and intentions be transformed in God; thus he becomes a child of God. But those who want to arrive at this must act according to the counsel of the holy Gospel, where our Lord says: "Anyone who wants to come after me, let him deny himself, take up his cross, etc." (Matt 16:24). Whoever wants to live according to the spirit must crucify his flesh. And whoever wants to save his soul must lose her in many temptations and anxieties; thus he shall save her in glory. He should constantly be turned inward to God, as a child toward his Father, in order always to ask his help. He should have a childlike fear so he can leave evil behind, and a childlike love of doing good; he should always keep a close watch on his five senses. He must have such knowledge of God and of himself, too, as is prescribed, and he must know all the faculties of the soul and order them to their proper places; he must always be simply recollected, not flying high or probing what is not his to probe, or he shall be humbled by the Holy Trinity.

He must also be taught and instructed by the secret friends of God, following the Spirit of God within and of people without, so that there remains nothing of his own within him; for he is stripped of himself at once, if he can humble himself. The Lord has regard for the humble, and the proud he knows from afar. Whoever can thus humble himself to learn this art shall make rapid progress. He shall be taught within a special way by the Spirit of God, much more than any writings and people could ever teach him. This is certainly a blessed humiliation through which we can learn such a noble interior art! How much more shall this person be zealous to learn this interior art (which Jesus Christ himself has taught and modeled) with inner courage and an obedient, submissive soul, and a pure, patient body in all virtue and uprightness of life, so that the example of Christ might not be given to us in vain and we be ungrateful for his benefits! For the one who has received much should give much in return. So that pearls may not be thrown before swine, we should entreat God to make all his gifts fruitful in us and to help us so that he might carry out in us and through us all that pleases him. Though by reason of infirmity one might be deterred from doing good and from practicing virtue, one should nevertheless not delay in taking up a virtuous life and in making close acquaintance with the truth. For St. Bernard says: "He whom the light of knowledge does not illumine here below shall not be illuminated in eternity. Whoever lives without knowledge shall be damned without knowledge." For this reason each person should strive first of all to know God and himself, and steadfastly to cleave to God; he should take a serious look at himself and examine himself on all that he knows might deter God from flowing into him or working within him. He who does not want to make this examination cannot be illuminated or receive any savor in spiritual goods; instead, he feels an aversion, for he is filled with the cold food of sensuality. If we correct ourselves, turning to a spiritual life, savoring the sweetness of God, ruminating the words of the Gospel, we would not loathe spiritual goods but would hunger all the more for a virtuous and upright life.

# Chapter 7

*How we are invited by Our Lord to come to him.*

Oh, let us listen carefully to how our Lord invites: "If anyone hungers and thirsts after righteousness, I shall fill him with inward spiritual savor, so that you shall no longer hunger after temporal things. Through the sweetness of my love, I shall make you so drunken that you shall never thirst again for passing things. Come to me, all you who labor and are burdened; by my love's wounds I shall cure the wounds of your soul. Come to me, you who are oppressed; I shall console you within, so you can disdain all consolation from creatures, considering it as nothing. If you do anything for my sake, no matter how small, you shall receive an eternal reward for it. If you trample down and erase your faults, and make your flesh submissive to the spirit, you shall receive a hundredfold reward for it, and hereafter possess eternal life. If, for my sake and out of love, you conquer yourself in the face of your enemies, you shall be endowed with secret heavenly bread."

Oh, is this not greatly and overflowingly offered! Oh, it is certainly a lamentable thing that our ears are partially stopped up against these interior divine voices! Our outward conduct shows that we neither hear nor follow them, for we are so often ensnared by sensual things and are so concerned about our honor and comfort and the body's lusts. Oh, therefore, the empty wisdom of this world can certainly be called foolishness before God! Oh, let us no longer walk in insecurity! Rather, let us cast aside the works of darkness and put on the armor of life; let us cast off all self-will, self-conceit, and our wisdom in order to be enlightened by the eternal Wisdom and thus be considered foolish and useless by those in whom the sensual wisdom of this world abides. For the greatest blessedness that the soul receives is the light of heavenly Wisdom, through which her inward eyes are opened in the recognition of God's goodness and her own shabbiness and her hidden abysmal faults. She sees how dangerously she lived and what subtle snares are laid for her—snares by which all self-willed and self-conceited people (who are not naked and stripped of self) are entrapped, and from which no one extricates himself but one who is little and humble, who bows down and creeps through the meshes, and so escapes the net.

# Chapter 8

*How people of interiority see and recognize the harm done by their neighbors.*

These humble people are enlightened by eternal Wisdom and recognize how perilously those of this world live, and how they spiritually remain caught in their sinfulness and do not enter into their ground where they could become aware of God and be dead to all created things. To most people this reality is little known; they bear the name and appearance of spirituality with so very little fruit that one must lament for God.

Those who are disdained by the world because they are enlightened by God's Wisdom, and who are knowers and lovers of God, experience in themselves what happened in Christ Jesus, for they are disdained, condemned, stoned, and crucified by the lovers of this world with their backbiting words and false witnesses; by their unjust works they obliterate the lovers of God. Thus, these humble people suffer with Christ; they have patience in the body, and interiorly they flee into God, for they do not pay heed to those who can kill the body, but rather they give it to him who can give life to souls and take it away; him they fear and consider as a friend. Though in the lowest part of their soul they feel measureless pain and anxiety out of pity for the harm done by their neighbor and the dishonor done to God, and because God, for whom all are created, is so little known and loved (because of this they suffer great torment and an untold number of spiritual deaths), nonetheless, in the highest part of the soul they feel, with Christ, a limitless peace and freedom. For the soul always has God within her, and she is always in God; she always takes her rest in her Principle, in the divine Source with that simple essence from which God never departs nor does the simple essence depart from God. The faculties of the soul may be obliged to turn outward and be busy with a multiplicity of things, but her essence abides in God.

In the highest part of the soul the faculties are one spirit and one love with God; they are penetrated by God's power and by divine love and knowledge, and enlightened by divine radiance in spirit, in soul and in body. They continually abide with the heavenly spirits in God's presence and are fed on knowledge and love of him, ready to do God's commands and to carry out the service of the angels; whatever they are commanded to do, they do it faithfully, out of love; and in fear, they omit whatever is forbidden. Thus they are heavenly spirits and earthly angels.

# Chapter 9

*How the soul should remain properly ordered and take cognizance of all the inward admonitions and chidings from God.*

This ground about which we have written earlier is useful and necessary for all, no matter what their state or rank may be, if they would possess much discernment and knowledge:

- of both God and themselves,
- and of where the image and likeness of God is to be found,
- and of why God dwells essentially in them,
- and on what they should fix their heart's gaze if they want to adore God in spirit and truth,
- and of how their faculties and affections are and ought to be,
- and of how God shines down, out of this essential ground, with his light, in their reason and conscience (this light is a divine power),
- and of how it always gives them a conscience in all they do: if they do good, it results in happiness, for nothing is happier or more joyful than a good conscience; if they do evil, the result is heaviness and accusation, for nothing weighs heavier than a bad conscience;
- and of how they should always follow that light,

- and of what it admonishes them to do, and where it is leading and drawing them.

It may be the case that the soul at times is drawn into the innermost ground and union of the spirit and there is taught by God's Spirit in a thousand ways. At times the soul is taught:

- how she should remain in God and become one spirit with him,
- how she should die and God will live in her,
- how she should rest, and God will work in her and through her,
- how she should keep silent, and God will speak within her.

Sometimes, the soul is sternly chided and admonished for her failings. It may be for wandering thoughts,

- or for desiring special knowledge,
- or in that one's intellect has fruitlessly occupied itself in outward things,
- or for lack of submission to God's will in some way, or for self-will,
- or for evil desires,
- or for lack of simplicity, for scrupulosity and multiplicity of reason,
- or for hardness and inflexibility of heart,
- or for impropriety of one's affection, if they have uselessly gone to extremes in hope or fear, love or hate, joy or sorrow, or shame,
- or for carelessness and laxity of conscience,
- or for instability of heart,
- or for carelessness of the senses,
- or for bad intentions,
- or for disordered sorrow concerning spiritual and temporal affairs,
- or for misuse of God's gifts,
- or for ingratitude for God's benefits,

- or for neglecting one's spiritual advancement,
- or for having badly kept God's commandments and counsels,
- or for unlikeness to the image of Jesus Christ crucified.

For these and many similar failings God chides and corrects a person from within, for his own good and happiness. On this account, one must earnestly commit himself to remain quiet and calm within, and to listen to where God is drawing or leading him. For if you are chided and judged by him now, you will have a peaceful dying day and a merciful Judge. It is necessary and profitable for all to exercise this ground; what they are lacking to this ground here in this life is the measure of what is lacking to their blessedness. For they shall find as much blessedness as they know and love God, and know themselves, and resemble the image of Christ. This is how happy they will be, and no more. However much is lacking to them here is the measure of how much they must suffer in the pains of purgatory until they clearly recognize this. Therefore, this ground and its exercise are necessary for all. But you should know that a person may lay aside or take on exercises there insofar as it is to his benefit, insofar as he has time, place, and opportunity, insofar as he himself feels that it hinders or helps him, and insofar as he feels that it interiorly reveals or affects his ground.

# Chapter 10

*On three things that will save a person.*

First: that he neither fly high nor try to understand things that are beyond him. Otherwise he cannot be conscious of the infinite good within him which is always inclined to flow down and to fill up and to shine upon the person of simplicity.

Second: that in the work of God he remain still in his innermost being, not giving consideration to his thoughts, nor chasing after them, nor allowing himself to be led astray by them into anything that would entice his intellect. But wherever the light shines within us, we can always obtain new knowledge of our faults and become aware of our shabbiness.

Third: that we always remain calm but never idle in perceiving interiorly or exteriorly, always having a good exercise with which to enkindle the fire of love—whatever would be useful to each person according to his state or rank. Let us always keep God in our mind, prayer on our lips and work in our hands.

# Chapter 11

*On three things against which a person should be on guard.*

You should know that everyone who desires to come to this ground must beware of three things.

First, one should not spread oneself too widely into many things and exercises. He would easily be distracted in this way, his spirit would be hindered and burdened, his heart would become unstable, he would forget this ground, and the light would become dim. One should praise all exercises, but follow only as many as help a person to find this ground, the love of God, and self-disdain.

Second, one should beware of arrogance, self-conceit, dejection, and detraction of his neighbor's life. The heart is thereby embittered, and the human senses and nature are weakened. Through such faults, one always gets a gnawing prick at his conscience, and one's reason is blinded so that good cannot be distinguished from evil. From this there comes much disturbance in the community, and one does himself great damage, unless his conscience nags him and he does penance for it all and forgets himself.

Third, one should not depart from God, following the counsel of the wicked (that is, the backbiters and enviers of good), and he should not linger on the path that leads to such evil or sit on the throne of evil (that is, he should not set his pleasure in fleshly, sensual things). He should set his will on the law of the Lord and should meditate on his Law day and night. Thus he shall be like a tree planted by the water, bearing fruit in due season (Ps 1:2–3).

Therefore, always serve the Lord with fear, and rejoice with reverence.

# Chapter 12

*On three sorts of spiritual persons.*

The first ones who will experience the above-mentioned exercises are those who courageously and joyfully give up their own
nature and all creatures, and who are touched in the pure ground of
their soul, and who have learned through instruction how to discern
how their faults lie in the deepest ground of their nature and in the
hidden recesses of their heart, where these roots lie deeply beneath
the three lower faculties and have deformed, falsified, and sickened
the soul; how God is present in the deepest essential ground of their
soul and has ennobled her and works through the three higher faculties; how he punishes and corrects the lower faculties, chides and
enlightens conscience, and makes the heart pure, bringing it back to
its first purity and conforming it to follow the image of Jesus Christ,
both within and without. They are constantly interiorly aware of
God and forget themselves totally, always following the will,
desires, and intentions of God. They keep watch over their heart
and senses, repressing their faults, and they no longer consider
themselves free but as always standing under the fear of God. They
experience and feel an infinite good that God himself gives and they
must persevere. And they always live in self-annihilation, making
themselves small, desiring to be nothing in the eyes of all men, so
that God may be revered. That is how the self-conceit of nature is
put to death and kept subject to the spirit. In this way they find the
greatest freedom and ascent of their spirit in order to cling unhindered to God. The humble should like to camouflage and conceal
this, but love cannot hide it and floods humility with the flames of
love. It wants everyone to recognize that such a treasure, namely,
God himself, is present there. For we have him entirely in the
essential ground and image of our soul, and he has saved us all and
purified us by his bitter passion, so that the Godhead might once
again shine and work through us. But not all recognize this, nor do
they apply themselves to it; that is why so few arrive at their source
and point of origin. On account of this, love and humility have a
great struggle so that the human heart is often scarred and wounded;
it may even sometimes fall into unconsciousness because of the

force of love when a person is not instructed about this and if he does not possess the virtue of discretion, which governs humility and love. Humility is the heart's little hollow in which the tiny coal of divine love is kept and concealed. Humility is the mother from which love and all the other virtues are born. They are strengthened by love and ruled by discretion. When these three virtues dominate, all vices give way and virtues progress. The sweetest food of the soul—the sweetest thing that is in God—is humility and love. Love forces God, and humility inclines God, to flow powerfully in the soul, so that she becomes drunk in her love, disdains herself and all creatures, and lives discreetly and orderly.

### On the second sort of people

The second sort of people are those who have heard that God is essentially in the ground and image of the soul (the holy scripture from the Old and New Testaments witnesses to this many a time; it introduces strong progress of soul to all who practice it, and this is clearly taught). But they turn to the merits and passion of Jesus Christ in this ground, so that they feel what they have believed through good practice. And there once again by their sensuality and instability and inattentiveness they have hindered their senses so that they do not feel this in themselves. And since they turn inward again with difficulty and are distracted and multiple, they can neither be united with that simple goodness nor be ignited by its love. Or else, within them is only honor or pleasure or love or favors of creatures that they do not want to renounce entirely. In their hearts these people become aware of a measureless heaviness and anxiety that they have not often felt. And then they think: Shall this ever go away? I have never felt so beclouded; what can this be? How does this come upon me so surprisingly; this cannot be from God. I should gladly have done the best thing; I felt much better in my simple practices. I cannot make use of these lofty and deep things. Oh, let us neither think nor speak so foolishly, for we would deceive ourselves. That is our sensuality and the counsel of the evil spirit. For we are all created unto the highest good in order to know the love and the abysmal goodness of God. And let us there not be downcast in that we are enveloped in a dark cloud with Moses. For then we are certain to await the light, if in our dark anxiety we hold on to God until the humors of sensuality are consumed.

When our heart is laden with continual desires of our earthly nature's burdensomeness, and in that we thus are miserable in this persistent wilderness of our heart where we hunger and thirst and the waters of grace are lacking to us, let us then neither murmur nor be impatient with God nor with our fellow human beings nor with ourselves. But let us attentively pray to God and hang on him in our oppression and temptations, and pray to God without ceasing until the time that God is pleased to hear us. Indeed, when our nature is thus oppressed and our soul does not cease hanging on God, then shall she be fed and filled to overflowing with the heavenly bread. And when all doubt goes away and the soul believes firmly in God, the vein of living waters then springs up in that hardened heart. And she is led into the promised land that is in the most interior, essential ground in which the superessential life shall go on forever. And thus all oppression and poverty disappear, and they rejoice on account of the past labor. And this is the conflict of spirit and nature. For the spirit wants to hang onto God and the flesh onto sensuality. And when the spirit understands that such a precious good is in it, then "abyss calls out to abyss" (Ps 41:8). The abyss of the Godhead calls the abyss of the soul into it, and wants to possess and rule it entirely. But when the soul is still hindered by hanging onto creatures and does not prune away the unfruitful branches, then it cannot mature in love so that it cannot enjoy God according as it would want. And because it is not empty, God cannot come into it to possess it. Nevertheless, we shall not be downcast if we are hindered and hung up with passing things and unfit for this inward exercise and for observing this inward turning. But therefore we shall pray God that he draw us inward through the merits of his holy passion and through his joyful spirit and through his holy afflicted soul and through his holy wounded body so that he would make our spirit fit for him to rest therein, and that he would steer our soul aright, with all its faculties, and that he may possess it and rule it according to his desire, and that he may make our body pure and submissive to the spirit so that he may dwell therein and accomplish thereby what he likes.

In these three things shall all our practices stand, if with Christ we always have a freely uplifted spirit hanging onto God without means by uniting of the spirit. An obedient submissive soul subject to the divine will, and a pure patient body always ready to follow the spirit so that God may have joy in our spirit, peace in our soul, and satisfaction in our body, and thus work in us and through us according to his desires and intent: this is the highest and most useful practice that one can have. Whoever flies higher and seeks farther than these three does himself damage and is a hindrance to himself. And what he receives in these three and what is wrought in him he shall not doubt that it is the grace of God. And shall humbly sink down and bow under the goodness of God and remain with that mirror and view of the soul in God's presence, so that he wants to know what pleases him there. And thus he shall let himself be illuminated by God, and thus he is swallowed up in him in spirit, soul, and body. And so we have put on Jesus Christ. And we feel in ourselves what there is in Christ, who is the door through which we shall enter into the Godhead and by the help of God follow his humanity. And through this door may we again turn inward just as far as we are turned outward; and no matter how much we are distracted, if we again turn and desire grace and pray the Lord by his holy merits that he will make us as pure as we were when we flowed forth from him so that we may once again flow into him.

*On the third sort of people.*

The third sort of people are those who enter into themselves and have no knowledge of God as to how he is in the ground of the soul; nor do they know how they are constituted within. A watch keeps its ordained time if it remains steady in its point. But when it is not functioning correctly and does not remain steady in its point, then it runs without proper ordinance. And so, too, it is with the soul that does not remain in its point, that is, God. For all the soul's faculties and affections are unknown to it, so that they run on by themselves so that they cannot keep the right ordinances of a good life; nor do they know of that light of the discernment of conscience, or where their faults are rooted and have their original seat. Nor do they know how God is superessential, without means, in the point of the soul. Of all these they have no correct knowledge. But they have taken on all their practices in outward ordinances and in

238

ownness, in praying, in reading, in thinking, through manifold images and forms that one can take in and feel with outward understanding and through the senses from without. And thus they remain stuck in their nature. And if they receive any grace from God, they enjoy it for their own pleasures and gratification and thus mingle the precious balm with worthless manure. But if they would leave themselves to God that he might do what he wills and if they were thus submissive to God and co-workers with the help of God so that they did their works with God and God with them, then their works would become godly and fruitful. But since they do not learn to know themselves deeply and hence follow their own lust and desire, therefore they never arrive at their best; that is, they do not arrive by way of the images and means of their nature at the high level of virtues to which they are created. And they shall nonetheless become blessed if they persevere in their practices out of love of God unto their death; and then they shall receive unmeasured reward for which there has been the most labor and industriousness. But the more they have sought themselves, the less shall be their glory and the greater their purgatory. And they shall suffer unmeasured torments and purgatory until they recognize that in this life they were not right. Knowing brings about loving, and in heaven there can be nothing but loving and knowing; if we learn to know God here, so shall we also love him well, and loving, enjoy him. And out of love is born fear and humility, and patience and meekness, sobriety and purity, and all the other virtues as well. Therefore, let the one who stands in the love of God see to it, with the fear of God, that he not fall out of the love of God. Unto this may God help us. Amen.

# Chapter 13

*How the soul should bathe herself in the precious blood of our dear Lord Jesus Christ, and how she should climb up, by three rungs, through Christ Jesus.*

But since we are always inclined to faults now, as long as our soul is in the body, and since by ourselves we never cease to fall, we should therefore always remain near to the Master Physician and often wash our souls in the precious bath of his dear blood which he prepared for us. Within it unceasingly flow countless streams and the five fountains, with fullness of grace. There we must cleanse our souls, if we would enter into his presence, for no one can ascend the mountain of the Godhead but those who have washed their souls in the blood of the Lamb, and who are innocent and clean of heart, and who preserve their souls from vanity and live according to the truth. These are the ones who are brought to the mountain of the Godhead, are received by the holy of holies, are set before the face of the Lord, their original place, and receive the paternal blessing.

# Chapter 14

*First, how one should ascend by means of Christ's wounded body.*

Christ Jesus is the first ladder, by which we approach the mountain; he is a threefold stairs, which we should climb in three rungs, namely, the active, the spiritual, and the divine life.

First, we must purify ourselves in this fountain and then scale the first rung to the mountain by means of the wounded body of Christ; there, we should pray for mercy for all misuse of our members and or five senses, and climb up in this way.

· We should first approach his feet, with which for thirty-three years he so humbly sought after us; now he has allowed himself to be nailed on the cross in order to remain near us forever. Let us pray for pardon on our sinful lives, and pray that from now on we may walk the right path.

Next, let us go to his knees, which for our sake he so often bent night and day before his heavenly Father; let us pray that he would forgive our sloth.

After that, approach his holy body, which for our sake was so pitilessly treated by imprisonment, bonds, blows, scourging, crowning and crucifixion, and shameful death, in order thereby to purify us with genuine purity.

Next, to his loving heart, which was opened with love as wide as heaven so that we might dwell therein; here pray that he would purify our hearts from all evil thoughts and warm our cold hearts in affection and gratitude.

Next, his holy hands and arms, which he so often extended in prayer and in works of mercy, and which now, for the sake of our soul's salvation, are nailed to the cross; pray him to make all our works righteous and resplendent with mercy.

Then, to his holy mouth, by which, with many cries, he brought forth the true teaching of life and sought our souls with so much thirst that he drank vinegar and gall for our sake. Pray for pardon for the excesses of our words and for our excessive satisfaction with food and drink; ask him to adorn us with genuine, sober wisdom.

Then, to the eyes of his mercy, from which fountains of tears welled up so abundantly because he saw the great dishonor that would be done to God, the great harm to souls, and the immense grief given to his beloved Mother. Pray for pardon for having so often turned the eyes of our hearts away from him; ask that he would enlighten our interior eyes and fasten them upon himself.

Next, to his holy ears of patient purity, with which he heard the mockery, frightful din and shouting of the Jews, and the sorrowful mourning and sobbing cries of his beloved Mother and all his friends. There ask for pardon in that we have not turned our interior ears to his divine speech within us and to the admonitions and instructions of our superiors.

Next, to his holy head, which he allowed to be baptized in the Jordan, through which our own baptism was made holy, that head, which is now so cruelly pressed under the crown of thorns and horribly pierced by those thorns and overflowing with blood in order to purify the baptism we have tainted. There pray for forgiveness for the misuse of our baptism and of our five senses; ask him to purify them and enclose them under his crown of thorns, and to baptize us in his holy blood so that he would deign to dwell in us and conceal and transform our bodily nature in his human nature, to keep it safe in his tabernacle from all the attacks of the enemy.

Note well, this is how the sensual lower man has climbed his ladder, by means of the body of Christ, and stands at the foot of the mountain; he can come no farther in this life.

Therefore, we are people who are always beginning and must remain in the active life, according to the humanity of Christ, who was always doing good.

# Chapter 15

*How we should climb up a second time, on the second ladder, by the sorrowful soul of Christ.*

The second ladder that we climb to the entrance of the mountain is the soul of Christ, which was so brimming over with interior suffering and pain that, on the interior cross of love, she was outstretched in love with all her powers, even to the heights of heaven and the depths of hell, to the breadth and length of the earth. How great this suffering was is written in no book other than in the Book of Life, which is closed and sealed with seven seals, and no one can undo them but the Lamb seated upon the throne (Rev 5:6–10). And how his soul, together with all loving souls, was opened and pierced, and what it felt no one can describe; the interior suffering by which the soul of Christ was crucified and outstretched was as different from his exterior suffering as heaven is from the earth. The exterior suffering was uncommonly great, but his interior suffering was immeasurably greater, insofar as he loves souls more than bodies. The wounds of his soul were ineffably greater, wider, and deeper and bled much more with overflowing love and mercy than did the wounds of his body with blood.

The cries of his soul penetrated to the secret abyss with the loud sounds of his sighs and cries for lost souls, with many loving and appealing words, etc.

The poverty and desolation of his soul was so great that she had no support, no sustenance, no consolation from his Godhead. But he hung, naked and exposed, pitilessly abandoned by the Godhead and by all souls, his veins rent open from love, his members broken by the lost souls, so that he had not a single soul upon which he could rest his head, or with whom he could satisfy his thirsty soul.

Therefore, exteriorly, he cried out pitifully, but even louder interiorly: "My God, my God, why have you abandoned me?" (Matt

27:46). O noble soul, think over and take note of this cry; it should make you abandon yourself and all things for his sake, who for your sake was so pitilessly abandoned because you had abandoned him.

Listen to how he says "God" twice. The first "God": O omnipotent God, let yourself be won over by love for the soul for whom you abandon me (whom you love so much), me so poor, and for whom you deliver me up and name as security for her in order to retrieve her. O powerful love, which can thus bend and wound the almighty God, make him drunk with love and so freely overflowing!

After that, he says a second time "My God," and calls inwardly to the soul: "O noble soul, made after my image and God's; you who are my child, my sister, my bride, soul in which I have united myself with you, hidden in the image of your soul. Soul with whom I have made an eternal covenant, in order to be with you eternally. Soul, who are so like unto me and whom I love so much, why have you abandoned me? I pursue you, even into hell. O soul, how often have I longed to gather you under my wings, but now you run after a little pleasure and abandon eternal pleasure. Oh, my soul thirsts after you, so that I may pour out floods of life for you. Oh, come to me; my sorrow is complete, for my heart lies totally opened; the door of life I have opened to you, and I have prepared a place for you; all my servants are waiting for you. And I stand with outstretched arms of affection and desire to embrace you and to press you to my heart, so that you may feel the heat of my love, and so that I might clothe you in the raiment of my beauty, bedeck you as a bride, and make you one spirit with me, for I am a Father of souls. Now, O Father, into your hands I commend my spirit. O fatherly Might, into your wisdom and goodness I commend myself and all the spirits and souls saved by my suffering; keep them in your hands, make them one spirit with you, as we are one, so that I may renew my life and suffering in them."

If the soul understands this, she rises up with all her might and reaches out, embraces the interior cross, and desires with all her strength to cleave to her Bridegroom and to follow him. She gives herself over to him entirely so that he may possess her and rule her as he desires.

Here, by the soul of Christ, the soul has climbed the second rung, that of the spiritual life, up to the entrance of the mountain.

# Chapter 16

*What sort of hindrances the soul may expect in its ascent.*

A person's lower nature cannot come this far, for his nature is too weak and cannot bear it. If the human heart insisted on swallowing up that which is flooding the soul and what is wrought within her, then it would choke and fall into unconsciousness. The soul would thereby be hindered in her ascent and the spirit would be lost at the entrance, and the lower faculties would no longer progress unto Reality.

Therefore, guard against thoughtless passion of heart and of nature. It would drive you away from the foot of the mountain, that is, from likeness to Christ's humanity, and it would drive you into harmful nature, leading to your eternal perdition. Here, one must wisely take care and ask counsel of the mountain dwellers, of whom there are few. (Nonetheless, many are called, but almost no one risks traversing the way that leads to so much blessedness and eternal life, which if we do not gain here, we must forfeit forever.)

Therefore, let your nature climb alone into Christ's humanity, and let it remain there, walking, acting, learning, undergoing and suffering, dying and living with him.

And let your soul ascend with the soul of Christ into a spiritual life, and let your spirit enter with Christ's spirit into a superessential divine life. Thus you are guarded in all your ways—that is, if you savor nothing more in your passage upward, downward, and inward than you are granted or is promised to you.

So that you may be preserved herein, say and pray: "O Lord, incline your ear and hear me; preserve me in all my ways, for I can do nothing of myself. Preserve my soul, for it is sanctified by you. Preserve my spirit, for I have hoped in you, my Lord and my God."

If the soul has ascended in this way, as it is described above, she must remain there in her ground and go no farther forward or backward.

# Chapter 17

*The third ladder is the joyful spirit of our Lord Jesus Christ.*

The third ladder by which we enter the mountain of the Godhead is the spirit of Christ, which remains fixed and immovable in the perfect joy and delectation of his Godhead, in the essential unity of his higher powers, in plenitude of weal, which he never leaves even for an instant, no matter what suffering and abandonment his soul and body experience. With a joyful spirit he was ready to deliver up as many bodies to death as stars in heaven, drops of water in the sea, grains of sand on the seashore, and grass on earth, as Bonaventure writes, and to remain in the same sufferings unto the last day in order to save just one soul, if his justice had required it.

With perfect joy he looked at himself in the divine abyss, in the mirror of the Holy Trinity. He recognized himself face to face, that is, spirit to spirit. It is here that our spirit is exalted and, with Christ's spirit, is brought into the mountain of the Godhead; it returns to its true home and is welcomed back to its origin, embraced and surrounded by the Holy Trinity. Here the spirit is inundated in the superessential good, in the light of the truth, fixed before the face of the Lord in simplicity of thought, purity of mind, and with imageless love, in endless contemplation of God in the spirit's hidden ground and innermost recesses. In this superessential abyss the spirit is overwhelmed and illuminated throughout, in knowledge of radiant truth that flows through spirit, soul and body, heart and senses, and transforms a person in divine knowledge and clothes him with divine light, the first garment of purity. There, the spirit sees itself surrounded by infinite light, and its vision penetrates to its hidden ground; there it sees the obstacles that hinder it and how it ought to conduct itself from now on. The spirit also recognizes the same in others, for all things exist for it in that light.

At this time all the senses of scripture and all hidden grounds are revealed to it, for he contemplates God face to face, in the hidden abyss in all the ends of the earth. That is, it looks at God simply, in the secret, deep abyss in the innermost recesses of the spirit and in all the grounds of the souls and of the hearts of men, all of whom God desires to draw unto himself, where they are free of every hindrance. Hence, the person who knows exceedingly great pain in his soul, always thirsting for the soul's blessedness and human salvation, is nevertheless never distracted by the image of anyone in his soul. He is encircled by simple truth, which is God himself; therein he has the happiness, peace, and satisfaction such as God has in his saints. For God has fed humans on himself and entirely clothes them with spirit, soul, body, heart, and senses; he transforms them and makes them by grace what Christ is by nature. He has united human will with his divine will, human desires with his divine desires, human intentions with his divine intentions, human nature with his divine nature. He is born in him, lives in him, walks in him, works therein, suffers there, rises and rejoices there in the fact that he has found a human person after his own heart.

In this, a person is emptied of all his actions and omissions, words and works, and has lost his form but not his essence, and he lives now no longer, but Christ lives in him. That a person is thus annihilated and lives for God alone is the spirit's highest happiness. Just as when a good person dies, his soul is loosed from his body and blood, raised up, welcomed into God's arms, and introduced into heaven (for God, who himself is the heaven of heavens in the soul, draws him unto himself), so also the Godhead has illuminated this soul, filled her to overflowing, raised all her powers to himself, encircling her with divine radiance, so that the soul lives more in God than in her own body, and the Godhead lives more in that body than does the soul herself. Her conduct is more in heaven than on earth, for she walks steadfastly in heaven with God, that is, in the original ground of the soul, which is a heaven in which God dwells. This is the heaven into which St. Paul was caught up, when he saw God directly, without intermediary, in the third heaven (cf. 1 Cor 12). That was in the primary essence of his soul, for St. Paul was not dead; his soul was in his body. But his soul was caught up in the primary essence of his soul where he saw God essentially, above all understanding and above all images, and above likenesses in his naked essence, just as he now sees him in eternal life.

The spirit is caught up and introduced into this third heaven, that is, above the three higher powers of the soul; above memory, which contemplates there by way of understanding; above intellect, which contemplates there by way of images; and above will, which contemplates there by way of likenesses. Here, the spirit is entirely in an essential nakedness, and it sees God directly, without intermediary, in the simplicity of the divine essence in the innermost essence of the soul, without any activity of the understanding, without images, without likenesses.

Here the soul is illumined and lifted up in the same light in which Adam lived and was clothed in paradise, to which the soul is now reintroduced by Jesus Christ. In this light the soul understands truth in a way none can understand but he who has climbed these three ladders through Jesus Christ, and she is introduced into the third heaven, into the mountain of the Godhead.

How blessed is this soul that has climbed up here, who has been brought in, has died to herself, and is buried in God! How pure she is of all creatures, of all alien desires! How peaceful of heart, how pure from sin, how free of all torment, how far from all fear, resplendent with all virtue, enlightened in understanding, exalted in spirit, united with God, and forever beatified!

# Chapter 18

*How a person has found God in the house of his soul.*

This person may certainly say, with the loving soul: When I passed by all cares and turned into the house of my soul, I found him whom my soul loved. I have found him, and I shall not let him go. I shall lead him into the chamber of my spirit and into the kingdom of my soul and into the house of my heart, and I shall not let him go before he has blessed my soul. I shall hold him and embrace him in the arms of my spirit, and in the arms of my soul, and in the arms of my heart.

When she embraces him in her spirit, through receiving admonition, illumination, and instruction, she embraces him with her concupiscible and irascible powers. And when she embraces him in her heart, through welcoming his divine intentions in all its works, she embraces him in prosperity and adversity. She is so aware of him and seeks his honor in all she does or omits (eating, drinking, sleeping, or waking) that she does everything for love of him. In turn, he is keenly aware of the soul, and in turn leads her into his chamber and into his essential unity; there the soul enjoys his rest, and he embraces her in the arms of his spirit, and with the arms of his soul and with the arms of his heart. Here, love is embraced by Love; here, love is honored by Love; here, love is watched over by Love. Oh, what stronger bond and knot is there? Take note: we can come this far if we intend to be earnest in his service. For if we do not stay near what is highest, then we are unworthy of what is lowest. Oh, what shall be required of us?

# Chapter 19

*How the soul should respond to God's grace.*

Now, in order to respond to the grace of God, we must cleave to God and conform ourselves to him in all earnestness, with all our powers, and enter through Jesus Christ. That is, in our body, we must be purified by his pure, wounded body; we must don his holy body and follow him in purity.

Through his holy soul, our soul with all her powers must be justified and re-created.

Through his spirit, our soul must be freed and introduced into the deepest ground of the soul, in which the uncreated light of the Godhead dwells.

It is here that one must lay down his very self before the divine abyss and give himself up with simplicity of spirit, with his faculties subjugated, with simplicity of heart. This must occur without any understanding, image, and likeness. For if one enters through the image of Christ to the abyss of the soul, there must hereafter be no other image than a simple onefoldness, for God himself is onefold there. Faced with this abyss, one must lay down his very self and sink into his nothingness. Then grace bends down to him and draws him unto herself, undoing all his own works; grace then performs a divine work in him, and for that same work she will eternally reward a person.

How noble this intervention of grace: that a person can thus break through into the very abyss of truth, and that God would see

248

fit to do his work in him! Nobler still than his flowing out of himself is the fact that he flows out from God, to whom we must all come.

That we may all be purified and washed in the bath of his bitter suffering and precious blood, and may ascend by these three ladders, be brought to and watched over in the arms of the Bridegroom and attain that real ground written about above, may the Son of Man, Jesus Christ, who for our sake came down from heaven, help us; Jesus Christ, with whom we all should be united and through whom we should climb and enter into life, if we wish to be saved, for he himself says: "No one enters heaven except through me, unless the Father draw him, through me" (John 6:44; 10:9). Oh, woe to those who do not walk in this way! What fearful, horrible ways are prepared for them! In the hour of their death, their souls, ensnared by darkness, fearfulness, and terror, will be rent from their bodies, and they will find the door locked.

Therefore, as long as time is lent to us, let us make our ascent in this way.

# Chapter 20

*How this ladder reaches from earth to heaven, and how heaven is in the soul.*

This threefold ladder that is Jesus Christ reaches from earth to heaven and to heaven's entrance, and into heaven, and into the essential abyss, that is, from the body to the starry heaven of the soul in which God continually dwells and which is broader than all heaven.

It is there that the human faculties shine like stars in heaven, illuminating earth's dwellers, that is, the human heart and senses. This ladder, then, reaches up to the entrance of heaven, that is, the heaven where the soul lives in God. It is there that the powers flow out of their original Source; it is there that the Holy Trinity works in the higher powers.

Then that ladder reaches up to and proceeds into the abyss of the Godhead, into the essential unity of the spirit, where the spirit is angelic and divine, and dwells more in heaven than on earth, for its place is in God and its work is God, and it is God by grace. On one side of itself, its deepest ground, it is not itself.

Then, it reaches up into the beloved ground in which God dwells; this is so divine and so immersed in God that there is nothing there other than divine unity and simplicity. This is the resting place of the pure essence of God alone. Here my soul is closer to heaven than to earth, though, on the one hand, she still lives in the body and has a life that is "of the earth" and earthly, and that shall return to the earth; and she is sustained and fed and clad from the earth, by God's creation, and she tastes and sees, hears and smells and touches earthly things. How is it that the soul is not closer to the earth?

Nonetheless, on the other hand, she is nearer to heaven, for God dwells in the soul, makes the soul to live, is a heaven of all blessedness, the heaven of heavens in which all heavens are encompassed. In him all spirits are united and immersed, and they see and enjoy God in their own innermost essence; in this heaven the soul now lives and is one with God; she has flowed forth from God, shares his divinity, and flows back into God; she is a heavenly spirit, feels, thinks, and understands heavenly things with the angels, and hears, smells, tastes, and feels divine things eternally. In this heaven the soul shall contemplate God forever. This is how the soul is closer to heaven than to earth.

When the soul now dons Christ's humanity, she then stands between divinity and humanity, between heaven and earth, and she longs to be wholly of heaven and to hide her entire earthly dwelling within Christ's humanity so that there is nothing in the soul but God and man, and so that she dwells nowhere else than in God. But no one may find this kingdom of heaven and this treasure in himself but through the key of David, that is, Jesus Christ, the son of David. And no one can approach this heaven unless he climbs up to it through Jesus Christ and enters through him; it is in this way one finds this treasure and the kingdom of heaven.

With this key we unlock all hiddenness. What it opens, no one may shut. Therefore, let us ever carry this key with us and enclose it in the little shrine of our hearts, so that he will bring us back and enclose us with his inheritance. This is the foundation and key of all cloisters and enclosures.

# Chapter 21

*How one should mount this aforesaid ladder in nine rungs.*

Using this aforesaid ladder, we climb up in three "ways of life," namely, the active, the spiritual, and the superessential. Each includes three rungs.

Some people lead an active life, but they act out of fear, for the sake of reward, not out of love or with discernment of virtues.

Some people are indeed in a spiritual life, but they cannot overcome their passions or control them by gentle patience, nor do they know themselves, nor do they disdain what the world loves and desires.

Some people indeed lead a contemplative life, but they are sterile; that is, they gaze too rationally at image and likeness, but not at the essential bareness and at simple rest.

Therefore, if we want to make progress in these three lives and their nine rungs, we must climb up by our ladder, Jesus Christ (its rungs have been perfected and fulfilled in him), and climb up to the nine choirs of angels, by whom this ladder is surrounded. Around each ladder there are three choirs of angels who help a person and faithfully assist at his ascent of the nine rungs of virtues, and at his new birth, and they watch that his birth may be renewed and multiplied, from birth to birth, that is, they see to it that he climbs up from one choir to the next.

For in each choir to which he ascends, his birth is multiplied and his progeny is increased, proceeds from birth to birth and from generation to generation.

Here people are purified in such a way that our beloved Lord bemoans the fact that "the children of this world are more shrewd in their strivings than the children of the kingdom in their births."

Therefore, cast off all hindrances and climb up this ladder of nine rungs to our kingdom and fatherland, for which we were created and fashioned.

# Chapter 22

*The first rung of this ladder is the fear of God.*

The first rung of this ladder is the fear of God. For the beginning of our blessedness is the fear of the Lord, for the one who fears God in all his ways does nothing neglectfully.

Now, those who fear God and keep his commandments climb the first rung and into the first choir, that of Angels.

They do this by observing Christ Jesus, who is our head. We who are his members must follow our head, if we do not want to be cut off and cast into the eternal fire; so we must follow him and climb up with him, and observe how he always respected his heavenly Father and was obedient to him and submissive in fulfilling everything that was entrusted to him, with childlike fear and reverence and veneration. Then why should we, poor little worms, not fear and fulfill all he has commanded us? Now observe in what a horrendous state are those who do not fear God, what great anguish awaits them in their last hour, which is soon upon them! When that dreaded judgment shall come upon them, they will not be able to excuse themselves.

But those who fear God in childlike fear will be welcomed into the first choir of Angels, and that not only when they are dying, but straightaway, for their place is prepared for them there, as long as they do not fall off this rung into mortal sin; as long as they remain in childlike fear, they remain in the first choir of Angels and all the angelic choirs rejoice in the fact that their number is increased.

And they assist a person so he does not relapse. The Father rejoices that the lost sheep has returned to the fold; the Son rejoices that his precious blood was not spilled in vain; the Holy Spirit rejoices that his love is fulfilled; the Holy Trinity rejoices that its image is re-created, and that there God can mirror and illuminate his countenance; there, too, the Eternal Word can enlighten it.

# Chapter 23

*The second rung is the love of God.*

The second rung is that of divine love, and those who serve God out of love and keep his counsels enter into the second choir, the Archangels. They do this through the ladder Jesus Christ, who performed all the works of our redemption out of love. Through this rung we are united with him in our works and are welcomed among the Archangels; there we shall have more joy than all the Angels in the first choir have. The Archangels here guard man very carefully lest he fall out of the love of God.

# Chapter 24

*The third rung is distinction of virtues.*

The third rung, by which one ascends to the third choir, namely, the Virtues, is that one does what is good, neither out of fear nor out of love, but rather that one performs all good and practices virtues with discernment and is discreet and well-ordered in one's service, so that one can make progress in virtues, and so that one does not repress or mortify one's nature but rather roots out and kills one's faults, and serves not with the body but with the spirit, and is obedient and works neither for one's own renown nor according to one's own comprehension and plans, but according to the illumination of the holy admonitions from God and according to the works of his humanity.

Here a person has climbed straight up the first ladder through the humanity of Christ, who acted with discernment in all his works. He is received into the choirs of the Virtues and is protected by all the holy angels of these three choirs of the first hierarchy that surrounds our ladder, Christ, and preserves a person in fear, love, and discernment of virtues. Here the lower man has mounted up the three rungs into the active life and has become one with the humanity of Christ, through whom all one's works are perfected in active life.

# Chapter 25

*How we should proceed from the active life to a spiritual life.*

Now we must climb higher, using the second ladder, into a spiritual life, by the soul of Christ; for whoever does not climb up and go forward must necessarily go backward. Whoever is not better one day than the next is not worthy of his bread. Therefore, we should not cease to make progress until we arrive at the highest rung of virtue, unceasingly following our Bridegroom into the highest and most sublime choir of the angels, in which the Supreme Good ever rests, in the innermost abyss of the spirit, until our soul finds rest.

There alone is joy of spirit, peace of soul, and rest of heart; we have many aids to arrive at this. The Father draws us; the Son enlightens and teaches us; the Holy Spirit imparts himself and rules; the Holy Trinity embraces us, and the essential simplicity draws us inward;[2] all the saints of God pray for us; and the angels serve us and always stand by us.

# Chapter 26

*The fourth rung is humble patience.*

The fourth rung by which we climb to the first level of the spiritual life into the fourth choir, that of the Powers, is humble patience in all suffering. Humble patience does not lose its peace in adversity, that is, in the irascible faculty of one's left side, where, when one reaches this level, so much suffering overcomes a person that it is incredible. This occurs through the work of the devil, who envies the fact that anyone should reach this state from which he has been cast out. It is not a question of only one evil spirit but of all the evil spirits who have fallen from the choir of the Powers. All together they bear man much hate and envy, and persecute him with a vengeance and opposition. What the devil cannot visit on a person himself he does through other men, and especially by means of those who are easily moved to envy, anger, and dissatisfaction.

This way they often produce such great turmoil that a person hardly knows which way to turn.

And no one will be able to understand himself in this condition; from it there comes a great profit to the soul, for if one offers oneself interiorly to God in all suffering, and lets oneself be stretched out on the interior cross and suffer joyfully all suspicion and disdain and says: O dear Lord, for my sake you have suffered in this way and had to go, crucified like this, into your kingdom. How much more fitting it is that I, poor little worm, should suffer and be trodden underfoot by everyone! For the servant is no greater than his master. Therefore, O Lord, extract and kill all that the world loves in me; ransom with your passion what I have deserved to suffer, for you have abundantly paid for me, so that I, as though innocent, could suffer with you. Grant that I may overcome all my enemies by meekness so that I may not be overcome by evil but may overcome all evil with good, and so that I may overcome those who persecute me and not cease to pray for them. This is the basis of spiritual life, and by it all our enemies are overcome by humble patience.

These persons are welcomed into the fourth choir, the Powers, through Jesus Christ, who overcame all his enemies by humble patience. And they rejoice that their company is increased; they preserve us in peace and subdue the evil spirits so that they do not harm us. And in this we have more joy in God than all the angels of the lower levels.

# Chapter 27

*On the fifth rung, which is disdain for the world.*

On the fifth rung, by which we mount to the fifth choir, the Principalities, we find those who disdain the world and themselves, situate themselves in God and in God's desires, and keep themselves pure, in no way pursuing their own pleasure or the inclination of their desires either here or hereafter, in order that God would have only joy and pleasure according to his desires; in all things they seek the honor and glory of God, and they use everything for sake of his love, with the purpose for which he ordained it.

These people are fruitful grains of wheat and have fallen on the earth, that is, Christ, and are dead to the world in themselves and produce much living celestial fruit. These people are welcomed into the choir of the Principalities, through Jesus Christ, who never pursued his own pleasure on earth or desired any honor either here or hereafter, but he sought the honor and glory of his heavenly Father; he overcame all the soul's inclinations and desires with his bitter death. He himself is the fruitful grain of wheat by which everything in heaven and on earth is nourished.

The Principalities have dominion over the world and direct those in authority; all these angels keep men from the world and from themselves so that they are not overcome. Here a person shall have more joy than all the aforementioned holy ones.

# Chapter 28

*On the sixth rung, which is patient interiority.*

The sixth rung by which one ascends to the sixth choir, the Dominations, includes those who serve God with a patient heart and interiority and who are introduced by the illumination of truth in all situations in which they find themselves or in whatever they do. These people are much suspected and persecuted by people who appear good and who are situated in exterior things with great semblance of virtue. These people of this latter group are a real burden to the former, and these latter want to have everything according to their own way and activity—which can never be the case. For eternal truth itself leads the former persons inward, and they are acted upon by truth. But these exterior people do not understand this, for they know neither the entrance nor the route thereunto. For this, Christ thanked his Father that he had hidden these ways from the wise and revealed them to the little ones. All holiness that is burdensome to others is not genuine. And all their virtues do not enrich the spirit; that is, those who perform and properly possess virtues with their own effort, and with an appearance of holiness, are not enriched by God's wealth, for they are not acted upon by God's Spirit.

But those who have been introduced by truth into their deepest essence and who dwell there above, with God, beyond all necessity of virtue, are themselves essentially all virtues. It is there that the spirit is enriched. And that is God's wealth: that our spirit is so enriched and acted upon by his Spirit. For God himself is all good and all virtue. So when he finds a spirit abandoned and poor, he draws it to himself and makes it by grace what God is by nature. All man's work counts as nothing; this person returns to his origin, that is, to all good, for which he has been created.

Even though these people exteriorly are oppressed and persecuted beyond what is right and just, interiorly they are consoled and exalted, and they suffer all opposition with joy of spirit, peace of soul, and rest of heart as best they can. In the lower part of their nature they always remain impressionable and sensitive; if they occasionally stray into faults due to human weakness, they immediately purify themselves again in our Lord's passion. These people are heavily burdened and bear immensely grave suffering interiorly, in their soul, and they feel a part of what Jesus Christ felt, for they are enlightened by truth. Thus they see how the kingdom of God and the path of truth (which leads into the soul) have become quite obscured and unknown, and that this happens not only to people in general, but also to spiritually learned persons, who ought to point out and reveal the path of truth, but, remaining in their natural way of understanding, they produce the letter and not the spirit, and live more according to their nature than according to the Spirit. These enlightened people also see how gravely these persons are ensnared and caught, according to their own nature. This is why the evil spirit wields such great power over them and brings them to do his will and lead them along with him, trapped by false appearances; for all faults issue from the fact that a person lives according to his nature. From this comes such an intense suffering to the souls of these enlightened persons that their nature cannot bear it. If they were to bear it in their bodies, their heart would surely break a thousand times out of compassion for their neighbors.

Nonetheless, their joy of spirit is not lessened, for if their spirit were not caught up by divine love, it would all be unknown to them, and they would not feel such suffering and affection on behalf of everyone.

These people are very dear and pleasing to God, for they are led by the Spirit of God; and they are welcomed into the choir of the Dominations, through Jesus Christ who bore all persecutions beyond right and reason, with great patience, when all good works were exchanged for the most wicked, and he prayed for those who put him to death.

These angels are inner intercessors and dispose the abyss of the Godhead to flow out in pity, and they possess authority and dominion over all the aforesaid choirs, and over religious superiors, and over all who are led by the Spirit of God, and they acquire for them patient interiority and enlightened discernment, in order that they might teach other people the path.

Here a person has climbed up into the spiritual life, which is practiced in the soul in three rungs: humble interiority, disdain of one's self and of the world, and patient interiority. Here one is encircled by the second hierarchy. And all the angels guard this person lest he fall off, for if they did not protect a person, he would immediately fall off through lack of patience, and because of all the opposition from evil (and even from good) people. These people must carefully watch themselves lest they become unwilling to suffer, and they must remain fixed and fastened on the rock, Christ, and hold tightly to the second ladder by which they climb, through the soul of Christ; and they must cry for help interiorly, and say:

O heavenly Father, strengthen and draw me.

O Son of God, eternal Truth, enlighten and embrace me, and protect me from any evil that might draw me away from you.

O Holy Spirit, direct me and fill my innermost self with your divine presence.

# Chapter 29

*On the seventh rung, where the will is given over and one proceeds through a spiritual life into a divine life.*

Now one must climb higher, into a divine, superessential life, by the third ladder, the Spirit of Christ, by which one ascends to the seventh rung into the choir of the Thrones, and into the first level of the superessential life. This includes those who have given over their will into the dear will of God and who have denied themselves completely in all things, not in appearances but in truth.

Not only do they have the desire to fulfill God's will, but they have immersed their own will with all its powers, with all that they are and can do, in the divine abyss, so that God may perfect his will in them. They have become a strong royal throne on which God dwells, rests firmly, and on which he praises himself and sits there as a king on his throne; there he performs all his works in the innermost ground in which he dwells immovably.

In this ground there is such peace and freedom that one is moved neither by weal nor by woe, for no one but God alone, who lives and works therein, can affect this ground; no angel nor saint, nor any creature, not even man himself can enter therein. And we all bear this hidden in our ground. But if we want to become conscious of it, and for it to become fruitful for us, we must be so recollected and interiorized, and deny ourselves so completely, that nothing but the will of God lives in us; so that God has always full sway to direct all our innermost selves as King in his kingdom, and to order all our senses for his service and worship; this ground in which God dwells, as on his throne, lies within us.

And these people become as pleasing to God as a thousand others who have not been wrought upon by the will of God but who prefer rather to work with the will of God. Therefore, they remain creatures whose works are faulty. But those who allow God himself to perform his work in them become divine and godlike persons, and are welcomed into the choir of Thrones through Jesus Christ, who fixed his will as so empty and abandoned into the will of his heavenly Father, as though he never had a will of his own, and always said: O Father, not my will but thine. And these angels preserve these persons in the divine peace and from inclining to any lower thing. They rejoice that their number is increased. In this they have more joy in God than all the angels beneath them.

# Chapter 30

*On the eighth rung, where simplicity of understanding is found.*

On the eighth rung to which one climbs is the eighth choir, the Cherubim. These are they who keep themselves free of all rational understanding and who contemplate imagelessly. They are turned toward their natural light and have retreated into their primary ground, into the divine darkness where the uncreated light ceaselessly shines, where the divine light rises up from the abyss and fills them with a penetrating brilliance, and shines on spirit and soul with all their powers, and casts its rays on the earth of man's heart and makes it ardent and fruitful.

Because of this the powers shine and burn like stars in heaven. Here the soul becomes simple and is clad resplendently with light and glory. Here the image of the Holy Trinity shines most brilliantly. Here the face of the soul is rendered fit to contemplate God simply and without obstacle. Here the simple eye of the soul always remains open and beholds the divine abyss with joyful vision, lacking all specificity, in the nothingness of one's self. Created understanding and the other powers can neither attain this nor enter here; nonetheless, they flow out of this simple divine ground as out of their source, and are unified and transformed by the uncreated light.

For those who wish to arrive at this, it will cost all that they have—their understanding, their will, and their works—and they must lay themselves so bound before the divine abyss and sink into their nothingness, and follow God into the desert of poverty. Now there are some people who have been led into this ground and who know this way, but they are artfully led out from it again by the created light, where their intellect still contains many rational objects imprinted on it and so it is brought out once more from simplicity to multiplicity. Thus, this ground is hidden and closed to it, and it becomes poor and miserable.

A true lover of God must watch over himself that he not respond to the intrusion of the natural light but respond to the only One in whom is all good and eternal life. These people are so entirely illuminated that all things are enlightened by that godly light through which they are enlightened by eternal Wisdom. And they are received into the eighth choir, the Cherubim, by Jesus Christ, the one who saw the uncreated Light most clearly, and who taught this way most marvelously when he said: "I am the way, the truth and the life. He who follows me walks not in darkness. He who walks by me shall not go astray. He who believes in me shall not be deceived. He who clings to me becomes a light with me" (John 14:6–7).

These angels preserve man in simplicity and gain for him clear knowledge of God and of himself, divine wisdom, and discernment both as to himself and others. And here he shall have more joy in God than all the lower angels.

# Chapter 31

*The ninth rung is simplicity of memory.*

The ninth rung by which one climbs up into the ninth choir, the Seraphim, includes those who keep their memory in God and who are so deeply immersed in God with their innermost thoughts that their spirit always tends and looks toward its source and always remains near God, in his presence, where it continually responds to eternity and dwells in its origin. Here there is nothing other than simplicity and divine union; memory burns and is inflamed in ardent love with the angelic Seraphim. Here the memory is divested, at rest and empty of all phantasms and lower things. This faculty is onefold and simple, exalted in pure light. Here, God speaks: "I shall show you all good, that is, myself. I shall give you knowledge of me." For when we cling to the loving, generous, heavenly Father with persevering spirit, he lets a light of incomprehensible brilliance descend into the innermost depths of the naked soul.

This light is a transparent medium between God and the loving soul. The simple bare memory is a living mirror in which this light shines without opposition, exacting of us likeness and union with God; it is a spotless mirror. Here plenitude of grace is poured into the essential unity of the spirit, grace by which the superessential, spiritual, and active life is made resplendent and ennobled, and it makes a person pleasing in all graces and at one with God.

In this state a person possesses supernatural unity of spirit as his own proper dwelling, and, in the divine essence, tends toward the highest unity. Here the soul is constantly renewed in the divine birth; the divine word is spoken now and always in the soul, and the soul is born with the Son of God; here all riches, wealth, divine knowledge, and all that can satisfy one are possessed without measure in this incomprehensible dwelling that is a tightly locked keep in which God dwells.

Here the heavenly Father rejoices exceedingly with this person, with the love by which he loved his only Son, and he speaks to the soul: "You are my son; today I have begotten you" (Ps 2:7); that is, now and in eternity you shall be my child and be with me. And I shall let the light of my countenance shine upon you and embrace and unite you in my love, and just as we three are one in the divine essence, so also you shall dwell in me and I in you, in the very center of your spirit. And I shall dwell there in your essential nature, with my divine nature, and I shall be with you and walk with you, for you are my beloved son in whom I am well pleased (Matt 3:17). They should listen to and follow you, and I shall renew my birth, life, passion, death, and resurrection in you. And I shall reveal myself to you and to all who are with you in likeness to your life, in unity of spirit. I shall make them all rejoice in a gladsome resurrection and newness of life. My life was full of suffering so that your life would be full of joy. In the world you will have opposition, but in me you will have joy. Therefore, abide in me; thus you have consolation and peace such as no one can take from you; thus you have joy in your spirit, peace in your soul, and satisfaction in your body; thus you become conformed to my joyful spirit, my holy soul, and my pure patient body.

Even though these people possess such joy and union with God, nonetheless they are not without suffering, for the more they suffer, the loftier they are in knowledge and in love, and they bear the cross of love in their soul out of compassion for their neighbor.

The more joy and love of God there is in their spirit, the more the soul's suffering and the heart's compassion out of love for all humanity. This is how they always walk: with a joyful, elevated spirit, with a soul crucified by love, with compassionate heart, and with purity and patience of body. This is how they follow Jesus.

These people are received into the highest choir, the Seraphim, by Jesus Christ, who was perfectly united in his memory and elevated in mind, and burning with love for his heavenly Father and for all humans. And these angels preserve a person in purity of memory, and in freedom of spirit; they gain for him divine love and make him burn with divine charity and with love of his neighbor. In this state he shall have greater joy in God than all these aforesaid choirs.

# Chapter 32

*How this person is surrounded by the nine choirs of angels and is introduced into divine freedom.*

By the third ladder this person has indeed ascended to the superessential life where one becomes most like unto God, through Christ's spirit, and he is surrounded by the third hierarchy.

The first hierarchy of the angels protects the body in the active life in three rungs: fear, active love, and discernment, through the life and passion of Christ.

The second hierarchy protects the soul in the spiritual life in three rungs: in humble patience, in disdain of one's self and all sensual things, and in patient interiority, through Christ's soul.

The third hierarchy protects the spirit in a superessential divine life in three rungs: in divine union, in clear knowledge, and in ardor of love, through Christ's spirit.

Here, the innermost, interior, and exterior man becomes divine and is surrounded by the nine choirs of angels, who walk with him before the face of the Lord. In this way a person should exercise himself in these nine rungs of virtues, which have nine corresponding places in a man, by which he should progress with the help of the saints and the angels and should climb up, through Jesus Christ, who himself practiced them and possessed them perfectly in himself, and who is for us the way by which we walk and our ladder by which we mount up to the Holy Trinity and enter by the door of life, by the power and the help of the Father, the wisdom of the Son, and by affective love and grace of the Holy Spirit, and by the work of the inseparable Holy Trinity and essential unity. Thus he becomes one spirit with God.

# Chapter 33

*How God imparts himself to this man.*

Oh, how lovingly these people are welcomed by the Supreme Good and are introduced into the kingdom of God, not only in the hour of death, but from this time forth. If they are thus dead and their life is hidden in Christ Jesus, and God alone lives in them, then the kingdom of God has arisen in their soul and they are brought into the secret place of the spirit, into the third heaven, where St. Paul was when he saw God essentially, and where Christ always saw his Godhead and rejoiced in his spirit and walked in heaven among the angels when his body and soul were in exceedingly intense suffering on earth.

Now, understand as you ought that for which we have received understanding: that we should know and understand the truth. The soul is an image of God and a dwelling of the Holy Trinity, in which God constantly dwells. The heart and body are temporal, and they are the earth in which the soul dwells. This is how the soul exists between time and eternity, between God and the body.

In the higher part of his soul, a person is divine and united with God; in the lower part, he is human and united with the body. Now it is true that the soul has more affinity with the fact that God dwells in her and makes her to live and savor things of eternity and to understand, than that she dwells in the body and makes it live (which life, nonetheless, it has also received from God).

Therefore, it is more correct for me to say that God is within me than that my body is around me. Oh, if only souls could know this as they should, how happily they would disdain all earthly things, render their body submissive to their spirit, disdain and forget what is external to it, and seek and love the kingdom of God within it! The pure Virgin Mary was turned toward that kingdom of God when she was greeted by the Holy Trinity and told that she would be a daughter of the Father, a mother of the Son, and a bride of the Holy Spirit, when the angel greeted her, and the eternal Word took flesh in her; she continually dwelt herein, and worshiped God in the ground of her soul.

Mary Magdalene was turned in this direction when the optimal and best part was attributed to her (Luke 10:42). Here, too, all the saints and angels contemplate God essentially.

Here it is that I desire to contemplate God for eternity and to be with him. In this heaven walk these aforesaid dear people who continually delight in God, who receive the blessing of every grace, and who in their engendering become as rich and increased as the stars in heaven. Thus they become fruitful by grace and fill heaven with the fruitful works of virtues that God himself works in them; they increase in their progeny like the sand on the seashore.

This way, in addition to their heavenly condition, they have communion with each other in God and all alike flow out of God, are made in God's image, and are united with God in one will, in one desire, and in one intention.

They also become so rich in grace and so generous in their innermost effusions that all their faculties and all the blood and marrow in their bones are wholly consumed and transformed in God's love, and in true abandonment to him. In turn, they receive new nourishment and divine infusion and are fortified by God so that they can bear the divine action within them.

They are anointed with the oil of gladness and receive the crown of joy, which no one can receive but the innocent and pure of heart, those who guard their soul from idleness and who cling to God in truth. They are so illustrious and joyful of spirit because of the Godhead's bright radiance shining from the head of souls having a divine crown.

And this is the gladness that comes onto their head. It is an exceptional crown that no one receives but virgins. They follow the Lamb wherever he goes. That is, in their souls they have received the light of heavenly wisdom, the living Word of the Son of God, and they follow with joy wherever that light leads, since Christ goes before them. They sing a new song that no one knows; that is, they have a secret hiddenness with God and always receive new grace and new knowledge of the truth. Because of this, they sing and praise God in the center of their spirit; God, too, praises himself in them for the gift of himself; he praises himself with the most sublime song of laud, with the sweetest voice of the loftiest joy, with new songs of praise for the gladness of his chosen ones. They are crowned by him with glory and honor, and written upon their foreheads they bear God's name, which is a savory wisdom, the fragrance and anointing of the Spirit, and of eternal life. This savor is not a taste for food or for drink, but a gladness and joy in the Holy Spirit, and assurance of eternal life. Here they receive the hundredfold reward that God has promised them, that is, an interior consolation and experience, knowledge of the perfection of virtue, and right discernment between good and evil, so that they can neither go astray nor be deceived, for they follow the radiant Lamb.

Is this not the hundredfold reward, that they are caught up by the Father's power and brought in, filled with the Holy Spirit, possess Christ in their bosom, bear the kingdom of God within themselves, and become children of election?

Is this not much more than a thousandfold reward that these people receive? And that not only once, but as often as one turns his inner soul to God in his interior ground, disdains himself, and considers all things as dung, then he is introduced by God into the secret holy of holies, to the hidden embrace of divine love, and he dwells in the innermost center of our Lord Jesus Christ, not with his soul in his body, but in the body of Christ.

Concerning this, St. Bernard says: "Here it is that the martyr receives patience, here he walks with total self-surrender and dwells with his thoughts fixed on the wounds of Christ." Even though the martyr's body be totally rent and torn, nevertheless he remains rejoicing and victorious. Where is the martyr's soul? In truth, she is in the interior of Jesus Christ, having entered through his open wounds. For were the martyrs in their own innermost center, they would have felt irons in such a way that they could not bear the torment but would be overcome and abandon God.

Likewise, God-loving people dwell with their thoughts fixed on the innermost center of Jesus Christ, by whom they are wholly protected and consoled in all their suffering. For how else would they be able to bear all the tribulations, slander, and adversity, and all temptations from the enemy, unless they were strengthened by Christ, through whom they are able to do all things, not only to suffer patiently, but also to endure gladly all sickness and suffering.

As the apostle says: "I can do all things in him who strengthens me" (Phil 4:13). Secret, heavenly bread is given to those who are thus victorious, and a precious stone is given to their soul, as the Spirit of our Lord says in the Book of God's Revelations that St. John wrote: He says, "The conquerors are those who overcome themselves and all things; to those who excel, I will give secret heavenly bread, that is, hidden savor and heavenly gladness. And, he says, I shall give them a shining stone, and on that stone a new name is written that no one knows but the one receiving it" (Rev 2:17). This little stone is called a pebble because of its smallness. For though man treads it underfoot, it does not harm him. This little stone is shining, bright, and red as a blazing flame, and it is tiny, round, and smooth. This shining stone we understand to be our Lord Jesus Christ, for according to his Godhead, he is a shining, eternal light, and the radiance of God's glory, and a spotless mirror in which all things live. Whoever overcomes and excels will be given this shining stone, and he receives radiant truth and life. This stone is also like a blazing flame, for the ardent love of the eternal Word has filled the whole earth with love; he desires to burn up all loving souls to nothingness.

This little stone is so small that people scarcely feel it even when they tread on it underfoot. This is why it is called *calculus,* that is, a pebble *(tredelinck).* Though these people are trodden underfoot, they are not broken; neither is anyone irritated by them. This noble little stone is smooth all around, and this roundness of spirit is divine truth that has neither beginning nor end. This is the shining stone that is given to these people who have thus climbed, by Jesus Christ, up the nine rungs of virtues by which we all must go if we are to be saved.

# Chapter 34

*How one should climb these ladders both upward and downward.*

Here a person has indeed climbed up in the three lives, to the ninth rung of virtue, into the ninth choir of angels, and has returned to his source through our ladder, Jesus Christ. This is the ladder on which Jacob the patriarch saw the angels ascending and descending and that is surrounded by all the saints and angels. This is the ladder we should continually ascend and descend. He who has ascended it should take care to remain steadfastly on it, and to make progress in virtue, and to guard himself carefully from all obstacles. He should descend it again in order to put into practice and show forth with works that which is wrought in his spirit, and also for love of neighbor and in order to share the fraternal love they have received from divine truth, and show people the way that has been revealed and laid open for themselves, where they walk in their Source. This is the Source to which they desire to draw all people, through the commandment of love, as is written, "You shall not see my face unless you bring the least of your brethren with you" (Gen 42:13).

Now, whoever has not yet mounted should be careful to climb up through Jesus Christ and to make progress in virtue. He should first purify himself in the fountain of mercy and remove his old clothing in order to climb up bravely and then he should sink down before a crucifix and there behold his unlikeness, show the Lord his manifold sins by which he has wounded the loving Lord, examine himself and confess all his misdeeds to the Lord of mercy, with a weeping heart, a sorrowful soul, and sighs of spirit, before the fountain of mercy in ways such as those that follow.

# Chapter 35

*A devout prayer, showing how a person should examine himself and expose his faults before God.*

Source of all goodness, have mercy on the abysmal sea of my wickedness, which makes me tend toward the depths of hell. For if your goodness had not preserved me, the abyss of hell would have swallowed me up on account of my great wickedness and evil works and bad intentions by which I have sought myself, looking for profit, comfort, and people's praise, when I should have had you in view and sought your honor and glory, and I have shamefully lost my precious time in which I should have served you and earned my salvation. And thus I have been robbed of purity, which is likened to that of the angels. And I have lost the garment of my first purity and innocence with which we must be clad if we intend to possess your eternal tabernacle and the halls of your eternal glory. I have stained the garment of my baptism and also the one I received at my profession, the garment with which we should also be clad. I have also robbed my soul of all virtue, and I have dishonored the image of the Holy Trinity (to which you have united yourself). Out of weakness I have sinned, blaspheming your majesty; out of blindness blaspheming your wisdom; out of wickedness blaspheming your goodness; and I have so often broken faith, which I promised you in baptism when I renounced the devil from hell and all his pomp. Because of this I am grievously wounded and have very poorly kept the faith which I promised you in my profession. And I have often broken my vow of chastity by adultery, namely, by all sorts of sinful desires. I placed my love in creatures, thereby letting my love for you grow cold, O blessed God, you who are creator of all creatures, and I have desired more to please your servants than you, my Bridegroom, my Lord, and my God.

And I have taken more notice of the beauty of creatures than of you, O blessed God, in whom is all beauty, and the one from whom all creatures have received their nobility and beauty. I have not kept the vow of voluntary poverty in spirit, in soul, and in body. I have often had all sorts of cares and desires for temporal things and for the body's comfort and lusts.

And I have labored more for spiritual goods and virtue for my own advantage than purely out of love for you. I have more desired your spiritual gifts and satisfactions and graces than love for you with all of the strength my soul and my whole heart, and thus I have robbed myself of that poverty of spirit proper to the kingdom of heaven. I have not kept the vow of obedience, in spirit, in soul, in body. For when you desire to work in my spirit, I have often been an obstacle to you there by all sorts of practices that I took on. I have often placed my own will and work before the divine working that you desired to perform in me, and I hindered you in your bringing about the interior rest of the spirit.

I have occupied my soul with all sorts of strange gods through which I have often been disobedient to your divine inspirations.

And I have thus hindered you from taking any pleasure from being in my soul and from ruling her according to your love and I have neither served you with my body nor been submissive to you; I have been disobedient and recalcitrant like a hedgehog toward my superiors.

I have not been helpful to everyone, either spiritually or temporally, and have not honored them as temples in which God dwells.

# Chapter 36

*A chaste prayer, showing how we should ask pardon and go out of ourselves.*

O dear Lord, I am the guilty one who struck you with all your wounds. Since I stand here with my misdeeds, have mercy on me and let all your wounds flow forth before your heavenly Father, to stream over my poor, deformed, sinful soul. Do not let them be staunched before you have effaced my sins and faults and those of all people, and consoled and enlightened all souls in purgatory.

O dear Lord, turn not away from me but incline your fathomless mercy toward me; gaze upon me with the eyes of your mercy as you gazed upon the Magdalene, and as you gazed upon Peter when he denied you, and on the murderer on the cross. Gaze upon me thus and grant me a true avowal of my sins and contrition, and receive me into the paradise of your grace; wash me in your holy blood; forgive me and take from me all that has disloyally occupied my ground, for you yourself have said, "When I shall be lifted up from the earth, I will draw all things to myself" (John 12:32). Therefore, I pray you, O Savior of my soul, draw me to you and purify me from my secret evil; shine brightly in the darkness of my soul.

Consuming fire, consume all the sins and faults in me. Come and visit my sick soul, purify my conscience, and make your dwelling in it. By your sacred incarnation and birth, make me pure; adorn my soul so that you, O eternal Word, may be born in it, for that is why you have made me. By your sacred sojourn on earth, make me gentle and humble, so that your holy life and works may shine forth from me. By your sacred teaching and preaching, enlighten and teach me truly.

O eternal Truth, protect me from ever going astray, from all unbelief and heresy. By the love that impelled you to leave yourself in the holy sacrament, receive yourself in me, and change me wholly into you. By your bitter passion, make me patient in suffering, to suffer in turn for your sake all that you will me to suffer, and in all suffering, grant me to rejoice.

By your miserable captivity, release me from all my misdeeds and fasten me to you with the bonds of your eternal love. By the cruel handling, slaps, and blows from the Jews, protect me from all the ambushes and snares of the wicked spirit. By the insults, shameful treatment, and disfigurement you endured, remake my deformed soul made to your image. By your secret sufferings, purify me from my secret sins. By the blindfolding of your divine gaze, uncover my interior eyes in a true recognition of my abysmal wickedness, and gaze upon me with the eyes of your mercy. By the painful suffering of being ushered from one judge to another, lead my soul away from all false paths, keep me within you, and lead me on the path of truth. By your humble silence and by the cruel mockery you endured, absolve me from all sins of my mouth and grant me to bear all mockery and contempt with silent meekness. By your bitter and merciless scourging and excessive effusion of your sacred blood, purify me and wash my leprous soul. By your countless wounds, heal and transpierce my heart with your love. By your burning love and hot blood, warm my cold heart in your love and bath all my faculties in your red blood. Shine through all my bones and marrow and make me fruitful in all virtues. By the crown of sharp thorns that was pressed onto your royal head, purify me of all misuse of my five senses and grant me to keep careful watch over my senses and always to press them under the crown of thorns of divine fear of you.

By the merciless judgment by which you, dear Lord of life and Creator of all creatures were, though innocent, condemned to death for my sake, forgive me all my sins, and be a merciful judge to me; keep me from judging others; grant me a low opinion of myself and always to accuse myself before you. By the heavy burden of the cross by which you were laden, and with which you fell so grievously to the earth, unburden my soul of all faults, and keep me from the fall of sins; help me to bear gladly all the crosses, interior and exterior, that come to me; by the shameful stripping and by your sitting in the biting wind, strip my soul of all adherence to creatures; make me rest only upon the stone which is you yourself. O loving Lord Jesus Christ, by the merciless stretching and nailing to the cross, nail me fast to you with true faith, hope, and love. By the lifting up of your wounded body and painful casting down onto the hard rock, soften the hardness of my heart; impress on it your disfigured image. O pressed Grape, press my soul in your naked, bloody arms; grant me to bear you always between my breasts as a bundle of myrrh; O transpierced Knight, how you were pierced with love for my sake and were so shamefully disfigured! Oh, what shall I return to you for all that you have given to me? I hand over my spirit to your rest, my soul to your love, and my body to your outward service.

O noble Pelican, who feeds your young with your heart's blood, feed my hungry soul then, which can do nought else but eat your flesh and drink your blood. O honey-flowing River of celestial riches, inundate all my innermost being; inebriate me so that I must die to myself and to all creatures and live for you alone. O exceedingly bright Mirror of the Holy Trinity, in which all the saints and angels desire to gaze, how dishonored you were for my sake, and became the scorn of men and rejected by the people! Oh, let me appreciate the high price by which you have purchased me and paid for me all that I owed; make me to be what you wish for all eternity.

By your goodness, through which you prayed to your Father for your enemies, forgive me all that I have done against you; grant that I may forgive whatever is done against me. By the mercy with which you promised paradise to the murderer, receive my soul into the paradise of your grace. By the great compassion for your beloved Mother by which you commended her to St. John, I com-

mend to you and to her my spirit, soul, and body, friends and rela-
tives, goods and reputation.

O all-beloved Father [sic],[3] by the terrible abandonment by
which you were forsaken by your Father, forgive me for having so
often forsaken you, and let me not be separated from you. By your
terrible thirst and the taste of vinegar and gall, grant me to savor
your divine sweetness; make all earthly things bitter to me; make
me always thirst for you. O Fountain of life, by the cry by which you
called out "It is finished" (John 19:30), help me so that your dear
will and complacence may be brought to completion in me according to your pleasure and desire.

O Father, into your hands I commend my spirit, and I pray: O
God, life of my soul, draw my spirit out of me into you; make it
totally conformed to your joyful spirit, so that you alone may rest
there immutably; draw my soul out of her tendencies toward lower
things; make her conformed to your holy soul, so that she may be
moved, possessed, and ruled by you alone; draw my body out of all
its faults; make it conformed to your holy, pure, wounded body with
all its faculties, senses, and members, so that it may be wholly dedicated to you, you alone may dwell there, and have your sway and
work with it as you sojourned, spoke, and worked through your
holy humanity. Work through it what pleases you. May I always go
out of myself into you, never more to return into myself; may I be
so irretrievably lost in you that I can never come out again.

# Chapter 37

*How God comes into the soul with all his grace.*

When I thus go out of all my poverty, then you, O my best-
Beloved, go wholly into me with all your richness, into the empty
dwelling of my soul, you raise up once more the fallen walls, restore
the broken pathways, close the doors and windows, set watchmen
before it, purify the ground of the soul, make your chamber within
the spirit, adorning it with flowers of virtues: faith, hope, and charity,
and the eight beatitudes, you surround her by the highest hierarchy
of angels: the Seraphim, Cherubim, and Thrones. They protect the

memory in pure thoughts, the intellect in clear knowledge, and the will in ardent love, in order for the Bridegroom to rest without moving, on the bed of the spirit, which is resplendently strewn with the flowers of the bright radiance of the beaming rays of the Godhead. This room is full of all the most wonderfully fragrant spices, which stream down into the house of the soul where the King dwells and rules the entire household, making her obedient to him. He fills the house with all the gifts of the Holy Spirit, adorning her with the four cardinal virtues and encircling it with the second hierarchy, the Dominations, Principalities, and Powers. This hierarchy stirs up reason to ardent prayer, strengthens desire to disdain the world like a prince and to subdue the irascible faculties and the powers of the evil spirit with the greatest meekness, so that they may possess his property in peace. He comes forth glorious as a bridegroom from his bridal-chamber, has his sojourn in the palace of the heart, adorns it with all grace and with the seven sacraments and all moral virtues, and surrounds his tabernacle with the third hierarchy of angels, the Virtues, Archangels, and Angels, who preserve the royal dwelling in discernment, in divine love, and in fear.

This is indeed a blessed going out, where God in turn goes in! This is why I know how to do nothing more blessed than to go out of myself. Therefore, I want to turn away from all creatures, and also out of my self and hide in the arms of the eternal Word, where I lose my name and am transformed in knowledge and in love and become one with the Bridegroom in his delectable rest and in his delightful sojourn in the nothingness of my self. O God, O Life and In-dweller of my soul! You are the one who knows my innermost spirit and the hiddenness of my soul and the depths of my heart; drive out whatever displeases you and uncover the ground of my soul, in which the holy of holies (which you yourself are) is hidden. Adorn the bridal chamber of Sion. Consecrate and sanctify the temple of my soul. Offer yourself in the holy place of my spirit, with all your holy works and merits, unto your praise and the glory of the Holy Trinity, for the consolation and salvation of all people, and for the release of all the souls in purgatory. Bless this house of the soul and fill it with heavenly grace and blessing. Preserve it by your love and grace.

# Chapter 38

*How we find these nine rungs of virtues most perfectly in Mary, and how we should pray to her.*

Oh, how perfectly Mary climbed up these nine rungs of virtues and was turned inward to the ground of her soul, where she found the kingdom of God, eternal life, and all perfection of virtue! It was there that she found and adored God without intermediary. She always dwelt there in her Source, and sojourned with the Angels. She was perfect in divine fear. She honored and praised God with all reverence and worship, and so she was in the choir of Angels.

She performed all her works out of divine love, and so she sojourned among the Archangels. She possessed the total perfection of virtue with discernment, and so she sojourned among the Virtues. She was most sweet and peaceful in all misfortune, and in this way she subjugated the evil spirit; thus she sojourned among the Powers. She forgot herself and all that was in the world; thus she sojourned among the Principalities. She was a person of interiority, persevering, and she always adored God in the ground of her soul, rejecting all the favor of humans; thus she sojourned among the Dominations. She yielded herself to God and united her will with God, and was a throne of God; and so she sojourned among the Thrones. She was so enlightened that she knew God, and she contemplated him most transparently in the center of her spirit; thus she sojourned among the Cherubim. She was immersed in God by divine love and sojourned in her Source and saw God perfectly in her own essence; thus she sojourned among the Seraphim.

O Mary, I pray you, crush the head of the serpent, and compel the evil spirit neither to harm me nor anyone on this way, nor to deflect us from it, so that by your example and the help of the holy angels, I may climb this ladder of nine rungs, by your beloved Son, through the nine choirs of angels, into that noble ground in which God dwells, and in which he is contemplated by all the saints and angels. I pray that by divine fear, love, and discernment of virtues, and by humble patience and self-contempt and patient interiority, by abandonment to God, union of my will with the divine will, by enlightened knowledge and ardent thoughts, I may find and preserve the kingdom of God and the divine Source in my innermost soul.

O Mary, Mother of grace, remain near me now and always, but especially when my soul will part from my body, so that she may not be deterred from this way of salvation and of truth, and may not wander away from unknowing into alien ways of darkness, and may not be caught in the hands of the evil spirit, but, by the bitter passion of your Child, may she be kept pure; by his holy merits may she be enlightened by divine radiance and incline herself into her hidden abyss where God's dwelling is; may she go with her essence into the divine essence, with her powers into the divine power, and into the arms of the eternal Word, and so be received by him as a child by her father, as a sister by her brother, as a bride by her bridegroom, all unto the glory of the Holy Trinity.

# Chapter 39

*A summary of the preceding, through faith. How God dwells in the soul and shall dwell there eternally.*

O God of my life, I believe that you dwell in my soul, that you are a heaven of richness there, a heaven in which all heavens are encompassed, and that you dwell in the heaven of my soul, where I now contemplate you and shall contemplate you eternally. When the cloth of our nature shall be rent, then the kingdom of God in the soul will be revealed. When mortal eyes shall fail, then the inner eyes shall be opened to see the God of gods in Sion, who is surrounded by all the saints and angels. This gate of Sion is the bare essence of the soul where she shall meet her Bridegroom in the hour of death and eternally; she goes in to him and is welcomed by him. This is the way, a short path which those who are united with God and are hidden in Christ walk and shall walk.

I believe firmly in this, O God of my life, and I desire to live and to die in this, for I have received witness from you yourself, from the Book of Life. Neither death nor life can part me from it, and it shall be for me for my great joy or torment. You have made an eternal covenant with me. If I now disdain myself and all creatures, and offer myself in turn, with all your gifts, in your essential unity where you dwell in the abyss of my soul, and if I abandon myself wholly to you, so that by the merits of your holy humanity you dwell in me, and if I am always careful to be aware of you and follow you in all things where you have gone before me (with your help, for without you I can do nothing), then your witness shall be for my eternal joy. But if I am heedless of your indwelling in me, and I do not cleave to you with all my strength, and if I am not obedient and submissive, if I do not bear your crucified life and passion in my heart and follow you, then your witness shall be for my eternal torment.

Oh! This witness is in all men, but they neither accept it nor follow it, but all who receive and follow it become children of God and receive the one thing to which we are all called; they become God's children and chosen friends, and they receive the essential reward, which is God himself. That we may all arrive at this, may the One who continually calls us in order to bring us to this, help us.

# Chapter 40

*How we should always cleave to God in the ground of the soul and always maintain an essential introversion.*

Now we have heard many times how the kingdom of God is in the soul and that every just person is a heaven for the Holy Trinity where God unites him to himself in the noblest part of the soul. No one but the Holy Trinity, according to whose image we have been created, may enter there; there, God has breathed into her the Spirit of life and has poured forth the light of his countenance on her, namely, his mighty Word, a fountain of Wisdom.

The Source of life and blessedness is in the ground of the soul. The soul is created in such a way that she should delight in, and cleave to, her Source. God's throne should be in the spirit. He should possess the kingdom of the soul and have his dwelling in the tabernacle of the body.

Therefore, let us turn inward and cleave to the fathomless goodness of God, for he is the Source from which we have flowed without intermediary. He is the Source in which we remain, by our union with him; our soul cannot part from him, as far as our innermost essential ground is concerned. If we want this blessedness to act in us and to gather and preserve virtue, we must always maintain this free introversion, from which there springs forth charity, the bond of love that binds God and soul together. In this union God gives the light of his grace by which all the faculties of the soul are purified and the conscience is cleansed. Out of this introversion the highest part of the soul is continually lifted up in God, in a stillness, in blessed divine delectation; there she savors the nobility of God's richness. Because of this same introversion, the soul, with all her powers, bows deeply before the lofty, majestic, worshipful God. With all reverence she immerses herself in deepest lowliness. With a prostrate heart, mature behavior, control of his senses and humble conduct, this person bows before God and before his neighbor, always keeping God in view and whatever God desires of him.

This is how a person is rendered capable of receiving additional grace and gifts from God. For this reason we should continually abide in the presence of God according to our ability, with reverence; then that blessedness can bring it about in us that we can have such a precious good, such a strong helper, such a faithful Indweller in our souls.

Therefore, let us always keep our eyes on his dear will and on what he wants us to do, to omit, or to go through, and let us always keep a watch on the tendencies of our hearts and on what God brings to light in our ground; let us turn inward with all our powers. Then God can lead us along his hidden secret path, which leads into the ground of the soul; this remains hidden to all other people who do not turn inward. God then shows him his adorable light by which he can see, note, and know his faults in that ground and in the medium between God and him, for that light enlightens us so that we may know both God and ourselves. For if our heart is lifted up in God, and our spirit is simple, free, and turned inward, then the divine Sun of justice shines in us and through us, purifies our conscience, and teaches us, in that ground, what we ought to do and omit. It teaches us a particular exercise by which we leave behind the practices we had taken on, full of images and multiplicity, and instead we follow that simple, onefold Light that leads us into the

278

ground of Truth. This is the way it must always be for one who desires to live according to the heart of God.

Now, some people say: How do I know if that light is from God or from the Angel of Darkness? We will know it in this way: If the light is enlightening you within, from the ground of your soul so that in that light you know God's goodness and your own shabbiness, have no doubt that it is from God, lest you be ungrateful for that light and be a hindrance to God. For the evil spirit may not mislead us, no matter how much he can do externally, in transforming himself into an angel of light and producing a sweet sensation in the soul, exteriorly in the body or in the blood. But no one but God alone can enter our heart or our soul.

Since God, out of his own goodness, endows the soul with his grace, no one on that account dare exalt himself, for no one is so holy as he who experiences this and yet can humbly bow before God and all creatures. It is here that God is found superessentially, he occupies that ground: all that a person has is then so submissive to God that he may work with it as with a living instrument that opposes him in nothing. This is how one obtains a steadfast hope and perfect confidence in the Supreme Good and the grace of relying uniquely upon the Giver, not upon his gifts. Oh, let us eagerly seek after this hidden treasure that leads us to all blessedness. Let us night and day seek after him with passionate love and pure intention so that he may draw all our innermost selves unto himself and gather all our powers into their proper place and that our interior selves may abide in his presence and our outer selves may be virtuous and honorable in conduct, following his perfect example, for he has gone before us in his holy humanity both interiorly and exteriorly. Amen.

# Chapter 41

*On the profit of seeking the kingdom of God before all else.*

It is particularly important to do this in the morning when we rise from sleep. An interior soul should take care that God be its first thought and awareness. From this there spring forth the vein of love and the flood of life so that one turns more intensely inward and is more attentive to cleave to God the whole day long, has more fortitude in following his life and suffering, becomes more prompt in obedience and more zealous for all good.

This is why everyone should take care to offer the first fruits to God, immediately offering God oneself, with ardent praise, as a living sacrifice and recommending oneself into God's hands so that God may never forsake him but rather always protect him in his fatherly arms, strengthening his memory, drawing his desires unto himself, enlightening his understanding, teaching his reason, uniting his will to divine love, making his affections strong in all virtue, controlling all the motions of the soul, casting out the heart's impetuosity, drawing a person's whole self into himself and transforming him in his love.

It is here that is found the secret way that leads the soul into the hidden abyss of God and into the hidden riches of his divine truth. This is found in very few people, for they do not take the first step inward to the very Source of truth. This way is also hidden from the evil spirit, for he does not know what is happening there in the soul. But he does see and recognize from a person's exterior that an exceptional work is being performed in him. He recognizes it by the light of grace shining from that person, which he must avoid and flee. That is why he takes so much care to hinder that noble inward turning, especially in the morning, when the mind is calm, the faculties recollected, and the senses closed. In order to busy the mind, oppress the faculties, and distract the senses by filling them with images, he introduces many things to hinder that introversion, and this occurs frequently even by means of good things! The purpose is to keep that which is better and divine concealed from the soul. But a person should be as wise as a serpent and simple as a dove against this.

Wise: to watch closely not to stray off into foreign paths that would separate us from the living mirror of truth which is put in the ground of the soul and is a light for our createdness.

Simple: directed toward inwardness, as when a person is suspended in God with simple imageless bareness; by it the spirit is exalted in divine freedom and dwells in God's presence through faith, affective love, and mutual knowledge.

280

From this, the soul becomes holy and blessed, and unhindered and rid of images, tending toward and sinking into her divine origin, where she is swallowed up for all eternity and transformed into brilliance and truth, consumed in love, so that nothing remains but seeing—looking out and looking in—into the imageless bareness of the divine nature in simple divine truth, where the soul's countenance is illuminated by the countenance of God, and the spirit is exalted in loving freedom, united with God, and endowed with the Holy Trinity.

The memory, which is there united with the Father, is exalted in imageless bareness in the divine fruition.

The understanding, which is united with the Son, becomes simple, exalted in radiant truth in the mutual knowledge of God.

The will, which is there united with the Holy Spirit, is freed of itself and exalted in divine freedom, where the spirit is transported into the Spirit of God and leans into the arms of the Eternal Word, in which it is held and preserved in God's hands.

Since it has given itself up entirely, with spirit, soul and body, heart and senses, then no one can remove it as long as it preserves its inwardness and keeps open the inward eye of its thoughts, which, above the soul has an imageless seeing into the divine freedom, and the eye of reason, which has an image-filled seeing-out onto the life and passion of his holy humanity. In this way the noble treasure, the kingdom of God, and the light of truth are found, known, obtained, and preserved in the ground of the soul.

These cannot be found, known, obtained, or preserved other than by the merits of our Lord Jesus Christ. That is clearly shown to us in the Old and New Testaments. For before the birth of our Lord, there was no one so holy but that he had to go to the antechambers of hell (limbo). For they had strayed away from the vein of living waters and from the straight path leading to the ground of the soul through the disobedience of our forefathers. If only Adam, who was darkened in this way when he sent his son Seth to paradise for oil of mercy, but believed and acknowledged then that the kingdom of God was in his soul, had addressed him interiorly and begged for grace! Nevertheless, he could not be enlightened or purified as he was before, but through the accomplishments and the merits of our Lord Jesus Christ, who has taken on our mortal nature and has shown us the way and the kingdom of God. As he says in the holy Gospel: "The kingdom of God is within you, and the treasure lies hidden in the field" (Luke 17:21). But if this treasure and that kingdom of God are to be found in our soul, it must happen through Jesus Christ, who is the door to it, the way, the truth, and the life through which we must enter the kingdom of God and into the union of the Godhead, if we are to be saved; this is the way we must walk if we want to come to a blessed end.

And if our life is to be pleasing in God, then we must bear Jesus Christ in our heart; it is through him that the kingdom of God in us is revealed to us. Through him the garment of nature is rent asunder and the holy of holies is discovered in the ground of the soul. That light shines in the darkness, but the darkness comprehends it not. That means the people who are outward and multiple, the ones who neither understand nor know how God is in the inward ground of the soul, where the mirror of the Holy Trinity is always shining before the face of the soul, where the simple eye of the spirit is enlightened, and the eye of reason is illuminated and instructed by Christ Jesus who has merited it for us.

They know not that through the merits of his joyful spirit, our spirit should be exalted in God and united to him, and that through the merits of his sorrowful soul all the faculties of our soul should be gathered together again and ruled by God. And that through the merits of his wounded body, our heart and our body should be rendered fit for God to live in and to receive him there spiritually and sacramentally. And that we would become changed entirely into Christ Jesus and thus dwell in God and God in us.

But in order to do this, we must always keep our inward gaze fixed on the imageless divine unity, and our outward gaze on his noble dear humanity, in order to follow him entirely with spirit, soul, and body.

And this is the right grounding that gives entry into the ground of the soul where we are one with God, and we have right material and make progress in virtue if we always have Jesus Christ as a mirror and example before our eyes, and thus desire to follow him inwardly and outwardly.

May God help us to achieve this.

# Chapter 42

*On how a person ought to awaken early to God, if he wishes to find God in the kingdom of the soul.*

Whoever wishes to find God in the kingdom of the soul, and who wants to be united to him with the very core of his being, and wants to be and remain one spirit with God, and wants to be transformed into Christ Jesus and to dwell in him here and in eternity, must awaken early to God, for he himself says, "He who watches for me early shall find me" (Prov 8:17). This is why one must be careful to turn inward into the kingdom of the soul where God dwells and lives, and is the living life. And especially in the morning one should be industrious about directing one's first thoughts, affectionate love, desires and intentions, heart and senses, to God.

This is how one becomes receptive to God's visitation. Then the heavenly Father shows his divine radiance in the highest part of the soul and enlightens the spirit with the superabundant light of his eternal Word and inundates the soul with the fathomless love of the Holy Spirit, and sends out his bright and shining rays into all the soul's faculties; thus she is endowed with every sort of virtue, each one according to its own operation. God hereby adorns his kingdom and his dwelling. This is the best offering and sacrifice one can make to God: that one first, before all other things, seeks the kingdom of God and his justice. And this is God's justice: that one always stands in self-renunciation and offers into God's hands all one has, spirit, soul, and body. Thus God has us in his power, in order to effect an upright, virtuous life in us. Christ himself has taught us this: that one should, before all things, seek the kingdom of God and his justice and thus all things would be added to us besides. Is this not utterly imperative? He may well complain when he says, "The children of this world are wiser about their earthly sustenance than are the children of the kingdom about their spiritual birth" (Luke 16:8). Therefore, let us be wise about turning inward when the grace of God is born in us and the eternal birth is renewed in us. Since one is transformed in Christ Jesus, all holiness of work and of life emanates from him. That one should first unite himself with God in the kingdom of the soul God himself shows us in the Pater Noster. He teaches that one should first address God when one wants to pray to him, in that one first says, "Our Father who art in heaven" (Matt 6:9ff.). There one turns inward and reminds him that he is our Father who has created us and in whom we have eternally existed, and that he has impressed his eternal image on us and that he himself has made his heaven in us.

Should this not incite a slow, halfhearted soul to rise up to its beloved Father in the innermost chamber of her spirit? And offer herself up into his hands who will care for her in all things? And so the soul should pray, not for temporal but for eternal good. In "hallowed be thy name" the soul should pray that she may be suffused with the light of his eternal Word and be clad with the brightness of truth, and invite him to come into us, and say "Thy kingdom come" and to possess and rule the kingdom of our soul so that we may possess the kingdom of your glory in the hereafter. And that "the will of God be done in us as in heaven," where all the saints and angels are one spirit and one will with God; that we, too, may be one will and one spirit with God on earth. And afterward, one should pray for daily bread, for food and nourishment of soul and bodily necessities, and for forgiveness of all our trespasses and wrongs. And that we may not give consent to any temptations. And that he deliver us and protect us from all evil. In this we are shown that one should first turn inward to our merciful Father and remind him that he himself has his heaven in us and is inhabitant of our soul.

Ah! Is this not fathomless goodness of God, that he wishes to be an inhabitant and the food of our soul, for all our beatitude depends on whether we want to be an in-dweller and one spirit with God and want to walk worthily in his presence, cling fast to him, and pray him that his eternal Word may be revealed in us, so that his name may be sanctified in us and our soul may be deified (rendered conformable to God), and that he may enter her and adorn her and make her one spirit with him. And that he would feed her with himself and with all the fruits of the sacraments, and transform her entirely into himself, and purify her of all sin and deliver and protect her from all evil, so that she may remain unhindered, without intermediaries, with all the blessed and believing spirits before his divine and lovable countenance.

This is the true divine prayer by which one is introduced to the ground of the soul where one adores God in spirit and in truth. Here the mouth is silent, but the spirit cries out and implores unceasingly in the ground of the Godhead.

The outward prayer has a beginning and an end, but the inward prayer has neither beginning nor end. With the outward prayer, one offers fruits, but in the inward prayer that goes on in the innermost recesses of the spirit, one offers the tree with the fruits. This tree has three roots (that is, human will, desire, and intention) with which this tree is planted in fruitful soil and near the welling fountain of the Godhead, which renders all arid hearts fruitful, insofar as they are one will, desire, and intention with God.

Now, whoever wishes to enter this inward ground and to remain there must apply himself day and night with all care to rise up the first thing in the morning in the innermost chamber of the spirit and incline himself toward his original beginning in the dark power of our Father where he is suffused with the living Word and embraced by his loving goodness. There he should pray that God would draw and unite with himself all his innermost being and both his inward and outward self, so that he may follow him as he has gone before us and as he taught us to walk. And just as he always remained, as far as his holy humanity is concerned, an inward man in divine union and in freedom and in fruition of his Godhead. And from without, he did the works of his heavenly Father, and he did not overstep the tiniest commandment (He who is the highest freedom of the angels). That, according to the inward man, he, too, may remain in the divine union, and from without, live according to his example, and by his help never overstep the least commandment and ruling of superiors, so that he may be pleasing to God inwardly and outwardly.

And thus one must always be ready to turn inward and to offer God the first and the last fruits.

# Chapter 43

*On how in the morning one should practice all the outward means interiorly, and continue throughout the whole day and night.*

One who wants to love God above all things (which has to be the case if one is to enter into life), must be zealous to turn inward in the morning so that God may be the first thought and the first desire of the soul, the first intention of the heart, and the innermost motion of the spirit. This is how entrance to the spirit, soul, and heart is opened up to God. In order for one to love God with all one's thoughts, all one's soul, and all one's heart, the soul should first of all bow down in God's presence and offer herself entirely into God's hands. Just as one is outwardly aroused by a sign of obedience, so one should inwardly wake up to God, who prods, moves, and arouses the soul to the love of God. Just as one exteriorly raises his head, lifts his hands, and dresses the body, and covers the head, and girds himself, signs himself with the cross, bends his knees, and goes to God's service and gives himself to the works of obedience, likewise one should inwardly raise up one's mind to God in union with his love, and offer himself entirely to the dearest will and complaisance of God, and raise up all the faculties of the soul to thanksgiving and to praise of God, in that he has not cast him off but has chosen him for his service and has lent him time in which he can praise God, and become a person after God's own heart, and he should clothe his bare soul and put on our Lord Jesus Christ, with an exalted spirit, with a submissive soul, and with a pure, patient body, and cover his head with the crown of thorns, that is, that one close off the five senses and prick them with the fear of God. From this, there comes a happy, joyous spirit, for the cruel crown of thorns that was pressed into that adorable head of our dear Lord made his spirit even more joyous; and he should gird and encircle himself with the union of love remaining in the presence of God, and sign himself with the cross, that is, follow him in his crucified holy life and passion.

And in this way he should make the sign of the cross, by which he may be protected against sin, heresy, the evil spirit, all error, and danger. As one raises his hand to make the sign of the cross, he should have this thought for his heavenly Father, saying "In the name of the Father," that he would strengthen us by his paternal might and come to our aid.

And as he lowers his hand, that he would fill, enlighten, and teach our soul with his fatherly Word in the name of Son. And as he moves his hand crosswise again, that he would protect us by his lovable goodness and grace, and receive us with the Holy Spirit, in the name of the Holy Spirit. Amen. (May it happen to us.)

And incline and bend down with all reverence and worship under the almighty worshipful God, to pray that he would hold him in his fatherly hands and keep him imprisoned and bound in the love by which he kept his lovable humanity imprisoned and bound, in the hands of the Jews, on the column and on the cross, so that he may not incline away from the divine presence or from the lovable image of his holy humanity, or that he may not overstep the commandments of God or any command of superiors, but always remain in God's presence, to be one spirit with the will of God, and one spirit with the desire of God, and one body with the intention of God; and that he may accomplish all divine service and grateful praise and all the works of obedience with him, for without the divine assistance, he can do no good.

# Chapter 44

*On how we should leave ourselves to God, in order for him to work in us.*

In order that God would deign, in her and through her, to walk and to perform all the works of virtue, as he has done and suffered through his only Son Jesus Christ, the interior soul then should remain thus clad and well ordered the entire day, and have a zealous attentiveness for God's inward speaking and for the inclinations of her heart, and in all her affairs to seek to love and intend God and his glory in all things; and to follow his holy life and passion inwardly and outwardly, and to resemble him in all her conduct, for the only thing we have to do is to become conformed to him in our innermost soul, and our inward and outward man, and that by continual exercise of his holy life and bitter passion.

Therefore the soul should at all times closely observe him, as to how he conducted himself.

At Matins, Prime, Tierce, Sext, and None: What anxious fear, dread, pain, injury, insult, mockery, and reproaches, and how many stripes and wounds he had at these hours, and what a frightful death he suffered for our sakes; and how lovingly, humbly, meekly, patiently, long-sufferingly, benevolently, sweetly, peaceably, and sweetly he showed himself in everything for the sake of our re-creation; and to bring our wrongs and faults to confront this: that we are so cold in love, and can suffer so little, and become upset and disquieted so easily, and that we are so bitter of heart and so puffed up in spirit and so harmful in words and so ready to excuse ourselves and to take revenge for little injustices.

These and similar faults and the wounds of our soul we should often show to the heavenly Doctor and Master of our soul, so that he will heal the wounds of our soul, cast out all her faults, and adorn her with all virtues, such as true love and deep humility; and that he would grant us to go about sweetly, peacefully, and lovingly with all people, and to win over our enemies by meekness, and to suffer all injustices patiently, so that we might be stretched out on the cross with Christ Jesus with joy of spirit and with peace of soul, with sweetness of heart and with patience of body.

These three should continually be impressed on our heart, for it is with such exercises as these that one arrives at likeness to Jesus Christ; therefore, we should set this before all other exercises, and hold ourselves to it, no matter how high and how great the other practices appear; and give up all that reason grasps onto in anxious attentiveness, and leave off research into many writings, which lead a person out from the simple ground of truth into multiplicity.

Therefore, cling to this groundwork and whatever you receive in addition, take it for truth in deep humility. Take as much as makes you advance.

For this is the basis from which all the other exercises proceed, upon which they all stand and are preserved.

# Chapter 45

*How the devout soul should always dwell in the cross and in the passion of her Bridegroom.*

A devout soul desirous of ascending in these three lives and by degrees should continually dwell in the cross. In her heart should be

Mount Calvary, where all the passion of her Bridegroom is collected. Her soul should be a cross on which her Bridegroom is raised up, stretched out, and fastened. Her spirit should be lifted up in joyousness with his spirit, and thus she will be joined to him, and hang with him on the cross in the greatest poverty and abandonment from without, and in the greatest peace from within, and in the greatest freedom, and in the most sublime joyousness; so she should live on it as a queen in her palace and see through the gilded lattice of his five holy wounds, and through the windows of his many wounds, and see through his entire holy life and passion with inward compassion of heart, with humble lowliness, in inward joyousness.

So should she continually bear his passion in her heart and see by means of it. For the higher a person is, the more one sees far and wide; the more she approaches her Bridegroom and is continually near him, the more she loves him and the more distinctly feels his life and passion and becomes more like unto him. This active love seeks her Beloved everywhere and runs through every place where her Beloved has suffered, and she makes herself happy by compassion in the places where he suffered. And so, in the meantime, she often forgets herself, for she is still full of images in her exercises, but this essential love possesses her Beloved in all things, and changes all multiplicity to simple rest, and she reminds her Bridegroom on the cross of all that he suffered in many places; she prays that he will make her multiform and allow her to encounter the birth and the cross as one. In the cross she sees the birth, as she looks on the divine Word that is eternally born of his Father, and is conceived by the Holy Spirit, and born of the pure Virgin Mary, he who is the Sun of justice there, and the bright mirror of the angels. Him she then sees so piteously abused on the cross; in the birth she already sees his passion, for from the first hour that he was born, he was crucified and in his soul he felt everything that he would suffer in body until he died on the cross. Even though his body was not stretched out, his soul, nonetheless, was stretched out with love for all creatures.

Even though his body was not wounded, nevertheless his soul was dreadfully pierced and suffered the pangs of many a bitter death. Even though his side was not pierced, nevertheless his heart was wounded with love.

This is how a real lover should dwell on the cross. And with enlightened reason and loving desire look through the passion of her Bridegroom, and gather and draw it to herself and bear it between her breasts like a tiny bundle of myrrh (cf. Sg 1:12) and remind him every moment and at all times what he has suffered on her account, so that she should follow him and resemble him in everything.

*How the soul should resemble her Bridegroom during the seven hours, and at Matins give herself up as prisoner of his dearest will.*

At Matins the soul inclines inward into the abysmal divine darkness and gives herself up into his divine power, spirit, soul, and body, heart and senses, to be eternally imprisoned and bound in his love, he who on her account at the hour of Matins willed to be so miserably imprisoned and bound. Thus God has mastery over her so that he can renew in her his birth, life, passion, death, and rising.

*How she should resemble him at Prime, and proceed from one virtue to another.*

At the hour of Prime she should abandon herself entirely to God and take heed of the in-flowing of God, and of the fact that the eternal truth, the Son of God, who is born in her, who suffuses all her innermost self, embraces and draws her spirit, soul, and body, heart and senses, and transforms her into himself, so that he may live and walk in her, and lead her from one virtue to another, just as he was led from one judge to another. Thus the eternal Word assumes human nature every day and dwells spiritually in us.

*How, at Tierce, she should be transformed into his pain-filled image.*

At the hour of Tierce she hides herself in his pain-filled image in order to bear patiently all the suffering and disdain, all the scourging and crowning and condemnation and unjust accusations and everything that might come upon her within and without, through the power of the Father, the wisdom of the Son, and love of the Holy Spirit, for the honor of him who for her sake at the hour

290

of Tierce was scourged, mishandled, and wrongfully condemned and laden with such a heavy cross.

*How, at the hour of Sext, she is crucified.*

At the hour of Sext she observes how, for her sake, he was very cruelly stripped and seated on the cold stone, and was nailed to the cross, was stretched out, and was lifted up. Here she strips herself again of all that is not God and places her life and sufferings upon the stone, Christ, in order to be nailed, stretched out, and lifted up on the cross with him. She takes her highest happiness and strength in this. This is how the world becomes a cross to her, and she to the world, and all those in whom the world still lives crucify and persecute and blaspheme her. Here she becomes black, deformed, and as nothing in human eyes, but she is all the more beautiful and shining white in God's eyes. But to human eyes she seems useless and fruitless; from the outward shame and confusion she receives inward joy and happiness and reckons that nothing is more honorable and glorious to her than to share in bearing her Bridegroom's shame and hurt, and to glory in the cross of Christ. Thus God allows the stars of heaven to become black. These stars are God's chosen ones, those who, through good works in the firmament of the holy Church shine like stars in the heavens. These God allows to become black from all sorts of tribulations in which they are exercised. This is a blessed blackness; through it the mind is elevated to God, and the spirit made joyful, and the conscience pure and shining white; through it the whole person is transformed into Christ Jesus. In this blackness, all the suffering and disfigurement and deficiencies and lack of resemblance are consumed. It makes her interiorly rejoice in all suffering. Even though it is true that nature moans and weeps, the soul nevertheless is always consoled by taking her joy in the cross.

*At the hour of None, she should die with him and live in the Spirit.*

At the hour of None she reminds him, with deep attentiveness, of the terrible, bitter death that he suffered in order to make her live. Here she is careful to purify her conscience from all that displeases God and that might weigh heavily on her in the hour of her death. And she is eager to die to herself again on account of him, and to live for him alone, so that in that hour she may be sure of life.

# Chapter 46

*How the soul should take her midday meal on the cross.*

Here she takes her midday meal on the table that is prepared before her face and anoints her head with the oil of gladness, because through his death she has obtained life. And she eats the bread of sorrow and drinks from the chalice of his bitter passion, and is fed on the fruitful wheat on that roasted flesh that was rent and cut upon the column, was salted by the spittle, and crucified for love, and sated by his precious blood. And on the roasted lamb that was pierced through by the crown of thorns and with the boring of the nails, and was roasted on the cross in the fire of love.

See, these are the dishes that are set before the loving soul at noon. Oh! Let us all together go in and drink from the fountain of life, that we may never again thirst after earthly things. Let us now be joyful; this is the golden year in which Christ has given himself to us, his flesh as food and his blood as drink. Let us listen attentively to how sweetly the Bridegroom sings and how enchantingly he plays on the harp of the cross the seven little songs that are so full of the sweetness of love that they make the loving soul melt away and flow back into him. All creatures are consoled and made happy by this, for they resound through heaven and earth and invite all creatures to table. And the Bridegroom is here, so generous that he gives all that he has and is opened up so wide that he is much more ready to give than we are to receive, for our soul is often unprepared and the vessel of our heart unclean. This is why an interior soul shall be zealous to purify herself and to bathe in his holy blood, and to acquit and pay all her debt by his passion, and to adorn herself with his virtues and to enter through him, and to be received at his dinner.

Especially at noon, when we go to bodily food, we should first inwardly go to this table for food and nourishment for the soul, and eat and ruminate the Word of God that we hear within and also without, and eat of the food of life and drink from the chalice of his open heart, which is full and overflowing with the crucified wine of love, and from the influx of the divine essence the best wine of the illumination of the divine radiance. Here the soul should, at every meal time, when she eats and drinks, seek and desire the embrace of God and be fed by his love, and take the bodily food with gratitude as a medicine by which the body is fortified in order to serve the spirit, to be submissive to it, and she should pray interiorly: "O dear Lord, let not this food and drink be for me food for sinning, but give it such power that is may strengthen me in all virtue, so that by it I may be more humble, more diligent, and more joyous, more grateful, in your service. For that is why you have granted me to enjoy it for your love's sake and to consume all my strength in your service."

Oh! May all people draw near to you, where you are lifted up on the cross, and once again take nourishment from your table, especially those who have done us good, both living and dead. And let the rivers of your grace and of your holy blood flow down upon the poor souls in purgatory, and release them from all suffering and guilt, and bring them into your eternal banquet. After the meal, let the soul then offer itself up again to God, with all the gifts and benefits she has received outwardly and inwardly from God, and lift herself up, with all her sufferings, onto the cross, and rest in that immutable good above all created things. Thus the essential love possesses God in all things and at all times, and dwells thus on the cross like a powerful queen in her palace, in which she has everything that she desires. She ever inclines herself before his divine power and shows him the image of his crucified self, in which the totality of all his bitter passion is encompassed. By it she begs a blessing for herself and for all humanity, and prays that he will transmute all suffering and every event to his beloved will and pleasure. She prays that by it he would come to the aid of all people and draw them to him, and strengthen them in all virtues by his fatherly power, and enlighten and teach and protect them by his eternal divine truth, and envelop them with his loving goodness, and make them one spirit, one soul, and one body with him, and that he would do this through his joyful spirit, and through his sorrowful soul, and through his wounded body. She should do this a thousand times a day and thereby obtain all that she and her neighbors need. She can obtain this generously from his holy passion, which is given to her as her own, in the measure that she is thoroughly given over to God and sinks herself into his divine abyss by his passion. Here no request can be refused; he must bless her and all who follow him.

*How she should purify her conscience at Vespers.*

At the hour of Vespers she so purifies and cleanses her conscience and carefully gathers all the herbs of virtues and opens up the lap of her desires and therein receives the wounded Knight who died on the cross for her sake. And she looks at all her dissimilarity to him and anoints and kisses his holy wounds with torment of spirit and with sorrowful soul, and with lamentation of heart. Then she presses him to her breast and embraces him in the arms of love.

*How she should anoint and bury him at Compline.*

At the hour of Compline she prays the dear Mother Mary to bury her dear child, and so she is careful to anoint him with all the herbs of virtues, along with the myrrh of total death to herself, and with the aloes of divine confession and with the balsam with which he is shining and radiant. And she winds him in the fine linen cloth of her pure conscience, which he has purified in his bitter passion. And she buries him with deep humility in the grave of her heart and closes the grave with a close watch of the five senses, and she buries and encloses herself along with him, and thus she is together with him immersed in the chamber of the Holy Trinity and buried in the abyss of the Divine Being. There she is raised up again in a new life of grace, and God arises in her and through her and clothes her in the garment of beauty and makes her to live unchangingly in him above all created things, to rest in his tabernacle, and ever to watch how her Bridegroom, who was born well before the hour of Matins in the night, was captured, arose from the dead, and is now one with the Father in glory, and is a lantern through which the Godhead shines, and by which the entire heavenly host is illuminated.

He who well before the hour of Prime lay before beasts and was led from one judge to another, and revealed himself to his friends, now leads all the heavenly company to the springs of the veins of the Godhead and lets them drink from the river of his wealth.

And he who at the hour of Tierce was circumcised, scourged, crowned, condemned, is now crowned with the glory and with honor and sits at the right hand of his Father, where he is adored by all the inhabitants of heaven and earth. And he who well before the hour of Sext was offered to the Father by his Mother, and hung on the gibbet of the cross, now is given all power in heaven and on earth. And he who well before the hour of None was baptized in the Jordan and died in disgrace on the wood of the cross is now the tree of life whose foliage makes all the chosen happy, and whose fruits feed them, and under whose shadow they take their rest and enjoyment. And he whose mother was denied lodging at Vesper time and who was also, when dead, given into his mother's lap, and taught his two disciples after his death, now shall never die again, but all the blessed souls have eternal life through him. And he who, at the hour of Compline, ate his last supper and was buried, and revealed himself to his disciples, the doors being locked, is now the hidden heavenly bread with which only the chosen children are fed. And he invites them to his supper where he, with all the saints and angels, makes good cheer and gives himself to be enjoyed as food and drink for eternity. His heart is opened wide to swallow up all the blessed spirits in it and to change them into himself, and to make them by grace what he is by nature. Thus the loving soul dwells in God and God in her, and is a living grape-stock planted in God, who brings forth abundant fruit in its season. In similar ways, each one should occupy himself in the evening, as he goes to supper, this is how he should go: In the innermost dining room of his soul, where Jesus desires to hold his supper, he should rest there upon the Lord's breast and there listen to the sweet words about the riches with which he has endowed us.

*How one should go to prayers and give himself up to the will of God.*

After the meal, he should think on how Jesus said: "Stand up and let us go" (Matt 25:46). And on the way he said: "My soul is sorrowful unto death" (Matt 25:38). And meditate on the cause of that sadness, and go with him to the Mount of Olives; when he gets there, he should fall upon his knees and worship God in spirit, and give himself up to God's desires and will in total dedication, keeping zealous watch over himself within and without. Where he failed in anything, inwardly or outwardly, he should pray insistently for speedy forgiveness by the bitter passion of our Lord Jesus Christ, especially in the evening.

# Chapter 47

*How a person should examine his conscience in the evening, and pray for grace.*

This is how an interior soul should turn inward and survey her innermost depths as to whether she has followed or resisted the admonitions of God and the motions of the Holy Spirit: whether she has extinguished or resisted the light or the urgings of conscience; whether she has cleaved to God with her innermost self and has been submissive and obedient to him with all her faculties; whether she ever, with any member of her body, stepped away from the living mirror of truth; whether she has ever outwardly overstepped any rule or ordinance; whether she has ever been an obstacle to anyone by word or by work, or lessened his good reputation by any slander, or has disparaged anyone in anything; whether she has followed the pleasure of the flesh, or the desire of the eyes, or the pride of life in anything, secretly, under cover, whether in words or in works, in going or in coming, in eating or in drinking; whether in all her affairs, where she should have intended and loved God, she secretly sought or followed her own senses and desires, for the root of our evil intentions sinks very deep into the ground of the heart. Therefore, one must pay close attention to the ground of the heart, as to whether one's intentions are right and pure before God and ask herself if she has ever let anything enter through the five senses by which unrest and oppression enter the soul.

With these and similar faults, and those that one discovers daily within himself and in which he recognizes that he is at fault or deficient, then he should humbly pray for forgiveness and ask for grace before God; that he may have mercy on him by his bitter passion and redeem all he has done wrong, complete all he has left undone, by the merits of his wounded body and of his sorrowful soul, that by them he would render him pure and rightly disposed in spirit, soul, and body; and that he would feed his hungry soul and would transform him entirely into himself.

# Chapter 48

*How one should enter into rest with God.*

As he goes to his rest, he should bow down and shut himself up in the innermost chamber of the spirit, and strip and denude himself of all past things and occupations that might hinder him in the morning when he should direct his first thoughts to God; then he should bow down and lie down in the unity of the divine plan and in the arms of the eternal Word, covering himself with his [the Son's] bitter passion. Thus he can say with the bride: "'I sleep but my heart keeps watch' (Sg 5:2); 'in my bed I have sought him whom my soul loves' (cf. Sg 3:1); I have sought and found him in the house of my soul, and I shall never let him go before he gives sleep to my eyes and rest to my head; thus I can rest with him from all outward things." When a person thus goes to rest with God, then he can freely wake up to God and say: "Where art thou, O my Beloved?"

# Chapter 49

*A prayer: how the soul shall speak to God interiorly as she falls asleep in bed.*

"O noble In-dweller of my soul, you who are there and will to remain there, life of my soul, deign to remain with me with your love and grace. And let the shining rays of your Godhead shine in and through me; by them, purify my soul and all my innermost being; come and feed my hungry soul, which can do nothing but eat your flesh and drink your blood; for without you my soul cannot live in the life of grace. When my soul is not fed by you, then it becomes infirm and lax in all virtues. Therefore, come, O Food of my soul, O Nourishment of my spirit, O Strength of my heart, O Guardian and Keeper of my body, transform me into yourself and make me by grace to be that which I am not by nature, so that again all my innermost being may praise you; may you receive as many praises from me as my breath goes out and in, like fiery arrows of prayer and burning torches of love. As often as I take a new breath, may my soul receive you with new graces; as often as I exhale, may my soul go out of herself and be received and held by you. Let all people be preserved in your love and grace, for you are in each one, unite them with you as we are united, and do the same unto all believing souls. Let your Godhead shine in them and through them as those in limbo shone, by your noble soul, so that all their pains depart and the evil spirits may flee from them. Grant them eternal rest; may the eternal light (which you yourself are) shine upon them." This is how he shall take his rest in the Lord in order to strengthen his nature for the service of God.

# Chapter 50

*How the bride should invite the Bridegroom into her chamber, whereby she is ennobled.*

For the soul which thus rests in the Lord, her night shall have no darkness if she thus raises her eyes to the Lord and fixes them on her Bridegroom. This noble soul, a friend of the Holy Trinity, shall sweetly invite her Bridegroom, the only lover of her heart, to come in, so she may enjoy his presence. For he is the generous outpouring and abyss of divine sweetness, the most exalted, the omnipotent, the most beautiful, the noblest, the sweetest, the most generous, the most lovable, the most desirable Lord, and he is heaven of riches, a heaven of sweetness, a heaven of consolation, and a light that fills that whole kingdom of the soul with celestial brightness. This loving soul should remind her Bridegroom in her chamber that he has suffered much for her sake, so that, for his sake, she might learn to suffer; she should review for him all the benefits he has shown her. Also, she should ask him if he is as noble, as beautiful, as rich, and as gracious to love as she has heard, and when he hears that, he will grant her to know him in her senses and to be gifted by him; as often as the heavenly bride invites her Bridegroom into her chamber, he gives her a morning present, a precious jewel of grace. She should also frequently invite her Bridegroom so that his friendship may not fade away, for if the bride neglects inviting her Bridegroom, it is a certain sign that another is resting in her heart, who knavishly wants to kill her soul. It is fitting for the bride to magnify the name of her Bridegroom and to rejoice when she hears him mentioned. Therefore, she should zealously ask him about the meaning of his name, about which the bride speaks so purely in the canticle, and about the nobility of his lineage, in words that the noble virgin St. Agnes uses to praise this beloved Bridegroom and say: "That family is very noble in loveliness of its beauty, in overflowing riches, whose Mother is a virgin, whose Father knows no wife; whom the angels serve and about whose beauty the sun and moon marvel. His riches have no end; the dead come alive at his fragrance; the sick become strong at his countenance. His love is pure; his embrace is holy; union with him makes one pure." With words such as these she praises her Bridegroom; the interior soul should look at her Bridegroom in praise and laud, and afterward speak of the many benefits he has given her and that he also gives to all believing souls who cling to him and who seek him above all else, disdaining all other pretenders, and she should answer all impure temptations of the enemy by [saying]: "Away from me, all food of sins and nourishment of death! Another lover has chosen me, whose race is higher, whose power is stronger; he is full of all grace and has espoused me with the ring of faith; I believe firmly in him, and he has imprinted a sign on my countenance that I may receive no other lover than him. (The countenance of the soul is the uppermost part of the soul, on which the Holy Trinity has imprinted itself on the soul and united itself to it, so that no other may be received there.) He has adorned my soul with all kinds of virtues, and he gathers me up in the bonds of his love; he has encircled my neck with precious stones, that is, with a pure, upright intention toward God, which is set on many virtuous works; he has clothed me with a mantle of woven gold, that is, he has clothed my soul with his holy life and passion; and he has adorned me with countless jewels, that is, his perfect virtues and example and the treasury of his holy merits. I have received honey and milk from his mouth. He has fed my soul on the honey of his Godhead and on the milk of his sweet humanity; his blood has colored my cheeks, that is, the remembrance of his bitter passion makes the soul's cheeks red and sparkling white, so that they shine before God's countenance. These cheeks are the remembrance, and I am embraced by his pure embrace, and my body is joined to his, and he has shown me countless treasures that he promised to give me, so that I should constantly remain with him. My soul will then find her rest in the richness of his divine essence, and she will dwell in his inheritance and in the recesses of his tabernacle."

Ah! Should this not rouse the indolent soul and make her wake up to God and make her always seek and adore the countenance of God with great longing? She should appear before the most high King for his eternal service, and carry it out with loving inwardness and inspiration. Then the spirit is ignited and embraced in divine love, which flows through the soul and gathers the faculties and strengthens them with the food of love. The conscience is thereby purified and the heart cleansed, and nature is transformed in grace.

In it the straight path is found, and the living vein in the soul is opened up; no one can stop it up as long as one always watches and prays. That is the ground, the right foundation, and the beginning of all spiritual life. Anyone can often practice it as long as such a spirit and ground move him to do so, but one should especially attach himself to the inwardness, and inward sinking of the spirit, and the gathering of all the faculties, and the bowing low of the heart with upright intention in all works, and the discipline of the body, and control of the senses.

# Chapter 51

*A prayer: How the noble soul should direct her first thoughts to God upon awakening.*

Now wake up, devout soul, with all inwardness, in the secrecy of the spirit, adore the infinite Godhead and say: I believe in God.

O fathomless Goodness of God! I have been existing, even when I was uncreated, in your fathomless goodness, for you have known me and chosen me from all eternity; therefore I, in turn, must acknowledge you. Thus I shall be chosen by you and I shall dwell in you and you in me, you who are sweeter than all the world's riches! O my best-Beloved, in whom is contained everything one can imagine, who are you then? You are the almighty, supreme Good, whom no one completely knows but your own triune Unity, in which you hold all loving spirits; but they cannot contain you; they, on the other hand, are swallowed up by you and consumed in love. O eternal, infinite Goodness! I have been in you for all eternity without knowing myself, and now you are within me! O noble In-dweller of my soul! you have so united yourself and enclosed yourself in the uppermost part of my soul that you do not desire ever to part from her. You are almighty in my soul and want to strengthen me; [you are] all-wise, and you wish to enlighten me; all-loving in the soul, and you want to change me into love! Therefore, O heavenly Father, you who are there and wish to remain in my thoughts, unite and establish my thoughts, and draw my affections to you, and help me that I may neither think nor desire anything but what you will. Do this by the merits of your Son and the love of your Holy Spirit. O Son of God, you who are there and wish to remain in my understanding with true knowledge of you and of myself, enlighten my reason, purify my conscience, and direct all my affections to your service, so that I may follow the light of truth and may learn nothing other than what you will. Grant this by the power of the Father and the love of the Holy Spirit.

O Holy Spirit, O Bond of Love between Father and Son, you who are there in my free will, I give myself unto you as entirely your own; unite my will entirely to your love; strengthen my irascible powers to work industriously for all virtue; and help me to say nothing but what you will. Do it through the power of the Father and the wisdom of the Son, who has promised me to send you from his Father to console me; make all temporal things bitter for my soul; lead it inward and make it one spirit with you, you who there are the love bond of the Father and the Son.

O Father! O Son! O Holy Spirit! you are three Persons and one real God.

O blessed God, unite me always unto yourself, so that nothing may come between us.

O Father, into your hands I commend my spirit.

I pray you, O Son of God, by the merits of your joyous spirit, and your sorrowful soul, and your wounded body, to make my spirit, soul, and body fitting so that it may be a pleasure for you to be in me. Let your Godhead shine in me and through me; drive out of me all that is displeasing to you; take yourself unto yourself in me in the Holy Sacrament, and change me wholly into you by the merits of your joyous spirit, your sorrowful soul, and your pure wounded body, so that I may thus become and remain one spirit, one soul, and one body with you, in divine union with you, and be obedient unto you with all my strength, that I may hold up before my soul the living mirror of your holy life and passion in my heart. That is the book of life. In it is written all perfection; may your disfigured image never leave my heart; may I never turn away from it, but may my soul at all times give pleasing praises.

With similar exercises, one is entirely grounded in God and becomes fitting and receptive for all other exercises in which a person might want to exercise himself, whether in reading, in praying, in thinking, or in other works of virtue, if this groundwork is ready and one continues to exercise there what God shows it, then all the works become divine and fruitful.

But whatever one practices without this foundation is not altogether agreeable to God, nor does it maintain a person in right spiritual life. In this ground the innermost part of a person is fixed on God and in God, and remains immovably in the essential unity, and dwells in divine freedom. There the fullness of grace is poured out into the higher powers and flows down into the lower powers. There the inward man is filled with the riches of divine grace. There the outward man is changed, and his works become directed to the works of Jesus Christ, and his heart and senses are ignited with greater love than ever to exercise themselves in his holy life, in order that they might be drawn totally into his feeling, such as his pain, his miserable abandonment, his blasphemous ignominy, pitiful rejection, shameful death, unbearable fright of his heart, the piercing distress of his soul, and the immeasurable joy of his spirit.

In this a person loses his own feelings and feels nothing other than what was in Christ, and, with deep joyousness and compassion of heart, he looks with enlightened reason and loving affection at all his life and passion, and he praises and thanks him then at all times, and especially during the seven hours in which holy church praises God, for he is a member of holy church, and has entered into the highest part of the church, into the secret holy of holies, and he shows the blood of the Lamb for the sins of the people, and is enclosed in the sublime cornerstone, Jesus Christ, who is there as a shining lamp, the brightness of divine light, which enlightens heaven and earth.

# Chapter 52

*How the interior soul should exercise herself on the passion of her Beloved.*

It is fitting for an inward soul to bear the precious treasure of the passion of her Bridegroom on her breast and enclose that precious jewel in the shrine of her heart. By its fragrance all her wounds are healed; by it she is made pure and clean; and she is resplendently clad and nobly fed. She should keep this collected between her breasts like a tiny bundle of myrrh that brings her down in prosperity and raises her up in adversity. It makes her happy in the cross of suffering, and in all that is painful to the flesh and all poverty, abandonment, disdain, and embarrassment; by these she is purified before the eyes of God. Her mind is thereby uplifted and enlightened by radiant brightness and filled with delicious wisdom.

Therefore, my soul, work industriously; gather all the faculties of your soul, with all the vivacity of your memory, with all the subtlety of your understanding, with all the readiness of your will, and pour them out into the bitter passion of our Healer.

First of all, do it with continual exercises, in order to follow him as St. Paul says, "Feel within you that which was in Christ Jesus" (Eph 2:5), as if he wanted to say, With body, soul, heart, senses, and with works, follow your Savior. This is what the Bridegroom says in the canticle, saying to the bride: "Set me as a seal upon thy heart"

(Sg 8:6), loving me with all your desires, and uniting yourself to me with all the powerful desires of your heart, and set me as a seal upon your arms. By "arms" we understand "works," as though he were to say, It is not enough that you love me with your heart, but I desire and will you to show the love of your heart by works and follow my example.

Second, with deep compassion. If we turn ourselves to real compassion for the bitter passion of our Lord, then we will hereafter rejoice the most with him. Oh, who would not be seized with deep compassion when he thinks over the grievous things he has suffered for us!

Third, with a profound wonder at who it is who suffered there, and what he suffered, and by whom and for whom he suffered. Oh, is it not cause for marveling that this mighty Lord has suffered such great torment and such a shameful death? Oh, now keep continually before your eyes not only the mere humanity, but always think that he is God and your Creator, your Judge, your Hope, and your Bridegroom.

Fourth, with inward happiness and joyful refreshment of spirit. Oh, should we not say, and joyfully sing with the prophet: "My soul is freed from the hunter's snare; our help is in the name of the Lord!" (Ps 90:3).

Fifth, in a whole outpouring of yourself, so that all the faculties of your soul should melt fiery hot in the bitter passion of our Lord Jesus Christ.

Sixth, to a restful sweetness, so that the whole person may rest in it. That happens when he is so poured out into the passion of our Lord that the crucified Jesus always comes to his mind, and he never lets off humbly and ardently exercising himself on the passion of our Lord.

And lastly, (he is ignited) with ardent burning love, and with continual exercise, he sets his rest and sweetness in Jesus, so that nothing of this world, neither pleasure, nor tribulation, nor fright, disdain, sickness, health, prosperity, or adversity may have sway in the uppermost part of his soul, but he rests immoveable, so that he says truly with the bride: "I sit under the shadow of him whom my soul loves, and his fruit is a superabundant sweetness on my tongue and in my palate" (Sg 2:3).

And in this love he is swallowed up in that embrace, to rest in the arms of the Bridegroom. Then the Bridegroom is forced to cry out, "O daughter of Sion, I adjure you not to disturb my friend from her slumber, but let her rest in my arms as long as she wants" (Sg 8:4). Here the soul sleeps, free of all outward preoccupations, and her going in is unto the divine fruition and union of spirit, and her going out is unto the passion of Christ, in order to follow the life and passion of Christ. The Son of God himself taught us that and did it himself, for he always enjoyed the face of the heavenly Father in the greatest joyousness of his spirit, and in soul and in body he fulfilled and accomplished the will and obedience of his heavenly Father. This, too, the noble, pure virgin Mary has done. She united her spirit and all the faculties of her soul entirely in the best-beloved will of God and was ready to serve God in soul and body; even though the Son of God assumed human nature in her and rested in her virginal body, and had his contentment in her, she bore him and served him and raised him and was near him in all his passion and dread and shameful death (by which her soul and heart were pierced through).

Nevertheless, her spirit remained in the most sublime freedom of spirit, and she adored the Holy Trinity in spirit and in truth, and adhered to God with sweet freedom, and was an example of total perfection. The holy angels who serve God and men for the love of God do likewise; they always enjoy the essence of the Holy Trinity. The chosen friends of God have done likewise. Paul, Augustine, Bernard, Francis, Agnes, Catherine, Barbara, Cecilia, and many others. These had their going in in God, and their ground and going out in the life and passion of Christ, and they have followed him.

This our mother the holy church also observes both outwardly and inwardly. For where there is "outward" but not "inward," it is not right; and "inward" without "outward" is also not right. This is why we should have both Christ's life and his passion; that is the foundation on which all virtues are constructed. Without this groundwork, no virtues remain in existence, and on this foundation, all virtues are henceforth constructed.

# Chapter 53

*How we should bear the passion of our Lord and imitate it.*

O my soul, if you wish to be saved, then you must lay this foundation in yourself, and go in through Jesus Christ, who says there, "I am the door; he who enters through me will be saved (John 10:9). I am the way, the truth, and the life (John 14:6). He who walks by me shall not stray. He who believes in me shall not be deceived. And he who cleaves to me becomes one spirit with me and shall have the light of life, and going in and going out he shall find pasture." Just as though he said: It is not enough for you to be concerned with the humanity alone, but you should also go in into the noble essence of the Godhead. For the humanity is not apart from the Godhead, and therefore God became man so that men should become gods. Going out in my noble humanity you shall be fed sweetly by my teaching and example.

For through the life and passion of Christ, we are all freed and redeemed, heaven is opened, and the power of the enemy is removed, for nothing is more pleasing to God or holier for us and more harmful to the evil spirit than that we continually bear the passion of Christ in our hearts. This is why everyone should exercise himself in it as best he can and become accustomed to have the passion of Christ in his heart in everything he does, as a mirror and example of all perfection. Then he shall make more progress and learn more truth than from all the books and professors of this world. For he is the fountain from which we draw everything. If we can study this book well, we shall certainly learn all perfection, and follow his example with ardently burning love in humility, meekness, obedience, mildness, purity, abandonment to God and sobriety; and exercise ourselves every day in the passion of our Lord with inwardness and with gratitude, as if it were always Good Friday.

For in the Old Law it was forbidden under the ban to let the fire go out on the altar. Likewise, no Christian should ever let depart from his heart what the Son of God has undergone, suffered, and taught for our sakes. It was also commanded that they should keep Sabbath with locked doors. Likewise, every soul who desires to obtain the innermost Sabbath, that is, the loving union with the bitter passion of our Lord Jesus Christ, should lock the doors of her five senses and not turn outward to levity, to laughter, and to joking words, but always keep the loving image of our Lord Jesus Christ before her eyes, and within, his fathomless love for us.

# Chapter 54

*On the fruits of this exercise and on the faults which hinder us.*

With such an exercise on the bitter passion of our Lord Jesus, one is rightly grounded in divine charity; here one is renewed, born again, and brought into God's presence and established therein. One is totally bound to God with all one's powers, inwardly and outwardly, with spirit, soul, body, heart, and senses. There the spirit is made happy by the divine Sun of justice, to dwell in divine freedom; the soul, with all its powers, is illuminated and enlightened; the heart is enriched by the influx of divine generosity.

This raises a person up above all creatures and above himself, and makes him disdain all creatures and adhere to God. But a sensuous person thinks that this is difficult and impossible, for he adheres to many things, such as his own comfort in words and works, and he relies on his own honor and desire to be something for others, and he clings to creatures, which is an exceedingly harmful thing.

For the soul who is taken up with creatures against God's will becomes so disfigured and ugly that she resembles the evil spirit. And as often as she approaches the holy sacrament (in this spirit), she does God such great dishonor, as if she were to trample the little Child Jesus underfoot; even though God often warns such a soul interiorly, she takes counsel within herself and excuses herself of guilt, thinking: I will wait a little longer, and then I will break it off, and turn myself totally inward. But when such people intend to do it, they cannot do it, for they have spurned God's help, without which we can do no good nor can we avoid any evil, as God himself says, "Without me you can do nothing" (John 15:5). And since her intention is not right, and her love is not pure, but rather is more driven by fear of hell and of the judgment than by the love of God, therefore she easily falls whenever the occasion arises.

When such a soul is admonished by others about this, she says: "I am a poor person; these things are far too high for me. I do not understand them. I will stick to what is lower and will say: he who walks simply, walks safely." This is what such people call humility, but this is rather pusillanimity, for they do not dare to do a thing.

Oh, how much they will regret when they die that they did not break away, part and parcel, while they were still alive. But they should be ashamed before God and before man for saying, "I am a poor person, and do not understand these things" and for the fact that they wear the habit of the spiritual life and do not understand the things that pertain to the spirit and to the inward life. They say that one who walks simply walks safely, but simplicity of spirit and security of a pure conscience are unknown to them. Therefore, those in religious life have become so very cold in the love of God! But they adhere very closely to temporal things, relying on them and on an outward mode of life, and they pay no attention within to inwardness. For in proportion to our attachment to these faults and to like things, so much do we have to die. But this dying shall not be as difficult for us if we live in loving union with God. For love makes all things easy; through love, faults easily fall away, making all love for creatures and for any temporal things bitter for us.

# Chapter 55

*How the soul is called by God and tested by abandonment.*

Oh, if only you would hear the voice of the Lord within, harden not your heart, but follow him in the way that he has gone before you, no matter how difficult, how hard, or how dark it may seem to us, or how unfruitful. For the more difficult it seems to us to be, the safer sign it is that we are on the right path and that the heavenly Father draws us and wants to draw us, through his only Son, who has gone before us on the most difficult path. He was as forsaken by his heavenly Father as though he had not been the Son of God at all.

Nevertheless, he was always prepared to be still more for-saken, had it been the will of his heavenly Father. He was ready to remain in forsakenness until the Last Judgment. This is why a real lover of God will not become anxious, no matter how strange this may feel. For God allows those whom he wants to lead along the right path to taste and feel similar things, so that they think they are being deceived, and they think that they are caught in a hundred snares and that everyone but themselves has taken the right path. It seems to them that they lose their time in vain and that they come closer to the gates of hell than to the portals of eternal life, and thus they are tempted to turn back to what they had left behind. For it seems to them that they felt better before than they do now that they follow God. For now they feel much aridity within themselves, which they knew nothing of before. If a person can persevere through this, whether for a month or even a half year, and with this forsakenness turn himself even more toward God than he did before, and transfer his will to God, then, if it were God's will, he would gladly stay in this forsakenness his whole life long. When God sees this good will and self-abandonment, he can no longer hold himself back. He flows through and floods over the whole innermost part of that person and enlightens him by his divine brilliance, so that from it he receives genuine security, and he sees and notices why God let him feel such things, so that his love should become more perfect and more pure. The more frightful and heavy his anxiety was then, the more his spirit is free now; the greater the darkness that accompanied it then, the more fruitful it now is for his soul. From all this, the soul obtains such great love and desire for God that were all her members individual bodies, she would gladly give them all up in forsakenness until the Day of Judgment. This is how she desires to follow the passion of her Bridegroom.

# Chapter 56

*How the devout soul thanks God for the light from him; how she should find, enjoy, and preserve the fountain of the Godhead within her.*

O best-Beloved! I have learned from one of our pilgrims a most suitable inward path toward our kingdom, and that at the end of this path lies the Sion Gate, this is, the noblest part of the soul.

On the one side, it lies within the royal city of eternity, and on the other, in the landscape of the body's temporality. If we now want to enter into our origins from all eternity, by this path, then we must denude ourselves of all temporal things and break through our nature, and turn down this path into the innermost ground of the soul and go through the Gate of Sion. Our soul no longer has to remain in aridity, for in its ground lies the vein of living water and the original fountain of the Godhead, and the bottomless well of the divine essence. But these waters are now so plugged with temporal things that the weeds of all kinds of faults have grown over them, so much so that we find it unbelievable, nor can others make us believe it either, that this living fountain is within us because of all the weeds that have grown up in our nature, such as unbelief, blasphemy, lies, slander, murmuring, unrest, despair, bitterness, unworthiness, spitefulness, quarreling, envy, creaturely love and lust. From all of these come evil, sorrow, and more of the like, which are too long to describe, whose roots lie very deeply in the ground of nature in the innermost part of the heart, where the three lower faculties are originally situated, and under which the seven deadly sins are rooted.

The appetitive faculty has under it three chief sins: gluttony, unchastity, and sloth. The irascible faculty has under it three chief sins of covetousness, hatred and envy, and anger; and under reason lies shame; and under that is pride, which wants to cover up and excuse all these weeds and throws them all together as though under a thorn bush, so that a person cannot enjoy his natural reason.

We must root out these weeds with sobriety, purity, alertness, poverty, peaceableness, patience, and humility, which is the mother and guardian of all virtues, and so on with all the moral virtues, so that the well of living water can once again be found in us. Then we must zealously and attentively dig through the earth of our heart. If it happens that we do not dig deeply enough, then no water can come in but it has to be brought in from outside. Water that is brought in immediately sinks out of sight.

This water signifies all the outward means and all that one brings in with the five senses; no matter how clear the water is, it is muddied and stinks if it just stands in the earthly nature. Therefore, let us dig on through the ground of the heart and through the sand

310

of the soul until we reach the quicksand, that is, into the really pure ground where lies the vein of living water and the original fountain and the fathomless well of the divine Being, so that the veins of living water shall always flow within, and we do not need to bring in any more water from outside but it shall flow of itself most generously, and we may share it with our neighbors: it is within us all.

He who becomes aware of this in himself finds therein all good and eternal life and more security and truth than all the professors could ever teach us. He who drinks of this water shall not thirst after earthly things any more. This is the water of which our Lord said: "The water that I give brings forth in thee a fountain welling up unto eternal life. And whoever believes in me, out of his belly shall flow living water" (John 4:14, 7:38). This water is so sweet and pure and it is so powerful that it expels all bitterness of faults, and it is so strong when it flows forcefully that it drives away all resistance of nature and flows through the whole kingdom of the soul and the landscape of the body and makes them fruitful. This is the pool that, when it is stirred and moved by the Holy Spirit, cures and makes whole all the faculties of the soul. If we want this fount to be preserved now, and no longer plugged up or stopped, then we must intercept it and cement it up with the foundation of a firm faith, with the marble stone of inward attentiveness, so that memory cleaves so tightly to the fountain that God may flow into it with divine thoughts; and with a carbuncle stone, to fix the intellect on the fountain so that God may flow within it with divine knowledge; and with ivory in the free will, so that God may flow into it with divine love and may be, as it were, brought into one with it with loving union, so that the fountain is led to flow into the kingdom of the soul, to render the reason simple and enlightened, to make the irascible faculty gentle and humble, and all the affections fitting and orderly, and the conscience pure, the heart clean, and the whole kingdom of the body fruitful. Since this fountain is so precious and costly, it must therefore be guarded and enclosed, and covered over by the tabernacle of the wounded body of Christ, for this is the solid stone without which no construction of virtues can remain standing. By it, all virtues and good are obtained and preserved.

Oh, admirable goodness of God! How countless are the benefits that you have given me! How could anyone, with heart and mouth, think on them and express all the goodness you have shown toward me? Nevertheless, Lord, I confess that I am more moved and inflamed since you have allowed me to meet this pilgrim and have sent me your chosen friend, for I know well that you have nothing against praise for your bride, but it pleases you when anyone praises your servant, for it is certainly right to praise and to laud this pilgrim by whom you have led me out of error, and who has made your benefits known, for I had eyes and did not see your light; I had ears and did not hear your voice; I had hands and neither felt nor carried out your works; I had feet and did not follow your example; nor did I follow in the path of your commandments. I believed you to be one God, but even the Jews and some unbelievers believe this, but I did not believe you to be in me. I also believed in Christ, but I did not do Christ's works. I believed what the holy church believes and celebrates, but I did not celebrate or hold it within me, which is its whole point. And this you have revealed to me through the enlightened pilgrim and through your help and grace; you have removed the scales from my eyes, the sadness from my ears, the hardness of my mouth, and the slowness of my hands, the unsteadiness of my feet, the unbelief of my heart, so that I may now see your light with the inward eyes of the spirit and hear your voice through the inward ears of my soul, by which you have aroused me to remain in you. For what good would it have done me to be eternally uncreated in your thoughts, in your knowledge and your love, and to be made after your own image and likeness where you have united yourself to me, and to be redeemed, and to be given yourself as food, and to be chosen out of a thousand and called to this state, to be cared for by you in soul and body, and to be so often invited to your table, since I have done so many similar things that are inexpressible? What good would it have done me to be eternally in you, if you had not taught and instructed me by your friend as to how I ought to flow back entirely into you, and do it by your holy merits, and keep you in my thoughts, knowledge, and love; and since you wish to remain in me, that I also should be united with you by your holy merits, and remain in your presence in order to serve you always with the blessed spirits, and to be obedient and to be of service to humanity for your sake in all good things, and to do it not only on account of human respect or friendship, but only on account of your love happily and simply to be helpful to each and every one, even though it frequently is received ungratefully and misunderstood. That is no reason for me to stop; I shall do as the angels do, who are such helpful spirits, and so simply obedient that if God wanted them to read the leaves on the trees, they would be ready. Thus they serve God and good and evil people, and no matter how ungrateful these people may be for it, yet they remain just as ready to serve.

Furthermore, you have taught and instructed me by your friend how I should become one spirit with you and sink away into the abyss of your divine love, where the spirit is baptized and made free in your spirit, and where my will dies there in your divine will so that I can will nothing but your divine will. This is the root of right charity; and that I am so born of the Spirit that my spirit ought to be lifted up in love and in divine freedom, above all care, and above all fear and death, of hell and of purgatory and of everything that could befall soul and body in time and eternity, whether good or bad, living or dying; and that I should remain subject to lovable, peaceful, joyous freedom, and always remain poor of spirit, so that in me nothing should live but the love of God; and I should be thus poor of spirit and exalted in mind, and be always peaceable, gentle, humble, and obedient in soul, pure, sweet and calm and lovingly inward of heart, virtuous and honorable of body, so that all my works may be ennobled by your works, so that I may come to follow you, conformed to your holy humanity if I become—and remain—pure and patient of body, obedient and peaceable in soul, and free and poor of spirit. And you have also taught me by your friend how I should discipline my nature in a spiritual life and should learn to put to death evil inclinations so that the flesh could become submissive to the spirit, and live according to the nobility and requirements of the spirit so that I do not bear the name of a spiritual person in vain; and I should always be inward and dwell in the Sion Gate; I should often lean toward the origin of the divine essence and carry on conversation with the highest good, which you yourself are, where you always teach me how I should carry in my heart all that you have done, omitted, suffered, and taught for my sake, and should always be transformed into the image of your holy humanity, and always bear in myself the sublimity of your spirit, the sanctity of your soul, and the purity of your body, so that I should follow the perfect example and the holiness of your virtues and spend my time fruitfully in the remembrance of your bitter passion.

And how I should pray (when my soul is burdened and heavy) that you would feed me with yourself in the holy sacrament, so that I may be entirely changed into you and become by grace what I am not by nature, and so be a "man after your own heart."

Also, that I should recognize and confess how hiddenly and secretly the faults die within me, and where the roots are to be found. And that they are very deeply rooted in the deepest ground of my nature, and you are in the deepest, most essential, purest ground of my soul, always ready to help me root out these faults and to plant virtues in their place.

And so many benefits and much more good you have done for me and shown me, and you yourself have taught me interiorly, and through your friend exteriorly. Even so, I have gathered so little fruit and have been so ungrateful. But forgive me and absolve me by your bitter passion, and make all your gifts in me fruitful, so that I shall not have received them in vain; for one who knows the will of the Lord and does not do it shall be buffeted with many buffets, and one who has received much shall be accountable for much. Let not pearls be cast before swine, O blessed God, I pray you, by the merits of your holy humanity. Help me in what you have taught and instructed me through your friend so that you can perfect it in me and through me, for up to now I have not made myself very fit for it. But since you are in me, act with me, in me, and through me; grant that this friend and all your friends may make progress in this state, and keep them long in your love and grace, for your honor and glory, and for the benefit of those here present, those who will come later, so that we may walk this inward path to our origin and come to the discovery of the vein of living water in us. May God help us to attain this.

# Chapter 57

*How one should understand and practice this book in a simple manner.*

The aforesaid material and exercises are frequently repeated with regard to some topics, for the purpose of better understanding.

Not that one should practice it a multitude of times, but rather, simply, in a onefold manner. But no one can arrive at a onefold, simple exercise unless he has first, with understanding, knowledge, and love, broken through all the multiplicity of worldly things.

Each one must empty his senses from multiplicity of spiritual goods.

Once a person, with his loving soul, has run the entire circle, that is, acknowledges and knows the commandments of God, the ordering of the spiritual life, the external exercises of fasting, watching, and praying, and all that a person should know and all that the Holy Trinity has wrought in the Old and New Testaments—once a person has this knowledge and has exercised himself in it, and still finds no essential rest and unity, then he should cast himself into the "point," that is, God, into that onefold simple Good, with simple inward exercises, and so in all his multiplicity he becomes onefold, and in all cares becalmed.

It is also frequently said in the aforementioned exercises that we should not stand on our own works and exercises but should let God work in us and through us. One cannot understand this, nor should one think this means to be empty of works, or of what we ought to do, following a rule or statutes, or that one should do no inward exercises.

If we should merely wait until God would do it through us and if we think that we want to be idle and not work with God, that would be to tempt God, and more a question of unbelief [than belief]; thereby one would arrive at even greater heaviness and blindness. For God wants us to be co-workers with him, and wants us to work with God, and God with us. For he created us without our assistance, but he will not redeem us without our assistance. God is capable of doing all things, but he has no power over our own human will. In hell, nothing will burn but our own will. Whoever, then, will not help himself and work with God, God will not help him, nor will all the prayers of the saints.

Therefore, we should adore God in ourselves with continual care, and give ourselves over completely to God to do with us whatever pleases him; thus he has power to work his divine work with us, since we add all our own assistance. If it should happen that from time to time we lose some awareness of God's in-working, then we should always, with God's help, do something good, something we know is very pleasing to God, so that we do not end up in harmful idleness. For this idleness is the cause of all sins and temptations.

This is why we should never be idle, but we should always have God in our thoughts, and in our senses, with burning love and with ardent desire, and we should have some work at hand that is suitable and necessary, so that we may be protected from the enemy of idleness. For no one can please God, or become holy, without good works. No one may be free without keeping the commandments and following the counsels of God, or without divine union in love and desire. And no one may be empty of God, or of the divine work. For the heavenly spirits are certainly never idle in their thanks and praise of God. So how much more, then, should we, poor little worms, be eager to do good, we who are set here in the field of battle, from which no one can exit as a saint without having struggled. Therefore we must struggle manfully and overcome all sensuality by sharp discipline and mortification of the flesh; overcoming all excess by sobriety, all pride by humility, and seek and intend the glory of God in all things. If we will struggle in this way, then our heart will be strengthened by God's might, and we can expect to be crowned by him with his glory. Therefore, let us always be careful and alert in good works, so that we may be acted upon by God, and that we may be found to be neither fruitless nor idle in the vineyard of our Lord. For the Son of God was not idle; he always sought and wrought the glory and the works of his heavenly Father, for his mind was united to the divine essence, and it remained so, in continual fruitful fruition, full of happiness, in onefold rest in the bright, shining Godhead. His soul was continually bowed down before the Godhead and upright with burning love and desire in thanksgiving and praise. In his body he was always active in praying, in fasting, in watching, in preaching, in teaching, in consoling, in laboring, and in service, being helpful and submissive to everyone—he who was the Son of God and Creator of all creatures! If he was so careful and industrious for our salvation, how much more should we, poor fragile little vessels, always cling to God and pray with inward mind and exaltation of spirit in the fruitful enjoyment, in onefold rest, and incline our souls before the sublime majesty of God, continually upright with love and desire, in thanks and in praise, and in body—with praying, fasting, and watching, and in laboring as much as necessary to attain freedom of spirit and to be of service to everyone in soul and in body, and to incline ourselves before God and before all creatures, and always remaining in poverty of spirit, since we have nothing of ourselves nor can we do anything of ourselves unless it is by God's help, with which we can do all things. The good that God works by us we cannot claim ourselves. That is what holy scripture testifies to us, and the Gospel in which Christ says: "The works that I do are not my own but the Father's, who sent me" and "Apart from me you can do nothing" (John 14:10; 15:9). This is why all good belongs to God alone, for God performs it with us, and he does not accomplish that good without our help. This is why we must gather together all the powers of our soul and body, joining to him all the vivacity of our memory and the subtlety of our understanding and the readiness of our will, and with all care and eagerness be co-workers with God. Then we are ready for God to work with us. For nothing is more pleasing to God than his own work, which he has wrought through humankind. The prophet says, "Lord, Thou hast wrought all our works!" (Isa 25:12). The whole spiritual life is ordered to arrive at this, and all gifts are given us so that we should be the instrument of God, but be annihilated ourselves and die to our nature so that God should live in us.

For out of the dying and the harshness to nature, there comes life and sweetness of spirit. And out of the bridle and constraint of the rule and discipline there comes lovable freedom of spirit. One should not be as a servant under the law, then, but as one set free under grace, for where the Spirit of the Lord is, there is such freedom that a person does not overstep the commandments of superiors, or the fixed ordinances, but, by the power of the Spirit, one transcends and fulfills all the statutes and commandments out of love, which another would do out of fear or force.

It is the work of the Spirit that our spirit is always being taught by the Spirit of God to be one spirit with God, and always to adhere to him with loving freedom within, and to follow the crucified image of our Lord Jesus Christ without. In this way all spiritual ordinances are established and remain in force. But since we now forget so very much and seek external profit, and maintain exterior modes, and entrust ourselves to exterior holiness: all this is why spiritual religion has become so lax. Therefore let us act according to the counsel of the holy Gospel and seek before all things the kingdom of God and his justice, and all things will be added unto us besides; and cast our cares on God. Then we shall be enlightened within, and free by divine truth, and protected by the power of God, so no one should disturb us in our progress. As a result, we should then be gathered into the unity of the spirit in the bonds of love and peace, and thus this spiritual life may well be called a paradise. For God is in their midst and they are like a strong army fortified against all the power of the enemy.

These people are adorers of the world, for with their common prayer, they penetrate heaven. Each of them should be a citizen of heaven, a companion of the angels, a throne on which God desires to rest, a kingdom God desires to rule, a tabernacle in which God desires to dwell, and an instrument with which and in which God desires to work spiritually just as he has worked through his holy humanity.

Oh! If we only considered rightly for what state we were created and how easily love would come to us, love would compel us to separate from all temporal things and to enter into eternity. Fear should make us tremble when we turn toward earthly pleasures; then we would live in blessed peace. May the Father, the Son, and the Holy Spirit grant us this by the peace our Lord Jesus Christ has made on the cross and by the prayer and the merits of his blessed Mother, and all his dear friends in heaven and on earth who are united with him. Amen.

# Chapter 58

*This is the conclusion of the book.*

Almighty God, without whose grace and favor we can do nothing, grant to all those who desire it, that they can be improved by this and they should live this way and not stay fixed in their own will and reason, and on the exterior letter. But they should turn inward toward the Spirit, who makes the letter live and who pours into us the streams of his teaching. When we interiorly turn toward him, we do not need to search through many books.

For multiplicity is distracting and is discouraged in all spiritual books. Seldom do those who always abide by their own counsel come to the simple light. The entire multiplicity of exercises with all that one can perform regarding God and regarding inward exercises is to be all gathered up into one, and in it everything is already enclosed, that is, in the emptiness within, in the renunciation of all things, to embrace God alone in the naked ground of the soul, and to be buried with spirit, soul, and body, heart and senses in his lovable humanity and to resemble him in everything.

He who practices this does all that is prescribed, and he will be justified by God. He who overcomes, says God, shall possess it all, and I shall be God, and he shall be my son. May God help us do this unto blessed eternity.

*On the grievousness and multiplicity of Jesus' bitter passion.*

There is nothing more beneficial for all sinful people than often and devoutly to consider the grievous passion and the great love of Christ toward us, with which we easily can repay all our guilt and can earn all grace and glory. So, here follows a brief sketch of the grievousness of his holy passion as God revealed it to a devout person. But to know perfectly everything that our Lord suffered on our behalf and what blessedness is hidden therein is impossible for all angels and humans. Blessed is the one to whom he reveals this daily in his heart, bearing it by faith, hope, and love (in order to follow him), and by the sacraments of holy church. Our Lord Jesus Christ, for our sake, wept 26,200 tears. In the little courtyard after the Last Supper he sweat 97,305 drops of blood because of the great anguish caused by the magnitude of our sins.

His body received 6,666 wounds. Or, as other books maintain, 5,470 wounds. His neck was beaten and poked 120 times. His face was struck 110 times. His mouth, 30. Stinking spittle was spewed in his face 32 times. His back was struck and poked 388 times. His breast was struck and beaten 43 times. His head was beaten 85 times. He was kicked by their feet, like a dog, 170 times. His side was struck and beaten 38 times. On his armpits and shoulders he was struck and beaten 62 times. On his hips and loins, struck and beaten 28 times. On his legs, beaten and struck 32 times. On his arms, beaten and struck 40 times. Thrown savagely down to the ground, 13 times. Pulled by the hair, 350 times. Pulled by the beard, 58 times. In the crowning (with thorns), received 300 wounds. He lost 85,200 drops of his most precious blood. He wept and sighed 900 times. He sighed at death 19 times. Had mortal anguish 162 times. Underwent mortal pangs 6,667 times. Had dying throes from great torment and anguish 19 times. Had interior mortal blows to the heart 7 times. Such as 2 in the courtyard when he sweat blood; 1 during the scourging; and 3 on the cross, hanging there so long in great pain and torment. At the first blow on the cross, heaven and earth quaked. At the second, the graves sprang open and the rocks split. At the third blow, he gave up his holy spirit and died a shameful bitter death for the sake of our salvation, without guilt, from great love, humbly and patiently. For this also all his holy bones were pulled one from another, his veins, sinews, and arteries broken, and all his members and senses, both outer and inner, were filled with unspeakable torments.

*On the immensity of the inward passion of Jesus.*

However, the inward passion and the dread in his soul far surpassed the outward sufferings, as far as heaven is above the earth; for each sin that was ever committed or ever would be committed, with all the heavy torments, anguish, and forsakenness that all the souls in time and eternity should suffer for their sins, the sweet Lord clearly saw all this and bore them in his soul, suffered fully for them and made satisfaction according to the requirements of his wisdom and justice, and his love for us, which was measureless.

The gravity of these sins and their punishment and satisfaction were so grievous and so great that Jesus had to let his soul be plunged into the most extreme forsakenness, anguish, sadness, and fear, that it escapes the grasp of any created understanding but his, for every mortal sin wounded his heart with five wounds:

- because his heavenly Father [whose glory he sought] was dishonored by sin;

- because the souls [whom he purchased at such great cost] were stained and destroyed;
- because the grace of God [that he merited for us] was thereby lost;
- because peace [which he had established between God and humanity with such great difficulty] was thereby broken and it aroused the wrath of God over us;
- because noble souls were thereby liable to eternal damnation [from which he had saved them]. Because the gravity of one mortal sin and the eternal damage to souls that comes as a result is beyond comprehension, so, too, Jesus' inward passion, which he willingly accepted in his soul for so many hundreds of thousands of mortal sins of the whole world, is beyond comprehension.

Some write, and it is pious to believe it, that if Jesus' inward passion were distributed among all creatures, they would all immediately die of it.

He also had incomprehensible sadness and compassion for his dear Mother, and for the suffering that all his elect would ever suffer for his sake. He foresaw it all and bore it upon himself; with great suffering, he offered it to God so that it might be fruitful for us.

He also had great terror and fright on account of his passion, which still was to come, and which he clearly foresaw. But he suffered all this from such a great eternal love for us that what he did suffer was all too little for him. This is why he surrendered himself on the cross, to remain suffering even to the Last Day, or even eternally, were it necessary, so that we might be saved from eternal punishment [that we had deserved].

And he is also ready to do and to suffer the same for every single soul, were it necessary, and it greatly pleased God to save us thankless people.

So I say again: no one can plumb the blessedness hidden in the passion of Jesus. Blessed is the one who has a share of it in time.

*On the suffering of the venerable Mother of God.*

Mary the venerable Mother of God, in her sorrow and compassion, wept 30,900 tears. But her inward suffering was also great; as some devout theologians write, it was more than all people together could suffer, since she had more love for her God and Son than all other people collectively. But the Holy Spirit enclosed this great suffering in her virginal soul. Otherwise her virginal heart would have broken a thousand times, and the sorrow would have overflowed into her holy body. Therefore, she is now exalted above all pure creatures and has the power to help us poor sinners, by her holy prayer and merits. Amen.

The aforesaid material and practice was learned from the Holy Spirit and on my own from an enlightened man who has himself practiced it many years, and so he, by the assistance and grace of God, has received great progress in virtues, as his daily conduct and life certainly demonstrate, and it is easy to see that he is a man after the heart of God and directed by the Spirit of God.

May the word of the Lord be fulfilled upon this person, where it says in the Gospel, "Thy light shall shine before man" (Matt 5:15). This person thus has not wanted to put this exercise under a basket but upon a candlestand, and has revealed it in order to benefit his fellowmen, driven by the urgings of love for those who desire to cleave to God and to become one spirit with him in the ground of their soul, according to the strictest truth. He wanted them to be taught of this and informed about walking the right path to God, which opportunity [in loving, and in all one's doings and in undergoing] is clearly written in this book.

And since this was not written out of audacity and my own understanding, but out of love, so, too, may everyone who reads it do as the bee, which draws out the honey from the flowers and not the poison. If anything is written here which displeases anyone, ascribe it to the onefold simplicity and unlearnedness of her who has written it out. For it is always open to improvement from superiors and theologians, whom God has commanded to govern his holy church. In obedience to which, by the grace of God, we wish to live and die. Amen.

# The Temple of Our Soul[1]

*The same anonymous author who wrote the* Evangelical Pearl[2] *also wrote the* Temple of Our Soul *(Die oeffeningen vanden tempel onser sielen). However, the* Temple *has had a far lesser distribution than the* Pearl. *The text has been printed only once.*

*It contains a series of reflections according to the structure of the liturgical year on the complexity of the encounter and the relationship between God and humanity. In the present translation chapters mainly from Advent and Christmas have been selected, which form a unity in the book. The basic idea underlying this spiritual theme of the liturgy structuring the interpretation of the relationship with God is obviously that of 1 Corinthians 3:16: "You are the temple of God." The reflections correspond to a theme that is almost constant in all Christian spiritual literature, and one that is also clearly present in the mystical tradition of the Low Countries. In thirteenth century* mulieres religiosae *circles it was expressed as follows:*

> *One day, the blessed virgin [Ida of Louvain] had a vision, when she was in rapture. She saw her own soul as a grand temple, which extended more and more so that its wide dimensions... resembled that of a splendid church. She could see it from within and while she was observing sharply and with amazement all its wondrous details, reflecting that she had never seen something as beautiful as this, she looked at the altar because it seemed the most beautiful of all....She could see the priest coming to the altar, dressed in the solemn liturgical vestments.... This priest was the only and most high Priest, after the order of Melchizedek, Jesus Christ, perfect God and man, born from the virgin Mary.*[3]

*And Erasmus (1466–1536), a famous contemporary of the anonymous author of the* Pearl *and the* Temple, *expressed it thus:*

323

*Nothing is said in the Gospel that does not concern us. Nothing happens there that does not happen daily in our life—in a more hidden but more real way. Christ is born in us, and Herods are not lacking to seek the life of the tender baby. He grows up and becomes older. He cures all kind of disease, if only one calls for his help with confidence. He does not reject lepers, or the possessed, or anyone who suffers from a flow of blood, or the blind, or a cripple. There is no vice so horrible or incurable that he cannot take it away, if only we say sincerely to him: "Jesus, son of David, have mercy!" and "Lord, if you want, you can make me clean!"*[4]

*For the present translation, I follow the critical edition by Albert Ampe, SJ,[5] and use several valuable suggestions in the modern Dutch translation by Joseph Alaerts SJ.[6]*

# THE TEMPLE OF OUR SOUL

## Chapter 1

*How God has made the soul his temple and has adorned it with many graces and gifts.*

(1) "The eternal Wisdom has made a house for himself and has carved seven pillars" (Prov 9:1). This house is the rational soul, which the Master of eternal Wisdom has carved out of the mountain of eternity, out of the almighty abyss of the Father, out of the eternal providential wisdom of the Son, out of the abundant riches of the Holy Spirit. Thus, he has made for himself a most fitting mansion for his noble divinity, just as the prophet says: "O Israel, how vast is the house of your God, how broad the scope of your dominion. Its height is immeasurable, its end is eternal" (Bar 3:24). (2) Even though this is to be understood as heaven, nevertheless one can reasonably understand it also as the soul, which is a heaven of the Holy Trinity, just as it is written: "Heaven is my throne, the earth is my footstool" (Isa 66:1) and "The One whom the heavens cannot contain wanted to be worshiped in Solomon's temple" (2 Chr

6:18). Is not the soul of the righteous a seat of Wisdom? Therefore, where there is a pure conscience, there is the seat of God. (3) The pillars of the house are the three faculties of the soul, each a room for the Holy Trinity, where the Holy Trinity dwells with all its sweet grace—which is for the soul life, nourishment, and support, and which works therein its hidden mystery. The other four pillars are the four elements that compose the body and that the body may use when the spirit is united with God. (4) The pillars are based upon the three divine virtues and the four cardinal virtues. Faith, hope, and love are called divine virtues because they unite the spirit with God—who is one, eternal, almighty, supremely good—and make it deiform in as far as he has made the soul similar to himself, so that by these virtues it can overcome all that is in the world, and also be one, almighty, supremely good. (5) Thus, by faith the soul has a pure gaze on God, who is the first object and enjoyment of the spirit; by this eternal good it disparages everything that the world desires and tramples on it. By faith it lives steadfast in God, in the immovable mountain, on which the house is founded, and where God himself lives: "Its foundations are in the holy mountains" (Ps 87:1). Thus, this house is founded in God, and, through faith, God is founded in this house. "Whoever believes in me," Jesus said, "rivers of living water will flow out of his belly" (John 7:38) (that is, the inner part of his spirit). And that, because it is becoming to God's honor that it has its fountain in itself. (6) By hope all pride of life is overcome, as far as one trusts firmly all that one has found in that unity. "Whoever trusts in me has eternal life in him" (John 7:38). (7) By love of God one overcomes voluptuousness, sensuality of the flesh and of nature, because "strong as death is love" (Sg 8:6) and "whoever remains in love, remains in God and God in him" (1 John 4:16). (8) Thus, one becomes divine by these virtues. These three divine virtues are like the pillars that unite the spirit—the higher part of the temple—in God and fix it, and alienate it from all lowly things and make it one in God.

(9) The other four pillars are the four cardinal "virtues that support the soul so that it does not incline to fleshly desires, but rather to divine obedience. The first virtue is justice. This is poured in the soul and sustains it at its origin and first beginning, so that it walks rightly before its God: in holy thoughts, in surrendering its

will, in a pure desire, in a pure intention of the heart. The Book of Wisdom says: "The Lord will guide the just man in righteous ways, and will show him the kingdom of God that is in us. The souls of the just are in the hand of God, and the torment of death shall not touch them. The blessing of the Lord rests on the heads of the just" (Wis 10:10; 3:1). (10) The second virtue is wisdom. It is a light and discernment in the soul to come to know God and itself and to have wise insight in all things, and to discern and embrace all that is good, and to hate all that is evil. That is why the eternal Wisdom has poured the light of his face into the soul, and has made an eternal covenant with it, and poured great clarity in it, so that it lives in that wisdom and walks in that light, just as the prophet says, "O Lord, in your light we see the light" (Ps 36:10). Happy is the man who will dwell in wisdom and meditate in justice" (Sir 14:22). "God the Lord will nourish him with the bread of life and understanding and give him the water of learning to drink. He will sustain him so that he will not bend down" (Sir 15:3). "The eye of the wise is always in his head, that is, in God" (Eccl 2:14). The wise man says, "O Wisdom, I love you beyond gold and beyond the riches of this world; from you all good things came to me" (Wis 7:9–11).

(11) The third virtue is temperance. It keeps a mean between too much and too little, careful to keep God's commandments and not to trespass what is forbidden. (12) The fourth virtue is strength, with which the house is strengthened by acquiring and keeping the virtues. Because the house is besieged on all sides by the vices and often assaulted and contested, it must be strengthened by the noble in-dwelling of God, and be relieved. Because the prophet says: "The Lord is my strength and my help (Ps 18:2–3). I will fear no harm, for you, Lord, are at my side (Ps 23:4). The Lord is my life's refuge, of whom will I be afraid? (Ps 27:1). The one who dwells in the shelter of the Most High, abides in the protection of the God of heaven" (Ps 91:1). (13) These then are the seven pillars with which the soul, the dwelling place of God, is supported. They are silver pillars in the soul, where the whole spiritual building is supported in the loftiness of the virtues, and they make it interiorly shining for God and exteriorly for men. They become gold by the sweet gifts of the Holy Spirit, so that whatever this person does, he does with insight and wisdom, with knowledge and deliberation,

with fear, grace, peace, and benevolence. (14) In this temple is established a golden throne on the seven pillars of the virtues. This throne is the deiform mind, irradiated with divine clarity. "The seat is ivory, the arms gold" (2 Chr 9:17–18). This chair is the pure mind, silently burning in divine love, where the peaceful King of eternal Wisdom rests as on a royal throne, who establishes the mind in an eternal light beyond all thought, and immerses it in silent love and freedom of spirit, and he renews all things in the soul, and goes through all the faculties and senses and makes them god-enjoyable.[7]

(15) The sanctuary of this temple is the unity of the spirit, where the Holy Trinity is ever honored and worshiped. The altar is the hidden wealth of the Divine Being, where the imageless divine abyss is worshiped. There, the eternal Word, continuously born in time out of the paternal heart, is dedicated and offered as a sacrifice. There the inner soul dedicates itself, and all graces that it has received from God, to the praise of God in the hidden *sancta sanctorum*, which is surrounded by all the angels and saints, who stand around the sanctuary and the royal throne and the temple of God and watch over it day and night, and honor and praise God there with joy because God has such a dwelling place on earth—though more in heaven because the heavenly things are more exercised there. (16) Rejoice, you inhabitants of earth, you have become God's temple; rejoice, because God rejoices in you. He says through his prophet: "I will keep my sanctuary. I am a defender of my realm. I do not want my temple desecrated by any image, or any pestilence to come near my tabernacle" (Ps 90:10). (17) This is the New Jerusalem that John saw coming down from heaven, prepared by God as a bride adorned for her husband: "Behold the tabernacle of God is with the human race; he will dwell with them. I will be their God, and they will be my people (Rev 21:2–3). Rejoice, O Zion, the great and holy God of Israel is in your midst" (Isa 12:6). (18) This is the temple of Solomon, the blessed field, the heaven of wealth, the golden chair, the joy of the angels, a royal city and a dwelling place of God, a house for the Holy Trinity, the Ark of the Testament where the soul is the table on which the Ten Commandments are written (because it is the precious stone with which the heavenly Jerusalem is built) and the golden jar of the pure heart wherein is the heavenly bread—that is, the bread of angels, the unity of the

divine essence, with which the soul is fed—and the staff of Aaron: the living Word of God that makes the soul fertile, on which the Holy Spirit rests with his sevenfold gifts. So many hidden holy things are in the temple of the soul, and it is a fruitful vineyard of God. (19) In this temple live those who truly worship God, namely, inward, holy people. In this temple our Lady lived continually, and she drew all her faculties therein, and there she adored her only Son in spirit and truth. She acknowledged to him that she could not honor him worthily. Therefore, she desired that he honor himself in her. And whoever could look into her virgin heart would have there contemplated God, in essential mode. (20) "Happy those, O Lord, who dwell in your house, they will praise you forever" (cf. Ps 84:5). Nevertheless, you are yourself your highest praise, where you respond to yourself in the rededication of all your gifts. "O Lord, I love the splendor of your house and the tenting-place of your glory" (cf. Ps 26:8). (21) O soul, which has become a temple for God through the adornment of virtues, why do you search outside for the One whom you have fully in yourself? You carry in yourself the One who has created all things!

# Chapter 8

*How the exterior liturgy in the holy church is carried out for the sake of the interior liturgy.*

(1) Our high feast in this miserable world is not found with genuine joy but is full of sorrow. Worldly hearts, inclined to vanity, look forward to holy feasts but don't celebrate them in the right way. They look outside for what they should seek within. But a person who exercises the virtues has always a high feast in himself, because he rejoices in the truth in which the angels rejoice. No sadness can take away such joy. It is always a feast day for a righteous person.

(2) Indeed, consecration of the church is accomplished only in the most intimate part of the soul, in the same place that God has reserved for himself and united to himself, where neither angel nor human person nor any other creature can enter—that is the noble

superessence of the soul—and that same place he desires to have for himself alone, and he does not want to share it with anyone else. For the eternal God always lives ardently in the pure soul with his consolation and with his divine grace. For he speaks, "It is my delight to dwell with the sons of men" (Prov 8:31). (3) Therefore, my dearest beloved in Christ, the one who desires a pure consecration of the church should bring the house of God, namely, the most inner part of the soul, to freedom for God and unity. Only in unity can the Most High and unique One, God himself, be united with the soul. Therefore, when the soul has cast off all self-love and all that is creaturely, and stands completely naked and empty of all multiplicity, purely in the truth, then the unique One, God himself, responds to the unity of the soul, so that there is nothing else in the soul than purely God alone. (4) Therefore, when the human person is disposed in such a pure way that his heart and soul are anxious about nothing but God, and what his own physical needs demand (which he in a rightly ordered way can take by God and have with God), then such a union between God and the soul comes into being, and they become together as one, as St. Paul says, "Whoever is joined to the Lord becomes one spirit with him" (1 Cor 6:17).

(5) The exterior temple is made for this inner temple. Everything that is disposed in it has no purpose other than to come to this inner temple, and all that is celebrated in it has no aim other than to be perfected in this inner temple. (6) The exterior temple is made by human hands; this one by the hands of the eternal Wisdom. That one is of inert stone; this one of rational, living stones and founded on the immovable mountain of the Divinity and the unfaltering rock that is Christ; it is protected by the heavenly spirits whom he has set as strong guards of these walls. The prophet says, "Upon your walls he has stationed strong watchmen" (cf. Isa 62:6). That one is adorned with perishable good things; this one with imperishable virtues. (7) In that one the servants tire, but in this one the heavenly servants do not, and God himself does not cease to glorify himself there. The organ in the external temple, and all the instruments, are played by human art, but in this one the Holy Trinity plays the organ of the soul, where the heavenly master of love brings about his praise, with the sweetest melody in the innermost part of the soul. In that one the sacraments are given and

received through human efforts, but in this one they are given, served, and received by God himself, who has become for us a blessed offering. In that one high feasts are celebrated and pass away, but in this one they are celebrated and remain in the essence [of the soul]. In that one the feast of the dedication of the church is celebrated once a year, but in this one the stational rite is ever celebrated, and there is ever the affluence of God's riches and graces.

# Chapter 10

*On the interior Advent, and how the soul should prepare itself for the solemnities.*

(1) In the outer temple, one celebrates Advent by looking forward to the coming of the Lord with eager desire. But in the inner temple, the Lord is always present, ever to announce to the soul the divine birth with a new promise. There, he is desired; here enjoyed. In that temple, there is hungry and thirsty indigence; here, one is satiated and replete with abundance. (2) Nevertheless, as long as we are on earth in our low human nature, in our mortal condition, we need to take this mutability as it is; and thus we resemble the Church Militant. Indeed, the human person cannot endure always the fullness of grace that is poured into the highest unity of the soul, where we resemble the Church Triumphant, where the heavenly Jerusalem is, where one ever celebrates the high feasts with full joy, and where they last forever essentially and pass not away. (3) Nevertheless, on every high feast the soul overflows with this fullness of grace, and in all creatures that turn themselves to this the soul brims. And thus, the most intimate part of our soul—where we resemble the heavenly Jerusalem—is given new joy on that high feast, and the Church Triumphant—with which our soul is compared—is renewed and fortified against all vices, to fulfill the desired glory of God. The Church Militant is given new delight and new ointment of the Spirit; heart and senses are renewed and the taste of the divinity permeates them. Thus, the Lord desires to make us resemble his divine majesty. (4) Human nature cannot endure these joys, especially when they are overflowing all three.[8]

The constant joy and inpouring abundance of God consume the faculties and weaken human nature. Our earthly dwelling place cannot endure this, and therefore it suppresses the spirit when nature endures violence. However, these joys can remain essentially in its highest part, in a simple celebration of our spirit, but not in the lower faculties of the soul. There, the human person suffers its mutability and the absence of the Bridegroom, and there begins the desire for his advent. While on the one hand the soul would like to have him and on the other it does not have him immediately, it grows weak and becomes negligent. (5) In this it is admonished by the friend of the Bridegroom: "It is the hour now to awake from sleep. Throw off the works of darkness and put on the armor of light. The night is advanced, but the day is at hand, that we might conduct ourselves properly in the day" (cf. Rom 13:11–13). That night is our ignorance. Christ is the day. Therefore we will throw off this tepidity and clothe ourselves with Christ our Lord, who is the true light that enlightens all human persons, and enkindles with the fire of his love hearts that have became slow, and draws them to himself to adorn them with the Lord of virtues, so that they walk in the newness of life.

(6) Now is the time for renewal. That is why the soul begins to be exhausted with yearning desires for the advent of the Bridegroom. And he comforts it in many ways by his saints, and says: "O Jerusalem, devout soul, your salvation comes quickly. Why are you wasted with sorrow? I will save you and deliver you. Fear not.[9] City of Jerusalem, weep not; for the Lord has grieved over you, and he will take away all your distress. See, here comes with power the Lord, who rules by his strong arm.[10] The Lord comes forth from his holy throne.[11] He will come and save his people from their sins (cf. Matt 1:21). I will put salvation within Zion and give to Jerusalem my glory.[12] Even if a mother should forget her only child, I will not forget you (cf. Isa 49:15). Rejoice, Jerusalem,[13] see: your king shall come to you (cf. Zech 9:9; John 12:15).[14] Of him the prophets have spoken, the angels worship him, the Cherubim and Seraphim cry to him: "Holy, holy, holy."[15] O Judah and Jerusalem, do not fear: tomorrow you will go out, and the Lord will be with you.[16] Remain firm in your confidence, and you will see God's help coming upon you.[17] O Jerusalem, stand up, climb the heights (cf.

Bar 5:5), behold the joy that comes to you from the Lord your God.[18] Lift up your eyes and see the joy that is coming now to you from the Lord. Fear not, Zion, see, your God will come, hallelujah![19] Jerusalem, open your eyes and behold the power of the king.[20] See, the Lord will come from Israel and protect our blessedness, he shall have a glorious crown on his head, he will rule from sea to sea, from the flooding rivers to the ends of the earth.[21] The heavens must sing out and the earth will rejoice. You mountains, break forth into praise, for the Lord will come and show mercy to his poor.[22] You, mountains of Israel, spread out your branches, and blossom, and bring forth fruit, for the day of the Lord is near.[23] See, the Lord will come and all his saints with him. On that day there will be a great light,[24] and from Jerusalem they will come, as a mighty stream. See, he will come with great power and majesty" (cf. Luke 21:27).

(7) O desired soul, how is it possible that you have not completely turned yourself with all your desires toward him who draws you so deeply, and urges you to be fully his, and for that reason sends all his messengers to you, even though they were sent to announce the physical birth of Christ? He was born once physically, so that he be born always in you spiritually. (8) That is why to every soul is said what the prophet Isaiah said: "For Zion's sake I will not be silent, for Jerusalem's sake I will not be quiet, until her vindication shines forth as a bright light, and your savior flares as a torch. You shall be called by a new name. You shall be a crown of the kingdom in the hand of your God. No more shall you be called 'desert,' your land shall no longer be called 'desolate,' but 'my delight shall be in him' and 'your land will be inhabited,' for the Lord delights in you (cf. Isa 62:1–4). Say to those whose hearts are frightened: God himself will come, and will save you. Then the eyes of the blind will be opened, the ears of the deaf be unstopped; then will the lame leap like a stag, the tongue of the dumb will be loosened. Streams will burst forth in the desert and rivers in the wilderness. What was dry has become a pool, and what was parched has reached the banks of the river (cf. Isa 35:4–7). The one who has sent me has anointed me to comfort all who mourn, and to strengthen those in Zion who weep, to place on them a crown instead of ashes, oil of gladness in place of mourning (cf. Isa 61:1–3). See, I am sending my angel, to prepare the way of the Lord before you and to make straight the paths toward him" (cf. Mal 3:1; Isa 40:3;

Matt 11:10). (9) This angel is the light of prevenient grace, clearing the way for God in the soul, and opening it, doing away with all that is displeasing to the advent of the great Lord, and bringing in the soul all good that is becoming for the advent of the lovable Lord. Indeed, what can we do or what do we have that we have not received from him? Oh, how lovely are the feet—the inner light of the divine truth—that bring the message of peace and all good to the soul, which make it love and desire more fervently, so that it calls to him, in its most intimate part, where the kingdom of God is, and where he has hidden himself.

(10) "O you who are above the Cherubim, wake up your might and come! O Lord, tear open the heaven of my dark mind, enlighten my senses and my powers, sitting in the darkness and the shadow of death. O Lord, rend the heavens and come down here, and make me humble myself for you. (11) Drop down dew, you heavens, from above. O glorious Holy Trinity, who have united yourself with my mind, send the dew of your mercy, and make my barren heart fruitful. Hosea says: 'They who dwell in your shade, shall be honored, and I shall be like the dew for them. Israel shall blossom like the lily and the vine' (Hos 14:6–8). (12) Let the clouds rain the Just One. O you radiant cloud of the fatherly heart, flow through my inner self with the fertile rain of your sweetness, and let the just seed rain down on me, which you have sown in me, and open the earth of my heart, so that it may bring forth the just. Come, O Lord of virtues, send the rays of your light, and renew this earthly dwelling that your enemies have invaded, destroying all its virtues. (13) Come and make your throne in my spirit, your seat in my soul, your tabernacle in my body, by the merits of your holy joyful spirit, of your sorrowful soul and your wounded body. As you are the re-creator of the world, make for yourself a becoming dwelling in me, and adorn your temple to be fit for such a king. Make my spirit, your impressed image, noble again, adorn my soul, your realm and seat, and purify my body, the work of your hands. Oh, come, and bring with you all that is good, as appropriate for high lords, for you are the King of the angels and the Lord of all lords. (14) Who could prepare himself worthily for your advent, or be able to welcome this advent worthily? O my soul, you could not host a worthier, nobler, sweeter lord than the King of the angels, in whom you can find all that is distinguished, desirable, and satisfac-

tory. And to you, O Lord of life, will be given no bride other than the soul, in whom you have impressed your image, whom you have married with the light of truth. You have put for yourself the sign of likeness to you on her face, and you have established the light of your face in her, so that you can leave her no more. (15) O Lord, you can take everything away from me, but not yourself, because you are the life of my soul. You have created my soul so that in it you could give birth to your eternal Word. Therefore I pray you, make it ready for your eternal birth. How near to one another are God and the soul, and yet how dissimilar!"

(16) When God and the soul thrust such arrows of love at each other, when there is such prayer, attention, and preparation for the coming high feast, then the mind and soul of the human person is dilated and made larger and ready for the high feast. Then this feast can let its riches and delicious graces flow into the realm of the soul. For those the door is opened; they are immediately welcomed by the Bridegroom and placed in the joy of heaven. And he transforms them and impresses on them the fruit of the high feast, so that its memory will always remain with them. (17) But those who still need to prepare themselves when the moment comes to enter with the Bridegroom, will remain locked out, and remain in their own nature, and he will pass by. Indeed, a person should prepare for the high feast according to how he wants it to be.[25] (18) The day of the wedding meal will not be a day of preparation, but a day of becoming united in love, of sinking into and being embraced by the Truth, of which St. Bernard says: "Sanctify yourself today and be prepared, for tomorrow you will see God's glory in you. Today is the moment for sanctification. Tomorrow will not be a day of sanctification or of preparation, but one of contemplation of the divine glory in you. Today we exercise justice, but tomorrow the justice will respond to us. Today justice is cultivated; tomorrow it will yield its fruits. For what a person has not sown, he will not reap. He who now despises sanctification will not see the glory of God then. And in the one in whom the sun of justice has not risen, the sun of glory will not come up. For the one in whom the light of today does not shine, the light of tomorrow will not shine either. The One who is made by the Father as our justice, he will reveal our life, and he will take us to himself, so that we may appear, together with him, in his glory."[26]

(19) All this should happen in receptivity. Someone who wants to invade violently, without preparing himself, without readying himself for it by inner attention, will remain outside. But the one who renounces himself, his exercises, and what is proper to him, and who at the same moment turns inward, in this person God can find that his ground is bare. If not, he will remain in his own nature at the moment that he had to enter with him [Christ] into inner joy. (20) What a great art, to have the spirit freed and unhindered with the Lord—not only freed from its faults and unhindered but also from the burden of nature. If someone wants freedom of spirit, he must judiciously and carefully deal with his nature in such a way that nature is joined lovingly and harmoniously to the spirit, so that without violence both can be united by God's loving ordinance. Then, the spirit can enjoy unhindered the mysteries of God, and be readied for the blessed high feast.

# Chapter 11

*On the inner silence of the soul, its harmful running outward and the unification of the senses and faculties.*

(1) "When all things were in the midst of a silence and the heaven had spent its course, the almighty, eternal Word came down from the royal throne."[27]

(2) The soul has similarity with all creatures. Its senses assume unseemly liberty and associate with all things. They enjoy what is improper, in an improper way, according to an appetite they have for what is improper—and this is never without harm. They run outward and lose themselves in the multiplicity of things that should be considered in simplicity. In simplicity, one can possess God in all things. So long as the soul loses itself in the multiplicity of things, it is not well ordered. (3) Therefore, the senses and faculties must be turned inward and recollected in a simple silence. If God is to speak, then all things must be silent. If God is to enter, then the soul should go out, out of itself and all creatures. If God is to accomplish his noble work in the soul, then the soul must be withdrawn and empty and surrender to God. (4) The most noble work the soul can achieve is to sur-

render itself to God and to become purely patient of God's activity. To allow God to do his hidden work, to surrender oneself to it, to undergo God's noble work for the length of one Pater Noster, that is more noble than what all creatures have wrought from the beginning of the world. Indeed, God's work goes beyond all the works of creatures. (5) The hidden friends of God abandon themselves and become God's most beloved children. They allow God to work with them and reach the apex of their souls. They possess together with him the essence of all virtues and thus reach the highest nobility. Those who keep themselves do their works with great labor. They never reach their highest beatitude; they ever remain servants. Now, what is better: to be God's children, or to be his servants?

[When all things were in the midst of a silence]

(6) The bride says: "I compassed the circle, and could not reach the end (the circle is the outward activity of the Trinity); therefore, I have thrown myself toward the center" (cf. Sir 24:5), that is, into the essential unity and the rays that come out of that center. That unity separates out and liberates my soul, and draws it, with all its senses and faculties, inward into that center. (7) Light designates the attention of the soul; it is so empty that it is not concerned with virtues and vices. When the soul is so empty, then it knows whatever enters into it on the highest level. God sends his light into the soul in order that it may know that he knew it before it existed, that he loved it when it did not yet exist. That will be a great incentive for the soul to go out of itself. Whoever does not live in this light is not struck by love. (8) So free and empty the soul should be, when God shines his noble birth in it. But God should help it attain this freedom. And he does that with pleasure for the one who is willing to renounce himself and be immersed in the center, that is, God's Divine Being which has united itself with the essence of the soul. In this way all creatures must be silent.

[The heaven had spent its course]

(9) Then, everything is silent in the soul, and the heaven has fulfilled its course—this heaven is the inner mind, in which the Holy

336

Trinity has portrayed and hidden itself, and with which the Trinity has united itself. This heaven cannot rest, neither can it stop its course, before it is united again in its source and origin, the Divine Being, before the Holy Trinity dwells with fruition in its chamber, before the faculty of the soul that is called *memoria* is united and fixed with the heavenly Father, who gives it true joy and certain peace; before the other faculty, which is called intelligence, is united with the Son, who shines his light through it, so that it becomes so clear that it need not search the origin hereof but finds this in itself; before the third faculty called will is one with the Holy Spirit, liberated with him, united with him in silent love, and free of all things that could trouble the city. (10) [The heaven cannot stop its course] before it becomes free of itself and does not resist God any more, so that it can say, "I am nobody's soul, and nobody is my God." Indeed, it has sunk from itself into the nameless being of God. God possesses the city of the soul. The Holy Trinity works in it, and the soul has become a dwelling place and an instrument of the Trinity. With the heavenly Father, it wants to remain there steadfastly. And only with the Son it wants to go out: to rest and to let him work, to be silent and to let him speak, to die and let him live. (11) The soul has a hidden way of entering into the divine nature, where all things are annihilated for her. Jesus himself says: "Be perfect just as your heavenly Father is perfect" (Matt 5:48). There, the soul is beyond all desire, beyond all yearning, beyond work, beyond practice. It is empty because God fulfills it and works even more. Indeed, it can suffer God's activity more than work by itself.

[The almighty, eternal Word came down from the royal throne]

(12) Well then, understand now the superessentiality of God in the soul. God gives birth to himself in the soul. Then the soul is stripped of all images, deprived of its createdness, and transformed in the eternal work of God, which God works in it. There, the soul is the Son of God, whom the Father, by a gracious union, gives birth to in the soul—yet it remains a creature. In this rebirth of the Son, the soul must go out of itself and all foreign beings. Here the soul is blessed. (13) A master says that the soul has a noble capacity: subtly it flows out of God, and returns into God and comprehends God in its being. Indeed, nothing is closer to the soul's being than

God, for God is in the being of the soul. (14) The soul that is turned therein lives in the land of freedom, in the inner world. God lives here, and he enlightens all people who come there. This inner world is the image of the soul, which God has essentially in him, without modes and without intermediary. In it God is beyond all modes in order to bring beyond all modes the soul that lives in the outer world. God became man for that reason, and has given and taught modes so that with modes he could bring man beyond modes. Here the soul has completed its course. God has waited to find the soul pure and empty, and like a virgin. (15) The soul, which in this way is empty of all creatures and separated from all things and free and united in God and married and secured, is truly a pure virgin. "Whoever is joined to the Lord becomes one spirit with him" (1 Cor 6:17). "You are all-beautiful, my beloved, there is no blemish in you" (Sg 4:7). Indeed, God has taken away all its stains. God's near presence and union with him makes the soul even purer. With the Pure it becomes pure, with the Holy it becomes holy, and with the radiant clarity it becomes a pure light. Oh, how good is it for the spirit to be found in this rich and pure knowledge! This knowledge is unknown to all who are not pure. (16) God is free, unchangeable, and one; nevertheless, he maintains all things, rules and brings them about, and remains one with himself. In the same way the soul can be occupied with heaven and earth and neverthe-less be free and immovable—provided that the soul is not given to these things and does not assume them. Then it has God in its authority and has authority over all things. For this, the soul is cre-ated, to be able to walk these divine ways. In God is nothing that is impossible for the soul, if it wants to search it. (17) Augustine says that for the soul nothing is more useful or blessed than to walk in the knowledge of the Holy Trinity.[28]

# Chapter 12

*How the inner soul is chosen by the Holy Trinity as a spiritual Mother of God; how it is turned inward, greeted and made pregnant for the divine birth.*

(1) The soul that is thus empty and free is chosen by the whole Trinity to live in the Trinity and to be an intimate family member and an heir of God. It is made free by him, and introduced into the hidden chamber of the Holy Trinity, where God gives it his secret mystery. The heavenly Father chooses it as a daughter and gives it his divine dominion. The Son chooses it as a mother, and gives it all his merits. The Holy Spirit chooses it as a bride, and gives it all his wealth and riches, and leads it further into his hidden bedroom, into the hidden unity of God, into the hidden silence, into the secret unity. There God speaks with it. A heavenly light shines upon it, and it receives a new wondrous message. The soul is greeted by the [divine] clarity, turned inward, embraced, penetrated, flooded by God, and united to him. It receives the Lord of life, and is blessed and honored in the abundant blessings of the Holy Trinity. That is the meaning of the angel's salutation. (2) When *Ave* is sung, the melody indicates that this word is turned inward. *Ave* is a single immersion in the hidden unity of God. *Ma* is a descent into God's depths. *Ria* is a loving embrace by the Holy Trinity. *Gratia* is an illumination, and an overflowing fullness of the richness of God. *Dominus tecum*, that is, the soul is filled by and fruitful with the Creator of the world. *Benedicta* means that, by virtue of the blessing of the Holy Trinity, the soul is united with the divinity by its most blessed fruit and pregnancy.

(3) The soul is startled that God honors it so much; it humbles itself, makes itself small, and wants to sink away from itself for God. It considers itself as small as dust compared to the whole sun. If it could annihilate itself, it would have disappeared immediately by making itself even smaller. But that is impossible—for the soul is eternal—and because God has created it for this, it says with humble fear: "How does this happen to me that the majesty of the Lord should come to me? Oh, I am not worthy. If I were all that you are, I would prefer to let it be yours, and to be the handmaid of you and of all creatures, and to have your will done in me and in all creatures" (cf. Luke 1:29, 38, 43). With this humility the soul pierces God and wounds him with the wound of love. (4) And the almighty eternal Word comes down from his royal throne and, in turn, pierces the most intimate part of the soul. He notices all its humility and wants it elevated in its divinity. He wants it to dwell in his

divinity, and himself to dwell in its humanity. (5) The Word has become flesh and dwells in us. God says, "Man, for your sake I became man; if you do not become God for my sake, you do great wrong to me. You will bury your human nature in my divine nature, so that no one will be able to discern your human nature."

(6) Now, the soul will enter into God that he may work all the works of the soul. Whoever wants to obey God, to honor him, to delight Mary and all the saints and angels, to console all people and save all souls, must turn inward, renouncing and denying himself, so that God may accomplish his noble birth in him. Love compelled God to be born once in human nature. The highest honor that we can give to him is to have him be born in us always in a spiritual way. (7) Blessed are those whom you have chosen and adopted as your children for this. They will dwell in your spacious forecourt, and be fulfilled by your birth in the fruitfulness of your house, and rest in the bosom of the paternal heart, and be immersed in the eternal Word, fulfilled with the marrow and clarity of the fatherly heart, and become pregnant with the Son of the Father by the collaboration and embrace of the Holy Spirit, who overshadows them. (8) Blessed are you, virgin soul, who carry the Lord, the Creator of the world. You give birth to the one who made you, and you remain virginal eternally with him. You carry the one who reigns over all in the innermost part of yourself, by the power of the Father and the love of the Holy Spirit. You enclose the supreme architect, who sustains the entire world. (9) This soul can indeed say: "In all things I sought rest, and in the heritage of my Lord—that is, in the unity of the Divine Being—I will dwell. The one who created me, rests in my tabernacle" (cf. Sir 24:11–12).[29]

# Chapter 13

*How God is born in the human person in three ways according to the three unities.*[30]

(1) Here, the soul is so filled with God that he must be born from it. He cannot remain entirely hidden. The virgin Son must shine forth from it. As the soul has received nothing but God, and

is filled with God, it can give birth to nothing else than God, who is born from it in three ways—nevertheless, he is and remains essentially one, just as the Holy Trinity is three in persons but remains essentially one. (2) Indeed, there are three unities in all human beings, and each unity is in God. The first unity is that of the inner being of the soul. The second is the unity of the higher faculties. The third is the unity of the heart. In good people, God is present in a superessential way, for all the vigor of spiritual work comes from here. Whoever lets himself be directed from here, is directed by God, and becomes a spiritual and divine person.

(3) Now, the highest unity of the being of the soul hangs always in God—one life—and is united with the Divine Being. It is one and unwavering, because God dwells in that unity as in an eternal "now." If the soul were always to be united here, the human person would remain forever young. This unity cannot become old; on the contrary, in itself the soul remains always young, in an eternal newness, and remains always a virgin. It is indeed simple—beyond all determination—and it is without determination or characteristics. In the same way God is there in the soul simply, with no distinctions of names or persons. He is there in no other way, and in this part the soul is similar to God. There, God ever gives birth to himself, in a superessential way, and he keeps the essence of the soul fixed to his unity, so that it is free and stripped, without name or form. The essence of the soul is simple and does not intermingle with anything, so that one cannot reach it in a determined way. And here the Father gives birth to his only Son, as truly as he does in himself, and the mind is continuously embraced in the divine unity. The one who experiences this in himself finds all good and eternal life. In this lies all freedom and abundance of wealth. It is not limited, it is wider than all the heavens, and it is a streaming flood, a bottomless source from which all living rivers flow forth. (4) In this way the Son to whom the Father gives birth is ever born. And that is the meaning of the first Mass sung at midnight, in the dark night unknown to the created intellect. This intellect is unable to reach it, because it is as a darkness to it. And in this dark silence a simple light reveals itself, and the Father speaks, "You are my Son, today I have begotten you" (cf. Ps 2:7). Here the spirit is born again, and taken up in its divine origin, where it has been from eternity. There

it is God with God, where God gives birth anew to himself—in the mode of simplicity, in the highest unity.

(5) The middle unity is that of the higher faculties, which emerge from the first unity. They have their origin and foundation in the Divine Being. In this unity, God dwells with his Holy Trinity, and he works in this unity according to distinctions of the Persons. The Father is the power and being of memory, and keeps it in an eternal attention. The Son is the clarity and the being of the intellect, and keeps it in an eternal light. The Holy Spirit is the burning spark of the will, and keeps it in loving inclination, in an eternal adherence to God. He unites the spirit with God in the bond of love. (6) And here God gives birth to his Son in a hidden brightness, with which the spirit is clarified. That light gives the spirit knowledge of God and of itself; it discloses the senses of scripture and teaches the content and the modes of all spiritual exercises and spiritual life. It gives all this to enlighten the soul. This birth is the sense of the second Mass, where we sing, "Light will shine upon us today."

(7) The last unity is that of the lower faculties and the heart. God dwells in this unity by his inner illumination, which comes forth from the higher faculties. This illumination guides all that is in the soul and in the human person. It shines through, keeps reason in discernment, so that with God it wisely probes and disposes all things. It keeps desire in a pure orientation toward all that is good, in order to adhere to him with all its strength. It maintains the irascible force in its inclination to God, in its composure and discernment. It also keeps conscience in the light of knowledge, in order to be joyful in all virtues and to allow nothing else. It collects the heart's sensitivity, with all the senses of the human person; it purifies them, makes them inner senses, and unites them with God. In this way God takes up our humanity and, in turn, gives us his divinity in order to be born spiritually from us, and so that we may apply ourselves to his human birth and become similar to it. He gives us all his life, virtues and loving birth in order that we might be united completely with him.

(8) Oh, wonderful union of God and soul! That he deigns to take the soul to himself and to be born of it! That he gives it his divinity and the merits of his holy humanity, to make the human

person a reflection of his works! And this spiritual birth is the content of the third Mass, where we sing, "To us a child is born, to us a son is given" (cf. Isa 9:6).

(9) The soul is a virgin when it conceives God and gives birth to him in this way. But now it must be a wife too, by returning this birth and all these gifts back to God, from whom it received them.[31] The fruitfulness of the gifts lies only in gratitude for the gifts. The soul becomes a wife by grateful praise, when it gives birth again in God. Virginity is not useful unless it sinks again in God with all the gifts. Otherwise the gifts decay, and no fruit can come from it. But this virgin wife bears fruit a hundred times daily, and merits a hundredfold, even infinitely, by giving birth again. For it is fruitful from the very best ground, yes, from the same ground as that of the Father giving birth to his only Son: the soul gives birth together with the Father. For Jesus is the light and the reflection of the paternal heart. This Jesus is united with the soul, and it with him. And it lights and radiates together with him as a unique and pure brilliance in the heart of the Father. (10) St. Bernard says: "This is the new person, who does not become old. Even they, whose bones are old, are renewed again."[32] (11) God and all the angels and saints rejoice at this. And God desires that his birth be renewed in us. And Mary's joy and desire is that all that happened physically and spiritually in her be realized again and renewed spiritually in the soul.

# Chapter 14

*How the heavenly spirits lull the divine birth of the new baby with a hymn.*

(1) Angels surround the spirit, and they rejoice, and honor God because of this birth. With sweet melodies and voices they lull the baby in the tiny manger of the paternal heart and in the bed of the virginal mind. They sing: "Glory to God in the highest." (2) And just as one sings nine times *kyrie eleison*, the nine choirs of angels herald God's praise at the threefold birth.

At the superessential birth the highest choirs sing:

343

*Kyrie*—God is born
From a chosen virgin.
Therefore we rejoice
Forever.—*Eleison.*

(3) At the divine birth the middle choirs sing:

*In dulci jubilo.*
Sing and rejoice!
All the desire of our heart
Lies *in presepio.*
*Ergo merito*
All hearts
Will be taken up *in gaudio*, etc.

(4) At the spiritual birth the lowest choirs sing:

A child is born to us
Therefore we all rejoice.
Let us serve him with fine heart,
For his name is Jesus.
*Vala sus, vala sus*
*In ore.*

# Chapter 15

*The fruitful virginity of the soul.*

(1) "Blessed are you, virginal soul, for the Sun of Justice is born from you." And "as a fruitful vine you bring forth abundant fruits of honor and commendation." And "God chooses it and makes it dwell in its tabernacle." And "he wants to dwell in the center of it and make it unchangeable." "Honorable virgin, Mother of God, you were worthy to carry the Lord of the angels, to suckle him with the fruitful interiority of your spirit." "Holy, immaculate virginity, I do not know which praises I can express to you, for you drew into your womb the One whom the heavens cannot encom-

pass." (2) Here the soul is filled with God, and her being deiform. All her faculties enjoy God, and her heart is full of love; it is brought into a pure light and contemplation of his divinity and humanity. It dwells with God in the land of freedom, in the inner unity.

(3) St. Bernard says: "How indescribable the benevolence of God, whose high majesty bends down to such humble meekness! He who created us is born in us. And, as if it were not enough that God be our Father, he wants us to be his mother. 'Whoever does the will of my Father,' he says, 'is my brother, my sister and my mother. He is my brother when he is obedient; he is my mother when I am born in others by his good teaching' (Matt 12:50).

(4) O good, faithful soul, enlarge the womb of your heart, enlarge your desires, do not be cramped interiorly, so that you can conceive Christ, whom the world cannot encompass. He is conceived daily in us through faith since the time that the blessed Virgin Mary conceived him. By good preaching he is begotten, by good inner life he is nourished, by love he is kept. The conscience should be pure, so that it can bring God into its inn. The soul should also be careful to serve its Son, so that the high divine Majesty could not refuse to rest in its womb. It should also be inner, to intend God alone, and never depart from him. Such a conscience is a joy for the soul, and pleases God. The angels hold this conscience in esteem. In itself, it is peaceful and quiet."[33] The conscience should also be pure, because pure love of Christ makes even the impure pure. Those honorable in their nature, he makes most pure.

(5) Intend now to what is still lacking to your blessedness, knowing that the child is embraced and received by the mother, father, daughter, brother, and sister—under many names. It is wondrous that so many mothers have one son, and so many daughters one brother, whom one cannot separate according to time and space, yet whom each has nevertheless completely and indivisibly. I think we rightly give birth to Christ when we have received of his fullness. He is born first in his words; then the soul bears fruit, when he is born by the soul's works, as St. Paul says, "My children, for whom I am again in labor until Christ be formed in you" (Gal 4:19). Christ was once carried by his virgin mother in a physical

way, and she gave birth to him physically. Now, he is ever conceived spiritually by holy virgins, and they give birth to him spiritually.

(6) O wondrous virginal beauty, there is nothing comparable! What more delightful than the splendor of a blossoming soul? What more beautiful than a pure body? What other is this most precious gem, mounted on pure gold, than a soul in a pure body, drawn inward?

# Chapter 16

*How we may carry Christ in our hearts and nourish him.*

(1) The stains of sin are dispelled by no exercise more than by the constant practice of inner union with God. Since Christ is the Word of the Father, you carry Christ in your heart as often as you delight in the words of life. How could space for sin remain there, when you carry the fountain of life within you? The one who carries Christ in his heart, in a hidden manner, need not be concerned about death.

(2) Now the soul should see to it not to depart from the unity of the spirit, or to go out of this fruitful house, or to draw any member away from the lovable image of his holy life and passion, by which Christ has transformed the soul. The soul is then guarded by Christ and by his holy servants, so that neither it nor the tender members of the Child are hurt, or that the rest of the Child's growth is hindered. Indeed, if the merits of Christ had not led the soul inward and adorned and made it fruitful, then this birth could neither happen nor be protected.

(3) Where could you find a king able to prepare for his bride such a palace and an adorned dwelling and unique chamber, as this King of glory does? He himself has prepared the chamber for his bride, led her in, united himself with her, and made her pregnant for a divine birth, so that she births the King of angels. (4) This chamber is ever surrounded by angelic spirits, that the King of peace may rest there, in the bed of the mind, strewn with herbs and flowers of the virtues, and bathed in the beaming rays of the Divinity, even as it is written, "Our bed is one of flowers (Sg 1:16).

As the king rested, my nard gave forth its fragrance" (Sg 1:12). When we remove our thoughts from earthly things, and turn to the memory of God, then we make a bed for the King of peace, and he enjoys his mystery there. The heavenly spirits ever sing the delightful song of love at the bed of this virgin. Here, lover is united with the beloved, and the beloved embraced by the lover. She gazes upon him in divine attention.

(5) She carries him in the arms of her soul with pure desire and pure love. She has wrapped him in the divine light and heavenly garment in the womb of her heart, by her deiform intention. She feeds him with inner thoughts, with pure desire and love, with religious practice and pure intention, with righteous works, mercy, and benevolence, and with all the works of the virtues that make one obedient to God and man.

(6) In the canticle is written: "The Bridegroom is nourished among the lilies" (Sg 2:16; 6:3), that is, in a pure heart. He delights to rest in a virginal body as in an arbor of green and fragrant flowers. St. Bernard says: "Nothing is more pleasing to the Bridegroom then to rest in a virginal womb."[34]

(7) When Christ is pleased with its good works, the soul feeds him.[35] It feeds him with desires, as it is written: "My people have satisfied me with desires, and have sated me with perfumes." This food nourishes and revives his members with examples when other people are edified and improved by its example and holy life and behavior. It nourishes and strengthens these members with prayer when they receive from God the grace that comforts them and builds up their salvation. It nourishes them with doctrine when it strengthens them with sermons and teaches them to savor eternal things. It nourishes them with advice, when it comforts people, and raises up with mild admonitions those who are sad, and stimulates the good with conversation. It nourishes them when it speaks to anyone about good things, and shuns as much as possible useless words, or when it speaks in the assembly words that edify, and gives matter for a holy converse, and zeal for charity and peace, and does not lend ear to backbiting, but sorrows upon hearing such. This way a holy soul nourishes and edifies Christ and his members.

. . .

# Chapter 22

*First Sunday after Epiphany.*

The child grew to perfection, to the honor of God, as the Gospel says, "The child grew and became strong, filled with wisdom, in favor with God and man" (cf. Luke 2:40), that is, in his own person and in his assumed humanity. And he still does this, in a spiritual sense, in the pure mind and the faultless heart of people with whom he has enrobed himself. For his part, he clothes the human person with his divinity. Thus he renews all his works, and he works all the works of the human person. And he wants to conform that person to his holy dealings and manner of life, just as he himself was. Because he is the essence of all virtue, he draws the human person, and teaches him, and brings him to all virtue. In this, the human person has nothing to ascribe to himself. Then he will let himself undergo God's works. Whatever happens to this person happens to God. It cannot happen to this person unless it first happens to God and affects him. All this the person undergoes with joyful pleasure because God has put on the person, and made the person put on God. The Holy Trinity rejoices at this. The Father speaks, "This is my only son, with whom I am well pleased" (Luke 3:22). The Holy Spirit finds joy in resting upon him. Jesus Christ finds joy in dwelling in him.

The child stayed behind in Jerusalem, "the city where I have chosen to put my name," in the soul. Somewhere else he says, "It is my delight to be with the children of men" (cf. Prov 8:31). The inner soul is a spiritual Jerusalem, the true place for prayer, where one is accustomed to worship the Father in spirit and in truth. That Jerusalem is the inner part of the mind, where God's temple is. Herein the eternal Word is kept, and it will dwell there eternally.

# Mystical Sermons[1]

## The Manuscript

*Manuscript Den Haag, Koninklijke Bibliotheek, 133 H 13, contains a unique collection of mystical sermons. Several scholars have drawn attention to this collection, but no extensive study of the codex or its content has ever been made.[2] Only one sermon has been edited.[3]*

*Nothing is known with certainty about the original provenance of the manuscript. There are no ownership marks, and the sermons yield practically no information about the place and context in which they were written and read. The codex in its present form dates from later than 1545; the stamps that were used to make impressions on the binding are dated 1545, which means that they were made in that year. Watermark evidence suggests that the codex was written around 1560.*

The Mystical Sermons, *as they might justifiably be labeled, are written in a distinctly eastern Middle Dutch dialect. The manuscript, therefore, probably originates from Gelre, a region that is now almost evenly divided between the Netherlands and Germany. Furthermore, there is even reason to believe that the manuscript was written in the St. Agnes convent in Arnhem, a city located in the heart of the Gelre region. The script is very comparable to if not identical with that of Alberta van Middachten, a scribe of several other manuscripts who was "custos librorum" in St. Agnes around 1560.*

## The *Mystical Sermons* in Their Spiritual and Historical Context

*No fewer than 162 sermons are written on the 381 leaves of the manuscript, making it the largest known collection of Middle Dutch sermons according to a recent repertory.[4] The sermons are organized according to the Proper of the Season and the Proper of the Saints. They have been an important source of mystical vocabulary for the* Middelnederlands woordenboek *(Middle Dutch dictionary).⁵ The* Mystical Sermons *are of high literary and spiritual value and are probably of great significance for the history of Dutch—and French—spirituality and mysticism.*

*The most important evaluation of the content thus far was formulated by De Vooys: "(The sermons) manifest on every page the influence of fourteenth-century mysticism, especially through lavish use of Eckartian and Ruusbroecian terminology."⁶ It is worth mentioning that Ampe points to strong parallels in the spirituality of the* Mystical Sermons, Sister Bertken, *and the author of the* Evangelical Pearl.

*Several sources of Late Medieval mysticism seem to merge in these sermons. Influences from the "essential" mysticism of Eckhart, the bridal and trinitarian mysticism of Ruusbroec, the unassuming mysticism of Lebemeister Tauler, and the negative mysticism of Pseudo-Dionysius the Areopagite can be clearly traced. This distinct synthesis of several mystical currents quite unexpectedly starts to blossom from the early decades of the sixteenth century, following on the heels of more than a century of spiritual writings marked by asceticism and moralism. Reaching back over two centuries, the mystical teachings of the sermons are closely connected to the mystical writings from the heyday of fourteenth-century mysticism. The Gelre mystical culture and the text and book culture connected with it had hitherto not been identified as a coherent phenomenon. The cultural and historical circumstances that contributed to this rebirth of mysticism also need to be analyzed in detail. A promising research perspective is the relation of this mystical renaissance to the Counter-Reformation activities of the Cologne Carthusians and the then-new Jesuit order.*

*The collection in* Mystical Sermons *is the material and conceptual link between the Brabantine and Rhineland mystical sources and a public with a new receptivity to mystical texts in sixteenth-century Gelre. The fact that mysticism is molded into the genre of sermons addressed to women suggests that this receptive audience was found in a community of women with a yearning for mysticism.*

*The sermon collection in the Hague manuscript is the product of a mystical renaissance that seems to have occurred in some closely connected convents in Gelre. Numerous manuscripts from the convents in places like Arnhem, Nijmegen, Nazareth, and Gaesdonck attest to this blossoming of mystical culture. The Arnhem convent seems to have had a place of prominence in this movement. It owned remarkably good copies of the works of Jan van Ruusbroec, and works from the Rhineland mystics Eckhart,*

*Tauler, and Suso were also available in manuscript form. The same St. Agnes convent might also have been home to the author of the* Evangelical Pearl.[7] *Thus, there is ample evidence to suggest that this convent was one of the centers of a mystical renaissance that took place from the second quarter of the sixteenth century onward.*

*No renaissance regenerates in the exact same shape and form what existed earlier. Through a combination of fourteenth-century Brabantine and Rhineland "essential" mysticism with sixteenth-century christocentrism a new and unique blend of mysticism came into being. In the first half of the sixteenth century spiritual life became intricately entwined with the rhythm of the yearly liturgical cycle, and thus there was recurrent contemplation on the stages of the life of Jesus and on their spiritual meaning for the life of the believer. Perhaps more explicitly than in any previous period, the contemplative and mystical life were coupled with the liturgical cycle. The stages of the life of Jesus were spiritualized; not only were they historical events, but more important, they became symbolic events in the contemplative life.*

*There are conspicuous resemblances in spiritual content between the* Mystical Sermons *and contemporaneous texts, first and foremost the works of the author of the* Evangelical Pearl. *In this, her magnum opus, the empathy with and the centrality of the life of Christ are striking. Her second major work,* Den tempel onser sielen (The Temple of Our Soul), *is characterized by a mystical reliving of the life of Christ through a spiritual celebration of the liturgy in the "temple of the soul." These are precisely some of the most noticeable characteristics of the* Mystical Sermons.

# Sermons in the Religious Community

*No genre brings one into more immediate contact with the spiritual life of a religious community than a collection of sermons spoken and listened to for spiritual nourishment. A sermon collection provides immediate entry into the spiritual core of a community's religious life precisely because the aim of a sermon is to address the central spiritual needs and aspirations that all members of the community share. The priest speaks the community's language; he formulates sermons using terminology and concepts that the community members use and understand themselves. As a consequence, a sermon collection is representative of the spiritual life within a religious community. Such a collection becomes a historian's tool that can be instrumental in identifying the actual spiritual life in a community, as well as its spiritual ideals. The subject matter and language of the liturgical sermon are the material that is used in shaping the mystical content of the sermons.*

*It is entirely feasible that these sermons are not actually preached sermons, but rather texts used for contemplation that have simply borrowed the literary form of sermons to shroud their content. In reading these sermons one will notice that the double density of mystical-theological content and literary expression is most likely too much for a listener to grasp and digest. If these "sermons" are indeed contemplative texts—which should be the subject of a thorough study—then this collection of contemplative texts might well be unique to the early sixteenth century. The explanation for this dressing up as sermons would be a spiritual culture in which women devoted to God engaged in a very intimate "spiritualization" of the liturgical cycle. A further hypothesis would then be that these sermon-like texts were not written by a man, as one would expect at first, but by a woman with the capacities to be a spiritual leader, who was part of or connected to this community of religious women.*

## The *Mystical Sermons*: Central Themes and the Use of Allegory

*Since a thorough analysis of the* Mystical Sermons *is lacking, this introduction can only explore tentatively the content and nature of these sermons. Nevertheless, it would seem that the sermons are definitely worthy of inclusion in this book, as they are pure representatives of a spiritual culture that might well be labeled a sixteenth-century mystical renaissance.*

*Two very striking features of the religiosity expressed in the* Mystical Sermons *can be identified. First, there is a constant awareness of the ontological union between God and the human person in the uppermost part of the mind. The members of the community share the yearning to experience this union. Second, the members of the community strive to attain unity with God by trying to relive the life of Jesus through a spiritualization of his life's events. God became man out of love for mankind.*

*God the Son reconciled mankind with God the Father through his life and suffering. The sermons advocate not just meditation on Jesus' life, but a spiritual reliving of it in connection with the feasts of the liturgical year. This reliving takes place in the temple of the soul, to which the author of the Mystical Sermons devotes some of the finest pages.*

*These characteristics and objectives lie behind the most conspicuous stylistic feature of the sermons: the unremitting allegorization of all concepts, substantives, and actions as found in the text of the biblical theme or the pericope. This systematic allegorization is expressed in its purest and simplest form when the mention of a substantive or phrase from the pericope is immediately followed by the Middle Dutch words "dat is" (that is) accompanied by the given allegorical meaning. Some examples: "the daughter of Zion, that is, the faithful soul"; "Mary, that is, the mind"; "the Son of man will be seen coming on the clouds, that is, in the frailty of our flesh"; "there must be signs in the sun, that is, in our mind; in the moon, that is, in our soul; and in the stars, that is, in our humanity," and so on. The key to the quality of the sermons is that the author is able to devise allegorizations for every single element of a pericope and that those allegorizations can then be put together to form a coherent and meaningful whole in light of the mystical teachings the author wishes to expound. This is a "technical" quality that the author possesses, but on top of that the author manifests a touch of literary brilliance in the expression of the most complex of mystical concepts, such as the interconnection of intra-trinitarian processes with mental processes in the uppermost part of the human mind.*

*The sermons are plain yet profound, simple yet sophisticated. No authorities are cited—a lone reference to Augustine left aside. It is as if all authorities pale and become superfluous in comparison to the "authorities" mentioned numerous times on every page: God and Jesus. The allegorizations seem to sprout fresh and new from the mystically imbued mind of the author, who appears to step in nobody's footsteps. The sermons are among the best products of Dutch literature. They are Vermeer in writing.*

# MYSTICAL SERMONS

## Sermon 1: On Advent. How an interior soul should not just receive God interiorly, but how it shall be with Mary an interior, pure, God-bearing young woman, and prepare herself with our dear Lady, so that God may be born from her. Nota bene.

Dearly beloved, *now our salvation is nearer than when we became believers. Therefore, let us lay aside the works of darkness and put on the armor of light.*[8]

Now every interior soul shall sincerely turn into itself and examine its creatureliness from the highest to the lowest, that is, from that part and innermost essence of its mind, by which it has rested uncreated and eternally in God, all the way to the highest and lowest creatureliness of its capacities, which spring forth from the essence of the mind; and it shall note how they are deformed by the perverted disposition of its nature; and it shall rise from that and acknowledge that its salvation and rescue are present. And this acknowledgment will be a fundamental throwing aside of the works of darkness, so that the innermost essence and form of the mind will again sink purely and barely into God, its origin, as it has been there from eternity and still is; and it shall flee there from all the distractions of memory, all images of reason, all desire of the will, and shall seek and desire to once again be attached to the highest good with the proper intention, and to put on the armor of light, such as the strength, wisdom, and the love of God, and to carry out justice in our lord Jesus Christ. If now the interior soul is inflamed in God in this way and has put on the armor of God, then it shall offer its frail, sordid body as a donkey to carry the burden and weight of the Lord. Then the soul sees with the inner eyes of its rational mind that the Father in the Godhead comes and takes away from that body its meekness and frailty and wants to possess it with his omnipotence and give it likeness to the body of his clarity, which is his Son. And this happens truly each day in the receiving and the transformation

354

of the holy sacrament. Because of this the holy church says daily during Advent: "Tell the daughter of Zion," that is, the faithful soul, "do not be afraid, because your king is coming" (cf. John 12:15). This we shall constantly be aware of: how the fatherly omnipotence arrives gently with all that it is, has, and is capable of into our feeble flesh and wants to rest therein.

O interior soul, you, who are the true Zion, contemplating God, you, who have received and carry God in you, prepare yourself with Mary, the true mother of God, so you may give birth to God inside and outside of you. Because it is not enough for you only to be a God-receiving woman and God-bearing woman, but you also must be, like Mary, a "God-birthing" woman.

Mary, the mother of Christ, was a betrothed woman, because she had been given and joined to Joseph, but before they were married she was found to have conceived by the Holy Spirit.

Similarly, you must also be a woman engaged to God, for even if your soul has been given to you and joined to the body—which is identified with Joseph—still it must remain married and committed to God, the heavenly Father. Because through his omnipotent might, with the help of his spirit, he has conceived the fruit of his life, which is his eternal Word, in which we all live, and which is the life of our soul. But Joseph, our humanity, recognizing that the fruit of the soul is God himself, is fully subservient to Mary, that is, the mind, and carefully sees to it that his senses or body do not obstruct the mind with any of its actions, and makes sure that in reverence and humility he is fully devoted and deferential.

And the mind that is constantly introverted with Mary looks upon the fecundity of the fatherly nature and upon the inspiring and working of the lofty Holy Trinity, and raises itself constantly up with all creatures and all of God's gifts back into its origin, and sacrifices itself fully and relentlessly with the emanated Son toward the fatherly heart, in order to be born anew by the Father into the Son.

Behold, dearly beloved, this has been the constant work of Mary, who was the most fitting instrument of the Holy Trinity and was the fertile, living earth in which God the heavenly Father planted the Word from his fatherly heart to the benefit of us all.

Thus the interior mind that is truly filled with God's presence shall during this holy time continuously turn inward and consider

God's acts of grace with fervent gratitude. And Joseph, our humanity, shall mind and carry out all the humble, obedient works and outer duties of love, and carefully seek to fulfill all the external commandments with guarded senses, so that Mary, that is, the spirit, will not fail in any of her duties.

## On the Second Sunday of Advent

*There will be signs in the sun, the moon, and the stars.*[9]

O dearly beloved, let us look carefully at the signs that will be and how they will happen before the Son of Man will be seen coming on the clouds (cf. Matt 24:30; Rev 1:7), that is, in the frailty of our flesh. There must be signs in the sun, that is, in our mind; in the moon, that is, in our soul; and in the stars (cf. Matt 24:29), that is, in our humanity. What will those signs be that must happen in them before we will see God in our flesh? These signs are that, beyond what is natural, the in-shining and the perceptible workings of the Holy Trinity will be obscured in our mind, so it will seem—even though these take place continuously more or less as they take place in eternity—as if the Father will no longer generate his Son in the mind through the love of his mind. And the obstruction that hinders God in giving birth to his Son in the mind brings such darkness to the mind that it fears it will perish. For the presence of the fatherly strength and might, the in-shining of the light of the eternal wisdom, and the stream of God's wealth are the essence and maintenance of our mind, and when they seem to hide themselves and draw away from our mind, then the sun of our mind is like a darkness beyond measure and human understanding, and does not know itself or God in any way. And this is a clear sign of its failing and perishing. And when our mind wholly loses its selfness in this darkness, then a supernatural, incomprehensible light comes into it, whose immeasurableness and clarity no reason can understand or heart conceive, but it fully takes hold of and devours and overshines all beings, substances, and forms in its own ground. In whatever way and mode the Father then gives birth to his Son in the mind, with the eternal, unmediated love of his uncreated mind for the created mind that is then known to some extent to God and the mind only.

The other sign will be in the moon, that is, in our soul. The moon receives its light from the sun; similarly the soul receives its light from the mind without intermediary. If then the mind is entirely covered in darkness, then the soul cannot receive any light at all; what is more, not just not receive light, but not even retain what it has, and it darkens to such an extent and becomes so impotent as to its faculties that it is unable and cannot be anything else than a darkness. And this darkness causes failing of the faculties of the soul and annihilation of its brightness and activity. If, however, the soul chooses this failing and annihilation willfully, and perseveres in it till the end, then it returns into its original limpidity and receives without the intermediary of the mind the in-shining of divine clarity. And this eternal birth features streaming and fecundity, both in the faculties of the soul and in the essence and the ground of the mind.

See, this failing and annihilation of all selfness are the signs that really need to happen in the sun of our minds and in the moon of our soul if God is truly to be born spiritually in us and we in him, and if he is to be seen and understood by us in the clouds—in our flesh—of the sky; these clouds we now take to mean the immeasurable darkness that the mind and the soul overcome in this way to be annihilated.

But there will also be signs in the stars, that is, in our human senses. What signs will happen in the stars? The doctors say that during the night there will such a big storm in the sky that it will seem as if the stars fell down (cf. Matt 24:21, 29; Isa 13:10).

Therefore, when the sun of our mind and the moon of our soul are thus disturbed, obscured, and failing, then the stars of our senses must also fail and fall in this dark night in the sky of their body, in such a way that all their shine, their work, and their power must fall and perish in them, and they must seem to be nonexistent. If, then, the bodily senses thus start to fail in their function to the extent that the subject does not desire, taste, or feel God, then because of this there will arise in this person fear and aridity, and such anxiety and depression of his nature that it will seem to him, and he will feel as if, the earth of his heart will perish.

357

But in case that this person endures this collapse in his lowest, middle, and highest part equably, patiently, meekly, and humbly, and perseveres in it till the end, then unquestionably there will arise in him a new, shining earth (Rev 21:1), with a lit-up new sun and moon, and shining, illuminated, new stars in the translucent sky of his body, so that his body will then receive and have a new clarity and unity with the body of Christ, in which the senses that perished before will again shine and gleam in the senses of Christ like the shining stars in the firmament of heaven, and the sun of the mind will shine with sevenfold more clarity than before.

If then the mind of a person will receive and possess, like the spirit of Christ, the sevenfold gifts of the Holy Spirit, and will be illuminated without intermediary with the highest and clearest light of the divinity, with an extraordinary outpouring and fecundity—in the moon, that is, in the faculties of the soul, with the full divine influence; and in the earth, that is, in the heart and body, with all the divine fruits of good thoughts and virtuous deeds—then there is the opportunity for God the heavenly Father to give birth through the love of his spirit to his eternal Son in human nature into our flesh and humanity and to transform us into him. For this reason God once became man, and remained God and man, so that we would be Godlike and united in him and remain with him what he is to us, God and man, though not by nature but by grace.

See, dearly beloved, these are the signs, such as the total annihilation, as we have seen, that need to happen in us if God is to be born in us and from us and if we are to be transformed into him. For since nothing can enter into God but God himself, similarly God cannot be born from, or be seen, by anyone but by those who are fully Godlike. Therefore, we must strive with total patience so that our annihilation and transformation may occur in us, as God pleases and carries it out in all, so that the Word from the Fatherly heart may be born into us and we be transformed into him, and that we may see him in our flesh in his own light and clarity, and the fear of stern justice will neither confuse us nor destroy us through our sins. May the Lord grant us this. Amen.

# Sermon 2: How Joseph and Mary obeyed the decree of the emperor. And how we shall with them look for shelter on the solemn Christmas Eve.

Mary and Joseph traveled from Nazareth to Bethlehem to be registered (cf. Luke 2:4–5). In like manner our mind and body shall gladly, placidly, and sincerely pursue the commandments of God and men, and not mind the amount of time, the scope of the work, the tiredness of the body, or painfulness of the limbs, but they shall with a willing attitude subject mind, soul, and body to obedience. For through simple, humble obedience one never neglects or fails the service to God, or God's praise and honor, but often one fulfills more perfectly what had been neglected.

When Joseph and Mary arrived in Bethlehem, they went about in the streets and looked from house to inn (cf. Luke 2:7; Sg 3:2), and they were turned away everywhere, because they were all full. Then they had to lodge in a run-down, despised, exposed little house that hardly had a roof or wall. Here the humble and pure Joseph happily entered in with the blessed mother of God, and they fell on their knees and thanked the heavenly Father that he had prepared and given them such a place to stay.

O interior, devout soul, now look upon yourself and do as Joseph and Mary did, and go round and round in the streets of your creatureliness and look for shelter from house to house.

When you enter into your humanity, go about the streets of your senses and ask from door to door, that is, from sight to hearing, to smell, taste, and sense, whether there is anyone who wants to house the grace of God. But no, alas, they are all full; God's grace, with its wealth, will have to pass by. For as long as they are filled with sensuous creatures and transitory goods, it cannot be born in them.

Then go into the streets of your words, and consult your prayer and speech. They are all full with all sorts of distraction, vanity, and idleness, and with other sorts of sinful company, so that neither the grace of God nor its wealth can enter into them.

Continue in the streets of your habits, and ask your wandering, your going, your staying, your lying and sitting, your eating and drinking, your sleeping and waking, your silence and your speech, if they can house you and want to receive God's grace and mercy and its wealth as retribution and payment. But they will answer: No. They are so engaged in lust, delight, and dissoluteness that they cannot accommodate God's grace. Because they cannot bear punishment and fear, contrition and acknowledgment, they have to follow and satisfy their desires; therefore they cannot house the retribution. They need to have their freedom, for they are in their younger days. Oh, sadly, God's grace must move on; there is no room for it here.

Finally, continue in the streets of your promises, from your baptizing to your profession,[10] and see whether God's grace could not find a place there, and whether the devil's whisper, advice, and deeds are also consistently resisted, whether the resolve, the spiritual preparedness, the purity, the obedience, the poverty, with all of God's commandments and counsels, are equally pursued. They will answer: Ah, well, God's grace can find no place; it is just not the right time. They are filled with despair and disbelief and other doubts, and idle hopes and refuges, with lust of the flesh and the world, and they are so full with all concupiscence and self-seekingness that God's grace with its stream will have to move on.

Oh, you interior soul, who now knows and sees yourself to be thus, what will you do, where will you and Joseph stay?[11] Do as Mary did. Do not be despondent; trust in the almightiness of the heavenly Father. He cannot abandon you, because you have his treasure hidden in you, namely, the Word of his heart, the life of all lives, and the subsistence of your soul. Therefore, thank the Father in the Godhead that he lets you criticize and know yourself in your weakness. Be content and of good spirit with your Joseph and enter together into the little open house of a good will, which you can see and acknowledge, inside yourself, from afar, and which hardly has any wall or roof of good deeds. See, in this house the heavenly Father wants to bring forth his Son through the love of his mind.

If, then, the interior mind sees this small welcoming house of the holy Father, then Mary and Joseph, that is, the mind and the body, enter it together. And as they fall to their knees of their fathomless insignificance, they thank the holy Father that, after all these occupied houses, he has given them such a small house of good will in which he wants to bring forth his Son.

# Sermon 3: On the Wednesday after Easter

*Throw your net on the right side of the boat and you will find some, Jesus said (John 21:6).*

O you, interior soul, who has gone out of the fatherly heart, where you had rested from eternity, and have come into this perilous sea of the sinful world to go fishing, that is, to acquire virtues and exercise them, and all night, that is, all of your life, you have not caught or obtained one essential virtue. Now, throw your net, which is nothing else than the lust, love, and desire of your senses and nature, and the intentions of your heart with its self-seeking; they are the knotted net by which you cannot truly or essentially catch any virtue in yourself or in God.

Now, throw this net of your own self altogether from you, at the right side of your ship, that is, go out with a voluntary movement of your spirit, beyond all love and lust of your sensuous nature and beyond all intentions of your heart and all self-seekingness and enjoyment and love of yourself, into the glorious, immovable, impassible, immortal, eternal beloved, who is the right side of your ship, being the essence and subsistence of your soul and creatureliness.

Into the depths of his abyss throw out the net of your selfness and let it sink, and let it sink again, float and swim in the wide immeasurable sea of your eternal, dearly beloved, until your whole created being is entirely filled with the true, essential holiness and virtuousness of himself; and toil as long in the ship of your strong hope, and row as forcefully with firm faith and burning love, until, with all that you are, you arrive through his created, true, essential holiness in the uncreatedness of his Godhead, where your createdness should aim to sink into the abyss of eternity. See, there the net of your selfness will receive, through the incomprehensible fishes, the almighty Trinity.[12]

Through its[13] own wisdom and love, the outpouring ground of the Fatherly Omnipotence gives to the net of your mind the immeasurable fish of its fatherly might, and makes the deiform mind and highest reason so fruitful and strong that the fatherly power immediately produces in it a host of fish of his eternal benefactions.

Through its own might and complacency the complacent, outpouring ground of the Eternal Wisdom of the Son gives to the highest reason the big, incomprehensible fish of its eternal clarity, and makes the imagelessness of the highest reason so informed and wise that it is immediately filled with all the fish of the lucid notions of Christ.

Through its own love and goodness the incomprehensible, outpouring ground of God's Love gives to the highest faculty of love the most magnificent fish of its love, and fulfills the highest love of the mind with such fullness, strength, and vigor that the Holy Spirit has to flow in and out with an endless stream of fish of his eternal love and loyalty.[14]

Thus this net, that is, the essence of our mind, is then completely filled with the host of big, incomprehensible fishes of Fatherly Might, Wisdom, and Love of God, and made fruitful with his eternal flow of love, riches, and grace. For our eternal image has in eternal newness received his image and our likeness, his similarity and unity. If we then have thrown the net of our creatureliness and selfness so absolutely into the immeasurable sea of our Eternal Beloved, at the right side of our ship, that is, into the eternal might of the Godhead, and he has fulfilled us with all that he is, then we are unable to haul in the net even with all of our might, that is, then we are unable to carry out the least good deed without the mercy of God.

Then how shall we act? John, that is, the most sublime, deiform person, who is entirely fulfilled with knowledge, taste, joy, and love of God, says to Simon Peter, that is, the professing soul, "It is the Lord God almighty (cf. John 21:7) who has fulfilled me with himself and whom I know, love and enjoy, and who is my entire aptitude." When Peter, that is, the interior soul, sees that John—that is, the most sublime, deiform person—perceives the Holy Trinity in pure unity and has entered into it with true love and pure understanding in loving enjoyment, and when he sees that the Omnipotence is his strength, the eternal Truth his Wisdom, and the Eternal Love and Goodness of God is his essence, possession, and

362

joy, then Peter—that is the rational soul—can no longer stay on-board the ship of the soul's imperfection but immediately throws on the mantle of the soul's imperfect faculties—for it is naked as in its original purity and holiness—and jumps headlong with all its powers into the fathomless sea of the love of God, and strides with true abandonment through all and beyond all toward God the Holy Trinity in the mind. If he wants it to submerge, drown, and perish, it is prepared to suffer this. It strides through the loving sea of the created soul of Christ into the purity of his essence, until it arrives in the land of the Godhead, where it shall find the Trinity one and the same in one essence, and even if the other faculties of the soul,[15] namely, memory, reason, and will, follow the soul in the boat, that is, in their own domain of arduous struggle and anxiousness, it is prepared to accept that. For the rational faculty leaves all effort and tribulation to the other faculties and hurries unmoved forward to the one it sees and notices.

And because the other disciples, that is, the other faculties, are not far from the shore (cf. John 21:8) of enjoyable rest, therefore they are not afraid of any effort, sadness, or misery; they get on board of the ship, that is, in their own being and frailty, and haul the net of their selfness—which before had been empty and void of all good, but which is, after throwing it out into the ground of God, entirely filled with the many, big fish of God's benevolence—onto the land, that is, into their own being, so as to rest in joy.

There they find charcoal prepared, with fish on it and bread (cf. John 21:9), that is, they find an immeasurable, burning glow of love, that has ignited and engulfed the essence and form of the entire loving mind as a fish, which the divine fire of love permeates with the flame of its love and heats so much that they are easily made into one to be devoured by God, the Holy Trinity, as one being; and together with this bread [is prepared], which is the glorious, created humanity of God, who prepares himself in a bread for angels and men, and who therefore wants to be eaten and devoured by the love of the soul, because he wants to transform the whole person fully into him. And he says to the loving soul as he says today to his disciples in the Gospel: "Bring some of the fish that you have just caught" (John 21:9), and he demands of the soul that it shall bring all of its created faculties, with all the intermediaries and deficiencies that the soul has caught with the net of its will since the soul has worked in the sea of the sinful world from the moment it went out of him by creation up to this moment.

Simon Peter climbed up—that is, thus a professing soul climbs up from knowledge of its fundamental insignificance to the summit of the mind, and hauls the net with the big fish, that is, all the soul's faculties with their big and manifold deficiencies, and brings them on land, through Jesus Christ up to the high Godhead into the perfect united essence of the three Persons, which stands for the perfect number of 153 fish in the loving soul. After that Jesus said, "Come and eat" (cf. John 21:12). Likewise he says to the loving soul: Come, that is, sink into me completely, and eat, that is, enjoy and use all that is mine and all that I am as if it were yours in you, so that I may devour what is yours as if it were mine in me, as I, the Son of God, am being divinely devoured by the Father in a union.

Then no faculty of the soul can continue to work or look out but in the innermost essence of itself, for it knows that it is the Lord who is all that there is.

That we may thus truly throw the net of our creatureliness and deficiency into Jesus Christ; that we may catch and retain God with all that he is in us, and remain godlike ourselves—may the Lord grant us this. Amen.

# Maria van Hout
## *Two Letters*[1]

*Maria van Hout was a beguine at the beguinage Bethlehem in Oisterwijk, a village near Tilburg (North-Brabant)—therefore, she is sometimes called Maria of Oisterwijk. For some time she was the superior of the community. Her spiritual authority was well known to many. We know of her correspondence with the Carthusians in Cologne and with some Jesuits (Peter Canisius, Cornelius Wischaven, and Adrian Adriaensens), who called her* mater nostra. *In 1530 the Carthusians invited her and two of her companions to come and live in Cologne because the situation of the beguinage in Oisterwijk had become too uncertain. Maria died in Cologne in 1547. Two works by her are known: "The Straight Road toward the Evangelical Perfection"* (Der rechte weg zo der evangelischer volkommenheit) *(Cologne, 1531) and "The Paradise of the Loving Souls"* (Dat paradijs der liefhavender sielen) *(Cologne, 1532). One work,* De novem gradibus simplicitatis, *is lost.* The Evangelical Pearl *is sometimes erroneously attributed to her. Gerard Kalckbrenner, the prior of the Carthusians of Cologne, edited her works, as well as a number of her letters. These letters have been re-edited by J. B. Kettenmeyer, SJ (Ons Geestelijk Erf 1 [1927]: 278–93; 370–95), and more recently by J. M. Willeumier-Schalij, De brieven uit "Der Rechte Wech" van de Oisterwijkse begijn en mystica Maria van Hout, Miscellanea Neerlandica 6 (Leuven: Peeters, 1993). Our translation of two letters is made using the edition and translation by J. M. Willeumier-Schalij.*

## TWO LETTERS
### Letter 12

To the Reverend Father, Prior at N.[2]

I wish you the blessed poverty of spirit, as a humble greeting, Reverend Father Prior. May God be thanked and blessed a hundred times because of you, since you humbled yourself to be my spiritual father. I cannot describe the joy that your letter has given me in the spirit. God has really helped me through you, because, as it is written in your letter, my spirit is now in such great poverty that I cannot express it. All active grace has abandoned me, and I am so reduced to nothing that I myself do not know what I am. I do not know how I could become more naked and bare with the Lord at the cross, and could come on the cross.

O father of my heart, what a miserable creature is a human person! I cannot understand how a human person comes to elevate himself in some things. Oh, if proud people could only understand what they are, they would be ashamed—since an intelligent person has a good insight into them. O Father, how wonderfully I understand the depth of the words in your letter. I hope to keep it respectfully with me as long as I live. Often, I have to write risky things; that is God's work, and I cannot rejoice in it. But when I hear someone speaking about that poverty, I rejoice so much that I cannot express it. O father, it seems that my heart lives in you; please write me another letter of that purport, just as God inspires you; command me as you wish, and punish me, and do not spare me.

Further, at this moment I am not able to write about your concerns, because I am purely in the spirit, and my body hurts so much that I can hardly write to you. Nevertheless, a spiritual person always wants something good from God, such as virtues, and with that God gives this person much work. Sometimes God makes people carry a cross, and sometimes a person is carried through so many burdens precisely by what is shown to him. Indeed, he hopes that he will receive it—thus, it is God who grants what he suffers because of it. And God wants to give the virtues and graces, which a person desires through God's goodness, that is, if this person truly believes in it and prays for it.

O father, there is no language to express how free a heart is that has no remorse. If we can come so far that we have no remorse or reproaches in our heart and our conscience, and that we have overcome all selfishness and all struggles, then a person should apply himself to simplicity of mind and be content with the way in which God gives or takes and not scrutinize how his relationship with God is. I would prefer to live in hope than to live in knowledge. O father, how valuable it is not to want, not to know, not to have, not to desire, so that a person can come to give himself to God in mere simplicity, and to surrender fundamentally to God and his judgments. Whatever the Lord does with us will be equally dear to us. May it be sufficient to us that he knows our situation.

Nevertheless, we will often pray that he indicates to us our shortcomings so that we can correct them. As long as we have something to long for, we have not yet reached the real poverty. God likes a capable and empty instrument, and he knows very well how to purify it, if only we let him do it, without meddling. But alas, a person is so reluctant to depart from himself! Why should I say more about this—you do not really need it. Forgive me, dearest father, that I write to you so boldly. It should be far from me to teach you, as you have sufficient experience in these matters. I did it simply as God inspired me. O father, how can I thank you for all that you, your son, and your community have done for me? I should be ashamed that you deign to associate with me, such a poor little person, unworthy of you, and in whom I can find nothing good. Nevertheless, I receive all that you give me completely, as if it were given by an angel from heaven, on behalf of God, so strongly am I convinced that both of you belong to God. Indeed, I have prayed to God so long with bitter tears that he would feed and fortify me with himself, or else that he would rectify my indigence—as he is doing now through you—so that I could give myself to him with all my heart. Therefore, thank all your dear children on my behalf, with all the gratefulness that I can give in God to all of you.

Written on Saint Martin's day, in the year one thousand five hundred thirty one.

[P.S.] All those whom you receive, in God's name and on my behalf, I offer them to Mary, Mother of God, and I pray that she would offer them henceforth to her dear Son, so that he may have mercy on all of you, concerning all that you may need both in spirit and in nature. If she would not hear us, I would give myself in exchange in order to be annihilated, or that she would have mercy on me because of your generous goodness. Tell this to all those who, through God and me, are willing to trust in whatever you advise them. Me too, I tell it to them on behalf of God; if they are able to put trust in it, then it will happen to them. Comfort all the lost sheep; tell them to have good courage. I hope the Lord will have pity on them.

# Letter 13

No one should be scandalized that this inner person writes such high things about herself to some of her hidden friends. St. Paul and other great saints have done that too. God obliges his friends to do it, in order to improve us. That aspect is also touched upon in this letter.[3]

Dear spiritual father, at present I am forced—both interiorly by God and exteriorly by you, so that I cannot avoid it any longer—to write about myself.

O heavenly Father, may you be honored by me, though I am a sinful creature, and may the people be improved! So accomplish your work, as I have prayed to you for so long. Indeed, O Jesus, people have not been willing to believe you. Then why would they believe a sinful person? Therefore, Lord, I pray you from the bottom of my heart, if this is your will, then let no creature ever believe me, and let your will be done in me, whatever that may bring me. For I do not want to serve for a reward. If I did everything I could, I would have done no more than what I owe you. O Lord, God Almighty, how will I dare to write what you command me interiorly? If it is your will, I would prefer that you made my heart break into pieces. Ah, ah, I wish I could crawl into a hole in the ground!

Ah, dear spiritual father, if you wish me anyhow to write—I am at present both God's prisoner and yours—I would like to request you that you take it well. I cannot make it better, though it sounds dangerous.[4] I have no more wisdom than a child. Then, I can see what goes through me, and I can simply say it or write it. I do not know anything more about it. Each one can take from it whatever is helpful to him. They say "simple faith is good faith," and "one should not dispute with the devil." Even though great and high things are shown to me, I am not more concerned about it than a child. But then I always look inwardly, in myself, whether I can take something from it that could be helpful, namely, to annihilate or to scorn myself, and nothing else remains in me. And thus I stand always empty and unknowing. Even if someone else would say about me what I should say myself, I would not know if I could believe it. Because my heart knows almost nothing about the words that I speak. And I am not able to know them beforehand or to invent them. Inwardly, I am so poor and miserable that I do not know myself what I am—just a nothing, a thing that is of no use. O father, do not be angry; I am ready to die and to stand before the judgment to confirm that I have never nourished any other thoughts, and that I remain steadfast on this ground. However, I am standing every moment in humble fear and watchful against myself, looking on attentively that I would not cause myself to fall. Who can be certain that, if he stands today, he will not fall tomorrow? I know nothing except of what is today! And there is nothing I can do about that, even though I sometimes speak intelligent words.

I cannot master myself more than a child can. Indeed, I am completely deprived of myself and united in God, as if I were not a human person any more, and as if it were not me who lives but the Lord in me. And God has imprinted so intensely this union to me, a sinful creature, on the feast of Corpus Christi, and has given so graciously a new spirit, that since then this has not been taken away from me. On the contrary, I see that it increases every day and does not decrease, so that I am lost to myself and to all things, not knowing what has happened to me. Afterward, such a great suffering arose in me that I cannot express it. Thus, dear father, you can deduce from it what God wants to give you. To me that is all the same, because the more one despises and rejects me, the more one presses me into God and the more he throws grace to me. And that what happens to me daily is wonder of wonders. I had thought to write you all this differently, but God has wanted it this way.

Then, about the things that you have written to me, please let me know what you would like me to do; I would not dare to do things otherwise, as I do not want to trust in myself or rely upon idle presumptions. I will trust in obedience, and remain steadfast with my faith in God. Mary remained firm under the cross, etc.[5]

# Notes

## General Introduction

1. Hadewijch and Ruusbroec have each been included in the Classics of Western Spirituality series. See James Wiseman, trans., *John Ruusbroec: The Spiritual Espousals and Other Works* (Mahwah, NJ: Paulist Press, 1985); and Mother Columba Hart, trans., *Hadewijch: The Complete Works* (Mahwah, NJ: Paulist Press, 1980). The critical edition of Jan van Ruusbroec's *Opera Omnia* (with English and Latin translations included) is now complete; see Jan van Ruusbroec, *Opera Omnia*, editor in chief Guido de Baere (Turnhout: Brepols, 1989–2006), CCCM, nos. 100–110. vol. 1: *Boecksken der Verclaringhe*; vol. 2: *Vanden Seven Sloten*; vol. 3: *Die Geestelike Brulocht*; vol. 4: *Dat Rijcke der Ghelieven*; vols. 5–6: *Van den Geesteliken Tabernakel*; vol. 7: *Vanden XII Beghinen*; vol. 8: *Een Spieghel der Eeuwigher Salicheit*; vol. 9: *Van Seven Trappen*; vol. 10: *Vanden Blinkenden Steen Vanden Vier Becoringhen; Vanden Kerstenen Ghelove; Brieven.*

2. John Van Engen has translated a number of key works in *Devotio Moderna*, Classics of Western Spirituality series (Mahwah, NJ: Paulist Press, 1988).

3. See K. Ruh, *Geschichte der abendländischen Mystik*, vol. 4, *Die niederländische Mystik des 14 bis 16 Jahrhunderts* (Munich: C. H. Beck, 1999), 138.

4. Appelmans teaches that Mary was free from original sin from the very moment of her conception (XII, 4), a teaching first defended by Duns Scotus and rejected by the Dominicans; his theology of the Trinity with its emphasis upon the fruitfulness of the divine nature also seems more reminiscent of Bonaventure (and Ruusbroec after him) than of Thomas Aquinas. Also, we find little evidence for Reypens's claim (in "Gheraert Appelmans' Glose op het Vaderons," *OGE [Ons Geestelijk Erf]* 1 [1927]: 119) that Appelmans had been a *Magister* before he became a hermit. Appelmans' theology of the Trinity seems somewhat confused.

After all, according to trinitarian theology the Persons are distinguished by their mutual relations, and calling the Son "Father in a Sonly way" (V) is hardly illuminating.

# Willem Jordaens, *The Kiss of Mouth*

1. Introduced and translated by Rik Van Nieuwenhove.

2. See the critical edition by Kees Schepers, *Ioannis Rusbrochii De Ornatu Spiritualium Nuptiarum. Wilhelmo Ordani interprete.* CCCM 207 (Turnhout: Brepols, 2004).

3. Apart from Ruusbroec, St. Bernard also exerted a considerable influence on *The Kiss of Mouth*. Other sources are Pseudo-Dionysius (on whom Jordaens frequently draws to develop his negative theology (especially in chapter 9), and, of course, St. Augustine. We also find occasional references to St. John Chrysostom, St. Jerome, and St. Gregory the Great. Finally, the treatise is permeated with ca. 250 scriptural sources.

4. L. Reypens, *De Mystieke Mondkus* (Tielt: Lannoo, 1967), 5–24; 121–40.

5. In this respect, too, Jordaens seems indebted to Ruusbroec. Part of the difficulty for the translator (and the reader) is that some of the key terms *ledich*, *ledicheyt*, and *onlede*, can be translated in a number of ways, sometimes with positive or negative connotations, depending on the context. For this reason I have usually included the key Dutch terms in my translation.

6. *The Divine Names*, ch. 7, § 3

7. *Onderstant ende onthout:* technical terms that denote the continuous creative presence of God in the soul, maintaining the soul in existence.

8. A classic theme from Augustine's *Confessions* 3.6 (11): "tu autem eras interior intimo meo et superior summo meo."

9. *Ghemeyne* (common) is a Ruusbroecian term, which denotes the universal, self-giving, generosity of God's love, and also our deified life ("the common life") in response to this love—a life of virtuous activity and contemplation.

10. *Ledich*. Jordaens is skeptical of an "affective," psychological mysticism that pays too much attention to inner feelings and

consolations. Herp will share his reservations in chapter 60 of *The Mirror of Perfection*, translated below.

11. "Mutual befriending" translates *ondervriendelijcken*.

12. *Een puer onghebeeltheyt der ghedachten* is translated "emptiness of the mind devoid of all images." Ruusbroec too rejected passive, quietist states when criticizing the so-called Brethren of the Free Spirit. See, for instance, *Die Geestelike Brulocht*, 2411–2584. For a discussion, see R. Van Nieuwenhove, *Jan van Ruusbroec, Mystical Theologian of the Trinity* (Notre Dame, IN: University of Notre Dame Press, 2003), 70–74.

13. The Douay version reads: "Now there was a word spoken to me in private; and my ears by stealth as it were received the veins of its whisper."

14. Jordaens's distinction between the essential being of the soul *(weselijc sijn)* and the soul's active existence *(werckelijcke sijn)* is adopted from Ruusbroec (See *Die Geestelike Brulocht*, 44–58 and 1626–69; for a discussion, see Van Nieuwenhove, *Jan van Ruusbroec, Mystical Theologian of the Trinity*, 104–11). The distinction is crucial in order to grasp Jordaens's (and Ruusbroec's) understanding of mysticism, and especially their rejection of passive, quietist mysticism. The essential being of the soul refers to God's continuous creative presence in the soul; the active existence refers to the soul as the living core of the faculties (that is, memory/mind, intellect, and will). Jordaens does not want us to pursue idle, empty mystical states in which the faculties enjoy a sheer passive rest in their ground—quietism—but rather he proposes a transformation of our loving soul in which we actively love God. This is, for him, true rest; this is why he is at pains to distinguish this true rest from quietist rest (see nos. 222–26). True rest remains active through our knowing and, especially, our loving; it is "an inactive activity" *(een ledeghe onledicheyt)*, as he puts it in no. 203.

15. "In-form" translates *geformt:* the objects bestow their form on the senses or powers, and thus shape or in-form them.

16. *Die werckelijcheyt,* "the reality of nature," derived from *werken,* "to be active, to work."

17. Again, immediately inspired by Ruusbroec. See *Die Geestelike Brulocht*, 1663–66.

18. *ghesielt*, literally, "en-souled."

19. "Intention" translates *meyninghe*, a crucial Ruusbroecian concept. It refers to the theocentric focus we should have in whatever we do. For a discussion see Van Nieuwenhove, *Jan van Ruusbroec, Mystical Theologian of the Trinity*, 61ff., 71–72, 170–74.

20. *Als haer natuerlijck onthout:* this refers to the way God keeps the soul in existence in his continuous creative act; hence it is called natural to distinguish it from the supernatural presence through grace in the active existence of the soul.

# Jan van Leeuwen, Two Treatises

1. Translated and introduced by Marcel Cock, with collaboration and assistance from Rik Van Nieuwenhove.

2. For an English translation of Eckhart's *Defense*, which was anything but a guilty plea, see B. McGinn and E. Colledge, eds., *Meister Eckhart: The Essential Sermons, Commentaries, Treatises, and Defense*, Classics of Western Spirituality (Mahwah, NJ: Paulist Press, 1981).

3. For a discussion of Jan van Leeuwen's arguments, see Th. Kok, "Jan van Leeuwen en zijn werkje tegen Eckhart," *OGE* 47 (1975): 129–151, esp. 134–35. The original text, *Een boexken van meester Eckaerts leere daer hi in doelde*, has been published by Th. Kok in *OGE* 47 (1973): 152–72—although this edition is, as Marcel Cock has discovered, not without its flaws. Another edition is by C. G. N. De Vooys, *Meister Eckhart en de Nederlandse Mystiek*, in Netherlands Archives for Church History, new series, part 3 (The Hague, 1905), 182–88.

4. For a discussion, see H. Dorresteijn, "De Phasen van het mystiek leven," in *OGE* 8 (1934): 5–29. The text *Wat dat een armen mensche van gheeste toebehoert* follows (30–38). Another edition (extracts) can be found in S. Axters, *Jan van Leeuwen. Een bloemlezing uit zijn werken* (Antwerp, 1943), 88–91.

5. Cf. Eckhart's Sermon 52, *Beati pauperes spiritu*, in Colledge and McGinn, *Meister Eckhart*, 199–203.

6. This statement may at first seem surprising and at odds with what is said about the kingdom of heaven in Matthew 13:31, Mark

4:30, and Luke 13:18. The next sentence explains it: the church is not like a mustard seed because she is as strong as God himself.

7. This is a fairly literal rendering of *daer selen wi sijn een wese-like ochte een overweselike raste Gods*. Perhaps the author means "there we will rest in God's essence, which surpasses our essence."

8. This title is somewhat misleading. It is the actual overall title of the treatise and applies to all chapters, not just to chapter 4, which deals with the twenty-fifth hammer blow: the preparatory disposition for our ascent to God. The title should be *Chapter 4: The first rung* (in line with the titles of subsequent chapters).

9. We take it that *een gheheel sterven ons selfs* (translated here as "dying to ourselves") refers to an ever-increasing detachment and renunciation, not to our actual death.

10. The meaning of the latter part of the sentence is not entirely clear: *ieghewelc in kinnessen der andere doecht*.

11. *Minne* here is interpreted as our love for God rather than God's love for us.

12. "In-spiration" translates the mystical-theological term *ingheesten*, the transformative operation of God on the soul.

13. Van Leeuwen here quotes from Eckhart's Sermon 105 (Pfeiffer 15). For a translation, see *Meister Eckhart: Sermons and Treatises*, vol. 1, trans. and ed. M. O'C. Walshe (Rockport, MA: Element Books, 1991), 129–34.

14. "Works come to life" means they are considered a source of merit.

15. Jan van Leeuwen omits in his translation *in der sie geschahen* from the German original.

16. This is an insertion by Jan van Leeuwen, not found in the original German text.

17. Jan van Leeuwen's translation somewhat obfuscates the original German by turning the two sentences beginning with "I say" into one and then adding unnecessarily "or work" in the second subordinate clause.

18. The manuscript omits the translation of *unde diu zit, in der sie geschahen*. This is probably due to an error of the copyist.

19. Jan van Leeuwen omits "the evil and the good." After this sentence he omits a large portion of the text by Eckhart.

20. The German has *der geist lediget sin wesen mit dem uzwirken der bilde* (the spirit empties its being by the working out of images), while the Middle Dutch reads *die gheest ledicht syn wesen metten wtwerkenden beelden* (the spirit empties its being with out-working [as adjective] images), which is less clear.

21. Jan van Leeuwen seems to use *bloet* (bare) as a noun; used in this sense it probably refers to the important Eckhartian theme of the desert, which refers to the nameless, undifferentiated limit-lessness of both soul and God. On this, see B. McGinn, *The Mystical Thought of Meister Eckhart: The Man from Whom God Hid Nothing* (New York: Crossroad, 2001), 48.

22. We can understand van Leeuwen's position to differ from Eckhart's as follows: whereas Eckhart (allegedly) proposes the pursuit of a still emptiness "beyond reason and without reason," van Leeuwen wants us to pursue the path of faith (that is, beyond reason) for which we nevertheless adduce reasons ("with reasons"). This path should be subject to the bareness *(bloet)*, not of undifferentiated stillness of the soul (as with Eckhart) but of truth, the bare truth *(bloeter waerheit)*. Ruusbroec too links being above reason with faith: "If we are to taste God or feel the life eternal in ourselves, we must go into God with our faith, above reason *(boven redene met onsen ghelove in gode gaen)*. See *Vanden Blinkenden Steen*, 529–30; and *Boecsken der Verclaringhe*, 517–19: "For though reason and all corporeal feeling must yield to and make way for faith *(wiken moeten den ghelove)* and inward gazing of the spirit and those things that are above reason *(die boven redene sijn)*, reason nevertheless remains without action in potentiality." Similarly, in *Spieghel der Eeuwigher Salicheit*, 2035–37, we find: "If we want to behold eternal life and find it in us, then through love and faith *(overmids mine ende ghelooeve)* we must transcend ourselves beyond reason *(boven redene)* to our onefold eye." In *What Pertains to a Person Poor in Spirit (Wat dat een armen mensche van gheeste toebehoert)*, we similarly find *en si dat hi es een godlike mensche ende sta opghericht in minnen en de in kinnessen boven redene ende sonder wise* (ch. 3).

23. The theme of the birth of the Son of God in the soul is shared by both Eckhart and Ruusbroec (for Ruusbroec, see, for instance, *Die Geestelike Brulocht*, 1774; *Vanden Seven Sloten*, 625–27; *Spieghel der Eeuwigher Salicheit*, 923–34, 1801–3. For the different

ways in which Ruusbroec and Eckhart develop this theme, see R. Van Nieuwenhove, "Meister Eckhart and Jan van Ruusbroec: A Comparison" in *Medieval Philosophy and Theology* 7 (1998): 157–93, esp. 185–86.

# Nicolas of Strasbourg, *The Sermon on the Golden Mountain*, and Johannes van Schoonhoven, *Declaratio*

1. Introduced and translated by Rik Van Nieuwenhove.

2. J. Gerson's two letters to Barthélemy Clantier, written in 1402 and 1408 respectively, have been translated by Brian Patrick McGuire in *Jean Gerson: Early Works*, Classics of Western Spirituality (Mahwah, NJ: Paulist Press, 1998), 202–10, 249–56.

3. For the edition and commentary, see S. Axters, "De preek op den Gulden Berg door den Leesmeester van Straatsburg," *Tijdschrift voor Taal en Letteren* 28 (1940): 5–58.

4. From *Sermon* 61:4 on the Song of Songs.

5. Cf. Pseudo-Augustine (= John of Fécamp), *Meditationes*, in PL 40:902–42.

# An Anonymous Treatise on Ruusbroec's Teaching

1. Introduced and translated by Robert Faesen, SJ.

2. For an edition of the text, and a brief commentary, see R. Faesen, *Anonieme teksten in een Ruusbroec-handschrift (Averbode, Archief IV 101, olim Bibliotheek 101 F 3)*, in *OGE* 74 (2000), 197–210. I was given the opportunity to translate these texts during the spring semester of 2004, when I held the MacLean Chair in the College of Arts and Sciences at Saint Joseph's University, Philadelphia, Pennsylvania. For the hospitality, the amicable support, and all the generous help that I received for this and all the other projects in that semester I am very much obliged. A special word of thanks is due to Fr. Frederick A. Homann, SJ.

3. The author means that a correct interpretation of Ruusbroec's doctrine should result from the same origin (*gront*) or hermeneutical source; that is, it should be understood in the same spirit as it is written. This "origin" has to do with the mystical experience of the love encounter of God and the human person, and the life communion with Christ. In other words, a hermeneutical framework that dismisses the possibility of such an experience necessarily leads to misinterpretations.

4. Namely, the third part of *The Spiritual Espousals*.

5. See *Opera Omnia* 3, p. 574, line c14–c16 (English text).

6. The anonymous author makes here a brief but brilliant suggestion by adding the word "partition" *(tusschenscheet)*. Readers trained in Latin always understood Ruusbroec's Middle Dutch word *onderscheet* as equivalent to the Latin *differentia*, which means "difference." Thus, the misunderstanding immediately originated that Ruusbroec was speaking about an ontological fusion between God and the human person. But, as the anonymous author correctly points out, the Middle Dutch word *onderscheet* should be understood as "partition." In that case, the misunderstanding can be avoided, and there is no longer any reason to doubt the correctness of Ruusbroec's teaching.

7. "Influx" refers to the activity of God within the inner life of the human person.

8. (1) the loving drawing inward of God, and (2) his own active love.

9. John 1:3–4.

# Gerard Appelmans, *Gloss on the Our Father*

1. Introduction and translation by Helen Rolfson.

2. Unfortunately, the provenance remains unknown.

3. Jer 3:19: *Et dixi: Patrem vocabi me, et post me ingredi non cessabis.*

4. The mutual in-dwelling of Father and Son *(perichoresis)* allows the author to call the Son "Father in a sonly way," and the Father "Son in a fatherly way."

# Hendrik Mande, *Apocalypse* (excerpts), *A Love Complaint*, and extract from *A Devout Little Book*

1. Introduction and translation by Thom Mertens.

2. *Ghy selt altoes sien ende merken wat die liefste wille gods is ende die meeste volcomenheit. Ende daerna sal en yghelic pinen <als in hem es. Want altoes pinen> na volcomenheyt, dat wart voir volcomenheyt gherekent. Want wy en moghen niet staen in den weghen. Wy moeten voert of wy moeten afterwaert gane. Ende niet voert te willen gaen, dat is afterwaert ghegaen (Van drien staten*, ed. MollM–XII 149–55).

3. Hendrik Mande, *Een minnentlike claege*, ed. Thom Mertens, Veröffentlichungen des Instituts für Niederländische Philologie der Universität zu Köln 6 (Erftstadt: Lukassen Verlag, 1984).

4. From *Een devoet boexken vander volmaecster hoecheit der minnen*, ch. 5

5. Because they have entrusted everything to love they are already rich.

## *Exposition on the Song of Songs* (extracts)

1. Introduction and translation by Kees Schepers.

2. Kees Schepers, *Bedudinghe op Cantica canticorum, vertaling en bewerking van Glossa tripartita super Cantica: Teksthistorische studies en Editie (Miscellanea Neerlandica)* (Leuven: Peeters, 2006). For an extensive evaluation of the text, see K. Ruh, *Geschichte der Abendländischen Mystik*, vol. 4, *Die niederländische Mystik das 14 bis 16 Jahrhunderts* (Munich: C. H. Beck, 1999), 195–206.

3. Kees Schepers, "Van 'Bedudinghe op Cantica Canticorum' tot 'Glossa Tripartita super Cantica': De vondst van een Latijnse brontekst," *OGE* 67 (1993): 82–93.

4. Kees Schepers, "The Genesis of 'Glossa Tripartita super Cantica,'" *Revue d'Histoire des Textes* 29 (1999): 85–139.

5. Bernard of Clairvaux, *Super Cant.*, Sermo 68, 1, ed. Leclercq, vol. 2, p. 196, lines 21–22. For an English translation, see

*Bernard of Clairvaux, Sermons on the Song of Songs,* Part IV, trans. Irene Edmonds (Kalamazoo, MI: Cistercian Publications, 1980), 17.

6. Cf. Gregory the Great, *Moralia in Iob, Ad Leandrum,* 4, *CCSL,* 143, p. 6, lines 175–77.

7. Augustine, *De Genesi ad Litteram,* V, 3. *CSEL,* 28, 1, p. 141, lines 25–26. For an English translation, see *Saint Augustine: On Genesis.* trans. E. Hill (New York: New City Press, 2002), 279.

8. Not identified.

9. Not identified.

10. Not identified.

11. Cf. Gregory the Great, *Moralia in Iob, Ad Leandrum,* 4, *CCSL,* 143, p. 6, lines 177–78.

12. The Latin source text makes clear that this paragraph summarizes what many authorities, not just Bernard, have said.

13. Proverbs.

14. Ecclesiastes.

15. Song of Songs.

16. Gregory the Great, *Expositio in Canticum Canticorum,* 9, *CCSL,* 144, p. 12, lines 191–200. For an English translation, see Denys Turner, *Eros and Allegory: Medieval Exegesis of the Song of Songs* (Kalamazoo, MI: Cistercian Publications, 1995), esp. 217–55 (for this quotation, see 223).

17. Bernard of Clairvaux, *Sermones super Cantica,* Sermo 1, 11, ed. Leclercq, vol. 1, p. 7, lines 25–p. 8, line 5. For an English translation, see *Bernard of Clairvaux, Sermons on the Song of Songs,* Part I, trans. Kilian Walsh (Kalamazoo, MI: Cistercian Publications, 1971), 6.

18. Richard of St. Victor, *Adnotationes in Ps.,* 136, *PL,* 196, 371A.

19. Bernard of Clairvaux, *Sermones super Cantica,* Sermo 1, 6, 3, ed. Leclercq, vol. 1, p. 5, lines 21–24; p. 4, lines 12–14. For the English translation, see Walsh, *Bernard of Clairvaux, Sermons on the Song of Songs,* Part I, p. 4.

20. Origen, *Commentarium in Cant. Cant.,* Prologue, 6–7, *SC,* 375, p. 84, lines 6–7.

21. Bernard of Clairvaux, *Sermones super Cantica,* Sermo 1, 5, ed. Leclercq, vol. 1, p. 5, lines 17–18. For an English translation, see Walsh, *Bernard of Clairvaux, Sermons on the Song of Songs,* Part I, p. 4.

22. Gregory the Great, *Expositio in Canticum Canticorum*, 4, *CCSL*, 144, p. 4, lines 38–43; p. 5, lines 49–52, 55–59; p. 13, lines 223–28, 234–36. For an English translation, see Turner, *Eros and Allegory*, 224.

23. Cf. Gregory the Great, *Expositio in Canticum Canticorum*, 12, *CCSL*, 144, p. 14–15, lines 254–58. For an English translation, see Turner, *Eros and Allegory*, 225.

24. Bernard of Clairvaux, *Sermones super Cantica*, Sermo 2, 1, ed. Leclercq, vol. 1, p. 8, lines 20–25. For an English translation, see Walsh, *Bernard of Clairvaux, Sermons on the Song of Songs*, Part I, p. 8.

25. Gregory the Great, *Expositio in Canticum Canticorum*, 4, 5, *CCSL*, 144, p. 4–6, lines 43–48, 61–73; p. 7, lines 93, 100–101. For an English translation, see Turner, *Eros and Allegory*, 220.

26. Gregory the Great, *Expositio in Canticum Canticorum*, 4, 12, *CCSL*, 144, p. 7, lines 91–92; p. 14, lines 254–57. For an English translation, see Turner, *Eros and Allegory*, 225.

27. Bernard of Clairvaux, *Sermones super Cantica*, Sermo 2, 8, ed. Leclercq, vol. 1, p. 13, lines 28–29.

28. "The wise man" *(die wise man)* denotes several biblical books: Proverbs, Ecclesiastes, Wisdom, Sirach, and Isaiah.

29. Bernard of Clairvaux, *Sermones super Cantica*, Sermo 2, 2, ed. Leclercq, vol. 1, p. 9, lines 9–12. For an English translation, see Walsh, *Bernard of Clairvaux, Sermons on the Song of Songs*, Part I, p. 9.

30. After the ecclesiological exegesis of Song of Songs 1:2, the moral-mystical exegesis now follows.

31. Thomas Gallus (c. 1190–1246).

32. In this paragraph there is an allegorical personification of the soul; therefore, I translate *si* with "she" instead of "it," as I normally do.

33. The text from "Vercellencis" to "with desire" was in its entirety—including the quotations from Dionysius and Origen—taken from Thomas Gallus, *Commentarius super Cantica*, ed. J. Barbet, in *Thomas Gallus, Commentaires du Cantique de Cantiques: Texte critique avec introduction, notes et tables* (Paris, 1967), 110–11. For an English translation, see Turner, *Eros and Allegory*, 319–39 (for this quotation, see 329-30).

34. Bernard of Clairvaux, *Sermones super Cantica*, Sermo 7, 8, ed. Leclercq, vol. 1, p. 35, lines 21–26, 28–29. For an English translation, see Walsh, *Bernard of Clairvaux, Sermons on the Song of Songs*, Part I, p. 44.

35. Gregory the Great, *Homiliae in Hiezechihelem*, ii, iii, 8, *CCSL*, 142, p. 242, lines 163–70.

36. Bernard of Clairvaux, *Sermones super Cantica*, Sermo 2, 2, ed. Leclercq, vol. 1, p. 9, lines 21–24. For an English translation, see Walsh, *Bernard of Clairvaux, Sermons on the Song of Songs*, Part I, p. 9.

37. Bernard of Clairvaux, *Sermones super Cantica.*, Sermo 7, 2/3, ed. Leclercq, vol. 1, p. 32, lines 6–14, 20, 23–24. For an English translation, see Walsh, *Bernard of Clairvaux, Sermons on the Song of Songs*, Part I, p. 40.

38. Bernard of Clairvaux, *Sermones super Cantica*, Sermo 9, 2, ed. Leclercq, vol. 1, p. 43, lines 11–15. For an English translation, see Walsh, *Bernard of Clairvaux, Sermons on the Song of Songs*, Part I, p. 54.

39. Gregory the Great, *Expositio in Canticum Canticorum*, 18, *CCSL*, 144, pp. 19–20, lines 358–62, 370–72. For an English translation, see Turner, *Eros and Allegory*, 229.

40. Here follows the moral-mystical explanation of Sg 1:15. (I have omitted the ecclesiological explanation.)

41. Gallus, *Commentarius super Cantica*, 129. For an English translation, see Turner, *Eros and Allegory*, 330-31.

42. Here, as in other instances, the Middle Dutch translation of the Song of Songs text is different from modern translations; in this case, for example, "because I am darkened by the sun."

43. Bernard of Clairvaux, *Sermones super Cantica*, Sermo 28, 13, ed. Leclercq, vol. 1, p. 202, lines 1–7. For an English translation, see *Bernard of Clairvaux, Sermons on the Song of Songs*, Part II, trans. Kilian Walsh (Kalamazoo, MI: Cistercian Publications, 1971), 99-100.

44. Bernard of Clairvaux, *Sermones super Cantica*, Sermo 26, 1, ed. Leclercq, vol. 1, p. 170, lines 11–14. For an English translation, see Walsh, *Bernard of Clairvaux, Sermons on the Song of Songs*, Part II, p. 58.

45. Hugh of St. Victor. Quotation not identified.

46. Robert Grosseteste (Lincolniensis), c. 1170–1253, English theologian and philosopher, bishop of Lincoln from 1235. Quotation not identified.

47. Not identified. A main theme in Sermon 28, 10.

48. Bernard of Clairvaux, *Sermones super Cantica.*, Sermo 27, 1, 2, ed. Leclercq, vol. 1, p. 182, lines 3–5, 11–12, 16–18; p. 183, lines 6–12. For an English translation, see Walsh, *Bernard of Clairvaux, Sermons on the Song of Songs*, Part II, pp. 74–75.

49. Bernard of Clairvaux, *Sermones super Cantica.*, Sermo 27, 3, ed. Leclercq, vol. 1, p. 183, lines 24–25. For an English translation, see Walsh, *Bernard of Clairvaux, Sermons on the Song of Songs*, Part II, p. 76.

## *A Ladder of Eight Rungs*

1. Introduction and translation by Rik Van Nieuwenhove.

2. For this translation we used the edition by A. Stracke, *Een Leeder van VIII Trappen* (Antwerp: Uitgeverij Neerlandia, 1929).

3. See, for instance, *In III Sententiarum Libros*, d. 16, a. 2, p. 3, conclusio (Quaracchi, III, 358).

4. See Bonaventure, *The Triple Way (De Triplici Via)*, §3.

5. A free rendering of a noted passage in Bernard's treatise *On Loving God*, 10.28.

6. The text mistakenly says "three" here.

## *The Nine Little Flowers of the Passion* from *Indica Mihi*

1. Introduction and translation by Rik Van Nieuwenhove.

2. See K. Ruh, *Geschichte der abendländischen Mystik*, vol. 4, *Die niederländische Mystik des 14 bis 16 Jahrhunderts* (Munich: C. H. Beck, 1999), 240–41.

3. The edition from which we translate is S. Schoutens, *Indica mihi. Handschrift der 15e Eeuw* (Hoochstraten: Van Hoof Roelens, 1906), 126–56.

4. Unidentified quotation from Richard of St. Victor.

5. Peter Comestor's *Historia Scholastica* was a major source for biblical research in the late Middle Ages and was also used by Ruusbroec.

6. Francis of Meyronnes (d. after 1328), a Franciscan theologian and student of Duns Scotus.

## *A Sweet Meditation*

1. Introduction and translation by Rik Van Nieuwenhove.

2. K. Ruh, *Geschichte der abendländischen Mystik*, vol. 4, *Die niederländische Mystik des 14 bis 16 Jahrhunderts* (Munich: C. H. Beck, 1999), 248.

3. For the translation we use the edition by A. Ampe, "Een Soete Meditatie hoe die verloren siele van den sone Gods vonden es," in *De Gulden Passer* 41 (1963): 48–82.

4. Or, more literally, "When we know the cause of love, it is also necessary to know how we can attain this love."

5. Sir 28:12: "For as the wood of the forest is, so the fire burneth."

6. The Dutch *ghebreck* can mean both "debt" and "shortcomings."

## Hendrik Herp, *A Mirror of Perfection*, Part 4

1. Introduced and translated by Rik Van Nieuwenhove.

2. K. Ruh, *Geschichte der abendländischen Mystik*, vol. 4, *Die niederländische Mystik des 14 bis 16 Jahrhunderts* (Munich: C. H. Beck, 1999), 228.

3. See L. Verschueren, OFM, *Hendrik Herp: Spieghel der Volcomenheit*, part 1. *Inleiding* (Antwerp: Uitgever Neerlandia, 1931), 148. Part 2, *Tekst*, contains the text from which this translation has been made (370–421).

4. See Jan van Ruusbroec. *Van den Geesteliken Tabernakel, Opera Omnia* Vol. 5, CCCM 105 (Tielt: Lannoo; Turnhout: Brepols, 2006), 4:398–412, pp. 367–69.

5. *Memory* here is used in the Augustinian sense as the seat of our personality and much richer than merely the power of recollection. Notice the trinitarian transformation of the three faculties, inspired by Ruusbroec (see, for instance, *Die Geestelike Brulocht*, b 1118–27). All references to Ruusbroec's works are taken from the *Opera Omnia*, ed. G. De Baere (Turnhout: Brepols, 1981–2006), if available.

6. The meaning of this sentence is not entirely clear. Perhaps we should ignore the double negation, and read: "It happens that in an inappropriate manner they desire to receive again the grace that has been withdrawn from them; they do not know that they had used in a careless manner the gifts that had been bestowed upon them."

7. *ST* I, 12, 1.

8. *ST* I, 12, 5 and 6.

9. What follows is taken from Jan van Ruusbroec, *Vanden Blinkenden Steen*, 752–80.

10. *Ontgeest ende overgeformt*, "breathed out and transformed." This concept is difficult to translate into English. It refers to the process of self-transcendence into God *(excessus)* that the soul undergoes. Ruusbroec uses the term in *Spieghel der Eeuwigher Salicheit*, 1895 and 2111.

11. See Jan van Ruusbroec, *Vanden Blinkenden Steen*, 943–48.

12. This is taken from Ruusbroec, *Vanden Seven Sloten*, 784–93.

13. See Jan van Ruusbroec, *Vanden XII Beghinen*, 1, 700–705.

14. Compare Jan van Ruusbroec, *Van Seven Trappen*, 1140–61.

15. See Ruusbroec, *Vanden XII Beghinen*, 1, 409–35.

16. See Ruusbroec, *Vanden XII Beghinen*, 1, 628–43.

17. "Forms" translates *beeldet*, "to imprint the image," a term with rich theological connotations among the Rhineland mystics.

18. This passage is derived from Ruusbroec, *Vanden XII Beghinen*, 1, 466–541.

19. See Ruusbroec, *Vanden XII Beghinen*, 1, 439–65.

20. See Ruusbroec, *Vanden XII Beghinen*, 1, 483–84.

21. See Ruusbroec, *Spieghel der Eeuwigher Salicheit*, 2037–40.

22. See Ruusbroec, *Die Geestelike Brulocht*, c 76–82.

23. See Ruusbroec, *Die Geestelike Brulocht*, c 88–92.

# Claesinne van Nieuwlant, *Conversation* (extract)

1. Introduction and translation by Robert Faesen, SJ.

2. What Claesinne attempts to say is that if God did not retain the body in its "littleness," then it would be elevated and follow the spirit in its upward movement (cf. the elevations of Teresa of Avila).

3. The text contains *etc.* many times because Pullen is summarizing in a written report his conversation with Claesinne.

4. The last part of this sentence is not translated because one or more words are lacking in the original text.

5. "Inner person" and "outer person" refer respectively to the inner and outer dimensions of a person.

6. "The highest human person" means the highest dimension of the human person.

7. *Gestorven/gedood.*

# Alijt Bake, *Four Ways of the Cross*

1. Translated and introduced by John Van Engen.

2. On Alijt Bake, see Wybren Scheepsma, *Medieval Religious Women in the Low Countries: The Modern Devotion, the Canonesses of Windesheim, and their Writings* (Rochester, NY: Toydell and Brewer, 2004), 197–226; R. Th. M. van Dijk and M. K. A. van den Berg, *Alijt Bake, tot in de peilloze diepte van God: De vrouw die moest zwijgen over haar mystieke weg* (Kampen: Kok, 1997); Karl Ruh, *Geschichte der abenländischen Mystik*, vol. 4 (Munich: C. H. Beck, 1999), 252–67; A. M. Bollmann, "'Een vrauwe te sijn op min selfs handt': Alijt Bake (1415–55) als geistliche Reformerin des innerlichen Lebens," *OGE* 76 (2002): 64–98 (an important close reading of the autobiography).

3. B. Spaapen, ed., "De autobiografie van Alijt Bake," *OGE* 41 (1967): 219–20.

4. The essential orientation now is in the original Dutch version of Scheepsma, *Deemoed en devotie: De koorvrouwen van Windesheim en hum geschriften* (Amsterdam: Prometheus, 1997),

251–64. I am preparing an English translation of the main corpus of her writings, which may help sort out some literary problems, though what is truly required is a thorough new edition.

    5. See B. Spaapen, "Middeleeuwse passiemystiek II: De vier kruiswegen van Alijt Bake," *OGE* 40 (1966): 14–16. My translation is of this edition, pp. 18–64.

    6. In the manuscripts this treatise has no title; virtually none of Alijt Bake's works does. The present title follows Spaapen's in his edition. Unlike Spaapen, I place the first sentence in brackets. It was, in effect, the rubric for this work, as supplied in BS, the manuscript Spaapen primarily followed. In B, the manuscript written, we think, in Bake's own hand, the work begins with the next sentence (2), and in another manuscript (H), often close to B, it begins with (3).

    7. See Rev 7:3–4 (the sealing of the 144,000 "servants of God").

    8. This is the first appearance of the term *gront*, for which I have found no other English word than "ground," though the meaning of the original is very rich: the core of a human being, that from which all things spring, also that in which and by which the human encounters the divine at the deepest level. Bake could have acquired it from any of a number of Late Medieval mystical writers, most likely Tauler.

    9. *inden gront van alder eyghenscap:* a common phrase in Late Medieval mystical writers, which I have translated as "self-possession."

    10. *"gelatenen gront"*: by contrast with a "self-possessing" ground. This raises another translation problem, here dealt with as "submissive" in the sense of "letting go" or "emptying" (cf. n. 15 below).

    11. This is the first appearance in this work of a term Alijt Bake uses regularly of the sought-for divine.

    12. I have left this untranslated; it refers of course to the "holy of holies," the innermost chamber of the tabernacle in which the ark of the covenant was kept (Exod 26:34).

    13. See 1 Sam. 3:10 (Samuel responding to God's call).

    14. This echoes (or anticipates) a passage in her "Beginnings and Progress," which is more explicit about her reading and her

reaction to it. She refers to her sense of abandonment, as unfit for religious life (amid her struggles). But this sense came to her, she goes on, "and that I know in all truth, not from her side [Alijt tells her story mostly in the third person] nor from her people on the other side, but out of the very highest nobility that one can practice in making the ascent. It was also so for the good cook [Jan van Leeuwen] where he grieved so much about love. But in all his ten books, and likewise in the books of Father Jan Ruusbroec, I cannot find that those people were set so far from their own human acts, in utter scorn of them, such that they had themselves to reject and scorn and drive from themselves their own active self. I do hear that they had people in the right way of letting be *(ghelaetenheijt)* under the work and allowance of God, if nothing better could happen for them. But that people had themselves to reject and scorn and repudiate [that acting self], as this one [Alijt] had to, that I do not get out of their books. But why they did not have it so, I do not know, unless they dared not perfectly believe because perhaps they had not experienced it, or dared not describe it owing to the infirmity of human beings who easily draw it in another direction and thereby come into deceptions that they copy falsely, or indeed that they did not rightly note the right distinction here, that God sometimes asks this of people owing to some hidden self-possession that is in them" (B. Spaapen, ed., "De autogiografie van Alijt Bake," *OGE* 41 (1967): 326–27). This is a difficult passage, as are many of Bake's passages in her autobiography, and my rendering differs somewhat from the version given by Ruh, p. 256, which, in my view, misconstrues some of the Middle Dutch, and that of van den Berg, pp. 93–94, which sometimes, I think, makes things too intelligible and accessible in modern Dutch. In any case this remarkable passage reveals something of Alijt Bake's reading and also her spiritual independence.

15. Here at the beginning of the Fourth Way Bake first mentions her signature triad: *laten en lijden en minnen*, letting go and suffering and loving. As with all mystical teaching written in Dutch and German in the Later Middle Ages, the word that presents difficulties of translation is *laten*. I have usually translated it as "letting go" or "letting be," a state of spiritual quietude or acquiescence, of emptying out.

16. Allow me to note here from MS H (not in Alijt Bake's own hand, but a copy close to it in many particulars) this addition, which only further work, editorial and interpretive, could help determine whether it too is the voice of Alijt: "Thus is the condition of those people who are signed with the pitiful, deprived way of our Lord Jesus Christ. They stand without consolation or help, those who are truly captive to him. They are also without desire, such that they may not ever again be able to desire that they become better. Because they also do not have faith or hope. They have lost it all."

17. This is a term Bake may have acquired from Ruusbroec's *Die Geestelike Brulocht* (p. 136, for instance), where this inner speech is contrasted with delusions that come from external fantasies and sensual images.

18. This may be Bake's own term, modeled on *inspreken*.

19. One of the manuscripts (H), often relatively close to B (ascribed to Bake), breaks off here and goes into a short alternative ending.

20. That is, a religious habit, giving only the appearance of religion or holiness.

# Sister Bertken, *Pious Colloquy* and a selection from her *Songs*

1. Introduced and translated by José van Aelst.

# *The Evangelical Pearl*, Part III

1. Introduced and translated by Helen Rolfson.

2. "Ende die weselijcke eenvuldicheit in leyt ons." Paraphrasing, this means the essential simplicity leads us inwards. We are drawn inwards by the essential simplicity.

3. "Father" here is an obvious error and should be "Son."

# The Temple of Our Soul

1. Introduced and translated by Robert Faesen, SJ.

2. See the introduction to the translation of the *Evangelical Pearl* in this volume.

3. Anonymous, *Vita Idae de Lovanio*, II, 34 (*Acta Sanctorum aprilis* 2, col. 180C–D).

4. *Opera Omnia Erasmi*, ed. J. Clericus, vol. 7 (Lugduni Batavorum [now Leyden]: Petri Vander Aa, 1706), ii.

5. *Den tempel onser sielen*, door de schrijfster der Evangelische peerle, ingeleid en kritisch uitgegeven, by Albert Ampe, Studies and Text Editions of Our Spiritual Heritage 18 (Antwerp: Ruusbroec-genootschap, 1968).

6. *Gods tempel zijn wij, door de Schrijfster van de Evangelische Peerle: Een liturgiebeleving uit de XVIe eeuw*, trans. and foreword Dr. J. Alaerts, SJ, Mystical Texts with Commentary 3 (Bonheiden: Bethlehem Abbey, 1980).

7. "God ghebruykelic" refers to the Augustinian *frutio* (as distinct from *uti*). In this context "God Ghebruykelic" means "capable of the enjoyment or fruition of God."

8. "All three," that is, the heavenly Jerusalem, the Church Triumphant, and the Church Militant.

9. *Breviary*, Second Sunday of Advent, Matins, resp. 1; cf. Isa 56:1.

10. Ibid., resp. 2; cf. Mic 4:9; Isa 43:1, Neh 8:9; Isa 40:10.

11. *Breviary*, Fourth Sunday of Advent, Lauds, Ant. 5; cf. Mic 1:2.

12. *Breviary*, Third Sunday of Advent, Lauds, Ant. 3; cf. Isa 46:13.

13. *Breviary*, Third Sunday of Advent, Ant. 2.

14. Cf. Zech 9:9; John 12:15.

15. *Roman Missal*, Sanctus; cf. Isa 6:3; Rev 4:8.

16. *Breviary*, Vigil of Christmas, Lauds, Ant. 1; cf. 2 Chr 20:17.

17. Ibid., Matins, resp. 2.

18. *Roman Missal*, Second Sunday of Advent, Communion; cf. Bar 4:36.

19. *Breviary,* First Week of Advent, Saturday, Lauds, Ant. Bened.

20. Ibid., First Week of Advent, Monday, Vespers, Ant. Magn.

21. Ibid., Second Sunday of Advent, Matins, resp. 5; cf. Ps 72:8.

22. Ibid., Second Week of Advent, Matins, resp. 5; cf. Isa 49:13.

23. Ibid., Second Week of Advent, Tuesday, resp. 1; cf. Ezek 36:8.

24. Ibid., First Sunday of Advent, Lauds, Ant. 3.

25. That is, one has to prepare oneself in accordance with the fruits one hopes to harvest, as the quotation from Bernard illustrates. In this passage we detect resonances of the parable of the ten virgins (Matt 25:1–12).

26. Bernard, Sermo 5, Vigil of Christmas, *PL* 183, 94.

27. Cf. Introit for the Vigil of the Epiphany (cf. Wis 18:14–15). While the Latin text of the Introit is "et nox in suo cursu medium iter haberet," the Middle Dutch text replaces *nox* by *hemel* (heaven).

28. Quotation unidentified by A. Ampe.

29. Cf. Ps.-Bernard, *Medit.* I, 2 (*PL* 184, 486).

30. The characterization of the soul in terms of three unities is inspired by Ruusbroec, *Die Geestelike Brulocht,* 41–106, 1626ff.

31. This passage echoes Meister Eckhart's Sermon 2 on the soul as virgin and wife.

32. Bernard, Sermo 6, Vigil of the Nativity.

33. Ps.-Bernard, *Tract. de interiori domo,* c. 10 (*PL* 184, 166–67).

34. Quotation unidentified by A. Ampe.

35. For this paragraph, see Ps.-Richard of St. Victor, *Explicatio in Cantica Canticorum,* chap. 12.

# Mystical Sermons

1. Introduced and translated by Kees Schepers, who dedicates the publication of this small selection from these mystical sermons to the memory of Father Albert Ampe, SJ, who led the way

into uncharted fields in the study of Middle Dutch spiritual literature, and whose width of text-historical knowledge remains unsur-
passed.

2. Cf. C. G. N. De Vooys, *Meister Eckhart en de Nederlandse
Mystiek*, in Netherlands Archives for Church History, new series,
part 3 (The Hague, 1905), 50–92, 176–94, 265–90, esp. 56–57; A.
Ampe, "De geschriften van Suster Bertken," *OGE* 30 (1956):
281–98, esp. 296–98.

3. C. C. De Bruin, *Middelnederlands geestelijk proza*
(Zutphen, 1940), 244–46 (edition of *Opten hoegen kerstnacht*), 345. It
is important to point out that this text already existed prior to the
sermon collection. The text, a sermon about Christmas, is the only
one in the entire manuscript of which several textual witnesses exist.

4. The sermons are listed with their incipit and explicit in M.
Sherwood-Smith and P. Stoop, *Repertorium van Middelnederlandse
preken in handschriften tot en met 1550 (Repertory of Middle Dutch
Sermons preserved in manuscripts from before 1550)* Miscellanea
Neerlandica 29, 3 vols. (Leuven: Peeters, 2003), 2:1079–1157.

5. E. Verwijs and J. Verdam, *Middelnederlandsch Woordenboek*,
10 vols. ('s Gravenhage, 1885–1928; reprint 1990–93, Flandria
Nostra, Zedelgem). Now also on CD-ROM *(Middelnederlands woordenboek)*.

6. De Vooys, *Meister Eckhart en de Nederlandse Mystiek*, 57:
"(de preken) tonen op elke bladzijde de invloed van de veertiende-
eeuwse mystiek, vooral door een overvloedig gebruik van Eckartse
en Ruusbroecse termen."

7. P. J. Begheyn, "De handschriften van het St.-Agnietenk-
looster te Arnhem," in *OGE* 45 (1971): 3–44; idem, "Is Reinalda van
Eymeren, zuster in het St. Agnietenklooster te Arnhem, en oud-
tante van Petrus Canisius, de schrijfster der 'Evangelische peerle'?"
in *OGE* 45 (1971): 339–75. The identification of the author of the
*Evangelical Pearl* with Reinalda van Eymeren, great-aunt of Petrus
Canisius, and possibly a nun in the St. Agnes convent, has been
emphatically put forward by Paul Begheyn. This identification,
however, cannot be proven. Furthermore the hypothesis seems to
present some insurmountable problems. Petrus Canisius was certainly held in high esteem in the St. Agnes convent, given that the
nuns produced a handwritten copy of his edition of (Ps.-)Tauler ser-

mons of 1543. This convergence of indications makes it safe to say that the mystical sermons spring from the same spiritual community to which the author of the *Evangelical Pearl* was connected in some way. This lends these sermons exceptional significance, since they could provide some insight into the spiritual ambience around the author of the *Evangelical Pearl*. Her works were first published by the Cologne Carthusians and henceforth became a major influence on French spirituality of the sixteenth and seventeenth century, and especially on Pierre de Bérulle (1575–1629) and Louis de Blois (1505–65) (see J. Huyben, "Aux sources de la spiritualité française du xviiᵉ siècle," in *Supplement à la 'Vie spirituelle,'* 25 [1930]: 113–39; *Supplement à la 'Vie spirituelle,'* 26 [1931]: 17–46, 75–111; *Supplement à la 'Vie spirituelle,'* 27 [1931]: 20–42, 94–122; D. Vidal, ed., *La perle évangélique* [Grenoble, 1997]). The *Evangelical Pearl* also became known in the German-speaking world through the translation of Angelus Silesius (1624–77).

8. Romans 13:11–12. From the Epistle on the First Sunday of Advent.

9. Luke 21:25. From the Gospel on the Second Sunday of Advent.

10. The word *profession (professien)* is a clear and concrete indication to confirm the hypothesis that the audience for these texts is monastics, most likely women.

11. In this phrase there is a sudden and complete identification of the soul with Mary, similar to what we find in mariological commentaries to the Song of Songs. In earlier instances both Joseph and Mary were mentioned; now the soul takes the place of Mary. For the audience of these texts the Song of Songs was not the only "book of experience" (Bernard of Clairvaux, *Sermons on the Song of Songs*, 3, 1), but the entire New Testament could be read from this perspective.

12. What follows is, in a very concise form, a theologically and psychologically extremely complicated passage. The three Persons of the Trinity and their primary aspects mirror the three highest capacities of the mind and their primary faculties. *Ground of the Trinity*, i.e., *Father* (omnipotence, gives might)—*ground of the mind* (might, fecundity); *Son* (wisdom, gives clarity)—*highest reason*

392

(knowledge, wisdom); Love, i.e., *Holy Spirit* (love, gives love)—*love of the mind* (fullness, strength, force).

13. That is, of the "fatherly omnipotence": God the Father is the source of the Son's wisdom and the Holy Spirit's love.

14. It seems that in this passage, too, there is a remarkable intermingling of divine Persons and the main faculties.

15. The soul has put on the mantle of the imperfect, lower faculties and has left behind the higher faculties: memory, reason, and will.

# Maria van Hout, Two Letters

1. Introduction and translation by Robert Faesen, SJ.

2. Petrus Blomevenna (Peter Bloemeveen, 1466–1536), prior of the Carthusian monastery of Cologne.

3. The introduction to this letter is by Gerard Kalckbrenner (d. 1566), procurator of the Carthusian monastery of Cologne, who prepared the edition of the letters of Maria van Hout.

4. *Aventuirlich* can be "wonderful" but also "dangerous." In the context of the sixteenth century the latter seems more probable.

5. The end of the letter is omitted by Kalckbrenner and replaced by a postscript referring to other passages about the Virgin Mary written by Maria van Hout.

# Index

# Other Volumes in This Series

# Other Volumes in This Series

# Other Volumes in This Series

# Other Volumes in This Series

**Richard of St. Victor** • THE TWELVE PATRIARCHS, THE MYSTICAL ARK, BOOK THREE OF THE TRINITY

**Robert Bellarmine** • SPIRITUAL WRITINGS

**Safed Spirituality** • RULES OF MYSTICAL PIETY, THE BEGINNING OF WISDOM

**Shakers, The** • TWO CENTURIES OF SPIRITUAL REFLECTION

**Sharafuddin Maneri** • THE HUNDRED LETTERS

**Sor Juana Inés de la Cruz** • SELECTED WRITINGS

**Spirituality of the German Awakening, The** •

**Symeon the New Theologian** • THE DISCOURSES

**Talmud, The** • SELECTED WRITINGS

**Teresa of Avila** • THE INTERIOR CASTLE

**Theatine Spirituality** • SELECTED WRITINGS

**'Umar Ibn al-Fāriḍ** • SUFI VERSE, SAINTLY LIFE

**Valentin Weigel** • SELECTED SPIRITUAL WRITINGS

**Vincent de Paul and Louise de Marillac** • RULES, CONFERENCES, AND WRITINGS

**Walter Hilton** • THE SCALE OF PERFECTION

**William Law** • A SERIOUS CALL TO A DEVOUT AND HOLY LIFE, THE SPIRIT OF LOVE

**Zohar** • THE BOOK OF ENLIGHTENMENT

The Classics of Western Spirituality is a ground-breaking collection of the original writings of more than 100 universally acknowledged teachers within the Catholic, Protestant, Eastern Orthodox, Jewish, Islamic, and Native American Indian traditions.

To order any title, or to request a complete catalog, contact Paulist Press at 800-218-1903 or visit us on the Web at www.paulistpress.com